INFINITY AND PERSPECTIVE

The MIT Press   Cambridge, Massachusetts   London, England

Karsten Harries

INFINITY AND PERSPECTIVE

This book was typeset in Janson by Graphic Composition, Inc. and was printed and bound in the United States of America.

Library of Congress Cataloging-in-Publication Data

Harries, Karsten.
 Infinity and perspective / Karsten Harries.
  p. cm.
 Includes bibliographical references and index.
 ISBN 0-262-08292-6 (HC : alk. paper)
 1. Perspective (Philosophy)—History. 2. Infinite—History. 3. Nicholas, of
Cusa, Cardinal, 1401–1464. 4. Alberti, Leon Battista, 1404–1472. I. Title.
BD348 .H37 2001
190—dc21   00-048034

In Memoriam
Hans Blumenberg
July 13, 1920
March 28, 1996

Contents

Illustrations

Preface

Although they address very different issues, *Infinity and Perspective* and my earlier book, *The Ethical Function of Architecture* (Cambridge, Mass.: MIT Press, 1996), yet belong together. I began the latter with the observation that "For some time now architecture has been uncertain of its way" and cited Alberto Pérez-Gómez, who linked such uncertainty to the worldview ushered in by Galilean science and Newton's philosophy, which he argued led to a rationalization and functionalization of architecture that had to turn its back on that "poetical content of reality" that once provided "any meaningful architecture "with" an ultimate frame of reference." *The Ethical Function of Architecture* attempted to open windows to that content.

But what is said here of architecture can also be said of the modern world: for some time now it has become uncertain of its way; and once again such uncertainty can be linked to the way a particular understanding of reality, bound up with science and technology, has had to turn its back on dimensions of reality we need to affirm to live meaningful lives. One goal of the present book is to open windows to these dimensions.

When we have lost our way, it is only natural to search for maps that might help to reorient us, to reflect not only on the goal of our journey, but even more on how we got to where we now find ourselves, and on roads not taken. *Infinity and Perspective* sketches such a map, retraces on that map the road traveled, locates the threshold of our modern world in order to hint at where we might have gone and perhaps should be going.

This book had its origin in reflections that forty years ago led me to write a dissertation on the problem of nihilism (*In a Strange Land. An Exploration of Nihilism*, Ph.D. dissertation, Yale University, 1961). In that dissertation already I included a discussion of Nicolaus Cusanus, in whom I even then sought pointers that might help us to step out of the shadow nihilism has cast over the modern world. The present book pursues these pointers. To be sure, Cusanus is only one of a number of thinkers discussed in some detail. Still, his work helps to mark this book's secret center: much more than the works of his great admirer Giordano Bruno, his speculations continue to challenge us.

I mention Bruno here to suggest how fundamentally my understanding of modernity differs from that of Hans Blumenberg, to whose work my own owes so much and to whose memory I dedicate this book. In *The Legitimacy of the Modern Age* (trans. Robert M. Wallace [Cambridge, Mass.: MIT Press, 1983]) Blumenberg presents Cusanus as a thinker who still belongs to the Middle Ages and lies more thoroughly behind us than Bruno, who is said already to have crossed the epochal threshold. But precisely because Cusanus straddles that threshold, he has more to teach us as we try to understand not only the legitimacy, but also the limits of modernity.

Some of the ideas developed in this book go back to my years as a student. I was fortunate to have found caring mentors in Robert S. Brumbaugh, Charles W. Hendel, George Lindbeck, George Schrader, Wilfrid Sellars, and Rulon Wells: in different ways they all helped me to find my way. A lecture course that I taught off and on for the past twenty years and that bore the same title as this book helped me to focus my thoughts and sharpen my arguments. Graduate seminars on Cusanus, Alberti, and Descartes helped me to test my ideas. I owe a debt to many more former students than I can now remember. I would like to single out Karl Ameriks, Scott Austin, Elizabeth Brient, Peter Casarella, Michael Halberstam, Hagi Kenaan, Lee Miller, and Dermot Moran. I lectured on related topics in a great many places and published a number of papers on Cusanus and Descartes, parts of which I have not hesitated to use in this book. Conversations with Louis Dupré, Jasper Hopkins, and R. I. G. Hughes proved especially helpful.

This book would still be in process had it not been for Roger Conover's enthusiastic response when I first approached him. Once again I was fortunate in being able to depend on Alice Falk's careful editing. I am grateful to both. And I would like to thank Jean Wilcox for her design work and Judy Feldmann for watching over the transformation of the manuscript into a book.

My deepest thanks go to my wife, Elizabeth Langhorne, who in her own way made me learn about my ignorance.

INFINITY AND PERSPECTIVE

1

Number mysticism has never managed to capture my imagination. My greatest concern, as we approached the year 2000, was that instead of crossing that much-discussed bridge into the third millennium with open eyes, I would be unable to stay awake until midnight. With all the excitement around me, I felt just a bit ashamed that I might be carried across that bridge asleep. But without giving undue weight to three zeros, are we not caught up today in a process that promises or threatens to transform our cultural landscape? And if so, should we not try to assume at least some responsibility for where we are heading, instead of allowing ourselves to just drift along?

That we are indeed crossing some important cultural threshold is hinted at by the terms "postmodern" and "postmodernism." What is postmodern would seem to follow what is modern, to have taken a step beyond it, leaving it behind. But any suggestion that we take such a step has to raise questions: for what do we mean by "modern"? Do we not call "modern" what is of today and up-to-date, as opposed to what is of yesterday and old-fashioned? "Modernism" thus suggests something like an ideology that embraces what is taken to be the spirit presiding over our world, over its progress, however spirit and progress are understood. "Postmodernism" then presumably means the opposite: an ideology born of dissatisfaction with that spirit, which would have us embrace what is other than modernity.

Like millennial fervor, postmodernism invites interpretation as a symptom of our civilization's discontents, of widespread dissatisfaction with this modern world. Such dissatisfaction may look backward, to some premodern past, or forward, to some postmodern future. That is to say, dissatisfaction may lead to nostalgia—regret that modernity no longer allows human beings to experience their world as a cosmos that assigns the individual his or her place on firm ground, regret that with what Nietzsche called the death of God our spiritual world apparently lost both founder and foundation and now is developing all sorts of cracks and fissures, falling into ruin as supposedly stable supports have begun to shift. Such regret invites attempts to repair or rebuild that spiritual house, to recover in some way or other what has been lost. But dissatisfaction may also refuse nostalgia, convinced that all such attempts to recover what has been lost fail to confront the changed shape of our world, which rules out such recovery; fail to confront the challenge and promise of an inevitably open future, fail finally to recognize that the problem today is not so much a loss of home but rather the ability of our modern world, this simulacrum of a once meaningfully ordered cosmos, to place us all too well, so that what may already have become a ruin, nevertheless still functions as a prison to stifle freedom. Ruin and prison: in these metaphors postmodern suspicion of all sorts of architectures finds expression (fig. 1).

To call something, say art or thinking, "postmodern" is then to suggest a refusal of what modernity claimed to have established and to display opposition to what now often seems the naive optimism of the Enlightenment, an optimism that has supported modernism as it has supported science, liberal democracy, and international communism. Gesturing beyond all that is merely modern, the term points to some nebulous "other," some hoped for brighter future that may already be announcing its coming, even though it has not yet arrived and its contours are impossible to read. But given what postmodern art and theorizing have produced, such an understanding may still seem much too hopeful, too close to Enlightenment optimism. Postmodernism and optimism do not rhyme very well. The horrors of the twentieth century have taught us to be suspicious of revolutionary fervor and of the conviction that drives it. Religious fundamentalism and totalitarianism are also born of dissatisfaction with the modern world, and in this sense they

. . .

figure 1

Giambattista Piranesi,

Prison (Carceri) (1745).

Credit: Beinecke Rare Book and

Manuscript Library, Yale University.

are also expressions of a postmodern sensibility. Small wonder then that the mood of what remains of the cultural avant-garde should have "changed from vehemence to decadence and weary cynicism."[1]

It would be a mistake to understand postmodernism as what temporally follows modernism. Postmodernism is a phenomenon of modernity's bad conscience; it betrays suspicion that modernity lacks legitimacy, suspicion that has shadowed the modern world from the very beginning. In the twentieth century such suspicion has grown apace, especially in the past three decades. Reinforced in this country by the profound disenchantment of the Vietnam years, which undermined America's naive self-confidence, reinforced all over the world by intractable economic and social, race- and gender-related, religious and ecological problems, the rhetoric of postmodernism communicates a growing suspicion that the road on which this logocentric, Eurocentric culture has been traveling leads to disaster. Despair and hope, the former more articulate than the latter, mingle in such self-doubt, where both tend to focus on modern science and even more on the ever-expanding technology that science has made possible.

I suggested that we moderns no longer experience our world as a well-ordered cosmos, resembling a house that shelters and grants us place. That simile invites us to think God in the image of an architect, the architect in the image of God, and the philosopher, who with his or her thoughts attempts to reconstruct the order of the cosmos, in the image of both. The philosopher, too, is a would-be builder, someone who edifies—and that very word "edify" should make us think: a word that once meant simply to raise a dwelling or structure, that later came to mean "to improve morally or spiritually," today tends to carry primarily a negative connotation. Why such suspicion of all sorts of edification? The word's shift in meaning and connotation invites us to interrogate attacks on architecture that have recently come into fashion. Take the word "deconstruction" and all it stands for. What, for example, are we to make of Bernard Tschumi's attempt to create an architecture against architecture in the Parc de la Villette or of Derrida's collaboration in that project? Denis Hollier suggests that "Such a project calls upon a loss of meaning, to give it a dionysiac dimension: it explicitly takes issue with what Tschumi describes as an essential premise of architecture, 'the idea of meaning immanent in architectural structures'; the park, a postmodern 'assault on meaning,' claims as its main purpose to 'dismantle meaning.'"[2]

But are we suffering from such a surfeit of meaning that we should thus want to dismantle it? Has meaning become the prison that denies us access to Dionysian ecstasy? How are we to understand the current vogue enjoyed by Georges Bataille's stance against architecture, where architecture stands for an order that imprisons us and should therefore be destroyed, even if such destruction threatens chaos and bestiality? (fig. 2). "It is obvious," Hollier

THE PROBLEM OF THE MODERN

. . .

figure 2

Cover of Denis Hollier,

Against Architecture:

The Writings of Georges Bataille

(Cambridge, Mass.: MIT Press, 1989).

quotes Bataille, "that monuments inspire social good behavior in societies and often even real fear. The storming of the Bastille is symbolic of this state of affairs: it is hard to explain this mass movement other than through the people's animosity (animus) against the monuments that are its real masters."[3] But if we admit that monuments sometimes inspire good behavior, perhaps even real fear, is it also obvious that they therefore deserve to be abolished? Does this society, does the world, suffer from too much "good behavior"? Ought we to let loose the Minotaur? Such convinction betrays a deep self-hatred. As Bataille recognized, this animus against the monuments that are our real masters is inevitably also an animus against ourselves:

And this is precisely what, in Bataille's view, the mythical figure of Acephalus was intended to show: the only way for man to escape the architectural chain gang is to escape his form, to lose his head. This self-storming of one's own form requires, in fact, an infinitely more underhanded strategy than one of simple destruction or escape. The image of Acephalus, thus, should be seen as a figure of dissemblance, the negative imago of an antimonumental madness involved in the dismemberment of "meaning." The painter André Masson drew this figure and Bataille wrote an aphorism to go with it: "Man will escape his head as a convict escapes his prison."[4]

Such an attack on architecture, which is also an attack on meaning, presupposes a gnostic desire to escape one's human form, this prison of the free spirit, even if the price for such liberation should be losing one's head. The reasoning that here makes the prison the paradigmatic work of architecture, a kind of lens through which to look at all architecture, is of the sort that lets Dostoevsky's man from the underground call twice-two-makes-four a piece of impudence and celebrate twice-two-makes-five as the ultimate refuge of a freedom that, resisting placement, dreams of labyrinth and chaos: has not our head become our prison? But must such a displaced freedom lose, along with body and head, in the end also itself? The problem of both modernism and postmodernism is at bottom nothing other than the problem of freedom.

2

That postmodern rhetoric should so often have included critiques of the Enlightenment and of its founding heroes—such "dead white males" as Kant, Descartes, and Copernicus—is to be expected. It is their legacy, their architecture that is now called into question because what they helped build fails to answer to something we deeply desire. One aim of this book is to cast light on the problem of freedom by addressing this ambiguous failure. Not that questioning such attempts to establish the modern world as a house built by reason is a new phenomenon: Nietzsche, postmodernism's most frequently cited precursor, was in 1887 already lamenting that "Since Copernicus, man seems to have got himself on an inclined plane—now he is slipping faster and faster away from the center into—what? into nothingness? into a *penetrating* sense of his own nothingness?"[5] The Greek or the medieval cosmos assigned human beings their place near the center, but the Copernican revolution would seem to have condemned us to an eccentric position. To be sure, eccentricity still presupposes a center: Copernicus (as we should expect, given his place still on the threshold separating our modern from the medieval world) was himself only a half-hearted modernist and continued to hold on to the idea of a cosmic center, as he continued to invoke the idea of a divine architect and with it the idea of a bounded, well-ordered cosmos; he only denied the earth that central place, giving it instead to the sun. But, as we shall also see, of more fundamental importance than the shift from a geocentric to a heliocentric understanding of the cosmos proved to be the authority granted to human reason, bound up with a self-elevation that frees the thinking subject from any particular place. Such self-elevation, a new freedom, and a new anthropocentrism go together with a new sense of homelessness. Nor are any of these features specifically Copernican: the foundations of the bounded, homelike cosmos of Aristotle and Ptolemy had been shaken long before it fell into ruin and was abandoned.

Nietzsche was hardly the first one to rhetorically exploit the nihilistic implications of the post-Copernican universe. Here is the beginning of volume 2 of Schopenhauer's *World as Will and Representation* (1819): "In endless space countless luminous spheres, round each of which some dozen smaller illuminated ones revolve, hot at the core and covered with a hard cold crust; on this crust a mouldy film has produced living and knowing beings; this is empirical truth, the real, the world."[6] Empirical truth, so understood—that is to say, our science—knows nothing of privileged places, of absolute values, of home. And if that truth is identified with *the* truth, then, if we are to escape from nihilism, shall we not have to cover up the truth or abandon it altogether? Could the insistence on *the* truth be an obstacle to living the good life?

Nietzsche appropriated Schopenhauer's dismal if sublime vision in the very beginning of his youthful fragment "On Truth and Lie in an Extra-Moral Sense," so popular with postmodern critics weary of all centers, which should lead us to ask ourselves why such weariness is preferred to nostalgia. One answer is given by a continued insistence on a quite modern freedom. This free-floating freedom, however, needs to be incarnated if it is not to evaporate; and so, suspicious of all surrogates of home, postmodernists have dreamed of losing themselves in Dionysian ecstasies.

But let me return to Nietzsche's retelling of Schopenhauer's tale: "Once upon a time, in some out of the way corner of that universe which is dispersed into numberless twinkling solar systems, there was a star upon which clever beasts invented knowing. That was the most arrogant and mendacious minute of 'world history,' but nevertheless, it was only a minute. After nature had drawn a few breaths, the star cooled and congealed, and the clever beasts had to die."[7] Nietzsche emphasizes the immense disproportion between our lifetime and the time of the world:[8] what does this universe, which threatens to reduce the time and space allotted to us to insignificance, care for us? It is this same disproportion that Turgenev lets his nihilist Bazarov express in *Fathers and Sons* (1862):

I'm thinking life is a happy thing for my parents. My father at sixty is fussing around, talking about "palliative" measures, doctoring people, playing the bountiful master with the peasants—having a festive time in fact; and my mother's happy, too. Her day is so chockful of duties of all sorts, of sighs, and groans that she does not even have time to think of herself; while I . . . I think. Here I lie under the haystack. The tiny space which I occupy is so infinitely small in comparison with the rest of space, which I am not, and which has nothing to do with me—and the period of time in which it is my lot to live is so petty besides the eternity in which I have not been and shall not be. . . . And in this atom, this mathematical point, the blood is circulating, the brain is working and wanting something. . . . Isn't it loathsome? Isn't it petty?[9]

Happiness here is tied to active, self-forgetful participation in life, nihilism to the self-preoccupied perspective of the thinker. Having the leisure to lie beneath his haystack, Bazarov experiences himself adrift in the infinite, a stranger unable to find a place to call his own. And what foundations are there to build on, what centers by which to orient oneself? Here, too, thoughts of the infinite universe are tied to nihilism and self-loathing.

A related sentiment is expressed by Nikolaj Kusmitsch in Rilke's *Notes of Malte Laurids Brigge* (1910). Kusmitsch is disturbed to discover that our seemingly so stable earth, this supposed terra firma, in fact moves:

Under his feet, too, there was something like a motion—not only one, several motions, warring in strange confusion. He froze with terror. Could this be the earth? Certainly, this was the earth. After all, it moved. That had been mentioned in school, though it was passed over in a hurry, and later on they had tried to cover it up. It was not considered good taste to speak of it. . . . Whether other people felt it? Perhaps, but they did not show it. Probably they did not mind, these sailors.[10]

To be sure, like all of us, Kusmitsch knows that the earth moves. But what he had learned in school had been covered up by society with its fictions of terra firma. So understood modernity is a hybrid, embracing science while covering up its existential implications. Postmodernism can claim to be more honest in its willingness to confront those implications. Nikolaj Kusmitsch is thus terrified by the experience that what he already knew moved did in fact move, that our earth is a ship.[11] As Pascal knew, in more than one sense we are at sea, embarked on a journey without discernible goal.

Hardly surprising then that Nietzsche should have linked Copernicus to nihilism: "Has the self-belittlement of man, his will to self-belittlement not progressed irresistibly since Copernicus? Alas, the faith in the dignity and uniqueness of man, in his irreplaceability in the great chain of being, is a thing of the past—he has become an animal, literally and without reservation and qualification, he who was, according to the old faith, almost God ('child of God,' 'Godman')."[12] As we shall see, there is also another, much more positive reading of Copernicus that enabled the Enlightenment to celebrate him as one of the great liberators of mankind. But the one response inevitably accompanies the other. Common to both is an understanding of Copernicus as marking the ambiguous threshold of our modern world, which presents itself as shadowed by the problem of freedom, a problem that is inevitably also the problem of meaning and its threatened loss.

Implicit in this understanding of the modern age is the conviction that it is in decisive ways different from the Middle Ages, separated from it by something that deserves to be called a revolution. To understand the origin of the modern world, its shape and legitimacy or illegitimacy, we need to understand the nature of that revolution—if indeed we have the right to speak here of revolution: I shall have to return to this point.

3

Nietzsche, as we have seen, links the Copernican revolution to a transformation of human self-understanding that remains far from complete because it has not yet confronted the full significance of the death of God; because it has covered up its own implications, much as Nikolaj Kusmitsch thought that "they" had covered up what he had learned in school about the earth's motion. To "them" his anxieties have to seem those of a madman, a domesticated successor of that madman of whom Nietzsche has this to say in the *Gay Science* (1882):

> Have you not heard of that madman who lit a lantern in the bright morning hours, ran to the market place, and cried incessantly, "I seek God!" . . .
>
> "Whither is God?" he cried. "I shall tell you. *We have killed him*—you and I. All of us are his murderers. But how have we done this? How were we able to drink up the sea? Who gave us the sponge to wipe away the entire horizon? What did we do when we unchained this earth from its sun? Whither is it moving now? Away from all suns? Are we not plunging continually? Backward, sideward, forward, in all directions? Is there any up and down left? Are we not straying as through an infinite nothing? Do we not feel the breath of empty space? Has it not become colder? Is not night and more night coming on all the while? Must not lanterns be lit in the morning? Do we not hear anything yet of the gravediggers who are burying God? Do we not smell anything yet of God's decomposition? Gods, too, decompose. God is dead. God remains dead. And we have killed him. How shall we, the murderers of all murderers, comfort ourselves? What was holiest and most powerful of all the world has yet owned has bled to death under our knives. Who will wipe this blood off us? What water is there for us to clean ourselves? What festivals of atonement, what sacred games shall we have to invent?[13]

God is dead, Nietzsche writes. This says more than just "We have lost faith in God." Such a faith could perhaps be regained some day. But the murdered God remains dead. Although it is we who killed him, it is not in our power to reawaken him to new life. The process is irreversible—an asymmetry that demands more discussion.

The death of God implies the rise of nihilism, even if this implication may take centuries to become manifest. Nietzsche thus understands the modern age as an age that has not yet confronted its own nihilistic foundation. Only such blindness allows us to still seek shelter in an architecture of values that is in fact already a ruin. "Everything we believe in has become hollow; everything is conditioned and relative; there is no ground, no absolute, no being in itself. Everything is questionable, nothing is true, everything is allowed."[14] Following Nietzsche, Karl Jaspers here describes nihilism as a fate in which we, the heirs of Copernicus, are all caught up, like it or not. But this description of nihilism as a fate we must suffer is called into question by Turgenev's description of his nihilist as someone who "does not bow down before any authority, who does not take any principle on faith, whatever reverence that principle may be enshrined in."[15] Turgenev's nihilist chooses to rely only on his critical intellect; applying that intellect to inherited values, he finds them wanting. Given that choice it is hardly surprising that his search for supports, guides, laws, and love should all end in disappointment. These could not be reconciled with what he chooses not to surrender: a freedom that recognizes no authority beyond itself, no ties binding it to some larger order.

Here we have an answer to the question of Nietzsche's madman: how then have we done this? As I shall show in some detail, we are beings able to rise above ourselves in such a way that the death of God—and with it the destruction of the medieval cosmos, and more generally the destruction of all sorts of architectures that would assign us our place—appears as the inevitable corollary of our freedom. This freedom would seem to be a presupposition of the pursuit of truth, and thus of our science and technology, even if (as Dostoevsky's man from the underground demonstrates) freedom may raise itself to a point where that pursuit itself is called into question. Freedom thus appears as both the ground that supports the modern world and as the abyss that threatens its destruction.

Are we able to bear the burden of this freedom?[16] Is it possible to remain a nihilist? Or will the loss of faith inevitably give birth to bad faith? And why call bad faith "bad"? What in the life of the nihilist can give it meaning and direction? Turgenev had no answer. Basarov dies because he is careless, a carelessness that springs from an inability to care sufficiently for life to protect it.

4

By now it has become customary to tie the revolution that issued in the modern world to the emergence of the scientific attitude in the sixteenth and seventeenth centuries, more especially to Copernicus. It is hardly surprising therefore that Hans Blumenberg should have followed his magisterial defense, *The Legitimacy of the Modern Age*, with his even more monumental account, *The Genesis of the Copernican World*.[17] My aims in this book are related. But concerned as I also am to defend the legitimacy of the modern age against some of its critics, I place greater emphasis on understanding the limits of that legitimacy, on understanding how modernist self-assertion is necessarily shadowed by nihilism and pointing to what it might mean to step out of that shadow. And also different, more Hegelian in some ways, is my understanding of the genesis of the modern world, whose general shape, I shall show, has its deepest foundation in nothing other than our everyday understanding of truth. This understanding is, *pace* Heidegger, far older than Plato or even the Greeks and bound up with the fact of freedom. Finally, my approach is different: I choose a much smaller canvas, take a closer look at a small number of texts as well as some paintings, drawing from them what I hope will be at least a perspicuous, if quite limited model—perhaps only a caricature—of the emergence of our modern world. It is my hope that like any successful caricature, it will cast light on what it caricatures: the thresholds that separate the modern not only from the premodern but also from the postmodern world.

More than Blumenberg, it was Alexandre Koyré who, often by provoking disagreement, provided a first orientation for my initially quite unfocused reflections on many of these problems. And so I conclude this introduction with a look at his introduction to *From the Closed World to the Infinite Universe*. Koyré begins that introduction with this seemingly unproblematic assertion: "It is generally admitted that the seventeenth century underwent, and accomplished, a very radical spiritual revolution of which modern science is at the same time the root and the fruit."[18] In his preface he speaks similarly of a "deep revolution," which in the sixteenth and seventeenth centuries "changed the very framework and patterns of our thinking and of which modern science and modern philosophy are, at the same time, the root and the fruit."[19] I disagree with this thesis: it would be more accurate to say that instead of being both the root and the fruit of that revolution, modern science is only the fruit, or still better, only one fruit. For its roots we have to look further back than the scientific discoveries and speculations of the sixteenth and seventeenth centuries. As Pierre Duhem had already demonstrated,

From the start of the fourteenth century the grandiose edifice of Peripatetic physics was doomed to destruction. Christian faith had undermined all its essential principles; observational science, or at least the only observational science which was somewhat developed—astronomy—had rejected its consequences. The ancient monument was about to disappear; modern science was about to replace it. The collapse of Peripatetic physics did not occur suddenly; the construction of modern physics was not accomplished on an empty terrain where nothing was standing. The passage from one state to the other was made by a long series of partial transformations, each one pretending merely to retouch or to enlarge some part of the edifice without changing the whole. But when all these minor modifications were accomplished, man, encompassing at one glance the result of this lengthy labor, recognized with surprise that nothing remained of the old palace and that a new palace stood in its place.[20]

The metaphor that links science to a palace we have raised invites our questioning: how does this palace relate to the world we actually live in? Did the medievals, or for that matter the Greeks, live in a different world? The answer, it would seem, can only be yes and no. We still get born, eat, make love, and die in ways that make us almost contemporaries of, say, the Socrates of the *Symposium* or the *Phaedo*. There is a sense in which we still live in the same house, even if that house hardly deserves to be called a palace. How does that house relate to the palace of science? Is that palace even habitable?

We shall have to return to such questions, but important as they are, they do not challenge Duhem's suggestion that the new science presupposes a changed world-understanding. To understand this change we must look beyond the history of the cosmological doctrines that Duhem chronicled in such illuminating detail, for every cosmology presupposes a certain world- and self-understanding. The world- and self-understanding of the sixteenth century has a long prehistory. Here the history of art, especially the history of the theory of perspective, provides helpful hints; and therefore I shall consider in some detail certain aspects of this history.

Even more important are theological speculations and, more generally, the Christian understanding of God. Our modern culture, including its present opening to multiculturalism, can only be understood as a post-Christian phenomenon. One thesis I shall defend is that the revolution that inaugurated modern science and helped shape our technological world follows and presupposes a shift in human self-understanding that announces itself more clearly in the sermons of Meister Eckhart than in the learned discourses of his more scientifically inclined scholastic contemporaries. Not that we need to single out Meister Eckhart: he just gives especially eloquent expression to what with Jaspers we may call the spiritual situation of his age. A very different and yet at bottom related expression of this same situation is found in Petrarch's only slightly later account of his ascent of Mount Ventoux. It, too, deserves a place in this account of the prehistory of the scientific revolution.

As such texts demonstrate, the shift in human self-understanding is inseparably bound up with a changing understanding of God and of God's relationship to man and to nature. When this prehistory is kept in mind, the revolution to which Koyré calls our attention seems much less revolutionary. We are more nearly right when we speak of modern science, and thus also of our own culture, as a product of the self-evolution of the Christian culture of the Middle Ages. Something of the sort is already implicit in Hegel's understanding of the modern world.

5

But let me return to the introduction and preface of Koyré's book: how can that radical spiritual revolution of which "modern science [and we can add "philosophy"] is at the same time the root and the fruit" be described? Koyré considers a number of commonly given answers,[21] all of which seem somehow right and deserve our attention:

1. Some have distinguished the modern from the medieval in terms of a "conversion of the human mind from *theoria* to *praxis*" (from theory to

practice), "from the *scientia contemplativa*," the contemplative science of the medievals, "to a *scientia activa et operativa*," a modern science aiming at domination and mastery. In support one could cite Descartes, who insists on just this distinction in his *Discourse on Method* (1637), where he promises his readers that

it is possible to attain knowledge which is very useful in life, and that, instead of a speculative philosophy which is taught in the Schools, we may find a practical philosophy by means of which, knowing the force and action of fire, water, air, the stars, heavens, and all other bodies that environ us, as distinctly as we know the different crafts of our artisans, we can in the same way employ them, in all those uses to which they are adapted, and thus render ourselves the masters and possessors of nature.[22]

To the speculative philosophy of the medievals Descartes here opposes a thinking that bridges the separation of philosophy and craft, wedding theory to technology. Characteristic of this bridging is Descartes's shift from Latin, the language of a small elite, to the vernacular, the language of the artisans. An early example of this shift in thought is Alberti's *On Painting* (1435). Alberti, as we shall see, also promises something like a mastery of nature through mathematical representation. Theory plays an important part in his treatise, but what matters far more is a new desire to put theory to work. Indeed, as far as the theory is concerned, it would be hard to find much progress over medieval optics in what Alberti has to say. Crucial is a new willingness to apply long-familiar insights to the problems faced by the painter in his attempt to create convincing representations of the visible. This tie between theory and practice, between science and technology is characteristic of the practical philosophy envisioned by Descartes. Artists were in the forefront of this development. As Leonardo Olschki demonstrated, Alberti's *On Painting*, which was followed by many similar treatises, thus deserves a place in the prehistory of modern science.[23] And painting was just one activity to draw mathematics into its service: merchants and bankers, masons and goldsmiths had come to insist on a certain mastery of mathematics. This embrace of mathematical speculation by a world pursuing worldly interests hints at the social changes presupposed by the shift from a contemplative science to one aiming at mastery of what is.[24]

2. A second characterization to which Koyré calls our attention is the often-noted "replacement of the teleological and organismic pattern of thinking and explanation by the mechanical and causal pattern." Once again Descartes offers an obvious example. But his insistence on explaining the workings of nature by mechanical models comes at the end of a long process, demonstrating how deep-rooted is the hold of teleological explanation. Consider the following argument by Copernicus: "the universe is spherical; partly because this form being a complete whole, needing no joints, is the most perfect of all; partly because it constitutes the most spacious form which is thus best suited to contain and retain all things; or also because all discrete parts of the world, I mean the sun, the moon, and the planets, appear as spheres."[25] The universe is spherical because this *forma perfectissima* is the best suited to contain all things, the natural form therefore of the heavenly bodies. Teleological reasoning is also evident in the following passage: "But in the center of all resides the Sun. Who, indeed, in this most magnificent temple would put light in another or in a better place than that one wherefrom it could at the same time illuminate the whole of it? Therefore it is not improperly that some people call it the lamp of the world, others its mind, others its ruler. Trismegistus [calls it] the visible God, Sophocles' Electra, the All-Seeing. Thus assuredly, as residing in the royal see the Sun governs the surrounding family of the stars."[26] We shall return to this metaphor of the family with its political implications; also to Copernicus's invocation of the authority of the legendary all-knowing Hermes Trismegistus, which hints at how long it took the emerging new science to disentangle itself from Renaissance magic.[27] But here I want to do no more than underscore Koyré's claim that characteristic of the evolution of a genuinely modern science is the rejection of the kind of thinking exemplified by these quotes. Just what it was that made this rejection so compelling demands further discussion, as does its possible cost.

3. Common, too, are interpretations of the shift to a distinctly modern worldview that appeal to "despair and confusion." The cited passages from Schopenhauer, Nietzsche, Turgenev, and Rilke illustrate this point. Keeping to his period, Koyré refers us instead to the "eternal silence of infinite spaces that frighten Pascal's atheistic 'libertin'"[28] and to the gloom with which John Donne greeted the "new philosophy" in his *Anatomy of the World* (1611):

And . . . new Philosophy calls all in doubt,
The Element of fire is quite put out;
The Sun is lost, and th'earth, and no mans wit
Can well direct him where to looke for it.
And freely men confesse that this world's spent,
When in the Planets and the Firmament
They seeke so many new; then see that this
Is crumbled out againe to his Atomies.
'Tis all in peeces, all cohaerence gone;
All just supply, and all Relation.[29]

There was, as already mentioned, also a very different and much more joy-ful reception of the new science of Copernicus. In the sixteenth century Bruno is its most articulate representative. Chapter 13 will be concerned with his celebration of the infinite.

4. Koyré's fourth characterization, challenged by Blumenberg,[30] invokes a supposed secularization of consciousness. "Secularization" first of all refers to an illegitimate appropriation of Church property by the worldly authori-ties: the world takes over what was once God's. Or rather, human beings at-tempt to put themselves in God's place. Using the language of tradition, we can say that secularization is inseparable from the sin of pride. The thesis that modernity involves a secularization of inherited Christian contents thus sug-gests another thesis: that modernity has its origin in pride. Once more a few lines from Donne's *Anatomy of the World* point to what is essential:

For of Meridians, and Parallels,
Man hath weav'd out a net, and this net throwne
Upon the Heavens, and now they are his owne.
Loth to goe up the hill, or labour thus
To goe to heaven, we make heaven come to us;
We spur, we reine the starres, and in their race
They're diversly content t'obey our pace.[31]

The modern astronomer appears here as someone who has appropriated nature, even the heavens, putting the stars through our paces, as a farmer forces his horses to do his bidding. The secularization hypothesis raises this question: is what here is called "secularization" to be interpreted in terms of the sin of pride, as a fall from grace, or rather as humanity's coming of age, we humans finally seizing what rightfully belongs to us? It is the latter that Descartes attempts to demonstrate and thus to put an end to the religiously motivated skepticism that marks the threshold of the modern age. His demonstration helped lay the foundation of the modern world. Skepticism was, however, to return, if now in a secular mode—as much postmodern thinking bears witness. Modernity thus presents itself to us as framed by skeptical reflections.

5. And finally Koyré calls attention to those who contrast modern subjectivism and the objectivism of the ancients and the medievals. To do justice to this point we shall have to look more closely at what is meant by "objectivism" and "subjectivism": there is a sense in which we moderns have become at one and the same time both more subjective and more objective than the medievals.

Koyré concludes with the suggestion that all these changes can be subsumed under just one or perhaps two closely related developments: they can be understood as a result of the destruction of the finite world of the medievals and of the geometrization of space characteristic of modern science. The two are indeed closely related. But more important to me is showing that the destruction of the medieval cosmos follows from a changed self-understanding, bound up with a new sense of freedom. A passionate interest in perspective and point of view helps to characterize that self-understanding and offers a key to the shape of modernity. That interest in perspective is in turn bound up with theological speculations centering on the infinity of God. Only when we learn to understand these presuppositions of the destruction of the house-like cosmos of the medievals do we begin to understand its justification (or lack of justification); only then can we begin to inquire into the legitimacy or illegitimacy of the modern world. Without such inquiry all attempts to take a step beyond that world remain ill-informed and blind.

Part One

POWER AND POVERTY OF PERSPECTIVE

1

Koyré calls modern science both root and fruit of the revolution that, so we are told, in the sixteenth and seventeenth centuries gave birth to the modern world. But that "revolution," if "revolution" is indeed the right word, has a long prehistory and presupposes an already changed understanding of the world that announces itself long before the sixteenth century. This changed world-understanding is inseparable from a changed self-understanding, which in turn can be linked to speculations concerning the Christian God. Here I am interested in the historical presuppositions of the new science. In tracing these presuppositions I want to use the theme of perspective as a guiding thread. It will lead us from the infinity of the world, to the infinity of the self, and finally to the infinity of God.

In the very beginning of *From the Closed World to the Infinite Universe*, Koyré tells us that

The conception of the infinity of the universe, like everything else or nearly everything else, originates, of course, with the Greeks; and it is certain that the speculations of the Greek thinkers about the infinity of space and the multiplicity of worlds have played an important part in the history we shall be dealing with. It seems to me, however, impossible to reduce the history of the infinitization of the universe to the rediscovery of the world-view of the Greek atomists which became better known through the newly discovered Lucretius (fl. 1st c BC) or the newly translated Diogenes Laertius (3rd c AD).[1]

The footnotes inform us that the manuscript of Lucretius's *De rerum natura* was discovered in 1417 and that the first printed edition of the Latin translation of Diogenes Laertius's *De vita et moribus philosophorum* appeared in 1475 in Venice, to be reprinted in Nürnberg in 1476 and 1479, although the translation was available before then.[2] No doubt these texts played a significant part in preparing the way for widespread acceptance of an infinite universe. But, as Koyré points out, the rediscovery of the worldview of the Greek atomists can hardly explain the destruction of the finite medieval cosmos. It rather raises another question: what accounted for the emerging interest in the idea of an infinite universe that allowed such texts to be taken seriously in the first place? Rediscoveries inevitably presuppose a new receptivity to ideas that often have been around for quite some time.

In this connection Koyré points to the fifteenth century cardinal Nicholas of Cusa, or Nicolaus Cusanus, as the thinker who is most often credited or blamed for the destruction of the medieval cosmos—and in these pages, too, he will be given center stage. Koyré himself, however, is reluctant to grant Cusanus that much importance: he wants the revolution that issues in our modern world to begin with Copernicus (that is, in the sixteenth century) and not a hundred years earlier. He does point out that Kepler, Bruno, and even Descartes all acknowledged Cusanus as a precursor, but if Koyré is right, there are features to the cardinal's thought that separate him decisively from the originators of the new science: "The world-conception of Nicholas of Cusa is not based upon a criticism of contemporary astronomical or cosmological theories, and does not lead, at least in his own thinking, to a revolution in science. Nicholas of Cusa, though it has often been claimed, is not a forerunner of Nicholas Copernicus. And yet his conception is extremely interesting and, in some of its bold assertions—or negations—it goes far beyond anything Copernicus ever dared to think of."[3]

In spite of such daring, what on Koyré's view prevents us from interpreting speculations by Nicholas of Cusa as anticipating those of Copernicus is above all the fact that they were not meant as contributions to science. And this much must be granted: as Thomas McTighe points out, Cusanus "did not make any truly substantive contributions to physics or astronomy."[4] But we should also note that the autonomy of science, today assumed to have nothing to do with theology, is itself a relatively recent development. Modern science has indeed become autonomous in a way that makes it possible to treat it and write its history without paying too much attention to the wider context in which it stands. But the same is not true of its beginnings. As *Infinity and Perspective* will show, any account of scientific change that takes such autonomy for granted rather than as itself a historical product must prove inadequate in considering the science of the sixteenth and seventeenth centuries and its prehistory. The speculation of Cusanus did have implications for and an impact on science.[5] Anyone who took them at all seriously had to reject the then still reigning Aristotelian understanding of science. And although first of all a servant of the Church, Cusanus did in fact have an interest in the technology and science of his day and in ways of advancing them.

But wherein lies the boldness of Cusanus's speculations? Once again I cite Koyré: "We cannot but admire the boldness and depth of Nicholas of Cusa's cosmological speculations which culminate in the astonishing transference to the universe of the pseudo-Hermetic characterization of God: 'a sphere of which the center is everywhere, and the circumference nowhere.'"[6] In this chapter I shall take a closer look at that metaphor, which does indeed offer us a key to Cusanus's speculations. Later I shall try to point out the conceptual link between these speculations and the new science.

2

Before turning to the metaphor of the infinite sphere, a few words about the life of this cardinal, who will figure so prominently in these pages, are in order.[7] His philosophical and theological writings demand to be read in the context of his life and times, for, more than perhaps any other philosopher since the pre-Socratics, Cusanus was a man of the world, a world that he saw disintegrating around him. Reformation was in the air,[8] and Cusanus saw his task as helping reform the Church in order to preserve it. His theological and philosophical speculations had no different aim. There is a sense in which in his life he, too, placed *scientia activa et operativa* ahead of *scientia speculativa*—though not in the Cartesian sense, to be sure.

Cusanus was born in 1401 in Kues (in Latin, Cusa,) a village on the Moselle, not too far from Trier, that today is best known for its wines. His family was apparently quite well-to-do,[9] making its living off the river, especially with shipping. This connection with the river is suggested by the family name, Krebs or Chryfftz, meaning "crayfish," an animal shown in the cardinal's coat of arms. We can still see those arms in a number of churches with which he was associated, and on the copper plate that in 1488 was placed over his heart, which, following his wishes, was buried in front of the altar of the chapel of the hospice he had founded in his hometown.

About the childhood of Cusanus we know little. There is some circumstantial evidence that he studied with the Brothers of the Common Life at the famous Latin school in Deventer, as Erasmus of Rotterdam was to do sixty years later.[10] We can assume that already in these early years he became acquainted with Rhenish mysticism. Cusanus was only fifteen, already a cleric, when he enrolled in the University of Heidelberg, a center of nominalism. After perhaps a year,[11] he was to leave Heidelberg for Padua, then the leading university in Europe, a center especially for the study of nature—where a hundred years later Copernicus was to complete his studies. Cusanus stayed six years in Padua, receiving his doctor of laws in 1423. Besides canon law, he also studied mathematics and astronomy. And in Padua he found a number of friends, the most important being the mathematician and doctor Paolo Toscanelli, to whom he remained close for the rest of his life. After a brief stay in Rome, we find Cusanus back in the Rhineland, where a number of benefices testify to the high esteem in which the young cleric was already being held by the archbishop of Trier. Thus supported, he was able to continue his studies in theology and philosophy at the University of Cologne in 1425, where Heimeric de Campo, an admirer of Albert the Great and Raymond Lull, appears to have become his mentor. At the same time Cusanus would seem to have made a name for himself as a teacher of canon law, otherwise it is difficult to understand the offer of a professorship at Louvain he received in 1428. He rejected it, perhaps because his archbishop, Otto von Ziegenhain, had other plans for him and by then had called him back to Trier (the invitation was repeated in 1435 and once again rejected). In 1427 Cusanus was back in Rome, now as the archbishop's representative.

In the following years Cusanus was to become very active in Church politics. The death of Archbishop Otto in 1430 had led to a contested episcopal election in Trier, which pitted the candidate elected by the majority of the chapter, Jacob von Sirck, against Ulrich von Manderscheid; the latter initially had received only two votes but could count on the support of the local nobility. It was a local repetition of the Great Schism that not long before had divided the Church for forty years between popes in Rome and Avignon (and for a decade a third pope, when the Council of Pisa ineffectively sought to depose the two rivals and elect its own candidate).[12] The Schism finally was ended only in 1417 by the Council of Constance, which asserting the superiority of such a general council over all individuals, including even the pope, replaced all three popes with Martin V. It was this pope who now sought to end the schism in Trier by appointing as archbishop his own candidate, Raban, bishop of Speyer, even though the cathedral chapter by then had united behind Ulrich von Manderscheid. Ulrich chose the young canon lawyer whom he had made his secretary and chancellor to argue his somewhat shaky case before the council that had convened in Basel to complete the work begun in Constance. Cusanus's interest in Latin manuscripts, which bore fruit in his rediscovery of twelve comedies by Plautus, had already secured him a certain reputation among Italian humanists. Although after many presentations Cusanus failed in his mission to persuade those assembled of the merits of his patron's case, he quickly emerged as one of the most articulate and influential politicians at Basel.

The Council of Basel was in turmoil when Cusanus first arrived in 1432. One of his old friends from Padua, now Cardinal Julius Cesarini (1398–1444), who in 1431 had been appointed by Pope Martin V to preside over the council as his legate, had resigned that appointment to protest the issuing of a bull by Martin's successor. Eugenius IV had dissolved the council, an action to which the council responded by reiterating the pope's subordination to a general council that had been proclaimed at Constance. Supported by the emperor, the council decided to suspend the pope—who forestalled the act by giving in to the council's demands and revoking his earlier bull of dissolution. Not surprisingly, given the cause that brought him to Basel, on his arrival Cusanus actively supported the council in its struggle with the pope—and as such a supporter he presents himself to us in his first work, *De Concordantia Catholica* (1433).

But famously, or infamously, Cusanus soon switched sides and backed the pope. Was it the loss of his suit that had turned him against the council? Or had its interminable discussions that seemed to accomplish very little taught him to distrust the democratic process and to put greater faith in autocratic rule? Given his lifelong striving for harmony, he must have been troubled by the divisions that rent the council, by its radicalization, its increasingly strident opposition to the pope. The council went so far as to set itself up as the Church's supreme governing body and to insist that papal tax collectors henceforth send their money to Basel, not to Rome, claiming for itself the right to grant indulgences and canonizations.[13] One issue that divided the council was its decision to democratize by giving a simple parish priest or master of arts the same vote as a bishop or cardinal—a development that caused most of the higher clergy to reconsider their challenge to the pope. What authority could such a divided council claim? Had Cusanus himself not argued that the mark of a valid council "was that it was concluded in harmony, by which he seems to have meant by unanimous agreement"?[14] How could negotiations that Aeneas Sylvius, one of the chroniclers of the Council of Basel, "compared unfavorably to drunkards in a tavern,"[15] claim superiority over the pope? In Paul E. Sigmund's words, "The council rent by divisions seemed to Cusanus to be not the church of God, but the synagogue of Satan."[16]

In a world in which centrifugal forces threatened to tear Church and Europe apart, Cusanus labored for unity; and so it seems fitting that his final break with the fractured and fractious council should have come after a tumultuous meeting in the cathedral (May 7, 1437), a meeting at which the majority, faced with the possibility of reuniting the Eastern and the Western Church, refused to honor the wishes of the Greek representatives, who for obvious reasons insisted that the final negotiations take place in an Adriatic seaport.[17] Cusanus left for Bologna with two bishops and the Greek representatives, seeking papal approval before traveling on to Constantinople to prepare for a council of reunification. When the pope later that year transferred the council to Italy, those remaining in Basel attempted to reassert their authority, suspending the pope and stripping his supporters, including Cusanus, of their ecclesiastical offices.[18]

No doubt considerations advanced by his older friend Cesarini, who also made his definitive break with the Council of Basel when it refused to accommodate the Greeks, reinforced Cusanus's decision to desert its cause. Was he also moved by opportunism, as his enemies charged? For whatever reasons, Basel changed Cusanus into an untiring defender of papal supremacy, a reversal that was to earn him the bitter and lifelong enmity of conciliarists like the zealous Gregor von Heimburg, the epithet "the Hercules of the Eugenians" from Aeneas Sylvius, and Pope Eugene IV's personal support, renewed by his successors Nicholas V, Calixtus III, and Pius II (Aeneas Sylvius). In these years we see Cusanus involved in various attempts to restore unity to Christendom. As a member of the council he negotiated with the Bohemian Hussites; the compromise he proposed, though initially rejected, became the basis of the agreement that was reached in 1436. I have already mentioned his journey to Constantinople for discussions with the Eastern Church, which, threatened by Ottoman expansion, was looking west for support. Fleeting union was in fact achieved at the Council of Ferrara, transferred to Florence in 1439—though it could not save Constantinople, which fell to the Turks only a few years later, in 1453. But whatever was achieved in Florence was shadowed by the increasing hostility of the Council of Basel, which answered the pope's decree that proclaimed the reunification of the Church by deposing him and electing its own anti-pope. The schism seemed to have returned; it kept Cusanus busy from 1438 on, asserting ever more strongly the pope's supreme authority and challenging the authority of the Council at Basel. The threat it posed to papal authority was ended only in 1448 by the Concordat of Vienna, followed by the resignation of the anti-pope Felix V and the final signing in 1449 of the agreements reached.

Cusanus's tireless work for pope and Church did not go unrewarded: around 1440 he was ordained a priest, which meant above all financial security; and just before his death in 1447, Pope Eugene IV named Cusanus a cardinal, an appointment reconfirmed by his successor Nicholas V, who shortly after investiture in 1450 also appointed Cusanus prince-bishop of Brixen (Bressanone), south of the Brenner. It was not a happy choice: from the very beginning the papal appointee was considered an unwelcome intruder by the Tyroleans, who had already chosen their Duke Sigismund's chancellor, Leonhard Wiesmayer, for their bishop but were forced by the emperor to accept the pope's decision.

Before he could assume his post in Brixen, Cusanus was sent by the pope on a legation to Germany and the Low Countries with the important mission of reforming a church very much in need of reform. The cause of conciliarism was still smoldering, supported by national interests that threatened Church and empire with disintegration, and there were countless abuses that needed addressing. The Reformation shows that Cusanus was less than successful as the centrifugal forces proved too strong to overcome; the center no longer would hold—a problem with which Cusanus struggled as long as he lived.

Only in 1452 was Cusanus able to settle in Brixen—although "settle" is hardly the right word: the stubborn cardinal's attempts to use threats, church bans, and military power to bring about the reforms he thought necessary in his diocese only led to counterforce, even threats to his life, and his eventual capture by the Tyrolean duke Sigismund. Sigismund's resolve to resist the pope and his appointee was strengthened by one of Cusanus's enemies from the Basel days, Gregor von Heimburg, who had become the duke's adviser. Released only after making concessions that he later revoked as coerced, in 1460 Cusanus left the Tyrol for Rome, where he was eagerly awaited by his old friend Aeneas Silvius Piccolomini, who with his support had become a cardinal in 1456 and Pope Pius II in 1458; the new pope had learned to respect and rely on the judgment of Cusanus, appointing his ally vicar-general for the Papal States in 1458.[19] Happy to have Cusanus with him once more, he kept him busy in Rome, although here, too, as again later in Orvieto,[20] Cusanus's attempts at reform proved ineffective.

Meanwhile the situation in Brixen remained unresolved. It took years and the efforts of pope and emperor to work out a compromise with the Tyrolean duke to allow Cusanus to return. But on August 11, 1464, two weeks before that compromise was to take effect, while on a mission for his pope to help care for remnants of an army that had gathered in Ancona in futile preparation for a crusade that never gained sufficient support to materialize, Cusanus died in Todi. His friend Pius II died three days later.[21]

The Italian humanist Johannes Andreas Bussi—for six years the cardinal's secretary, who with the cardinal's encouragement had established the first Italian printing shop in the Benedictine monastery of Subiaco (1465)—included a eulogy for Cusanus in the dedicatory epistle to Pope Paul II that accompanied his Apuleius translation (1469). In it he praises Cusanus, this

PERSPECTIVE AND THE INFINITY OF THE UNIVERSE

best of all men (*vir eo melior nunquam sit natus*), for (among other things) keeping "in his memory not just the works of the ancient authors, but also those of both the earlier and the later Middle Ages, right down to our own time."[22] This is apparently the first time that we encounter the term "Middle Ages" (*media tempestas*): an epochal threshold has been crossed.[23]

3

To return to the figure of the infinite sphere: it was of course not original with Cusanus. Borges sketched the history of this metaphor in a little piece in *Labyrinths*, "The Fearful Sphere of Pascal." In a few pages he traces its origin back to the pre-Socratics—to Xenophanes, Parmenides, and Empedocles. Skipping centuries he turns to the twelfth-century theologian Alan of Lille, who is said to have discovered the formula "God is an intelligible sphere, whose center is everywhere and whose circumference nowhere" in a fragment attributed to Hermes Trismegistus;[24] following him medieval writers are said to have used it as a metaphor for God. According to Borges, it was only after the discoveries of the new astronomy had shattered the closed world of the Middle Ages that, searching for words "to tell men of Copernican space," Giordano Bruno described the universe as an infinite sphere. But while Bruno exulted in this infinity, "seventy years later there was no reflection of that fervor left and men felt lost in space and time. . . . The absolute space that meant liberation for Bruno, became a labyrinth and an abyss for Pascal." Nature had "become a fearful sphere, whose center is everywhere and whose circumference is nowhere."[25]

The story Borges tells is in keeping with Koyré's claim for the new science: that it was not only the fruit but also the root of that revolution which established our modern world. I have already challenged this claim. And we also need to challenge Borges's little sketch, which requires correction as well as fleshing out. Borges is right to insist on the importance of "the history of the different intonations given a handful of metaphors" and right to single out the central shift in the history of the infinite sphere, its transference from God to the universe for special attention. But Borges was wrong to give the credit to Bruno—Bruno here was only following Cusanus. To point this out is not just to correct Borges's sketch but to give greater importance to that metaphor than Borges can. Quite in the spirit of Koyré,

Borges suggests that the metaphor's transference from God to the universe followed the astronomical discoveries and theories of the sixteenth century. The reverse was the case; the metaphor's transference preceded and helped prepare the way for the new astronomy. Nor should this surprise us; for these astronomical observations and speculations presuppose a new way of looking at the world. As Thomas S. Kuhn points out, "the very ease and rapidity with which astronomers saw new things when looking at old objects with old instruments may make us wish to say, that after Copernicus astronomers lived in a different world."[26] The last part of this statement is a bit misleading, suggesting once again that this new world had its foundation in the Copernican revolution. But that revolution was itself made possible only by a more fundamental shift in the way human beings understood their world, which opened up new perceptual and intellectual possibilities. What Koyré calls Cusanus's "astonishing transference to the universe of the pseudo-Hermetic characterization of God: 'a sphere of which the center is everywhere and the circumference nowhere'" is part of, and can furnish a key to a better understanding of that shift.

But is Cusanus's transference of the metaphor really so astonishing? Is it not rather, as I shall attempt to show in more detail in the next chapter, suggested by the metaphor itself? That is, the metaphor of the infinite sphere presupposes an understanding of God and human that had to lead reflection beyond the medieval cosmos. A deep historical and systematic connection links medieval mysticism to the new cosmology.[27] Unless this connection is recognized, the work of a thinker like Cusanus will seem a curious hybrid of still-medieval theological discussions and some very modern epistemological and cosmological speculations. (An analogous claim can be made for his political thought.) This dichotomy, however, is false. In Cusanus's writings the two studies are closely joined; theology leads quite naturally to cosmology.[28]

I will approach this claim by turning to the very beginning of the twelfth chapter of the second book of *On Learned Ignorance* (1440), *De conditionibus terrae*, "On the conditions of the Earth"—perhaps the most often cited and most widely discussed passage in all of his writings.

The ancients did not attain unto the points already made, for they lacked learned ignorance. It has already become evident to us that the earth is indeed moved, even though we do not perceive this to be the case. For we apprehend motion only through a certain comparison with something fixed. For example, if someone did not know that a body of water was flowing and did not see the shore while he was on a ship in the middle of the water, how would he recognize that the ship was being moved?[29]

Cusanus is inviting the reader to engage in a simple thought experiment. At the same time it must have held a very personal significance for him: as he tells us in the letter to Cardinal Cesarini that he appended to the book as a kind of epilogue, the fundamental thought of *De Docta Ignorantia* came to Cusanus during the winter of 1437/1438 while he was "at sea en route back from Greece" (p. 158), where he had worked toward the reunification of the Roman and the Greek churches, toward a reconciliation of their different perspectives. Recent memories of the haggling at Basel, of the way the different parties there focused on what divided them rather than on their common goal, the unity of the Church, must also have colored what he then experienced.

And because of the fact that it would always seem to each person (whether he were on the earth, the sun, or another star) that he was at the "immovable" center, so to speak, and that all the other things were moved: assuredly, it would always be the case that if he were on the sun, he would fix a set of poles in relation to himself; if on the earth, another set; on the moon, another; on Mars, another; and so on. Hence, the world-machine will have its center everywhere and its circumference nowhere, so to speak; for God, who is everywhere and nowhere, is its circumference and center. (II.12;1, p. 117)

The poles by which we orient ourselves are fictions, created by us. As such, they reflect what happens to be the standpoint of the observer, his particular perspective.

In the beginning of this passage Cusanus appeals to the principle of learned ignorance. I shall return to this idea in the following chapter, but the paragraph gives us already a first understanding of its significance: In what sense did the ancients lack "learned ignorance"? One thing they failed to understand was the nature and power of perspective. So they mistook perspectival appearance for reality. Their geocentric cosmology is born of this mistake. The earth, to be sure, appears to be the stable center of our life-world. This appearance makes it natural for us to believe that it must therefore also be at the cosmic center. But could not someone on the moon or on Mars or on any other star make the same argument and with equal conviction proclaim whatever heavenly body they happened to inhabit the center of the cosmos? Rest and motion, Cusanus points out, are relative concepts; what we take to be fixed depends on our point of view. By undermining the idea of a natural center, such speculation tended to undercut not only the geocentric cosmology of the Middle Ages but also the heliocentric cosmology of Copernicus and Kepler that was to replace it. For Cusanus, not only is there no good reason to place the earth at the cosmic center, but the idea of such a center is itself no more than a perspectival illusion, a human projection. Our life-world, to be sure, has its center, established by the accident of our body's location. But that location does not bind reflection. I can imagine countless places I might occupy, can place myself in thought on the farthest star. Were I to live there, I would experience that star as the center of the cosmos. And the same will hold for all beings like us, wherever they might be. In that sense Cusanus can say that "the world-machine will have its center everywhere and its circumference nowhere, so to speak." We may not confuse our life-world with this "world-machine": to us the earth seems fixed, just as the sun, moon, and stars seem to rise and set. But their motion is relative to what we have taken to be fixed; and we have no more right to claim that the earth is in fact fixed (or is moving, for that matter) than that traveler on the ship, out of sight of the shores can judge his motion. Can we see the shores of the "sea" in which the spaceship earth faces an uncertain future? But if we cannot even make sense of the center of our cosmos, we also cannot speak of firm boundaries.

The passage in *Learned Ignorance* invites comparison with one in Copernicus's *De Revolutionibus* that is designed to make the reader more receptive to the new astronomy.

And why are we not willing to acknowledge that the *appearance* of a daily revolution belongs to the heavens, its *actuality* to the earth? The relation is similar to that of which Virgil's Aeneas says "We sail out of the harbor, and the countries and cities recede." For when a ship is sailing along quietly, everything which is outside of it will appear to those on board to have a motion corresponding to the motion of the ship, and the voyagers are of the erroneous opinion that they with all that they have with them are at rest. This can without doubt also apply to the motion of the earth, and it may appear as if the whole universe were revolving.[30]

Ornamenting his remark with a reference to the *Aeneid*, Copernicus, too, uses the example of someone on a ship to call the reader's attention to the relativity of apparent motion. Reflection on the nature of perspective will teach us that whatever presents itself to the eye, to perception, is no more than subjective appearance. To get to "actuality" or objective reality we have to reflect on perspectival appearance. Reality cannot in principle be seen as it is. Reality, as it is, is invisible. Such distrust of the eye is one of the defining characteristics of the emerging modern understanding of reality and we shall have to return to it. More radical than Copernicus, Cusanus is led by such reflections to reject the idea of a cosmic center altogether. Does our understanding discover a center in space?

Such reflections may perhaps seem obvious to us; but to see how difficult they must have been, how much what then seemed obvious opposed them in the fifteenth and sixteenth centuries, consider Tycho Brahe's famous report of a new star that he had observed in 1573. Tycho, we should note, was supposed to have been the keenest observer of the heavens at the time—that is, before the advent of the telescope:

Last year [1572], in the month of November, on the eleventh day of the month, in the evening, after sunset when, according to my habit, I was contemplating the stars in a clear sky, I noticed that a new and unusual star, surpassing the other stars in brilliancy, was shining almost directly above my head; and since I had, almost from boyhood, known all of the stars of the heavens perfectly (there is no great difficulty in attaining that knowledge), it was quite evident to me that there had never before been any star in that place in the sky, even the smallest, to say nothing of a star so conspicuously bright as this. I was so astonished at this sight that I was not ashamed to doubt the trustworthiness of my own eyes. But when I observed that others, too, on having the place pointed out to them, could see that there was really a star there, I had no further doubts. A miracle indeed, either the greatest of all that have occurred in the whole range of nature since the beginning of the world, or one certainly that is to be classed with those attested by the Holy Oracles, the staying of the Sun in its course in answer to the prayers of Joshua and the darkening of the Sun's face at the time of the Crucifixion. For all philosophers agree, and facts clearly prove it to be the case, that in the ethereal region of the celestial world no change, in the way either of generation or corruption, takes place; but that the heavens and the celestial bodies in the heavens are without increase or diminution, and that they undergo no alteration, either in number or in size or in light or in any other respect; that they always remain the same, like unto themselves in all respects, no years wearing them away.[31]

Tycho shows himself here as being in many ways bound by the traditional understanding of the cosmos. Note the presuppositions that make it so difficult for him to accept what he sees: Tycho is committed to the view, rendered authoritative by Aristotle, that allows no generation or corruption in the world above the moon—the only exception is a divine miracle. Presupposed also is the heterogeneity of the cosmos. A mundane realm, which knows change and corruption, is opposed to a heavenly sphere, which does not know either.

Did Tycho's observations shatter that worldview? They certainly dealt it a serious blow. But more than a hundred years earlier Cusanus took belief in cosmic heterogeneity to have its foundation only in perspectival illusion and thus in ignorance. Consider the ending of chapter 11 of book 2 of *On Learned Ignorance:*

For example, if someone were on the earth but beneath the north pole [of the heavens], and someone else were at the north pole [of the heavens], then just as to the one on the earth it would appear that the pole is at the zenith, so to the one at the pole it would appear that the center is at the zenith. And just as the antipodes have the sky above, as do we, so to those [persons] who are at either pole [of the heavens] the earth would appear to be at the zenith. And wherever anyone would be, he would believe himself to be at the center. Therefore merge these different imaginative pictures so that the center is the zenith and vice versa. Thereupon you will see—through the intellect, to which only learned ignorance is of help—that the world and its motion and shape cannot be apprehended. For [the world] will appear as a wheel in a wheel and a sphere in a sphere—having its center and circumference nowhere, as was stated. (II.11; p. 116)

The thought experiment is designed to undermine belief in an absolute center. But without an absolute center we cannot speak of absolute motion.

The traditional hierarchical conception of the cosmos, on which Tycho Brahe still relies, depends on the notion of a center. As this idea is called into question, so is the idea of a hierarchically ordered cosmos. That idea had thus been challenged speculatively long before there were observations—like Tycho's of his new star—to support that challenge. More to the point, only the challenge presented by such speculation prepared the way for a science that was to take such observations seriously. Why did Tycho even bother to measure the parallax of his new star to show that it was indeed above the moon? Tycho's star was not the first supernova to be observed. That no earlier "new star" had had such an impact testifies that the intellectual climate had changed.

4

The cardinal's speculations presuppose an unusual interest in the phenomenon of perspective. Cusanus loved to play games of perspectival variation, to invite the reader to put himself in some other place—on the other side of the earth, for example, or on the moon, or on Mars, or at the north pole of the heavens. How would things appear to us given such a change in perspective? Historically and conceptually such interest in perspective and the boundless, objective, homogeneous space of the new science belong together.

In support of his thesis of cosmic homogeneity, Cusanus runs through a number of thought experiments to challenge the traditional view of the earth as low and base. Cusanus thus tries to show that the earth's darkness, supposedly proof of its baseness, is itself but a perspectival appearance:

Moreover, [the earth's] blackness is not evidence of its lowliness. For if someone were on the sun, the brightness which is visible to us would not be visible [to him]. For when the body of the sun is considered, [it is seen to] have a certain more central "earth," as it were, and a certain "fiery and circumferential" brightness, as it were, and in its middle a "watery cloud and brighter air," so to speak—just as our earth [has] its own elements. Hence, if someone were outside the region of fire, then through the medium of the fire our earth, which is on the circumference of [this] region, would appear to be a bright star—just as to us, who are on the circumference of the region of the sun, the sun appears to be very bright. Now the moon does not appear to be so bright, perhaps because we are within its circumference and are facing the more central parts—i.e., are in the moon's "watery region," so to speak. (II.12; pp. 117–118)

I cite this argument because it shows how completely Cusanus has broken with the Aristotelian cosmos, how convinced he is of cosmic homogeneity. To be sure, he still appeals to the traditional theory of the elements and their ordering, but something analogous is now said to hold for every star: every heavenly body, he suggests, will have, "so to speak," its earthy, watery, and fiery sphere.[32] If appearance would seem to argue against it, it does so only because of our special point of view. We know of course that in this case Cusanus is badly mistaken, that his perspectivism here greatly overshoots the mark: the differences between sun, moon, and earth are more profound than he makes them out to be. But we should keep in mind that the thesis of cosmic homogeneity that he presupposes remains very much with us: it is, for example a presupposition of our search for extraterrestrial intelligence, to which I shall return later.

In keeping with the thesis of cosmic homogeneity, Cusanus insists that the earth is a star among countless stars: "the earth is a noble star which has a light and a heat and an influence that are distinct and different from [that of] all other stars, just as each star differs from each other star with respect to its light, its nature, and its influence" (II.12; p. 118). To be sure, every star is different from every other; but such differences do not derive from some cosmic hierarchy. There is no reason to call one more noble than another. In an important sense all stars are of equal value and thus equivalent. In the same vein Cusanus denies that "the influence" the earth receives is "evidence establishing its imperfection. For being a star, perhaps the earth, too, influences the sun and the solar region, as I said. And since we do not experience ourselves in any other way than as being in the center where influences converge, we experience nothing of this counter-influence" (I.12; p. 119).

Nor are death and decay an argument for the baseness of the earth:

Moreover, the earthly destruction-of-things which we experience is not strong evidence of [the earth's] lowliness. For since there is one universal world and since there are causal relations between all the individual stars, it cannot be evident to us that anything is altogether corruptible; rather [a thing is corruptible only] according to one or another mode of being, for the causal influences—being contracted, as it were, in one individual—are separated, so that the mode of being such and such perishes. Thus, death does not occupy any space, as Virgil says. For death seems to be nothing except a composite thing's being resolved into its components. And who can know that such dissolution occurs only in regard to terrestrial inhabitants? (II.12; p. 120)

Koyré could have pointed to such passages in support of his claim that Cusanus does not write as a scientist. He is indeed engaging only in thought experiments: acts of imagining how things might present themselves, given radically different points of view, that are designed to prevent us from falsely absolutizing what happens to be our own terrestrial point of view. But to say that Cusanus here is engaging *only* in thought experiments is not to say that he did not want his readers to take them seriously. To do so, they had to be persuaded by Cusanus's claim that our experience of the world is limited by what happens to be our point of view and that we should not think that such a point of view gives us access to the way things really are: there are infinitely many other possible points of view, and to each corresponds a possible experience that would take itself to be at the center. We have no good reason to privilege one of these above the others. Our geocentrism is supported by no more than a natural illusion—natural because founded in the very nature of experience itself, which inevitably places the experiencing subject at what it does indeed experience as the center. Learned ignorance will unmask such centrist illusion as being what Francis Bacon later was to call an idol of the tribe.

Earlier I suggested that the thesis of cosmic homogeneity that Cusanus presupposes remains very much with us. In this connection it is worth noting that Cusanus already was led by that thesis to the assertion that other heavenly bodies, such as sun and moon, must be inhabited too; and even as he insists that "since that entire region is unknown to us, those inhabitants remain altogether unknown," he does not hesitate to speculate about what they might be like (II.12; p. 120). He is aware that all such speculations are only that—mere conjectures that should not be taken too seriously; and many of them are indeed quite fantastic. But the details are not important here: what matters is the reflection on perspective and how it is used to undermine the traditional idea of a center. With that undermining, the traditional understanding of cosmic heterogeneity also has to collapse. What significance did "up" and "down" now still possess? What place could one assign to heaven and hell in the kind of universe envisioned by Cusanus? The doctrine of learned ignorance thus not only leads to a rejection of the traditional geocentrism but also leaves heliocentrism far behind. In this sense Koyré is right to suggest that Cusanus goes far beyond Copernicus.

Chapter 12 of book 2 of *On Learned Ignorance* was often cited in the following centuries.[33] Cusanus was considered a forerunner of Copernicus. As such, it was hoped, he could help legitimate the new science: what a cardinal once was able to say with impunity should not now be held against the astronomer. Campanella thus uses him in his *Apology for Galileo*, as do Descartes, Mersenne, and Gassendi.[34] Of all these Bruno, as we shall see, was the most enthusiastic.

But in particular the view that there might be countless other heavenly bodies with intelligent inhabitants reappeared again and again in the following centuries, playing an important part in speculations that extend from Kepler to Kant. It is in this context that Cusanus appears in Burton's *Anatomy of Melancholy* (1621), as he does in Huygens and Fontenelle.[35] Among Enlightenment thinkers the view came to be almost taken for granted. And it continues to retain its appeal today, though in search of these extraterrestrials we now have to look ever farther away.

That we still have not found them has become by now something of an embarrassment for a science committed to the thesis of cosmic homogeneity.[36] In the late 1970s, astronomers, physicists, chemists, biologists, and space travel experts came together in College Park, Maryland, to address that embarrassment. Their conference bore the title: "Where Are They? A Symposium on the Implications of Our Failure to Observe Extraterrestrials." "They," of course, referred to those alien beings, who must, it was thought, be somewhere out there in space, and who, disappointingly, had not yet been contacted. Most participants felt compelled by this failure to give up a long cherished and taken-for-granted belief, we were told by the

New York Times.[37] At bottom, it called into question the belief not just in extraterrestrial life, but that principle of cosmic homogeneity whose implications Nicolaus Cusanus developed in *On Learned Ignorance.* Today such reflections might take something like the following form: Assume that matter exists more or less homogeneously throughout the cosmos. If there are processes that let life emerge from inorganic matter and intelligence from life, given the immensity of the cosmos and the homogeneity of matter, then is it not inconceivable, that such life should have evolved only once, here on earth? Must not the same processes have produced it again and again? To insist on the uniqueness of life on earth seems to be to fall back into a pre-Copernican geocentrism.

The article on the Maryland conference was headlined "Close Encounters with Alien Beings are Held Unlikely." The significance of that failure should now be clear: it invites us to reconsider the challenge to the uniqueness of the earth that is part of the Copernican tradition and is one of the presuppositions of our modern understanding of reality. I shall follow that invitation in this book's concluding chapter.

1

The cosmological speculations found in chapters 11 and 12 of book 2 of *On Learned Ignorance* rely on what I want to call the principle of perspective. In rather general form it may be expressed as follows: to think a perspective as a perspective is to be in some sense already beyond it, is to have become learned about its limitations. No longer will we understand what shows itself to us in that perspective as more than just a perspectival appearance of something that does not show itself to us as it is. To be aware of perspective is to be aware not only of what is seen, but also of the way our particular point of view lets the seen appear as it does—to be aware of the conditions that rule our seeing. The space of perspective has its center in the perceiving eye, more generally in the perceiving subject. Everything that presents itself in that space is relative to that subject, is the subjective appearance of some object. Whatever thus presents itself in this space is no more than the appearance of a reality that as such cannot take its place in that space. To show itself as it is, it would require a different kind of space, an objective space, where "objective" here is thought of in opposition to perspectival and means not relative to a particular point of view in space.

The awareness of how my point of view lets things appear to me as they do cannot be divorced from another realization: awareness of what constitutes a particular point of view inevitably carries with it an awareness of other possible points of view. To recognize the limits imposed on what I see by my location here and now, I have to be in some sense already beyond these limits, capable of imagining and conceiving other locations. As I look at the table before me, I am thus also aware that this table will look different, given different points of view. This shows that what happens to be my present location is not a prison. Not only am I able to move, but in imagination and thought I am able to transcend these limitations even without moving. This ability of the self to raise itself above the perspectives that first bind it leads to demands for more adequate—that is less perspective-bound, and ideally truly objective—descriptions; it thus leads to demands also for a conception of space that allows us to go beyond all merely perspectival descriptions.

I have suggested that once I understand the way what I see is relative to my particular point of view and to the makeup of my body and eyes, I will no longer be tempted to mistake appearance for reality. To lead us to such an awareness is the point of Cusanus' simile likening the earth to a ship in some body of water, where the shores can't be seen. Geocentrism is understood by him as but an expression of that tendency founded in the perspectival nature of all our experience to place us at the center, just as the perceiving eye is at the center of perspectival space. Cusanus thus seeks to show that the geocentric cosmology of Aristotle and his successors rests on a perspectival illusion.

Cusanus's doctrine of learned ignorance—on which, as he himself says, his cosmological speculations depend—is inseparable from this principle of perspective. To become learned about one's ignorance is to become learned about the extent to which what we took to be knowledge is subject to the distorting power of perspective. Cusanus himself reminds us of the relation between his doctrine and the teaching of Socrates, who "seemed to himself to know nothing except that he did not know."[1] But in book 10 of the *Republic* that same Socrates suggests a way in which we might be rescued from the rule of perspectival appearance. Socrates here charges an art that aims at lifelike representations of appearances with exploiting that weakness of the human mind which is inseparable from its embodiment:

And what is the faculty in man to which imitation is addressed?
What do you mean?

I will explain: The body which is large when seen near, appears small when seen at a distance?

True.

And the same object appears straight when looked at out of the water, and crooked when in the water; and the concave becomes convex, owing to the illusions about colors to which the sight is liable. Thus every sort of confusion is revealed within us; and this is the weakness of the human mind on which the art of conjuring and of deceiving by light and shadow and other ingenious devices imposes, having an effect on us, like magic.

True.

And the arts of measuring and numbering and weighing come to the rescue of the human understanding—there is the beauty of them—and the apparent greater or less, or more or heavier, no longer have the mastery over us, but give way before calculation and measure and weight?[2]

Socrates speaks of "the weakness of the human mind" that the artists exploit. This weakness arises because our access to what is, is furnished first of all by the senses. But the senses are unable to offer us more than perspectival appearances. If we are to gain access to reality as it actually is, we should not simply accept these appearances; they need to be interpreted. If we want to get at the truth, we will have to interpret what the senses provide us, represent it in a different medium, recast it into medium of thought, and we will have to do so in a way that will free the represented from all perspectival appearance. Such representation, Socrates suggests, will depend on the arts of measuring, numbering, and weighing, on a shift from quality to quantity.

What Socrates here has to tell us should seem obvious: as I look at this room I am also aware that each person entering and moving about in it will see it differently. And yet they all know themselves to be in the same room. Suppose one of these persons were asked to describe the room and not just its perspectival appearance. How would she go about it? She might give its dimensions, place it in the building, the building in the city, and so on. It is clear that the demanded description should avoid everything that makes reference to the individual's particular perspective. In its essentials it should be no different from the description someone occupying a quite different place might give. The place occupied by the description's author should not show itself in the description. Should such a description use color words? Are colors not by their very nature tied to the makeup of our eyes, that is to say, are they not part of perspectival appearance, even though the perspective in question may be one most human beings share? But must we not, if we want to get away from appearance, get away not just from colors but from all secondary qualities and describe objects in terms of their primary qualities alone? This, at least, is suggested by Socrates when he insists that we should turn to the arts of measuring, numbering, and weighing: primary qualities are precisely what these arts get hold of. But his insistence suggests in turn that if science is to get beyond appearance, if it is to get closer to reality, it will have to use the language of mathematics. Given such considerations, Aristotle's science of nature, be it his physics, be it his astronomy, has to be judged too tied to appearance. I shall have to return to this point. But enough has been said to suggest that if at the beginning of the modern period we find a repudiation of Aristotelian science, such repudiation is linked to a reappropriation of Platonic insights. The thought of Cusanus illustrates this point.

Let me restate the central point: the demand for knowledge implies a demand for liberation from the distorting power of perspective. Truth requires objectivity; objectivity requires freedom from particular points of view. Reality discloses itself to us only in the spirit's more objective reconstructions of what the senses present to us. The reflection on perspective thus leads to an understanding of reality as invisible as it is. In this sense one might also want to speak of the essential absence of reality. If presence is construed in the image of presence to sight, then reality as such remains absent, invisible. The invisibility of reality as it is, is a presupposition of our science. To ask, "What is the color of an electron?" is to ask the wrong sort of question.

2

When Cusanus invited his readers to imagine themselves on a ship, unable to see the shores, to think the earth in the image of that ship as a spaceship, or when he invited them to consider how the cosmos would look to a man on the moon or on Mars, he engaged in such thought experiments to weaken the hold that a geocentric perspective has on us humans just because we happen to be on earth. As we saw in the previous chapter, Copernicus makes similar use of a ship at sea to figure our mobile earth and thus to make the reader more receptive to his heliocentric view of the cosmos. But as this reference to Copernicus suggests, by themselves reflections such as these do not necessarily lead to the thought of an infinite universe. Heliocentrist that he was, Copernicus after all, like Kepler after him, continued to hold on to the idea of a center and the related idea of a finite universe. What then led Cusanus to his insistence on the boundlessness of the cosmos?

Once more consider chapter 11 of book 2. That chapter begins with an appeal to learned ignorance. It is learned ignorance that is said to have generated the principle that we cannot think either an absolute minimum or an absolute maximum. Here is the key passage:

However, it is not the case that in any genus—even [the genus] of motion—we come to an unqualifiedly maximum and minimum. Hence, if we consider the various movements of the spheres, [we will see that] it is not possible for the world-machine to have, as a fixed and immovable center, either our perceptible earth or air or fire or any other thing. (II.11; p. 114)

Cusanus, as we have already learned, does not argue for a heliocentric rather than a geocentric position. He instead challenges what both positions presuppose, that we are able to make sense of the idea of a "fixed and immovable" cosmic center. But if we are unable to gain a clear and distinct understanding of such a center, we also will be unable to make sense of something being absolutely at rest. For in the absence of such a center, what could that phrase mean?

But Casanus here advances a rather different consideration when he continues: "For the [unqualifiedly] minimum must coincide with the [unqualifiedly] maximum" (II.11; p. 114). With this we come not just to another puzzling statement but to an expression of one of the central doctrines of Cusanus, the coincidence of opposites. What sense can we make of it? Before I take up this challenge, let me return to the passage I have been quoting: "therefore, the center of the world coincides with the circumference." The center of the world is the minimum that coincides with the maximum, the world's circumference. Here we have that transference of the metaphor of the infinite sphere from God to the cosmos that explodes the finite cosmos of the Middle Ages and that Koyré finds so astonishing. That transference is here justified by an appeal to the coincidence of opposites. But before returning to that coincidence, I continue:

Hence, the world does not have a [fixed] circumference. For if it had a fixed center, it would also have a [fixed] circumference; and hence it would have its own beginning and end within itself, and it would be bounded in relation to something else, and beyond the world there would be something else and space (*locus*). But all these [consequences] are false. Therefore, since it is not possible for the world to be enclosed between [a physical] center and a physical circumference, the world—of which God is the center and the circumference—is not understood. And although the world is not infinite, it cannot be conceived as finite, because it lacks boundaries within which it is enclosed. (fig. 3)

Three points especially require further discussion:

1. What is meant by learned ignorance?
2. What connection is there between learned ignorance and the coincidence of opposites?
3. What justifies the transference of the metaphor of the infinite sphere from God to the cosmos?

3

As we have already learned, the fundamental thought of *On Learned Ignorance* came to Cusanus while at sea, returning from Greece, still burdened by the chaos of Basel but hopeful that his dreams of a truly united Church might yet become reality. This first and most significant of Cusanus's philosophical works was then finished in Kues on February 12, 1440.[3]

As Nietzsche knew so well, distance from what we take to be terra firma lets us wonder about just where we are and should be going. Thus he lets his Zarathustra address his doctrine of the eternal recurrence first to sailors, to those who, finding themselves at sea,[4] have left behind the familiar and readily taken-for-granted. Related is Wittgenstein's observation in the *Philosophical Investigations* that philosophical problems have the form, "I do not

. . .

figure 3

Camille Flammarion,

Un missionaire du moyen age raconte qu'il

avait trouvé le "point où le ciel et la Terre

se touchent. . . ." illustration from

L'atmosphère: Météorologie populaire

(Paris: Libraire Hachette, 1888), p. 163.

Often said to be a German woodcut, dating from ca. 1530 and repeatedly connected to the thought of Nicolaus Cusanus, Bruno Weber has shown convincingly that this wood engraving has to date from the 19th century and is probably based on a design by Flammarion himself, meant to illustrate his reference to a "naive missionary of the Middle Ages," who tells of how in search of the earthly paradise he came to the horizon where heaven and earth touch, found a place where they were not quite welded together, and was able to push his shoulders through the opening to glimpse what lay beyond. Weber traces the words "où le ciel et la Terre se touchent" back to the legend of Macarius Romanus, which Flammarion had related in his earlier *Les mondes imaginaries et les mondes réels: Voyage pittoresque dans le ciel et revue critique des théories humaines scientifiques et romanesques, anciennes et modernes, sur les habitants des astres* (1865) as an imaginative attempt to think the limits of the then-familiar cosmos. See Weber, "Ubi caelum terrae se coniungit: Ein altertümlicher Aufriß des Weltgebäudes von Camille Flammarion," *Gutenberg-Jahrbuch 1973,* ed. Hans Widmann (Mainz: Gutenberg-Gesellschaft, 1973), pp. 381–408, which includes a thorough review of the relevant, if often misleading, literature.

know my way about," a remark that refers us back to Aristotle who locates the origin of philosophy in wonder.[5] Philosophy has its origin in dislocation, in a leave-taking from what normally orients and grounds us, from the everyday world and its concerns. This leave-taking renders philosophy problematic in its origin. It is hardly an accident that Thales, the first philosopher, should also be described as the first absent-minded philosopher, who, gazing at the stars (which did not concern him) fell into a well, to be mocked by that presumably pretty Thracian maid for whom he had no eyes.

Cusanus had Aristotle in mind when he, too, begins *On Learned Ignorance* with the theme of wonder (*admiratio, admirari*). Addressing his old friend Cesarini as his ideal reader, he suggests that this learned cardinal, "extremely busy with important public affairs," might well wonder what would lead his younger friend to publish his "foreigner's foolishness" (*barbaras ineptias*) and to select him alone as judge. But Cusanus also expresses the hope that the novelty of the title would incite the cardinal's curiosity: "This wondering shall, I hope, induce your knowledge-hungry mind to take a look" (prologue, p. 49)

But should not such hunger for novelty be resisted? Cusanus invites suspicion that curiosity will only lead us away from what really needs doing. Busy serving the Holy See, Cesarini presumably has better things to do than waste his time on this "very foolish production" (*ineptissimum conceptum*). By calling attention to the novelty of his title and to the unusual, perhaps even "monstrous" things found in the book, Cusanus himself thus invites the charge that was to be raised by Johannes Wenck:

For if I behold the mind of the prophet: after the elimination of malevolent wars, which are repugnant to our God, and, moreover, after the weapons of treachery have been broken and knowledge is to be had of Christ, our peacemaker and defender, then comes the command "Be still and see that I am God." For He envisioned certain who were free to spend time in the Lord's vineyard and who are accused in Matthew 20: "Why do you stand here all day idle?" Very many *see*—not unto salvation, the end of our faith, but with regard to curiosity and vanity. [We read] about these [individuals] in Romans 1: "They became vain in their thoughts, and their foolish heart was darkened."[6]

Cusanus may well be right to claim that "Unusual things, even if they be monstrous, are accustomed to move us" (prologue, p. 49), but this is not to say that they will move us as we should be moved. As the story of Thales' fall into the well suggests, the wonder that Cusanus, too, would place at the origin of philosophy had been shadowed by the charge of idle curiosity from the very beginning. Cusanus, to be sure, agrees with Aristotle when the latter links wonder to that desire to know which he places at the very center of human nature. Isn't it precisely the ability to wonder that raises us above the animals? Giving a Christian turn to the Aristotelian "All men by nature desire to know," Cusanus claims that "We see that by the gift of God there is present in all things a natural desire to exist in the best manner in which the condition of each thing's nature permits this" (I.1; pp. 49–50). What lifts us humans above the animals is our intellect. Our noblest desire is therefore the intellectual desire to know. Would God have implanted such a desire in us only to leave it forever dissatisfied? Our desire to know cannot be vain; we must be capable of discerning the truth, where the mark of truth is the inability of a sound and free intellect to withhold its assent. Truth binds the freedom of the intellect. What we judge true presents itself to us as having to be as it presents itself to us. Necessity and truth go together.

But are we really able to seize the truth? Cusanus himself, repeating the Socratic profession of ignorance, would seem to deny it: "regarding truth, it is evident that we do not know anything other than the following: viz., that we know truth not to be precisely comprehensible as it is. For truth may be likened unto the most absolute necessity (which cannot be either something more or something less than it is), and our intellect may be likened to possibility" (I.3; pp. 52–53). We are separated from the truth as possibility is separated from necessity. What we know is that the truth will elude us— which is not to say that we are therefore altogether cut off from the truth. But if "we know truth not to be precisely comprehensible as it is," are we not capable at least of knowing that truth? "Truth," however, cannot mean here adequacy to some reality that transcends the knower. When Cusanus claims that truth is not "precisely comprehensible as it is," he links truth to transcendence: to say that the truth is not precisely comprehensible is to suggest that it functions like a regulative ideal that we approach more or less successfully; and to approach it we must in some fashion glimpse it, even though we shall never quite seize it. This indeed is the heart of the doctrine of learned ignorance: "Avoiding all roughness (*scabrositas*) of style, I show at the outset that learned ignorance has its basis in the fact that the precise truth should be inapprehensible" (I.2; p. 52).

To show this basis, Cusanus examines the intellect's mode of operation. The brief opening chapters of *On Learned Ignorance* give us a first sketch of Cusanus's theory of knowledge. Above, I linked the doctrine of learned ignorance to what I called the principle of perspective. The doctrine of learned ignorance may indeed be approached as an extension of that principle: just as the faculty of sight prescribes a particular mode of access to reality ensuring that what we see is never more than subjective appearance, so, if Cusanus is right (and here he offers what may strike us as an anticipation of Kant), the human understanding's mode of operation prescribes a particular access to reality, a particular perspective—but one of a higher order.

How then does the understanding operate? In *On Learned Ignorance* Cusanus observes that our understanding relies on comparison: "However, all those who make an investigation judge the uncertain proportionally, by means of a comparison with what is taken to be certain. Therefore, every inquiry is comparative and uses the means of comparative relation" (I.1; p. 50). All inquiry presupposes a great deal that is taken to be certain and allowed to go unchallenged. It presupposes something like a stable ground, the ground furnished by our language and the associated concepts, although this ground, if Cusanus is right, is ultimately no more stable than the earth on which we stand. It is in fact a shifting ground.

Consider looking at a tree. To see what is before me as a tree I must already know what a tree is. I measure what I see by what I already know, assign it a place in a conceptual or linguistic space. When I call something a "tree" I claim its membership in a class of objects of a certain type. That there should be such a word as "tree" in my language presupposes something like a seeing, not just of particular trees but of a family resemblance that allows me to group these trees together, to see each particular tree as a token of the same type.[7] Such identification of what is different implies a certain violence. To open oneself to such violence is to open oneself to the rift that separates word and thing. Not that such violence should be thought a defect of our language. Without such violence, language would lose its point.

It should be evident that the word or concept "tree" applies not only to this tree, but to an unlimited number of other possible trees. Essentially universal, our linguistic measures are in principle inadequate to the reality we encounter. To be sure, it is a tree that I see, but how much does this say? The word does distinguish it from a flower or a stone, but "tree" says much too little, though for most practical purposes such descriptions are good enough and such inadequacy does not matter. Still, the particularity of this thing eludes my words. I can of course refine my concepts, point out that this is an oak tree, that it is of a certain shape and height, I can go on finding ever more complex descriptions, but there will always be a still endless number of possible trees, besides the one that I happen to be looking at, that would fit the description. Insight into this fundamental rift between language (or the understanding) and being is central to the doctrine of learned ignorance. As Cusanus puts this point in chapter 3 of *On Learned Ignorance:* "[T]he intellect is to truth as [an inscribed] polygon is to [the inscribing] circle. The more angles the inscribed polygon has the more similar it is to the circle. However, even if the number of its angles is increased *ad infinitum*, the polygon never becomes equal [to the circle] unless it is resolved into an identity with the circle" (I.3; p. 52). A totally adequate description, Cusanus here suggests, would be nothing other than the tree itself. The gulf between being and understanding, reality and language would have been bridged. But such an understanding is denied to finite knowers. It characterizes the creative Word of God alone in which word and thing, logos and reality are one. Incomprehensibly, that Word communicates itself in our experience of things and measures our understanding.

I suggested that to think a perspective as a perspective is to be in some sense already beyond it. Applying this principle to these reflections we can say: to be aware that our words, too, provide only a perspective is to have an intuition of the translinguistic—that is to say, of the transcendence of reality.

4

Once more let me return to Cusanus's claim that we "judge the uncertain proportionally (*proportionabiliter*), by means of a comparison with what is taken to be certain. Therefore, every inquiry is comparative and uses the means of comparative relation (*medio proportionis*)." The terms *proportio* and *proportionabiliter* invite closer attention. Hopkins translates *proportio* as "comparative relation,"[8] but what is crucial here is that the relation be thought of as based on a common measure:

But since *comparative relation* (*proportio*) indicates an agreement in some one respect and, at the same time, indicates an otherness, it cannot be understood independently of number. Accordingly number encompasses all things related comparatively (*proportionabilia*). Therefore number, which is a necessary condition of comparative relation (*proportio*), is present not only in quantity, but also in all things which in any manner whatsoever can agree or differ either substantially or accidentally. Perhaps for this reason Pythagoras deemed all things to be constituted and understood through the power of numbers. (I.1; p. 50)

Cusanus seems to be relying on Aristotle:

Contemporaneously with these philosophers and before them [Leucippus and Democritus], the Pythagoreans, as they are called, devoted themselves to mathematics; they were the first to advance this study, and having been brought up in it they thought its principles were the principles of all things. Since of these principles numbers are by nature the first, and in numbers they seemed to see many resemblances to the things that exist and come into being—more than in fire and earth and water . . . , and numbers seemed to be the first things in the whole of nature, they supposed the elements of number to be the elements of all things, and the whole heaven to be a musical scale and a number. (*Metaphysics* 1.5, 985b26–986a2)

To say that the understanding thus traces definite relations is to insist that it is limited to the finite. Never will it succeed in comprehending what is infinite. *Propter quod infinitum ut infinitum, cum omnem proportionem aufugiat, ignotum est:* "The infinite, qua infinite, is unknown, for it escapes all comparative relation" (I.1; p. 50). The point is reiterated in the beginning of chapter 3: "It is self-evident that there is no comparative relation of the infinite to the finite" (I.3, p. 25). The following sentence provides the key to the doctrine of learned ignorance: "Therefore it is most clear that where we find comparative degrees of greatness, we do not arrive at the unqualifiedly Maximum; for things which are comparatively greater and lesser are finite; but, necessarily, such a Maximum is infinite." Since the infinite cannot be reached by such inevitably finite steps, it surpasses our understanding. Cusanus invites us to think the impossible thought of the largest number. As we struggle to do so, we come to recognize that we shall never arrive at that number, since whatever number we get to, we will always be able to go on to its successor. And what is true of our counting is true of all our attempts to understand reality, which partake of its form: never will we escape the finite. Our human perspective is radically finite and has room only for what is finite. It follows that we cannot comprehend the infinite and that means for Cusanus above all that we cannot comprehend God.

But in order to even make that claim, we must have some insight into the infinite. Once again what I called the principle of perspective applies: to think a perspective as such is to be in some sense already beyond it. To think the essential finitude of all we can comprehend presupposes some awareness of the infinite. But why, if the infinite surpasses comprehension, should we bother with it? Is it not idle curiosity that concerns itself with what surpasses our comprehension? One answer might be that by thus insisting on the limits of our understanding, we guard against wasting our time on excursions that can come to no good end. Kant gives such an interpretation of his own effort in the *Critique of Pure Reason* (1781):

We have now not merely explored the territory of pure understanding, and carefully surveyed every part of it, but have also measured its extent, and assigned to everything in it its rightful place. This domain is an island, enclosed by nature itself with unalterable limits. It is the land of truth—enchanting name!—surrounded by a wide and stormy ocean, the native home of illusion, where many a fog bank and many a swiftly melting iceberg give the deceptive appearance of farther shores, deluding the adventurous seafarer ever anew with empty hopes, and engaging him in enterprises which he can never abandon and yet is unable to carry to completion.[9]

And does not Cusanus counsel us similarly to content ourselves with life on this island of the understanding when he concludes his first chapter with the following defense of learned ignorance?

Therefore, if the foregoing points are true, then since the desire in us is not in vain, assuredly we desire to know that we do not know. If we can fully attain unto this [knowledge of our ignorance], we will attain unto learned ignorance. For a man— even one very well versed in learning—will attain unto nothing more perfect than to be found to be most learned in the ignorance which is distinctively his. (I.1; p. 50)

But there is a decisive difference. Kant calls his island the land of truth, while Cusanus insists that the perspective of human understanding does not allow us to ever seize the truth. And in support of his position Cusanus cites Aristotle: "Even the very profound Aristotle, in his *First Philosophy*, asserts that in things most obvious by nature such difficulty occurs for us as for a night owl which is trying to look at the sun" (I.1; p. 50). Here is what Aristotle had written:

The investigation of the truth is in one way hard, in another easy. An indication of this is found in the fact that no one is able to attain the truth adequately, while, on the other hand, no one fails it entirely, but every one says something true about the nature of things, and while individually they contribute little or nothing to the truth, by the union of all a considerable amount is amassed. Therefore, since the truth seems to be like the proverbial door, which no one can fail to hit, in this way it is easy, but the fact that we can have a whole truth and not the particular part we aim at shows the difficulty of it.

Perhaps, as difficulties are of two kinds, the cause of the present difficulty is not in the facts but in us. For as the eyes of the bats are to the blaze of day, so is the reason in our souls to the things which are by nature most evident of all. (*Metaphysics* 2.1, 993a27–993b11)

To say that no one is able to attain the truth adequately, even when he says something true about the nature of things and, given further inquiry, may get even closer to the truth, is to invoke the truth as the measure that gives direction to our inquiry. With all of this Cusanus would agree, and for that very reason learned ignorance with him cannot mean resting content with the limits set to our understanding, cannot mean anything like skeptical resignation and acceptance of our being forever cut off from the truth. Learned ignorance demands that we open ourselves to the transcendent logos that illuminates all inquiry, even as it remains incomprehensible.

5

Let me return to Kant's metaphor of those adventurous seafarers who leave the island of truth only at their peril. We leave that island whenever we attempt to comprehend the infinite. All such attempts can only end in shipwreck. The coincidence of opposites marks the site of this shipwreck.

Cusanus himself thus suggests that what he has to tell us may well be considered *monstra* by his readers, and there is indeed something monstrous about an argument like the following.

Now, I give the name "Maximum" to that than which there cannot be anything greater. But fullness befits what is one. Thus oneness—which is also being—coincides with Maximality. But if such oneness is altogether free from all relation and contraction, obviously nothing is opposed to it, since it is Absolute Maximality. Thus, the Maximum is the Absolute One which is all things. And all things are in the Maximum (for it is the Maximum); and since nothing is opposed to it, the Minimum likewise coincides with it, and hints the Maximum is also in all things. And because it is absolute, it is, actually, every possible being; it contracts nothing from things, all of which [derive] from it. In the first book, I shall strive to investigate—incomprehensibly above human reason—this Maximum, which the faith of all nations indubitably believes to be God. (I.2; p. 51)

Cusanus here asks us to think what, given what he has told us about the limits placed on our understanding, we are incapable of comprehending. "Since the unqualifiedly and absolutely Maximum (than which there cannot be a greater) is greater than we can comprehend (because it is Infinite Truth), we attain to it no other way than incomprehensibly. For since it is not of the nature of those things which can be comparatively greater and lesser, it is beyond all that we can conceive" (I.2; p. 51). By definition, nothing could possibly be greater than the Maximum. But if we take that definition literally, he is also saying that nothing could be smaller. Maximum and Minimum coincide. How are we to understand this? It should be clear that the thought of the maximum is inevitably a monstrous thought.

With finite things you can always imagine something greater or less. The maximum is by its very nature infinite.

Therefore, if anything is posited which is not the unqualifiedly Maximum, it is evident that something greater can be posited. And since we find degrees of equality (so that one thing is more equal to a second thing than to a third, in accordance with generic, specific, spatial, causal, and temporal agreement and difference among similar things), obviously we cannot find two or more things which are so similar and equal that they could not be progressively more similar *ad infinitum*. Hence the measure and the measured—however equal they are—will always remain different. (I.3; p. 52)

The attempt to measure the circumference of a circle with an inscribed polygon can serve as an example. It figures the attempt to offer an adequate representation, be it in words or in some other way of, say, a tree. An insuperable gap separates all finite things. But implicit in our understanding of this gap—of which the gap that separates measure and measured, word and thing, is but one expression—is an understanding of the gap between finite and infinite:

Therefore, it is not the case that by means of likenesses a finite intellect can attain the truth about things (*rerum veritatem*). For truth is not something more or something less, but is something indivisible. Whatever is not truth cannot measure truth precisely. (By comparison a noncircle [cannot measure] a circle whose being is something indivisible.) Hence the intellect, which is not truth, never comprehends truth so precisely that truth cannot be comprehended infinitely more precisely. (I.3; p. 52)

As long as we concern ourselves with a finite circle, with an inscribed (or circumscribed) polygon with a finite number of sides, circle and polygon will remain ineradicably distinct, incommensurable as straight and curved line must be. But as you increase the radius of the circle to infinity, secants (and tangents) will approach the circumference, as the circumference will approach a straight line. Similarly, in God logos and being, word and reality, so radically distinct for the human knower, coincide. In such a circle the center would indeed coincide with the circumference. The same of course would hold also of the infinite sphere.

It may be a bit misleading to translate *rerum veritatem* as "truth about things." To be sure, we call an assertion or a thought true or false when it agrees or fails to agree with the matter in question. So understood, truth may be said to be "about things." Such an understanding is quite in keeping with the traditional understanding of truth as *adaequatio rei et intellectus*, as "the adequation of the thing and the understanding." But that definition is ambiguous in that it may be read both as *veritas est adaequatio intellectus ad rem*, "truth is the adequation of the intellect to the thing," and as *veritas est adaequatio rei ad intellectum*, "truth is the adequation of the thing to the intellect."[10] For a medieval thinker the second reading has an evident priority: the human knower, to be sure, created as he is in the image of God, does justice to his essence when he measures what he thinks by the matter to be thought. But that matter in turn has its measure in the divine idea, which in the end cannot be distinguished from the thing itself: in God's creative Word intellect and thing coincide. On this view, *rerum veritas*, understood as *adaequatio rei (creandae) ad intellectum (divinum)* secures truth understood as *adaequatio intellectus (humani) ad rem (creatam)*.[11] Cusanus thinks the truth of things in the image of the circle, the human truth about things in the image of the inscribed polygon. The truth about things has its measure in the idea of the coincidence of human truth and the truth of things. "Therefore, the quiddity of things, which is the truth of beings (*Quidditas ergo rerum, qua est entium veritas*) is unattainable in its purity; though it is sought by all philosophers, it is found by no one as it is. And the more deeply we are instructed in this ignorance, the closer we approach to truth" (I.3; p. 52–53).[12] What we have to say about things is never fully adequate to them, could always be more or less adequate. But this condition presupposes another truth, where intellect is fully adequate to things because it is nothing other than these things, which are understood now as nothing other than the creative thoughts of God. Looking at these things, our intellect must be somehow in touch with that truth if it is to function as measure of our inadequate thoughts.

With his mathematical speculations Cusanus hopes to give us a ladder that will enable us to glimpse something of the infinity of God. The infinity of space is understood by him, we might say, as a symbol of the infinity of God. Given the logic of Aristotle, Cusanus knows that such speculations may well be dismissed as nonsense. But Aristotle's logic, if Cusanus is right, also defines only a perspective (though a higher-order perspective to be sure), a perspective that is constitutive of what our finite reason can grasp.

The absolute is said by Cusanus to be beyond the opposition of great and small. And if the minimum coincides with the maximum, it, too, will be beyond all opposition. But we cannot help but think in oppositions. When we try to step beyond them, as we must when we try to make sense of what Cusanus has to tell us about the Maximum, that is, about God, all sense threatens to dissolve: what can we say about a God who is said to be beyond "all affirmation and all negation" (I.4; p. 53)? Neither positive nor negative theology will do justice to his being. "Rational inference," *discursus rationis*, will not be able to make sense of the coincidence of opposites: "maximum" and "minimum," as used by Cusanus, "are transcendent terms of absolute signification, so that in their absolute simplicity they encompass—beyond all contraction to quantity of mass or quantity of power—all things" (I.4; p. 54).

6

We are now in a position to consider the transference of the metaphor of the infinite sphere from God to the cosmos, that Koyré found so astonishing.[13] Cusanus had found this metaphor in Meister Eckhart, who in turn refers us to the rather obscure and extremely brief pseudo-Hermetic *Liber XXIV philosophorum* (*Book of the XXIV Philosophers*), dating from the twelfth century.[14] Here we find for the first time the formulation "God is an infinite sphere, whose center is everywhere, whose circumference nowhere."[15] It is in this sense that the metaphor is used in the first book of *On Learned Ignorance*: "But those who considered the most actual existence of God affirmed that He is an infinite sphere, as it were" (I.12; p. 63). Chapter 23 develops that metaphor, which suggests that God's creative power is fully present in every thing: even in that tree we were considering, even in a dunghill, God is fully present. The metaphor of the sphere thus suggests that God is equally close, infinitely close to every part of creation; by saying that its center is everywhere, we assert not only that God is equally close, but that there is no distance at all between creator and creatures. That this metaphor has an explosive content when an attempt is made to fit it together with the hierarchical cosmos generally accepted in the Middle Ages should be evident. Taken seriously, the metaphor threatens to shatter every hierarchy. I shall return to this point in chapter 9.

But what about Cusanus's transference of this metaphor from God to the cosmos? I suspect that to Cusanus it seemed only obvious.[16] As a Christian thinker he believed that everything created has its origin and measure in God. As he puts it in book 2, chapter 2: "every created thing is, as it were, a finite infinity or a created god" (II.2; p. 93). Our tree, for example, is such a finite infinity. Like every part of creation it shares, if Cusanus is right, in infinity. It is a contracted infinity. Similarly Cusanus understands the universe as such a finite infinite: like God in its infinity, unlike God in that instead of divine unity, we now have multiplicity, a manifold spread out in space and time. If both oneness and difference are accepted, not only will the metaphor's transference from God to the cosmos seem justified; but, since the metaphor joins extension and infinity, it can be said that it does greater justice to the cosmos than to God, who is beyond extension.

The transference of the metaphor from God to the cosmos invites a reading not only with respect to space but also with respect to time. Such a reading suggests itself in one of Johannes Wenck's critical observations in his *De Ignota Litteratura*, linking Cusanus to Meister Eckhart and the heresy of the Free Spirit:[17]

See what great evils swarm and abound in such very simple learned ignorance and such very abstract understanding. Wherefore, John, bishop of Strasburg, on the sabbath before the Feast of the Assumption of the Blessed Virgin Mary, in the year of our Lord 1317, conducted a trial against the Beghards and the sisters in his own city, who were claiming (1) that God is, formally, whatever is and (2) that they were God—not being distinct [from Him] in nature. . . .

The first corollary of this first thesis [All things coincide with God]: "By means of Absolute Maximality all things are that which they are, because Absolute Maximality is Absolute Being, in whose absence there cannot be anything."

Eckhart, in his works on Genesis and Exodus, alludes to this [point] in the following way: "Being is God. For if it were other than God: either God would not exist, or else if He did exist, He would exist from something other [than Himself]." And he adds: "The Beginning wherein God created heaven and earth is the primary and simple *now* of eternity — i.e. altogether the same *now* wherein God dwells from eternity and in which there is, was, and eternally will be, the emanation of His persons. Hence, when it was asked why God did not create the world earlier, I replied: because He was unable to, since before there was a world, *earlier* neither could be nor was. How was he able to create earlier, since He created the world in the same immediate now in which He was dwelling?"[18]

The problem of thinking a beginning or end of space is closely related to the problem of thinking a beginning or end of time. Why did God not create the world earlier than he did? But like "smaller" and "greater", "earlier" and "later" make sense only given the perspective of our finite understanding. God is not subject to our time and therefore did not create heaven and earth in time. The time of creation is "the primary and simple *now* of eternity"; and just as the divine center is both infinitely distant from and infinitely close to every creature, so this eternal now is both infinitely distant from and infinitely close to every point of time. Just as God is both center and circumference of that sphere which is creation, so God is both center and circumference of time. Time, too, is an infinite circle, "whose center is everywhere, whose circumference nowhere." There is a sense in which Cusanus's doctrine of the coincidence of opposites gestures in the direction of Zarathustra's teaching of the eternal recurrence. Both are *monstra*, as Cusanus uses that term in the prologue to *On Learned Ignorance*.[19]

That such a move from the Christian God to the doctrine of the eternal recurrence is indeed invited by the thought of that "now wherein God dwells from eternity" is supported by some quotations collected by Georges Poulet in his *Metamorphoses of the Circle* (1961). Thomas Aquinas, for example, relies on the metaphor of the circle in this reflection on the relationship of eternity and time:

Eternity is always present to whatever time or moment of time it may be. One can see an example of it in the circle: a given point on the circumference, even though indivisible, nevertheless cannot coexist with all the other points, because the order of succession constitutes the circumference; but the center that is outside the circumference is immediately connected with any given point of the circumference whatsoever.

Or again:

Eternity resembles the center of the circle; even though simple and indivisible, it comprehends the whole course of time, and every part of it is equally present.[20]

Peter Auriolus, too, is well acquainted with the image of the circle as a metaphor for time: "There are those who use the image of the center of the circle, in its relation to all points of the circumference, and they affirm that this is similar to the *Nunc* of eternity in its connection with all the parts of time. By which they mean that eternity actually coexists with the whole of time."[21]

7

I have tried to show how the themes of perspective and infinity are linked in the thought of Cusanus. Depending on the different meaning given to perspective, we arrive at different interpretations of the infinite. From the ordinary, spatial meaning of perspective, we moved to the idea of an infinite universe; from an understanding of the perspectival nature of language, we moved to the infinite richness of each individual thing; from an understanding of the perspectival nature even of logic, we arrived at an understanding of God who dwells beyond the coincidence of opposites. The problem of thinking the infinite is in each case analogous: in each case discursive reason suffers shipwreck and frees us for an intuition of the infinite. This analogy enables Cusanus to link the infinity of space to the infinity of each individual and to the infinity of God. Thus the attempt to master the infinite, above all the age-old problem of squaring the circle, becomes with him an activity symbolic of the search for God.

I would like to suggest that it is similarly possible to interpret the attempts of painters such as Rogier van der Weyden to grasp something of the infinity of space as a symbolic activity, analogous to our attempt to grasp God. And what is true of the infinity of space is also true of the infinity of each individual. The boundlessness of space and the infinite depth of the individual are both experienced as epiphanies of God. It seems appropriate therefore that on the first page of *De Visione Dei* Cusanus should have called van der Weyden the greatest of all painters.

1

The previous chapter tried to show that reflection on perspective leads quite naturally to the vision of an infinite universe that knows neither center nor circumference. The challenge to the hierarchical conception of the cosmos that had ruled medieval thought mounted by such reflection should also have become evident: no longer is there any reason to divide the cosmos into a sublunar sphere that knows death and decay and a superlunar realm that knows only the perfection of untiring circular motion. One difficulty posed by the cardinal's transformed vision of the cosmos was this incompatibility with Aristotelian physics, which had furnished the Middle Ages with the outlines of its science of nature.[1]

Aristotle himself saw the incompatibility between his physics and such an infinite world quite clearly, it was one reason he felt he had to reject the latter:

All movement is either compulsory or according to nature, and if there is compulsory movement there must also be natural . . . ; but how can there be *natural* movement if there is no difference throughout the void or the infinite? For in so far as it is infinite, there will be no up or down or middle, and in so far as it is a void, up differs no whit from down; for as there is no difference in what is nothing, there is none in the void . . . ; but natural locomotion seems to be differentiated, so that the things that exist by nature must be differentiated. Either, then, nothing has a natural loco-motion, or else there is no void. . . .

Further, no one could say why a thing once set in motion should stop anywhere; for why should it stop *here* rather than *here*? So that a thing will either be at rest or must be moved *ad infinitum*, unless something more powerful gets in its way.[2]

Aristotle here seems to be entertaining the Galilean thought of inertia, only to reject it.[3] But if one were to break with the idea of natural movement so evident to Aristotle then Newton's first law of motion—which states that—if a body is at rest or moving at a constant speed in a straight line, it will re-main in that condition unless acted on by some force—would seem almost inescapable. Aristotle to be sure would have rejected any such suggestion as a fantastic hypothesis. His whole theory of motion presupposes that we can make sense of up and down, thus presupposes what Cusanus would consider no more than part of the natural illusion that lets us earth dwellers place our-selves near the center of the cosmos. But Aristotle is convinced that the space of geometry may not be confused with the space of physics, convinced that if we are to make sense of the world around us we have to recognize that there is such a thing as natural place. The four elements therefore each have their proper place in the sphere below the moon. It is natural for earth to seek to come down, for fire to rise; water and air have their places in be-tween. Depending on how a body is constituted out of these elements, it will seek its proper place.

We may wonder why, given this model, motion in the sublunar realm would not have come to an end long ago, when every element had finally found its proper place. What is the motor that enables continuing change? Aristotle's answer is that under the influence of the sun, the elements will transform themselves endlessly. Think of ice, which when heated turns into water; heated further, water evaporates and turns into air; while air, in turn, when cooled, condenses and falls down as water, which when cooled still further turns back into solid ice. And does not this cycle give us a first clue to the endless cycling of nature? When the sun, during the day and in sum-mer, warms the earth there will be a greater upward tendency; when, at night and in winter, it turns away from the earth we meet with the reverse. The revolutions of the heavenly spheres are thus responsible for the different times of day and the changing seasons, for growth followed by decline and death. The sun is the prime motor of the sublunar realm.

The above is just a sketch, far too simple to do justice to Aristotle's science of nature, but it should suffice to show that the vision of an infinite cosmos entertained by Cusanus is incompatible not only with Aristotle's astronomy but more generally with his science of nature, which depends on a hierarchically ordered cosmos, on the distinction between a superlunar realm and a sublunar realm in which the four elements have their proper places. All of these are denied by Cusanus's vision of the cosmos, which thus makes it impossible to accept Aristotelian science. Aristotle thinks the space of natural science in terms of place. That people have even entertained the idea of an infinite cosmos rests, according to Aristotle, on a confusion of the space of geometry with real space, the space of the world we actually live in. The space of geometry is the result of a flight of thought that loses touch with reality. When thinking real space, we have to think space in terms of place, where "place" means something like a container. Deny this view, Aristotle insists, and you will no longer be able to make sense of rest and motion and of their difference.

Someone might cite Cusanus's monstrous doctrine of the coincidence of opposites, which invites us to think the coincidence of rest and motion, as support for the soundness of Aristotle's position. Cusanus, to be sure, could invoke the authority of Plato among others to counter him, insisting that it is precisely the flight of thought beyond common sense that frees us from the illusions that rule ordinary experience. Rest and motion are for him relative concepts. There is no absolute motion. Space comes to be thought of as an infinite field that human beings attempt to master by projecting onto or into it poles and lines of their own construction.

2

It is the conception of space as infinite field that underlies Leon Battista Alberti's perspective construction. Addressed primarily to painters and those interested in understanding the craft of painting, his theory of perspective teaches us to create convincing representations of what we see, as it appears. What paintings represent then are not the objects themselves but their inevitably subjective appearances. Implicit in all such appearances is a particular point of view. All appearance is relative to the subject seeing.

Such insistence on the relativity of appearance is as characteristic of Alberti as it is of Cusanus. The following passage from *On Painting* reads almost as if it could have been written by Cusanus:

It would be well to add to the above statements the opinion of philosophers who affirm that if the sky, the stars, the sea, mountains and all bodies should become— should God so will—reduced by half, nothing would appear to be diminished in any part to us. All knowledge of large, small; long, short; high, low; broad, narrow; clear, dark; light and shadow and every similar attribute is obtained by comparison.[4]

We cannot know the absolute size of things. Indeed, we do not even know what such absolute size might mean. Our understanding of the size of some object is relative through and through. Alberti goes on to give a number of examples, such as the height of Aeneas, who stands head and shoulders above other men but seems like a dwarf next to Polyphemus. "Thus all things are known by comparison, for comparison contains within itself a power which immediately demonstrates in objects, which is more, less or equal. From which it is said that a thing is large when it is greater than something small and largest when it is greater than something large" (A55).

Is there then a natural measure that we can use to escape from such relativity? Alberti suggests that there is, although "natural" should not be confused here with "absolute." The natural measuring rod is the human body: thus we measure length by arms (*braccia*), ells, and feet. "Since man is the thing best known to man, perhaps Protagoras, by saying that man is the mode and measure of all things, meant that all the accidents of things are known through comparison to the accidents of man" (A55). Our accidental size provides us with the measure of all things. That our measures are in this sense accidental in no ways robs them of their usefulness, or propositions based on them of their truth. Protagoras may have recognized something of the sort.

I find this rehabilitation of the sophist Protagoras, so sharply criticized by both Plato and Aristotle, at just this particular time remarkable and shall return to it in a later chapter.[5] That Alberti welcomed the rhetorical force of this challenge is suggested by the fact that a similar reference is found in his *Libri della famiglia*, dating from roughly the same time. And thought-provoking, too, is the same rehabilitation of Protagoras found later in Cusanus, who in

De Beryllo, which appeared in 1458, explicitly defends the sophist against the critique of Aristotle. Did Cusanus here borrow from the younger Alberti? It would seem likely. I suspect indeed that Cusanus would have been aware of *On Painting* even when working on *On Learned Ignorance*.[6]

While I am not aware of any direct evidence that the two ever met, the circumstantial evidence suggests strongly that they must have known each other.[7] Consider their biographies. Alberti was born in 1404, in Genoa. At an early age, when he was only ten or eleven, he went to Padua to attend the school of the humanist Barzizza. Cusanus came to Padua in 1416; and though there is no reason to assume that he would have met the young Alberti at that time, the possibility cannot be ruled out altogether: people matured early in those days—recall that Cusanus was only fifteen when he enrolled in the University of Heidelberg. In 1421 Alberti enrolled in canon and civil law at the University of Bologna. In 1431 he obtained a minor position at the papal curia. Like Cusanus, he took holy orders, though there is little about his subsequent career that reminds us of this (not because of any scandal—he appears to have lived an exemplary life). He died in Rome in 1472, having established himself as a theorist of art and architecture and as an ethical thinker who emphasized not contemplation but striving, laboring, producing. He himself was active as an architect and an urban planner.

The suggestion that Cusanus must have met the somewhat younger Alberti is supported by the overlap in their circles of friends. Most important perhaps, they were both close to the great mathematician, geographer, astronomer, and doctor Paolo Toscanelli (1397–1482), who, a friend also of Brunelleschi, shared their interest in perspective. Toscanelli is known to have brought to Florence a copy of Biagio Pelicani's then much-discussed *Quaestiones Perspectivae* (ca. 1390), a theory of optics and vision that followed the teachings of John Peckham.[8] Both Brunelleschi and Alberti seem to have studied that text. And Toscanelli is now believed to have been the author of a treatise *Della prospettiva* (in the Ricciardi library) that had been included among Alberti's works, "cast as a summary, in 'vulgar' Italian, of the key concepts of medieval optics" and written presumably earlier than *De Pictura*.[9] Toscanelli was among those responsible for the revival of interest in geography, more especially in producing more accurate maps, an interest that both Cusanus and Alberti shared—indeed Toscanelli is rumored to have been the author of the chart that first encouraged Columbus to seek the East by going west,[10] a reorientation that anticipates the spirit of Copernican revolutions. We know that Alberti joined Toscanelli in making certain astronomical observations.

That Alberti and Cusanus dedicated works to Toscanelli—Alberti the *Intercoenales* (1429), Cusanus his first two geometrical treatises, *De Transmutationibus Geometricis* and *De Arithmeticis Complementis* (both 1450)—shows the high esteem in which they both held the Florentine polymath. Cusanus had first met Toscanelli in Padua, at the lectures of Beldomandi, the newly appointed professor of music and astrology. They remained friends and Toscanelli was the doctor at his bedside when Cusanus died in Todi. We have Toscanelli's critique of one of Cusanus's mathematical writings and also a little dialogue by Cusanus, *Dialogus de Circuli Quadratura*, which would seem to be based on a discussion between the two that took place in Brixen in 1457. Joan Gadol observes that "In the late 1450's Cusa's home in Rome was a gathering place for men of science like Peurbach, Regiomontanus, and Toscanelli; Alberti must have been a member of this group."[11]

What explains this relationship between mathematicians and painters? The answer is obvious in Alberti's case. His interest in mathematics is tied to the help it can give the painter in his attempt to master illusion, where the word "mastery" is meant to suggest two things: both to be able to produce convincing representations of the world as we see it but also to have understood the logic of these illusions. The theory of perspective teaches us about the logic of appearance, of phenomena. In this sense the theory of perspective is phenomenology. So understood, phenomenology lets us understand why things present themselves to us as they do. This is indeed how Kant's contemporary Johann Heinrich Lambert, to whom we owe the term, understood it. Phenomenology meant to him a "transcendent optics," the theory of perspective in the widest sense.[12]

There is something magical about the illusions that mastery of perspective was able to produce, so much more lifelike than the kind of representations one had grown accustomed to; and it seems only fitting that Brunelleschi, on whom Alberti depends, was considered by his contemporaries to have been a magician in the tradition of Daedalus: his epitaph in Florence Cathedral celebrates the architect for having "excelled in the Daedalian art," mentioning as proof not only "this celebrated temple with its marvellous shell but also the many machines his divine genius invented."[13] His systematization of perspective was just another of these inventions, devised not by a painter but by an architect who began his career as a goldsmith, trained to take care with his measurements. The theory of perspective was thus brought to painting by a comparative outsider.

Alberti dedicates the Italian version of *On Painting* to Brunelleschi, who is mentioned, along with Donatello, Ghiberti, Luca della Robbia, and Masaccio, as proof that nature was still capable of producing those "geniuses or giants which in her more youthful and more glorious days she had produced so marvellously and abundantly" (A39). There can be little doubt that he deserves most of the credit for working out the theory of perspective as it concerned painters and other craftsmen.[14] Here is Manetti's account of Brunelleschi's original breakthrough:

He first demonstrated his system of perspective on a small panel about half a *braccio* square. He made a representation of San Giovanni in Florence, encompassing as much of that temple as can be seen at a glance from the outside. In order to paint it it seems that he stationed himself some three *braccia* inside the central portal of Santa Maria dei Fiore. . . .
[A description of what is on the panel and of the excellent workmanship follows.] And he placed burnished silver where the sky had to be represented, so that the real air and atmosphere were reflected it.

Brunelleschi then drilled a hole in the center of the panel through which the observer was to look at the work with the help of a mirror.[15]

The point of this exercise was to demonstrate to an amazed public the power of the newly discovered system of perspective: the world seemed to have been created over again. The artist appears here as a second god, and so Alberti calls him.

3

Alberti begins book 1 of *On Painting* with a statement clarifying the relationship of his theory of perspective to mathematics. "I will take first from the mathematicians those things with which my subject is concerned" (A43). What he takes from the mathematicians is sufficient to allow him to develop a mathematical symbolism that establishes an exact correspondence between the shapes of things located in space and their pictorial representations.[16] A language had been created that allowed for an easy passage from objects in space to their pictorial representation, given a particular point of view, and conversely from the perspectival appearance of objects to the objects themselves, the objects that are the concern of science. Alberti, to be sure, begs the reader to think of him not as a mathematician "but as a painter writing of these things. Mathematicians measure with their minds alone the forms of things separated from all matter. Since we wish the object to be seen, we will use a more sensate wisdom" (A43). We could trace here the dependence of Alberti on the medieval science of *perspectiva*,[17] a science of vision concerned with the nature of light, vision, and the eye that relied on ancient, Arab, and medieval optics (pseudo-Euclidean optics, Alhazen, Vitellio)—a science no doubt mediated to him by Toscanelli. What matters more, however, is Alberti's promise of "a more sensate wisdom" than that taught at the universities. Practice here turns to theory not for the sake of insight into the true nature of things, but for the sake of mastery. As Descartes later was to oppose his practical philosophy to the speculative philosophy of the Schools, so Alberti already teaches a practical science that brackets philosophical questions when these have no bearing on the craft that concerns him, taking from the mathematicians only "those things with which my subject is concerned" (A43). In this respect *On Painting* belongs to a by then well-established tradition. J. V. Field explains, "At least from the late thirteenth century onwards such mathematical skills were recognized as useful in wider contexts and were increasingly taught in abacus schools specially set up for the purpose. These abacus schools did their teaching in the vernacular. . . . In Florence, one of the best abacus schools, in the late fourteenth century, was that run by the Goldsmiths' Guild."[18] Brunelleschi belonged to that guild.

Having delimited his concerns, Alberti proceeds to draw a distinction between those qualities of a space that are changed by a change of place and light and those that are not (A44). Perhaps we can say that he is drawing a distinction between the real and the apparent properties of a thing. The painter is concerned primarily with the latter. But appearance is ruled by its own logic. This allows us to have a science of its representation. Alberti goes on to introduce the idea of the pyramid of sight—its base whatever is being observed, its apex the observer's eye (see fig. 7). Once again we should note his unwillingness to get bogged down in unnecessary theoretical problems: "Among the ancients there was no little dispute whether these rays came from the eye or the plane. This dispute is very difficult and is quite useless to us. It will not be considered" (A46).[19] Alberti's practical science goes only as far as it needs to go to accomplish its aims.

Alberti likens the rays that connect plane and eye to hairs or a bundle and the eye to a bud, distinguishing between extrinsic rays, defining the outline; median rays, which fill in the area, and the centric ray, which is perpendicular to the plane. The more acute the angle in the eye, the smaller the object will appear. The greater the distance of some given object, the smaller the angle. He adds a note on aerial perspective, suggesting that the humidity of the air tires the rays, so that we see things as in a haze. Alberti goes on to suggest that the picture plane be considered as if it were made of transparent glass, a window through which we look at what appears to lie beyond. From this conception follows the crucial rule from which much of the following can be deduced: "Let us add the axiom of the mathematicians where it is proved that if a straight line cuts two sides of a triangle, and if this line which forms a triangle is parallel to a side of the first and greater triangle, certainly this lesser triangle will be proportional to the greater" (A52).

But let us turn to the construction itself (fig. 4):

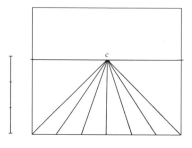

. . .

figure 4

Perspective construction.

Drawing by author.

First of all about where I draw. I inscribe a quadrangle of right angles, as large as I wish, which is to be considered an open window through which I see what I want to paint. Here I determine as it pleases me the size of the man in my picture. I divide the length of this man in three parts. These parts to me are proportional to that measurement called a *braccio*, for, in measuring the average man, it is seen that he is about three *braccia*. With these *braccia* I divide the base line of the rectangle into as many parts as it will receive. To me this base line of the quadrangle is proportional to the nearest and equidistant quantity seen on the pavement. Then, within this quadrangle, where it seems best to me, I make a point which occupies the place where the central ray strikes [C]. For this is called the centric point. This point is properly placed when it is no higher from the base line of the quadrangle than the height of the man that I have to paint there.

The centric point being located as I said, I draw straight lines from it to each division placed on the base line of the quadrangle. These drawn lines, [extended] as if to infinity, demonstrate to me how each transverse quantity is altered visually. (A56)

Alberti then discusses briefly a false construction apparently common in his day: a second parallel (b) is drawn to a line a, the distance divided into thirds, a third parallel (c), ⅔ of the distance between *a* and *b* above *b;* and so on. More important to us than this false construction is Alberti's gloss: "Know that a painted thing can never appear truthful where there is not a definite distance for seeing it" (A57). We should note that what the artist should strive for is not so much the truth as the appearance of truth.

But to return to the construction: how does Alberti draw his transverse lines (fig. 5)?

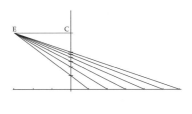

figure 5

Perspective construction.

Drawing by author.

I take a small space in which I draw a straight line and this I divide into parts similar to those in which I divided the base line of the quadrangle. Then, placing a point [E] at a height equal to that of the centric point from the base line, I draw lines from this point to each division scribed on the first line. Then I establish, as I wish, the distance from the eye to the picture [E–C]. Here I draw, as the mathematicians say, a perpendicular cutting whatever lines it finds. . . . The intersection of this perpendicular line with the others gives me the succession of transverse quantities. In this fashion I find described all the parallels, that is the square[d] *braccia* of the pavement in the painting. (A57)

Although I find what Alberti here has to tell us clear enough, many of my students have found this part of the construction difficult to follow. They find it hard to accept that Alberti means what he says when he writes: "I establish, as I wish, the distance from the eye to the picture." The procedure seems to them arbitrary. But Alberti does mean just what he says. *E–C* does not just represent but is equal to the distance of the ideal eye to the picture. And that distance the painter establishes as he sees fit, given, to be sure, his understanding of the painting's anticipated placement and use.

To check whether the construction has been done correctly there is an easy test: "If one straight line contains the diagonal of several quadrangles described in the picture, it is an indication to me whether they are drawn correctly or not" (A57; fig. 6). This test provides an alternative method of construction.[20] Once again "I establish, as I wish, the distance of the eye from the picture"; plot this distance on the horizon line from the centric point [C–D], where D (D_1 or D_2, depending on whether I move to the right or the left) will often fall outside the picture to be painted; and connect D to the division points on the base line of my quadrangle. All the diagonals of a properly drawn pavement meet in D (D_1 or D_2). But the distance of the eye from the picture has to be equal to C–D. Every painting with a pavement painted in accord with Alberti's construction gives us thus an easy recipe for determining the ideal point of view.

Alberti's construction provides the painter with a matrix in which the objects he chooses to represent can then be located. This space, too, is essentially homogeneous, though it does have its center in the perceiving eye; it

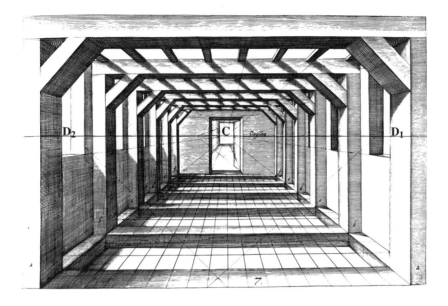

. . .

figure 6

Jan Vredemann de Vries,

perspective construction, *Perspective,*

(Leiden: Henricus Hondius, 1604).

is indeed the subjective appearance of the objective space of the new science. Note the arbitrariness of the adopted point of view! The body, to be sure, provides Alberti with something like a natural measure—recall once more his reference to Protagoras. The perspective construction of Alberti is essentially anthropocentric in more than one sense in that the human body provides both ruler and point of view and human reason provides the framework. This anthropocentrism is subject to criticism by those who demand a theocentric art, just as the anthropocentrism of the new science will be criticized by those who demand a theocentric understanding of reality. I shall return to this point in the next chapter.

. . .

Albrecht Dürer,

Artist Drawing a Nude in

Perspective **(1527).**

Credit: Foto Marburg/Art Resource, N.Y.

4

I would like to underscore the artificiality of Alberti's construction.[21] That his representation of space does violence to the way we actually experience things was noted already by Leonardo da Vinci. In Leonardo's *Treatise on Painting*, Hubert Damisch finds "the premonitory symptoms of a critical trope that has scarcely changed since that time, one that holds that *costruzione legittima* reduces the viewing subject to a kind of cyclops, and obliges the eye to remain at one fixed, indivisible point—in other words, obliges it to adopt a stance that has nothing in common with the effective conditions of perception, any more than it does with the goals of painting, as properly understood."[22] In Dürer's *Artist Drawing a Nude in Perspective* (fig. 7) the violation of both perceiver and perceived becomes image. Dürer does not just present here "the apparatus to which the painter should turn to facilitate rational construction,"[23] but accompanies such presentation with a critical commentary: note the different languages spoken by the two halves of the image—the contrast between the way the window on the left opens us to the promise of the bright world beyond, while in the window on the right a scraggly potted bush, threatening to burst the prison of its container, blocks our vision. Dürer knew very well that first of all and most of the time we experience space with our moving body and with all our senses; he knew also that desire is part of such experience.

Concerned as he is with painting, Alberti considers only the eye. And even here, to make his construction manageable, he assumes monocular vision and a flat earth. The violence his construction does to the way we actually see is evident: normally we see with two, constantly shifting eyes. Consider the way you look at some tall object, say a tree; you won't keep your head still but will tilt it backward as you try to get a better view of the top, thus shifting what Alberti calls the centric point of each eye. Alberti assumes one stationary eye. In his account of Brunelleschi's first demonstration of the power of perspective, Manetti thus calls our attention to the way that Brunelleschi ensures that vision is monocular by drilling a peep-hole into the center of his panel; important, too, is Manetti's remark that Brunelleschi decided to paint only what could be seen "at a glance." Ideally such a painting freezes time. The consequence of this decision for perspectival representation becomes clear when you want to represent a very tall building, say the Tower of Babel. Alberti's construction demands that all the different stories, assuming equal height, would also have to be given the same size in our painting, although this is of course not how we would ordinarily see them. And yet, assuming a stationary eye and a centric line parallel to the assumed ground plane, it is easy to come up with a proof of the correctness of Alberti's construction. But this problem only reminds us that everyday experience involves a lot of motion of eyes, head, and body, and every such movement means a shift of the centric point. For the sake of achieving his mastery of appearances the painter reduces experience to momentary, monocular vision and places us on a flat earth. The perspectival art of Alberti subjects what it presents to a human measure that has itself been subjected to the demand for ease of representation.

But in this respect perspectival art is not too different from the new science, which also has its center and measure in the perceiving subject. Alberti's understanding of the art of perspective thus offers itself as a figure of Cartesian method, perspectival painting as a figure of the scientific representation of nature. In this sense Aberti's *On Painting* may be said to help usher in what Heidegger called "The Age of the World Picture."[24]

ALBERTI AND PERSPECTIVE CONSTRUCTION

1

Alberti's perspective construction offers the painter a spatial matrix in which whatever objects he chooses to represent can be located. That matrix offers the perspectival projection of Euclidean space, which is also the infinite space of the new science. It, too, thus knows of no absolute centers or measures, though as we have seen, the human body (and specifically the position of the eye) does provide something like a natural measure, center, and point of view and enables the painter to escape from arbitrariness.

An Aristotelian would have us wonder how well this representation of space captures the space we actually experience and live in. I myself concluded the previous chapter by pointing to the artificiality of Alberti's rationalization of the natural perspective of our visual experience. Such artificiality is explicitly acknowledged by the title of the first printed treatise on perspective, published in 1505: Viator's *De Artificiali Perspectiva*.[1] The author first of all assumes monocular vision; second, a stationary eye; and third, a flat earth. That this rationalized artificial perspective does violence to the natural perspective that rules our visual experience is a fact of which a Leonardo or a Kepler was well aware. But such violence was a price gladly paid for greater mathematical control. An appeal to realism thus does not quite explain the triumph of the new perspective. What mattered more was that the painter was given an easy-to-use method to discipline his pictorial representations and fictions. The almost magical illusions the new method was capable of producing spoke for themselves, and soon *costruzione legittima* came to be pretty much taken for granted as a tool a painter was expected to have mastered—even if, more often than not, he bent it to his own purposes. But we should not lose sight of the doubly problematic status of an art willing to sacrifice reality to its rationalized representation, a sacrifice that anticipates the replacement, demanded by the science to come of the life-world with *its* rationalized representation.

Something of the questionable character of an art that replaces reality with simulacra is suggested at the beginning of book 2 of *On Painting.*[2] Alberti here praises the painter and the art of painting, which is said to contain "a divine force which not only makes absent men present, as friendship is said to do, but moreover makes the dead seem almost alive." A painting can offer a substitute for the absent or even dead friend: "Thus the face of a man who is already dead certainly lives a long life through painting" (A63). Painting grants life beyond death, although this victory over destructive time relies on the power of illusion. Alberti goes on to point out that painting has helped shape religious sentiments: "Some think that painting shaped the gods who were adored by the nations. It certainly was their greatest gift to mortals, for painting is most useful to that piety which joins us to the gods and keeps our souls full of religion" (A63). Later he quotes Hermes Trismegistus: "mankind portrays the gods in his own image from his memories of nature and his own origins" (A65). The reference is to the *Asclepius,*[3] an important source of medieval Hermetism, dating probably from the second or third century c.e., but then thought to go back to the ancient Egyptians, perhaps even to the time of Moses. The quotations from that text included by St. Augustine in his critique of magic in book 8 of the *City of God* had helped publicize its seductive if impious message.

Alberti, although eager to use the Hermetic text to rhetorically embellish his treatise, seems to have been unwilling to follow its lead and actually tie the art of painting to magic, as the *Asclepius* from which he cites so clearly does: "Do you mean the statues, O Trismegistus?" Asclepius continues.

Yes the statues, Asclepius. They are animated statues full of *sensus* and *spiritus* who can accomplish many things, foretelling the future, giving ills to men and curing them. . . .

These terrestrial or man-made gods result from a composition of herbs, stones, and aromatics which contain in themselves an occult virtue of divine efficacy. And if one tries to please them with numerous sacrifices, hymns, songs of praise, sweet concerts which recall the harmony of heaven, this is in order that the celestial rites may joyously support its long dwelling among men. This is how one makes gods.[4]

Had not Augustine called this art of making gods in the *City of God*, where Alberti is likely to have found the passage he cites, a "detestable art, which is opposed to divine religion" and which therefore "should be taken away by that religion"? Not that Augustine denies that there may well be such an art that, evoking the souls of demons or angels, "united them with these holy images and divine mysteries, in order that through these souls the images might have the power to do good or harm to men."[5] But had not Hermes Trismegistus himself recognized the incompatibility of such an art with true religion? Augustine, at any rate, leaves no doubt that such an art can only be born of error and incredulity. Alberti apparently would have agreed with this condemnation, though he could have welcomed the first part of the quotation, inviting us to understand works of art as "full of *sensus* and *spiritus*." But "spirit" here would have to mean the human spirit, not that of demons or angels. Art had replaced magic, and perhaps it was precisely to hint at this replacement that Alberti cited the archmagician Hermes Trismegistus. Be that as it may, the association of painting with magic, which must have suggested itself to any reader familiar with the *City of God*, shadows Alberti's treatise.

Even apart from the shadow cast on this passage by Hermetic magic, many an orthodox reader must have found Alberti's proto-Nietzschean praise of painting difficult to accept. There is the irreligious suggestion that painting may actually have shaped the gods, that pagan religion at least (Alberti speaks in the past tense and of gods) is a product of art. But what of the religion in Alberti's day? Did it not also rely on images? Think of devotional images of martyrs, the Virgin, or Christ. Augustine himself had found it necessary to conclude his critique of Hermes Trismegistus by contrasting the way the Egyptians worshiped their gods with the way Christians honor their martyrs. If art does indeed substantially strengthen religion, as Alberti asserts, must we not take care lest the piety it fosters be a false piety that sacrifices the transcendent content of religion, its real substance, to superficial appearance? Religion has thus often shown hostility to painting and sculpture, hostility that again and again erupted into iconoclastic furor. How did Christians of Alberti's day respond to the following proud claim: "Therefore, painting contains within itself this virtue that any master painter who sees his work adored will feel himself considered another god" (A64)? As a second creator the artist here threatens to usurp the place of God. The questionable character of this understanding of painting is underscored by the end of the paragraph, addressed not to the vulgar crowd but to those about to be initiated into the mysteries of the art: "For this reason, I say among my friends that Narcissus who was changed into a flower, according to the poets, was the inventor of painting. Since painting is already the flower of every art, the story of Narcissus is most to the point. What else can you call painting, but a similar embracing with art of what is presented on the surface of the water in the fountain?" (A64). Once again the *Asclepius* comes to mind, for it begins with Hermes Trismegistus, Asclepius, Tat, and Hammon meeting in secret in an Egyptian temple: divine wisdom is not for the masses. Something of this aura of secrecy is evoked by Alberti's suggestion that what he has to tell us is meant only for a small circle of friends. These friends, however, seem no longer to need magic, for which Alberti substitutes an art based only on reason and nature, a substitution that foreshadows Descartes's substitution of a science based only on reason and nature for the magical science of the Renaissance with its invocations of occult powers.

Perhaps more important, Alberti's understanding of painting here recalls book 10 of Plato's *Republic*, which had already likened the painter to a godlike magician:

And there is another artist,—I should like to know what you would say of him?
Who is he?
One who is the maker of all the works of all other workmen.
What an extraordinary man!
Wait a little, and there shall be more reason for your saying so. For this is he who is able to make not only vessels of every kind, but plants and animals, himself and all other things—the earth and heaven, and the things which are in heaven or under the earth; he makes the gods also.

He must be a wizard and no mistake.

Oh! you are incredulous, are you? Do you mean that there is no such maker or creator, or that in one sense there might be a maker of all these things but in another not? Do you see that there is a way in which you could make them all yourself?

What way?

An easy way enough; or rather, there are many ways in which the act might be quickly and easily accomplished, none quicker than that of turning a mirror round and round—you would soon enough make the sun and the heavens, and the earth and yourself, and other animals and plants, and all the other things of which we were just now speaking, in the mirror.[6]

For the real world, Plato's Socrates charges, the painter substitutes a world of subjective appearances. We can return to Alberti's invocation of the story of Narcissus: with his art the painter embraces mirror images, endowing them with a death-defying stability. In the myth, of course, what Narcissus tries vainly to embrace, having spurned the love of the nymph Echo and of Ameinias, is a reflection of his own beauty. To call Narcissus the founder of painting is to suggest that art has its origin in a self-love that, with its representations, wants to embrace its own reflection. There is, however, a sense in which the artist succeeds where Narcissus failed: the painter's attempt to embrace himself gives birth not to a child but to a work of art, understood here as a mirroring of self in nature.

Plato criticizes the imitative arts because they imitate only the appearances of objects that are themselves but imitations of the Forms. The artist is thus thrice removed from reality. It is a weighty charge: How can we take seriously art's claim to serve the truth? And was such service not central to the medieval understanding of art? We can understand why the philosopher Jacques Maritain should have mourned the rise of Renaissance art based on the newly gained mastery of perspective:

When on visiting an art gallery one passes from the rooms of the primitives to those in which the glories of oil painting and of a much more considerable material science are displayed, the foot takes a step on the floor, but the soul takes a deep fall. It had been taking the air of the everlasting hills—it now finds itself on the floor of a theater—a magnificent theater. With the sixteenth century the lie installed itself in painting, which began to love science for its own sake, endeavoring to give the *illusion* of nature and to make us believe that in the presence of a painting we are in the presence of the same as the subject painted, not in the presence of the painting.[7]

Maritain is quite willing to grant that great artists have always been able to overcome this danger and lie. But he also invites us to consider the mastery of perspective, which a Vasari could take for granted as an evident artistic advance, as a liability. For it is primarily the triumph of perspective that Maritain has in mind when he speaks of the theater. He is thinking of artful pictorial illusions that invite us to mistake them for reality, letting us forget their merely artificial being and at the time the reality of the work of art as a material object in the world. The artist here usurps the place of God, substituting for God's creation his or her own. Human artifice substitutes simulacra for reality. With the turn to perspective, art threatens to obscure reality.

Having its measure in the beholder, artificial perspective has to mean a secularization of the visible. Thus it provides an obstacle to attempts to place the visual arts in the service of divine transcendence. This is the problem faced by the religious art of Renaissance and Baroque: cut off from transcendence by its subservience to perspective, it yet seeks to use that same perspective to incarnate transcendence. But is the power of such incarnation given to the artist? If so, the painter would draw close to the Hermetic magician. But can art offer more than an illusionistic theater (fig. 8)?[8]

2

Maritain would have us consider the single step that carries us from the rooms of the primitives to those holding the masters of the Renaissance as a crossing of the threshold that separates anthropocentric modernity from the theocentric Middle Ages. That Alberti has already crossed this threshold is shown by his rejection of the use of gold in painting. Soon the gold backgrounds of medieval art were indeed to disappear, as demanded by Alberti's understanding of proper representation: "There are some who use much gold in their *istoria*. They think it gives majesty. I do not praise it. Even though one should paint Virgil's Dido whose quiver was of gold, her golden hair knotted with gold, and her purple robe girdled with pure gold, the reins of the horse and everything of gold, I should not wish gold to be used, for

. . .

figure 8

Andrea Pozzo,

The Transmission of the Divine Spirit

(1688–1694). S. Ignazio, Rome, Italy.

Credit: Alinari/Art Resource, N.Y.

there is more admiration and praise for the painter who imitates the rays of gold with colors" (A85). Illusion is preferred over reality. In the frame or in an altar's architecture Alberti allows the use of gold, but it is excluded from the picture, where it would insert a dissonant element and disrupt the pictorial illusion. "Again we see in a plane panel with a gold ground that some planes shine where they ought to be dark and are dark where they ought to be light. I say, I would not censure the other curved ornaments joined to the painting such as columns, carved bases, capitals and frontispieces even if they were of the most pure and massy gold. Even more, a well perfected *istoria* deserves ornaments of the most precious gems" (A85).

To understand what is at issue here we must keep in mind the significance of the gold background that was introduced into Western painting just before 1000—perhaps the only artistic innovation of comparable importance was the stained-glass window. Together they furnished medieval art with two critical metaphors—critical in the sense that they allow us to approach the essence of this art. Consider the double picture here reproduced, showing the *Holy Women at the Sepulchre Confronted by the Angel of the Resurrection* from *King Henry II's Book of Pericopes* (fig. 9; plate 1): women and angel belong to a realm that knows nothing of time. The gold background here has metaphorical power, hinting at eternal blessedness as it helps establish the timeless significance of representations drawn from the mundane. It invites us to look at what we see from a "spiritual perspective." I am using this expression, which I take from Friedrich Ohly's investigations into "the spiritual significance of the word in the Middle Ages,"[9] deliberately: Alberti's perspective invites us to look through the material painting as if it were transparent, a window through which we can see what the painter has chosen to represent. But this is very much a human perspective, which has its center in the observer: what we see is appearance for us. The spiritual perspective of medieval art would have us look through the painting in a very different sense: through the material to its spiritual significance. The mundane is transformed into a divine sign. Alberti's art is incompatible with this spiritual perspective. A God-centered art gives way to a human-centered art.

The tension between these two approaches is characteristic of the art of the later Middle Ages, occupying as it does the threshold that separates and joins modernity and the Middle Ages. As an interest in three-dimensionality

. . .

figure 9

Holy Women at the Sepulchre Confronted
by the Angel of the Resurrection. From
King Henry II's Book of Pericopes
(1002–1014).

Credit: Bayerische Staatsbibliothek.

and perspective begins to assert itself, the use of gold has to become ever
more problematic. Compare the three-dimensional solidity of both the angel and Mary in Ambrogio Lorenzetti's *Annunciation* (1344; fig. 10; plate 2)
with the flatness of the figures, enlivened by the gestures of wings, garments,
and hands, in the Ottonian miniature: a divine wind seems to blow through
these spiritualized images. Lorenzetti's angel possesses a very different solidity; firmly he has taken his place before the Virgin, his placement underscored by the way the orthogonals of the checkered floor seem to converge
in a single point, creating an illusion of depth.

Hubert Damisch points to the evident tension in the picture:

But the point toward which its orthogonals converge doesn't appear as such; it is dis-
simulated, or, to be more precise, obliterated, obstructed by a column in low relief

· · ·

figure 10
Ambrogio Lorenzetti,
Annunciation **(1344). Pinacoteca**
Nazionale, Siena.
Credit: Scala/Art Resource, N.Y.

that corresponds exactly with the panel's axis of symmetry and that, although an extension of the gilded frame, is nonetheless firmly planted within the painting, in the foreground, on its lower edge. In its spatial ambiguity, functioning as it does as a kind of mask or screen, this architectonic element is the lynchpin of an eminently contradictory structure in which the paving's recession is in open conflict with the flattening effect created by the gold ground—within which the vanishing point is geometrically situated.[10]

Alberti would no doubt have criticized such contradiction, as he would have pointed out the incorrect placement of the transversals.

The tension between the old and the new approach is even more striking in a *Conversion of St. Hubert* painted more than a century later by a follower

. . .

figure 11

Workshop of the Master of the Life of the

Virgin, *Conversion of St. Hubert*

(ca. 1480–1485). National Gallery, London.

Credit: National Gallery, London.

of the Master of the Life of the Virgin (fig. 11; plate 3). The rendering of the deep landscape with its aerial perspective demands an atmospheric sky. Here the gold background seems primarily a concession to a convention that by then had outlived itself. A need to justify the retention of a cherished tradition in terms acceptable to the new art is suggested by the many reinterpretations of the traditional gold background as a curtain made of some golden fabric. Related to this effort are attempts to represent halos as disks

. . .

figure 12

Rogier van der Weyden,

***St. Luke Sketching the Virgin* (1435).**

Credit: Museum of Fine Arts, Boston.

in space, a strange kind of golden headdress worn by saints, which the painter should take care to present in proper perspective.

In the work of the painter Cusanus admired most, Rogier van der Weyden, the new sense of space has pretty much triumphed, although awareness of point of view here does not mean subjection of space to the rigid scaffolding of Alberti's *costruzione legittima* (fig. 12; plate 4). In a painting such as *St. Luke Sketching the Virgin* the gold background has disappeared; so have the halos. St. Luke was the patron saint of painters: in representing the saint, van der Weyden was thereby also addressing the nature of his art. Of special interest here is the contrast between the saint, who lived in the presence of the Virgin, actually saw her, and the observer and the painter, who possess only a mediated access to the sacred event. The saint's line of vision is thus placed at right angles to our own, reminding us that we are no longer as favorably positioned as he was. Ours is a different, and less privileged point of view; his was a more spiritual perspective. How would he have represented the Virgin? The sheet in his hands holds no answer, but when in imagination we put ourselves in his position, we "see" the Virgin before the golden background of the fabric of her throne. A concern for different points of view offers a key to the organization of this painting: compare the saint's and the observer's points of view with that of the couple looking out into the landscape beyond. With their backs to the sacred event, outside the room that shelters the Virgin and to which we, too, as observers half belong, their attention is turned to the world with its infinite variety. They and the saint belong to different realms.

I called the gold background a metaphorical device meant to carry us beyond the familiar sensible world. It thus functions somewhat like the words "absolute," "perfect," or "infinite" added to predicates taken from the sensible world in order to make them more adequate to God. Such strategies make sense only as long as there is an assumption of some continuity between the mundane and the divine, or at least some commensurability. As a new subjectivism began to assert itself in the concern with perspective that Alberti systematized, the use of gold backgrounds had to appear an increasingly hollow convention. And something similar holds for the presupposed analogy of being.

This new anthropocentric art had to raise once again the old Platonic question: Given the self-consciousness that finds expression in the adoption of perspective and the transformation of the visible world into subjective appearance, how could art still claim to serve divine reality? Is art not tied by its very essence to appearance? And the fault would seem to lie not just with one-point perspective, but with the visible as such. We stand on the threshold of a conception of art that no longer places the work of art in the service of truth, but reduces it to a kind of entertainment. Similarly, we stand on the threshold of a conception of science that no longer demands of itself adequacy to the things themselves, but is content with a mastery of representations.

The Renaissance preoccupation with magic, seen in the appeal of texts like the *Asclepius*, may be understood as a refusal to settle for an art and a science cut off from reality, as an attempt to find in the Hermetic tradition an alternative both to the disintegrating medieval worldview that had come to be associated above all with Aristotle and to the soulless science that was to find its most thoughtful defender in Descartes.

3

Must an art that submits to the rule of perspective also cut itself off from reality? This is not a problem for the artist alone: if our experience, too, is ruled by perspective—that is to say, is an experience of mere appearances having their center in the subject—how do we get beyond appearances to reality itself? The self-understanding that expresses itself in the preoccupation with perspective is intimately linked to skepticism. Skepticism is, as I suggested earlier, the philosophical expression of the threshold of modernity; we can hardly be surprised that at the time, Cusanus's doctrine of learned ignorance was widely considered just another skeptical position.[11] The rival claims of Catholic, Protestant, and Reformed Christians had reinforced skeptical reflections, and this splintering of the old faith had its counterpart in the disintegration of Aristotelian science. How was it possible to distinguish among all the different claimants to the truth? This is not the place to review the skeptical literature of the age, but we should turn at least briefly to what is perhaps its most famous example, Montaigne's "Apology for Raymond Sebond" (1580).

According to Montaigne, there is a sad disproportion between the demand for truth, for real insight into what is, and the human condition. What the human being wants he cannot get:

The wretch has no stomach for effectively climbing over them [the barriers imposed on him by his nature]; he is trussed up and bound, subject to the same restraints as the other creatures of his natural order. His condition is a very modest one. As for his essential being, he has no true privilege or pre-eminence: what he thinks or fancies he has, has no savour, no body to it. Granted that of all the animals, man alone has freedom to think and such unruly ways of doing so that he can imagine things which are and things which are not, imagine his wishes, or the false and the true: but he has little cause to boast about it, since it is the chief source of the woes which beset him: sin, disease, irresolution, confusion, despair.[12]

The human being is indeed the *animal rationale*, the animal that has reason. But reason proves an ambiguous asset: as the rational animal, the human being is also the animal that is not at ease with itself and the world, the forever restless animal, subject to sin and despair. The disproportion between what we want and what we can get is particularly evident in the realm of knowledge. As Nietzsche was to say much later, we demand to know, but have no organ for the truth. Here is how Montaigne, whom Nietzsche admired, put this point: "Now, since our state makes things correspond to itself and transforms them in conformity with itself, we can no longer claim to know what anything truly is." This is but another variation on the principle of perspective. Things appear to us the way they do because we have subjected them to our merely human measure. That insight is expressed in the Protagorean "man is the measure of all things," invoked by Alberti. But to continue with Montaigne:

nothing comes to us except as altered and falsified by our senses. When the compasses, the set-square, and the ruler are askew, all the calculations made with them and all structures raised according to their measurements, are necessarily out of true and ready to collapse.

The unreliability of our senses renders unreliable everything which they put forward. And meanwhile who will be a proper judge of such difference? . . . if the judge is old, he cannot judge the sense impressions of old age, since he is party to the dispute; so too if he is young; so too if he is well; so too if he is unwell, asleep, or awake. We would need a man exempt from all these qualities, so that, without preconception, he could judge these propositions as indifferent to him.

On this reckoning we would need a judge such as never was.[13]

Montaigne goes on to suggest that since sense cannot decide the dispute, reason must do so. But where does reason take its reasons? Does it not have to rely on sense impressions? He concludes: "We have no communication with Being; as human nature is wholly situated, forever between birth and death, it shows itself only as a dark shadowy appearance, an unstable weak opinion."[14] Nothing is left of Plato's belief that human reason had access to the realm of true being, that it was therefore not victim to the deceptive senses, to the rule of time, and to the limits they imposed. Montaigne insists on these limits.

4

I began this chapter with painting and a question: how can an art ruled by perspective claim to reveal what is; how can it claim to represent reality? That this is also a problem for anyone who claims to know reality as it is, is shown by Montaigne. What renders both the new art and the new science profoundly questionable is hinted at by two paintings of the sixteenth century: Hans Holbein's *Ambassadors* (1533) and Pieter Brueghel's *Fall of Icarus* (1558). Holbein's splendid double portrait (fig. 13; plate 5) shows the French ambassador Jean de Dinteville and his intimate friend Bishop Georges de Selve, French envoys to the court of Henry VIII.[15] I shall not consider here the objects on the two shelves that speak of the cultural achievements of these two men and of the age—de Dinteville no doubt played a major part in deciding what was to appear in this painting, which was to hang in his palatial home in Polisy—but focus instead on the curiously elongated object in the foreground, which seems so obviously out of place, falls out of the picture as a dissonant "other." This enigmatic shape becomes legible when we assume a point of view to the left of the painting and slightly below: now it comes into focus as a skull. Here it is well to remember that the painter's name *Holbein* in German means "hollow bone," that is, skull, so that what we look at is no doubt also a witty way of signing the picture. But this explanation remains both obvious and superficial. Far more important is the way a change in the observer's position that leaves behind the generally taken-for-granted point of view (in front of the picture) reveals the real meaning behind the worldly pomp of the envoys and of the instruments with which they are associated: all this is only an appearance, a stage play. Death haunts this theater. The skull recalls us to what really matters.

This significance is underlined by other details. Quite theatrically the men pose before a green curtain, presenting themselves to us as actors on the stage of the world. The decorative pattern of the floor has been identified as that of the choir of Westminster Abbey. The worldly space of the theatrical setup is thus presented in a sacred space, though hinted at only by the pavement—and, if we look carefully, by the half-hidden crucifix, which we

. . .

figure 13
Hans Holbein the Younger,
The French Ambassadors of King Henri II
at the court of the English King Henry VIII
(1533). National Gallery, London.
Credit: Erich Lessing/Art Resource, N.Y.

barely glimpse in the painting's upper left-hand corner. The vanity of this life is thus revealed, as is its theatrical quality. Alberti's Narcissus, present here in the conceit of the signature, puts himself into question. By playing two perspectives off against each other, the artist lets us become aware of the illusory character not only of all perspectival representation, but also of our ordinary death-bound life.

Such confusing play with different perspectives helps define anamorphosis. As Shakespeare explains, "rightly gazed upon," such compositions "show nothing but confusion; eyed awry"—that is, looked at from the side—they "distinguish form" (Richard II, 2.2). A second, unexpected point

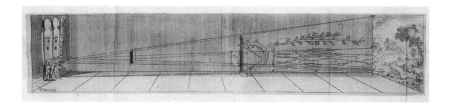

· · ·

figure 14

Emmanuel Maignan,

design for fresco in SS. Trinità in Rome.

From *Perspectiva Horaria* (1648).

Credit: Beinecke Rare Book and Manuscript

Library, Yale University.

of view reveals the hidden meaning. In Holbein's painting, to be sure, what we first see is not confusion but a splendid double-portrait, into which a dissonant, hard-to-read detail has been inserted. It is this detail that demands to be "eyed awry," confusing the apparently coherent picture. What is the significance of such games? The question becomes more interesting when we learn that the Paris monastery of the Minims, with which Descartes's friend Mersenne was associated and in which Descartes himself visited frequently before his departure for Holland, was soon to become a leading center of speculations concerning optics and perspective, with a striking emphasis on problems of anamorphic composition.[16] A number of large anamorphic frescoes were painted at the time. Niceron,[17] who like Mersenne was a Minim, painted two such frescoes in the cloister of the monastery of the Minims in Paris: one representing St. John the Evangelist, a repetition of a work he had done for the Minims in Rome two years before, the other a St. Magdalen, begun in 1645. Although these works have been lost, the St. John is illustrated and discussed in the *Thaumaturgus Opticus*. And one such fresco, dating from 1642 and by Emmanuel Maignan, has survived in the Minim Monastery of SS. Trinità in Rome (fig. 14).[18]

Why should such perspectival experiments or games be given room in a religious establishment? Is this interest in anamorphosis no more than a playful use of perspective? Facing such frescoes one sees very little: arabesques suggesting a landscape, but not coherent enough to be seen convincingly as such—riddles in search of an answer. That answer is given when the normal point of view is given up; a different point of view unexpectedly reveals the real significance of the work. Anamorphosis thus would seem to function as a metaphor for the world, which first presents itself to us as meaningless and confusing; only a change in point of view reveals its deeper order and meaning, in these cases very much a religious meaning. As we shall see in the following chapter, Descartes's method depends on a similar shift in point of view.

But a second point must be made: that such compositions call to our attention the power of perspective itself prevents us from trusting even the second point of view. It, too, is incapable of giving us more than appearance. What is therefore revealed is the deficiency of all perspectives. Anamorphic composition is art that by playing one perspective off against another, proclaims the insufficiency of the eye and thus of art. It resembles a theatrical performance in which the illusion is broken by an actor addressing us, reminding us that what we are watching is only theater; and yet that addresses, too, is part of the theatrical performance. Anamorphic painting should not be taken too seriously. It is born of a love of tricks and games. But it is precisely this lightness that gives it a particular adequacy in an age that had learned to distrust the eye and had despaired of the adequacy of the visible to the divine. Anamorphosis is closely linked to ornamental metamorphoses and to the rapidly changing images of the Baroque machine theater. All are metaphors for the labyrinthine character of the visible. By presenting the theater of the world as a labyrinth, such art gestures toward transcendence.

5

The labyrinth has of course a central place in the story of which "The Fall of Icarus" is but a chapter (fig. 15; plate 6). Auden has given us in "Musée des Beaux Arts" (1940) what has become the most familiar interpretation of Brueghel's painting:

. . .

figure 15

Pieter Brueghel the Elder,

***Landscape with the Fall of Icarus* (1558).**

Museum of Fine Arts, Brussels.

Credit: Scala/Art Resource, N.Y.

About suffering they were never wrong,

The Old Masters: how well they understood

Its human position; how it takes place

While someone else is eating or opening a window or just walking dully along;

How, when the aged are reverently, passionately waiting

For the miraculous birth, there always must be

Children who did not especially want it to happen, skating

On a pond at the edge of the wood

They never forgot

That even the dreadful martyrdom must run its course

Anyhow in a corner, some untidy spot
Where the dogs go on with their doggy life and the torturer's horse
Scratches its innocent behind on a tree.

In Brueghel's *Icarus*, for instance: how everything turns away
Quite leisurely from the disaster; the ploughman may
Have heard the splash, the forsaken cry,
But for him it was not an important failure; the sun shone
As it had to on the white legs disappearing into the green
Water; and the expensive delicate ship that must have seen
Something amazing, a boy falling out of the sky,
Had somewhere to get to and sailed calmly on.

But did the plowman turn away from the disaster? Did he even take note of it? To be sure, this painting is not an obvious example of anamorphosis, but it too makes a curious use of perspective. The scale jumps in ways Alberti would not have tolerated, the space falls apart as we explore the painting: its center will not hold. Try to fit the different scenes into one coherent perspective! We cannot easily get from one such scene to the next. Each individual seems caught up in his own private sphere. It is not, as Auden would have it, that they turn away from the disaster; they quite literally cannot see Icarus. They live in different private worlds, each governed by its own perspective and point of view. But note that the painter succeeds in revealing this imprisonment by his handling of perspective. This is a painting about many things, including perspective.

Why does the fall of Icarus in particular invite a meditation on perspective? Brueghel could find the story in Ovid's *Metamorphoses*. There we learn of Icarus, who together with his father Daedalus escaped from the island of Crete, home of the labyrinth, on wings Daedalus had made of wax. Human artifice was to carry them away from the isle of the labyrinth, which had come to be understood as a figure of this confusing world in which we have to make our way. By the time Brueghel painted this picture, Icarus had thus become a common symbol of knowledge that tries to raise itself beyond the lot of fallen humanity. In the famous emblem book of Alciatus, first published in 1531 and one of the most often reprinted books of the Renaissance, we find an emblem of Icarus with the inscription *In Astrolologos*, "Against the Astrologers," and an explanatory poem, warning that the astrologer should take care lest his attempt to raise himself with his knowledge above the stars lead to a fall (fig. 16). Icarus symbolizes prideful knowledge that must fall, "pride" being tied to the attempt to elevate oneself beyond the merely human perspectives illustrated in the Brueghel painting. The spectator, too, is invited by the painting to participate in an Icarus-like flight: the point of view is constantly raised as we move toward the slightly bent horizon. Alternatively, we can try to hold on to a single point of view, and then what we see becomes ever more toylike.

This painting especially invites us to place it in the context provided by the emblem books of the Renaissance. It is about the human condition, which, if we follow Montaigne, is one of imprisonment in a labyrinth of perspectives; and it is about the vanity of the attempt to escape from that labyrinth, as Icarus attempted to escape from Crete. Crete, the island of the labyrinth, figures the world in which fallen humanity finds itself, where the Fall is understood in terms of pride and thus of freedom, of the dislocating power of the imagination and intellect. The flight of Icarus compounds such pride and ends in death, though we should not forget Daedalus, who with his invention of wings "altered the laws of nature"[19] and who, by staying his course between heaven and earth, did escape.

But, as we are reminded by the partridge, visible on a branch just below the disappearing Icarus, the story does not begin here. As we learn from Ovid, it starts with a murder: in a jealous rage Daedalus had slain his supremely gifted nephew Perdix, who as a child had invented saw and compass and with whose education Daedalus's sister had entrusted him. But although Daedalus cast the boy "headlong down from Minerva's sacred citadel," the goddess, patron of human ingenuity, caught the falling boy and changed him into the low-flying partridge, which bears his name and is afraid of heights, replacing the "swiftness of intellect" with "swiftness of wing and foot."[20] The origin of the fall of Icarus lies thus in the fall of Perdix. The latter's fall, however, was born not of his pride but of Daedalus's unwillingness to tolerate a rival. Forced to flee Athens, Daedalus became both

figure 16

Andreas Alciatus,

In Astrologos (Icarus). **From**

Emblematum Libellus **(1542).**

Credit: Beinecke Rare Book and Manuscript

Library, Yale University.

a builder and a rootless wanderer: the two belong together. I want to underscore the restlessness of Daedalus: Bacon sought the key to the transformation of the world into a labyrinth in the restlessness of the human understanding.

Daedalus is not to be found in Brueghel's picture. Ovid does indeed suggests that he did not witness his son's fall. Still, another version of the picture, presumably a copy, "corrects" this unexpected absence, as it corrects the position of the sun that in our version is shown setting:[21] was it not high in the sky when it melted the wax of Icarus's wings? How high Icarus must have flown to have been falling for such a long time! Now night is about to fall. And if this painting is haunted by the impending triumph of the night, there is also a sense in which it is haunted by murder: how else are we to understand the dagger lying below the horse at the edge of the plowed—I am tempted to say "slashed"—field.[22] A more careful look reveals the head of a corpse lying in the field beyond. As dagger and corpse frame the horse, it is difficult not to see this tiller of the ground in the image of Cain. But Cain resembles Daedalus: led by jealousy to murder, he too becomes a fugitive and a wanderer, also a builder. Does the skyward-looking shepherd, so different from the dark earthward-looking peasant, besides answering to Ovid's account, also represent Abel? The seemingly so pastoral scene of plowman and shepherd thus invites interpretation as a Christian figure of Perdix's murder.

The murderer found a first refuge with King Minos on Crete, where he built the labyrinth to house the Minotaur, the monstrous offspring of Queen Pasiphaë's unnatural love for a bull (that love itself a punishment by Poseidon for her husband's unwilliness to sacrifice that bull, as he had promised). To help the queen consummate her lust, Daedalus is said to have constructed an artificial cow into which she could crawl. The craftsman here, too, meddles with the order of nature. Artifice gives birth to a deadly monster that needs to be imprisoned by further artifice. The invention of wings belongs in this context of the subversion of the natural order by human artifice. In the picture its monstrous consequences are visible in the ship's cannons, in the angler's fishing rod, in the iron plowshare, and finally in the dagger. In the *Fall of Icarus* Brueghel links these violent fruits of artifice to the setting of the sun. This land of the setting sun, illuminated by a pale light, is our *Abendland*, a land of evening on the threshold of the triumph of the forces of darkness. Death belongs with the labyrinth of perspectives.

6

As the story of Daedalus would teach us, the pride that leads us to refuse our place sets free something monstrous within us. Death, eroticism, and artificiality intertwine in stories of the labyrinth. For example, we hear of a dance, associated with both Ariadne and Aphrodite and said to have been invented by Daedalus, which imitated the windings of the labyrinth. The point of this dance, according to Virgil, was to lead men away from the regular; according to Ovid, it was linked to illusions that lead men stray. Masked balls come to mind, which similarly mingle eroticism and artificiality. Related to them is the widespread use of artful anamorphoses to conceal a pornographic content not considered a fit subject for pictorial representation. In such works it is the erotic, rather than death or the sacred, which is the "other" that anamorphosis is made to serve.

How are we to escape from the labyrinth, if indeed we want to escape and would not rather lose ourselves in Dionysian ecstasies? Three figures offer themselves as paradigms: Daedalus, Icarus, and Theseus. Theseus is able to leave the labyrinth because Ariadne gives him the thread that enables him to escape. The escape from the labyrinth here presupposes a gift. The cases of Icarus and Daedalus are different, for their escape is effected by artifice, by human ingenuity that would magically "alter the laws of nature." It is not at all surprising that in his *Rules* we find Descartes insisting that the method that he is advocating was given to him, as Theseus was given his thread. Descartes here is attempting to legitimate his theory by showing that it is not the product of a false pride. Similarly, in the famous dream in which the young Descartes tells how he came to arrive at his method, he declares that he received it as a gift. A gift from whom? Who is Descartes's Ariadne? We know that Descartes vowed in thanksgiving to make a pilgrimage to the Virgin of Loreto,[23] and we have good reason to believe that he fulfilled that vow. What speaks out of this vow is once again uneasiness about the legitimacy of theory and the new science that it was to found. The dream, as Descartes tells it, helped assure him that the method was not a delusion born of human pride, perhaps sent by the devil, but of divine origin—that he is not Icarus, nor even Daedalus the magician, but Theseus. At issue is whether the new science Descartes promises his readers gives human beings what is rightfully theirs or whether they are usurping the place of God, trading reality for simulacra. At issue is the legitimacy or illegitimacy of theory, which means also the legitimacy or illegitimacy of modernity.

1

In his once immensely popular *Labyrinth of the World and Paradise of Heart*, a kind of *Pilgrim's Progress*, the seventeenth-century pedagogue and reformer Jan Amos Comenius lets his pilgrim see the world through a pair of distorting spectacles. Their glass is the glass of illusion, their rims are the rims of custom.[1] Having discovered that what these glasses reveal are but shadows, that the truth will ever escape us mortals, Comenius's pilgrim throws away these "glasses of Falsehood," only to "behold awful darkness and gloom, of which the mind of man can find neither the end nor the ground."[2] Similarly Descartes, having freed himself from the distortions of the senses and common opinion by means of his method of doubt, finds himself as if he had fallen into deep water: "I am so disconcerted that I can neither make certain of setting my feet on the bottom, nor can I swim and support myself on the surface."[3] Comenius's pilgrim, too, enters "the innermost" of his heart to discover there, too, only darkness. But into this dark enters the light of God: the pilgrim is given a new pair of spectacles, its rims now the Word of God, their glass the Holy Ghost.[4]

Distorting spectacles let Comenius's pilgrim experience the world as a labyrinth. This conjunction of an optical conceit with that of the labyrinth is quite characteristic of Mannerism and Baroque: Balthasar Gracián thus speaks of a mirror that unmasks what we call reality as a labyrinth of chimeras,[5] while

Francis Bacon likens the human understanding to a "false mirror, which, receiving rays irregularly, distorts and discolors the natures of things by mingling its own nature with it."[6] The sciences, instead of seeking the path that leads us through the woods of experience to the clearing of axioms, are said to have lost their way, "either leaving and abandoning experience entirely, or losing their way in it and wandering round and round as in a labyrinth."[7] But even if common at the time, the conjunction of labyrinth and optical conceit is nevertheless puzzling: is not the labyrinth a region of darkness? Here the lack of light contributes to humanity's loss of way. Optical devices on the contrary presuppose light. The association of the two conceits communicates distrust of all attempts to improve our sight with artifice, a suspicion that such devices may serve only to pervert the eye, transforming light into dark.[8]

Unlike the metaphor of the mirror, which has been associated with illusion ever since Plato, the metaphor of spectacles belongs to the modern era. I have in mind not so much their relative chronology—the possibility of using lenses to improve human vision was discovered only in the thirteenth century—but their mechanism. Unlike the mirror, which reflects more or less adequately what can already be seen, spectacles attempt to improve on what nature has given us, extending the range of the visible. Human ingenuity attempts to correct what nature has left deficient.

There is pride in such an attempt. If God had wanted us to see better, would he not have given us better eyesight? And this pride is compounded in the late sixteenth or the first years of the seventeenth century by the invention of the telescope,[9] an instrument that not only makes the distant appear near, the small large—qualities that are among those Comenius attributes to his spectacles—but also, as Galileo demonstrated, enabled human beings to see what no one yet had seen. Or should these new sights, these new stars and "planets," be resisted as products of a false magic? Was the telescope perhaps a gift of the devil, as a legend telling of its discovery hinted? If God created the human eye defective, is it so clear that human artifice can or should even attempt to remedy such defectiveness? It is hardly surprising that the telescope was considered an instrument both of progress and of illusion.[10] The former view is exemplified by Joseph Glanvill, who, following Bacon and Descartes, saw these inventions as part of a legitimate effort to recover what humanity lost with Adam's fall.

THE THREAD OF ARIADNE

Adam needed no Spectacles. The acuteness of his natural Opticks (if conjecture may have credit) shew'd much of the Coelestial magnificence and bravery without a Galilaeo's tube: And 'tis most probable that his naked eyes could reach near as much of the upper world, as we with all the advantages of art. It may be 'twas as absurd even in the judgment of his senses, that the Sun and Stars should be so very much, less than this Globe, as the contrary seems in ours; and 'tis not unlikely that he held as clear a perception of the earths motion, as we think we have of its quiescence.[11]

Artifice will gain us back that clarity of vision Adam lost. Technology will help us undo the results of the Fall.

But is this very project not born of a sinful refusal to acknowledge the limits that God has set fallen humanity? And is such an attempt not likely to lead to error rather than truth? Our historical place may make it difficult for us to understand those critics of Galileo who refused to look through his telescope, such as Galileo's friend the Aristotelian Cesare Cremonini, who thought that it would only confuse him,[12] or Giulio Libri, the leading philosopher at Pisa.[13] But were they really so unreasonable? Galileo appealed to the authority of the eye, aided by an instrument. Yet philosophy had questioned the authority of that eye from the very beginning—recall Plato's critique in book 10 of the *Republic*—and optical instruments had long been associated with illusion and magic. Should such questionable evidence weigh more than logical argumentation and established science? I shall return to such questions in chapter 14.

Galileo's reply to such critics betrays his confidence in eye and telescope. He scolds those who "showing a greater fondness for their own opinions than for the truth . . . sought to deny and disprove the new things, which, if they had cared to look for themselves, their own sense would have demonstrated."[14] But surely such confidence must contend with that critique of the eye we meet with already in Plato. Distortion, as we have seen, is inevitable given that we experience the world from a place within the world and thus perspectively. Whatever we see appears to us as it does because we happen to be where we are and because our eyes happen to work as they do. Our human perspective is constitutive of what we see. The question that arises: do we not, when we uncritically accept the authority of the eye, submit to appearance? Is the brown of the table something that belongs to the table or is it something that we contribute? In the *Third Meditation* Descartes remarks of "things such as light, colours, sounds, scents, tastes, heat, cold and the other tactile qualities" that "they are thought by me with so much obscurity and confusion that I do not even know if they are true or false, i.e. whether the ideas which I form of these qualities are actually the idea of real objects or not (or whether they only represent chimeras which cannot exist in fact)."[15] To the extent that we base our knowledge on the senses, we would seem to remain imprisoned in a labyrinth of appearances. The natural light of the sun, let alone the artificial light of a candle, cannot dispel the darkness of this labyrinth. To find one's way in it requires a different kind of illumination. Only the spiritual light within can show us the way out of the labyrinth.

Similar considerations, as we have seen, had already led Plato to condemn mimetic art as an imitation of mere appearance, thrice removed from reality. Insofar as the artist accepts the rule of perspective he must surrender all claims to serve the truth. His art can be no more than "a kind of play or sport."[16] In his ability to create a second world the artist may seem like a godlike magician. Yet the power of his magic depends very much on the infirmity of our senses. And what of the telescope? Is it not perhaps, like the artist's perspective, a thaumaturgic device? Should the sights that it presents to us be taken for reality? Can it in any way helps us find our way out of the labyrinth of deceptive appearance? To find that way, we must free ourselves from the rule of perspective and from the limits imposed by the senses. To show us the way out is the point of Descartes's method. In the *Rules* the young Descartes therefore likens his mathematical method to the thread that guided Theseus.

2

And yet Descartes knows that his science is close to the art of Daedalus. This knowledge is at least suggested by the presence among the minor works Descartes wrote before leaving France for Holland, according to Baillet, the seventeenth-century biographer of Descartes, of a page bearing the title *Thaumantis Regia*.[17] The title also appears in the inventory of Descartes's manuscripts made in Stockholm just after his death in 1650.[18] Nothing of what cannot have been more than a brief sketch has survived. But the title gives us an idea of what Descartes must have had in mind: *thaumantis* suggests the art of conjuring. A letter dating from September 1629 enables us to be more specific. In it Descartes speaks of a branch of mathematics that he calls "the science of miracles." By means of that science, Descartes writes, one can cause the same illusions to be seen that, it is said, the magicians made appear with the aid of demons.[19] Descartes thus seems to place himself in the tradition of the artificial magic of Agrippa, Porta, and Campanella. At the same time he distances himself from that tradition by claiming that science will be able to achieve what the magicians were supposed to have accomplished. And while he admits that to the best of his knowledge this science is not yet being practiced, he does name a craftsman, an optician named Ferrier, as the only one he knows capable of it.[20] At least part of what Descartes was aiming at with his *Thaumantis Regia* appears to have been an applied optics, an aim not so very different from that of Alberti's *On Painting.*

The title brings to mind Jean-François Niceron's *La perspective curieuse*, which appeared in 1636. The subtitle of Niceron's book describes this curious perspective once again as a kind of magic capable of producing the most beautiful effects of which the art and industry of man are capable. Here, too, magic has been replaced by science. And though Descartes never met Niceron, the two were nonetheless very much aware of each other's work. Thus Niceron sent Descartes his *Perspective*, and Descartes reciprocated by sending his *Principles.*[21] Both were close to Mersenne, whom Descartes had known ever since his student days at La Flèche, where, as we learn from the *Discourse*, he "read through all the books that fell into his hands, treating of what is most curious and rare."[22] Mersenne shared this interest in and suspicion of these "curious" sciences. Seeking to serve both his Church and the emerging science, he was indeed at the very center of efforts to discredit Renaissance magic, with its basis in the Hermetic tradition.[23] Mersenne later was to give Niceron's *Perspective* its theological approbation and to supervise the posthumous and greatly expanded Latin edition of the work, the *Thaumaturgus Opticus* (1646). But it was in Descartes that Mersenne was to find his most thoughtful ally.

As we know from his early writings and letters, from the very beginning Descartes had an interest not only in optics, perspective, and painting but in using his knowledge of them to duplicate some of the effects said to have been created by the thaumaturgic magicians. Thus in the *Cogitationes Privatae* Descartes suggests that one could use mirrors to make tongues and chariots of fire appear.[24] Like such Renaissance magicians as Agrippa, Porta, Kircher, and Dee, Descartes appears here as someone who is interested in creating, as Plato would say, imitations of appearance, in optical tricks that would surprise and delight those unable to see through them. No doubt these tricks included anamorphoses.

As we saw in the previous chapter, there is something magical about anamorphoses, which reveal an unsuspected deeper meaning in a seemingly superficial appearance. But what Descartes must have found more significant is that such effects rest on a precise science. Magic has been replaced with optics; the demons that were supposed to have aided the magicians have been replaced with mathematical calculation. As already in Alberti's perspectival art, the imagination of the artist has been subordinated to science, which not only teaches us how to produce such marvelous images but at the same time enables us to see through the magic and delivers us from illusion. The science of anamorphosis yields the Ariadne's thread that guides us through the labyrinth of the visible.

Analogous considerations help dispel doubts concerning the reliability of the telescope. To decide to what extent the evidence it presents is reliable, one has to understand the workings of the human eye and of such instruments. Descartes's *Dioptric* is thus related to the projected *Thaumantis Regia*. Descartes knows that the evidence given to our senses is necessarily distorted. He also knows that such distortion is not arbitrary, but follows laws that can be understood. Such understanding helps us correct the natural defects of the eye. In the *Dioptric* Descartes invokes the analogy of vision with painting. In what sense can a painting be said to resemble the represented object? Certainly there can be no identity; "there would then be no distinction between the object and its image." To understand the perfection of a painting one has to understand its form of representation and thus the manner in which it differs from what it represents:

Thus, in the case of engravings, made of a little ink disposed here and there on the paper, we see how they represent forests, towns, men, and even battles and tempests, while yet of the infinity of diverse qualities which they make us conceive in these objects, the only one of the qualities to which they bear any proper resemblance is the quality of shape; and even this is a very imperfect resemblance, since it is on a completely flat surface that they represent bodies diverse in height and distance, and further that in accord with the rules of perspective they often represent circles better by ovals than by other circles, and squares by four-sided figures which are not squares, and similarly in the case of all other shapes.[25]

A representation may be more successful precisely because it departs from reality. It is in just this way, Descartes suggests, that we should think of images in the brain. Crucial here is the insistence that image and imaged must be different. To understand human vision we must understand its mode of representation, the mechanism of vision. Thus there is no need to assume that the dark or light-colored phenomena seen by us correspond to a world that is itself colored dark or light. Quite the contrary: color would seem to belong with appearance. Does it make sense to say of reality as it is in itself that it is colored? Secondary qualities have to be understood as effects and representations of primary qualities. Optics must be understood as part of mechanics. Once we have understood the mechanics of vision, we no longer need fear that the eye will deceive us.

The exit from the theater of appearances Descartes shows us is the same exit already marked by Plato: "And the arts of measuring and numbering and weighing come to the rescue of the human understanding—there is the beauty of them—and the apparent greater or less, or more or heavier, no longer have the mastery over us, but give way before calculation and measure and weight" (*Republic* 10, 602c–d).

3

When Descartes speaks of an artificial magic that is a branch of mathematics and that will enable us to produce the same appearances that magicians were said to have been able to raise with the help of demons, he refers the reader to a by then well-established tradition. Essentially the same claim had been made by Agrippa von Nettesheim in *De Occulta Philosophia* (1533), a book Descartes must have known. Agrippa, too, insists on the connection between magic and mathematics. Appealing to Plato, he claims that just by means of the mathematical sciences it is possible to create works like those of nature—for instance, bodies that will walk or speak and yet lack the power of life. He offers some examples from antiquity: the paradigmatic automata of Daedalus, tripods that moved, golden statues that served food and drink, the flying dove of Archytas, a brazen snake that hissed, artificial birds that could sing. He also tells of a brazen head cast by William of Paris when Saturn was rising that had the power of speech and prophecy. Mechanics and astrology fuse in characteristic fashion.[26] Similar lists were common in the sixteenth and seventeenth centuries. To the marvels of antiquity one could add such contemporary wonders as a fly and an eagle at Nuremberg that could raise themselves into the air or sculptures that could move, sing, or play instruments. Perhaps the most famous examples were found in the garden Salomon de Caus had created for the Palatine Elector at Heidelberg in the early seventeenth century, which was being celebrated as the eighth wonder of the world.[27] In this field, too, the moderns competed with the ancients. Salomon de Caus was the new Hero of Alexandria.[28]

The interest in perspective and optics belongs into this context. Agrippa had included appearances created by geometry and optics, such as illusions created by mirrors, in his list of thaumaturgic works. Similarly Salomon de Caus combined an interest in perspective, more especially in anamorphic composition, with his interest in mechanics, pneumatics, and hydraulics. In the same spirit Niceron claims in his *Perspective curieuse* that the marvels that can be created by the art of perspective should not be esteemed less than such works of artificial magic as the moving sphere of Posidonius or the flying dove of Archytas. Descartes's *Thaumantis Regia* would presumably have included instructions on how to fashion such mechanical marvels.[29]

We know, at any rate, that even as a young man Descartes had a profound interest in automata. In his *Cogitationes Privatae* we find suggestions as to how one might construct an automatic tightrope walker or the dove of Archytas. Particularly interesting is the reference to one such automaton in the *Thirteenth Rule:* having admonished the reader not to assume more or less than the data furnish, Descartes gives the following example:

So again, we must be on our guard when inquiring into the construction of a vessel, such as we once saw, in the midst of which stood a column and upon that a figure of

Tantalus in the attitude of a man who wants to drink. Water when poured into the vessel remained without leaking as long as it was not high enough to enter the mouth of Tantalus; but as soon as it touched the unhappy man's lips the whole of it at once flowed out and escaped. Now at the first blush it seems as if the whole of the ingenuity consisted in the construction of this figure of Tantalus, whereas in reality this is a mere accompaniment of the fact requiring explanation, and in no ways conditions it. For the whole difficulty consists solely in the problem of how the vessel was constructed so as to let out the whole of the water when that arrived at a certain height, whereas before none escaped.[30]

As long as we only look at such a statue its workings will seem mysterious and magical. But this magic rests on mechanics. As soon as the inner mechanism is understood, wonder gives way to an appreciation of the ingenuity of the engineer.

Automata not only provided Descartes with examples of deceptive appearance but also showed the way to the solution of the riddle they posed. As Descartes himself points out, they provided him with a model for understanding the human body. The body is like one of these automata; Descartes's God is like the creator of such machines. And just as the ignorant when faced with an automaton might be tempted to admire or accuse its creator as a magician, so someone who sees only the appearance of things is likely to think the world a labyrinth and its creator an artist like Daedalus, a demonic artificer who does not permit us to find our way through his labyrinth. The analogy between automata and bodies suggests that such a view is mistaken.

In the *Discourse on Method* Descartes invokes this analogy to make his physiology seem more plausible, which, he points out,

will not seem strange to those, who, knowing how many different *automata* or moving machines can be made by the industry of man, without employing in so doing more than a very few parts in comparison with the great multitude of bones, muscles, nerves, arteries, veins, or other parts that are found in the body of each animal. From this aspect the body is regarded as a machine which, having been made by the hands of God, is incomparably better arranged, and possesses in itself movements which are much more admirable, than any of those which can be invented by man.[31]

The analogy is further developed in the *Treatise on Man*, where he supposes that the body is nothing but a statue or machine of earth. Nerves are likened to pipes or tubes, muscles and tendons to engines and other devices to make such statues move, the animal spirits to the water that moves such statues, and so on. Descartes goes on to liken exterior objects that act on the body and thus cause sensations to strangers who, on entering some artificial grotto, cause the statues there to move without realizing what it is that causes such movement. Again Descartes has a specific example in mind (fig. 17): he speaks of a bathing Diana who, as the visitor approaches, hides among some reeds; as he pushes further to get a better view he is met by Neptune with his trident, while a monster appears from the other side and spits water at him.[32] Jurgis Baltrusaitis has shown that Descartes based his description on a grotto designed by Salomon de Caus and illustrated in his *Les raisons des forces mouvantes* (1615).[33] Faced with such creations we first marvel at what seems to defy understanding. Once we have grasped the mechanics involved, wonder gives way to admiration for human ingenuity. Similarly, by teaching us how the human body works, mechanics allays our doubts concerning the deceptiveness of the senses as it lets us admire the greatness of God's creation (fig. 18).

That we escape from the labyrinth of the world as we learn to see the world as a mechanism was a common thought. We find it, for example, in Comenius. The light of faith lets his pilgrim see the world as

a vast clock-work, fashioned out of diverse visible and invisible materials; and it was wholly glassy, transparent and fragile. It had thousands, nay thousands of thousands, of larger and smaller columns, wheels, hooks, teeth, dents; and all these moved and worked together, some silently, some with much rustling and rattling of diverse fashions. In the middle of all stood the largest, principal, yet invisible wheel; from it the various motions of the others proceeded in some unfathomable manner. For the power of the wheel penetrated through all things, and directed everything.[34]

For Comenius, as for Descartes, the path that leads to this vision requires an inward turn. Only within ourselves do we find the light that lets us see reality as it is, undistorted by perspective. The difference, however, is that according to Comenius, "corrupt nature cannot be mended by Worldly

figure 17

Salomon de Caus,

grotto of Neptune. From *Les raisons*

***des forces mouvantes* (1615).**

Credit: Beinecke Rare Book and Manuscript

Library, Yale University.

. . .

figure 18

Salomon de Caus,

machine for raising water. From *Les*

raisons des forces mouvantes **(1615).**

Credit: Beinecke Rare Book and Manuscript

Library, Yale University.

Wisdom."[35] Through faith alone we find the right way in the labyrinth of the world. Descartes, on the other hand, claims that we humans bear within ourselves the seeds of a science that will deliver us from appearance.

In the *Rules* Descartes thus makes an attempt to show that we do indeed possess an intuition that is free from the distortions of perspective. Such intuition is tied to an apprehension of simple natures, for which mathematics provides the paradigm. By their very essence such simple natures do not permit doubt as to what they are: we either grasp them or fail to grasp them. Their simplicity makes it impossible for them to be other than they present themselves to us as being. Out of such simples we construct models of what we encounter, which the young Descartes does not claim will do full justice to what they represent. But by their mathematical form they will avoid the illusions of perspectival painting. With its geometrical constructions the mathematical imagination mediates between reason and the sensible:[36]

Is there then any disadvantage, if, while taking care not to admit any new entity uselessly, or rashly to imagine that it exists, and not denying indeed the beliefs of others concerning colour, but merely abstracting from every other feature except that it possesses the nature of figure, we conceive the diversity existing between white, blue, and red, etc., as being like the difference between the following similar figures?

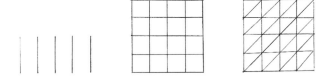

The same argument applies in all cases; for it is certain that the infinitude of figures suffices to express all the differences in sensible things.[37]

Descartes proceeds to the construction of mechanical models, which, he suggests, let us "understand how all the motions of the other animals can come about, though we can ascribe to them no knowledge at all, but only fancy of a purely corporeal kind. We can explain also how in ourselves all those operations occur which we perform without any aid from the reason."[38] Nature can be understood by us to the extent, and only to the extent, that it can be represented by mechanical models.[39] Such understanding will not only let us grasp the mechanism of nature but will enable us to repair and correct it.

Confident in the explanatory power of mechanical models, the young Descartes rejects not only the occult science of an Agrippa but also Kepler's appeals to psychological interpretations, which, Kepler thought, were appropriate when causal interpretations proved insufficient and reasons became effective in the world. Neither teleology, nor numerology, nor astrology has a place in Descartes' science of nature.[40] Renaissance Hermetism is banished: "Material phenomena may not be explained by means of spiritual concepts."[41] The sharp distinction drawn later between *res cogitans* and *res extensa* was meant to legitimate this exclusion. The new science was to have room neither for God nor for man.[42]

In *The Vanity of Dogmatizing* Joseph Glanvill praises Descartes for having "unridled" the "dark physiology of nature."[43] What Glanvill has in mind is not so much Descartes's work on the body; he speaks rather of shooting stars and meteors, which, once understood, offer no more ground for astrological speculations than does a flaming chimney. That progress in astronomy rests on the same principles as progress in physiology is indeed suggested in the *Thirteenth Rule*. After having shown how this rule enables us to look beyond the appearance of the Tantalus sculpture to the mechanism it hides, Descartes suggests that similar considerations will have important consequences for astronomy:

Finally, likewise, if we seek to extract from the recorded observations of the stars an answer to the question of what we can assert about their motions, it is not to be gratuitously assumed that the earth is immovable and established in the midst of the universe, as the Ancients would have it, because from our earliest years it appears to be so. We ought to regard this as dubious, in order afterwards to examine what certainty there is in this matter to which we are able to attain. So in other cases.[44]

By now we are familiar with this invitation to question a point of view that initially suggests itself as the obvious one. Such questioning undermines our confidence in the geocentric worldview by suggesting that it is no more than what Bacon called "an idol of the tribe." Descartes's admonition that we should not gratuitously assume the earth to be at rest follows the reflections of Cusanus.

Yet even as reflections on the distorting power of perspective reveal the world to be a theater of appearances, they also open the way toward a more adequate understanding. If first of all we see the world from a point of view assigned to us by our body and our senses, it is nevertheless possible for us to escape from these perspectives. Through our reason we can transcend the limitations of the here and now and arrive at a more objective mode of representing the world. As we represent the world we initially perceive as a collection of objects moving in an endless homogeneous space, the perspective-bound form of representation characteristic of painting is transformed into the transperspectival form of representation characteristic of science. The light of reason, the *lumen naturale* Descartes is so fond of invoking, is supposed to let us escape from the labyrinth. Are we not able to attain an understanding of reality that is objective? Perspective-bound everyday experience gives way to the descriptions of science. The thread of Ariadne turns out to be spun of mathematics.

4

But is the promised exit from the labyrinth to be trusted? Consider once more Cusanus's doctrine of learned ignorance and the challenge to the geocentric worldview to which it led. As Koyré points out, there are good reasons not to construe this challenge as an anticipation of Copernicus. Cusanus does not claim to give us *the true* account of the cosmos. Instead he forces the reader to put into question the very idea of *the* true account. Human understanding does not seem capable of giving such an account: it suffers shipwreck on the infinity of space. Cusanus thus does not ask us to exchange a geocentric for a heliocentric position. Rather it is the very idea of any cosmic center that has been undermined. And the same is true of the idea of absolute motion. But with this move, have we not also undermined the claim of astronomy to truth? What links a thinker like Cusanus to and what separates him from the new science should have become evident: what links them is their reflection on the perspectival character of what we experience—a reflection that, as I suggested, is the theme of learned ignorance, a theme familiar already to Plato; what separates Cusanus from practitioners of the new science is the latter's confidence in having found in mathematics the Ariadne's thread that leads out of the labyrinth of the world. But is such confidence justified? Is not the faith of the new science a naive faith?

Let me bracket this question for the time being. I shall return to it in chapter 15. It is clear that without such faith we cannot understand the confidence with which the founders of the new science sought to unriddle the secrets of nature. Such faith is presupposed by the outrage with which Giordano Bruno and Kepler were filled when they read the preface to *De Revolutionibus*—which claimed that Copernicus was trying to provide not a true picture of the cosmos, but only a device that would allow us to calculate more easily the observed motions of the sun and the planets. "Now when from time to time there are offered for one and the same motion different hypotheses (as eccentricity and an epicycle for the sun's motion) the astronomer will accept above all others the one which is easiest to grasp. The philosopher will perhaps rather seek the semblance of the truth. But neither of them will understand or state anything certain, unless it has been divinely revealed to him." Certainty is said to result only from divine revelation. Science aims at something less than truth, at descriptions and predictions that help us better cope with observable phenomena. The more elegant the hypotheses that provide these, the better.

Let us therefore permit the new hypotheses to become known together with the ancient hypotheses, which are no more probable; let us do so especially because the new hypotheses are admirable and also simple, and bring with them a huge treasure of very skillful observations. So far as hypotheses are concerned, let no one expect anything certain from astronomy, which cannot furnish it, lest he accept as the truth ideas conceived for another purpose, and depart from this study a greater fool than when he entered it.[45]

Once again the astronomer is denied access to the truth; the truth belongs to God, not to us humans. The astronomer must be content with models that make it easier to comprehend the phenomena. The outrage of a Kepler is understandable. As the main body of his book makes clear, Copernicus sought the truth.

We now know that Andreas Osiander, a Lutheran minister in Nuremberg who was interested in mathematics and astronomy and entrusted with the publication of Copernicus's work, substituted his own preface for the introduction Copernicus had written. He hoped by this substitution to make the work more acceptable to thinkers still tied to an Aristotelian conception of nature and to theologians who thought it conflicted with the evidence of Scripture. But such strategic reasons happily agreed with his own conviction. There can be no doubt that Osiander was convinced that astronomical propositions cannot claim truth, but serve only as the basis of calculations. There can be no doubt either about Copernicus's conviction that human reason is capable of arriving at the truth. Quite a few philosophers of science have sided with Osiander on this issue. Duhem, for example, explicitly agrees with Osiander's claim that truth is not attainable in the natural sciences, that hypotheses are only devices to save the phenomena.

To assess the strength of Osiander's position, think back to Cusanus and to his conception of boundless space. Of course neither Copernicus nor Kepler accepted this infinity, and in part their opposition to an infinite cosmos is motivated by the danger this conception posed to their understanding of truth: the infinity of space threatens to plunge us into a cognitive labyrinth. To quote Kepler: "We shall show them [those who, like Cusanus and Bruno, hold that the universe is infinite] that by admitting the infinity of the fixed stars they become involved in inextricable labyrinths." And again: "This very cogitation [the thought of infinite space] carries with it I don't know what secret, hidden horror; indeed one finds oneself wandering in this immensity, to which are denied limits and center and therefore also all determinate places."[46] Kepler, as Koyré tells us, also thought that he had good astronomical reasons for his view. To be sure, these reasons proved inadequate.

But what concerns me here is the threat that the infinity of space posed to the astronomer's claim to truth. Descartes himself was forced to acknowledge this. In the late *Principles*, as we shall see in chapter 15, he seems in places closer to Osiander than to Kepler. Thus he admits that we cannot finally establish the absolute truth of the Copernican over the Ptolemaic or the Tychonic hypotheses. We can only show that one hypothesis is better able to explain the phenomena. Because of its greater simplicity the Copernican is to be preferred. Important in this connection is a distinction Descartes draws between *moral* and *absolute certainty*. Moral certainty is defined as certainty that suffices for the conduct of life. Explanations that utilize mechanical models can never claim absolute certainty, since, as in the case of automata, we see only the surface appearance and have to reconstruct the inner mechanism it hides. Even if our mechanical models account for what we can observe, who is to say that some other model might not have served equally well. As Cusanus had insisted, we are separated from the truth as possibility is separated from necessity.[47] Duhem similarly suggests that to claim absolute truth for an idea or a hypothesis about the universe, we would have to prove that it permits no possible alternative. In the science of nature, however, proofs of this sort are unattainable. So we settle for less than absolute truth, settle for something very close to what Descartes called moral truth. The philosopher's place is not that of God. His is just a particular point of view; and even if he is unable to take any other seriously, he cannot therefore claim for it an absolute priority. We seem to be back in a labyrinth of perspectives.

It is therefore no surprise when Joseph Glanvill, a skeptic of sorts and at the same time a great admirer of Descartes, in *The Vanity of Dogmatizing* presents Descartes as a fellow skeptic. To Glanvill the mathematical sciences did indeed seem certain: "He that doubts their certainty, hath need of a dose of Hellebore." But that certainty did not mean that we have an equally certain knowledge of nature:

the knowledge we have of Mathematicks, hath no reason to elate us; since by them we know by numbers and figures, creatures of our own, and are yet ignorant of our Maker's. . . . And though the Grand Secretary of Nature, the Miraculous Descartes have here infinitely out-done all the Philosophers went before him, in giving a particular and Analytical account of the Universal Fabrick: yet he intends his Principles but for Hypotheses, and never pretends that things are really or necessarily, as he hath supposed them: but that they may be admitted pertinently to save the Phenomena, and are convenient supposals for the use of life.[48]

The infinite power of God cannot be imprisoned in our "shallow models." Descartes's method, according to Glanvill, does not lead us out of the labyrinth to reality itself; it just makes appearances more manageable. Why our models should enable us not only to interpret what has been observed but also to assert ourselves as the masters and possessors of nature remains obscure.

5

On this interpretation Descartes should be likened to Daedalus rather than Theseus: a proud artificer whose work may stupefy and may give us power, but the foundations of that power remain shrouded in mystery. Descartes himself would have resisted such an interpretation, and such resistance would have focused on his understanding of mathematics. Not only do mathematical demonstrations give us more than moral certainty, but, Descartes would insist, when using mathematics to understand nature we do more than impose on it our merely human measures. Mathematics is more than just a human creation. Descartes agrees with Galileo's claim that God wrote the book of nature in the language of mathematics: here, human thinking is in tune with divine thought. Mathematics thus possesses an ontological significance for Descartes that Glanvill does not recognize. I shall have to come back later to this point.

Here I would like to return to the way the idea of infinity threatens to deny the human demand for absolute truth. That is true of the infinity of space; it is even more true of the infinity of God, when that infinity is taken seriously—and Osiander, Descartes, and Glanvill do take it seriously. Recall Osiander's warning that if we claim truth for our astronomical views, we are likely to leave their study greater fools than when we entered upon it. It is of course the Lutheran minister who is speaking: *the* truth is the property of God. Our finite, human point of view is insufficient to enable us to lay claim to it. Behind that remark lies a very traditional suspicion of the legitimacy of theory. What human beings should really be concerned with is the health of their souls, a priority that the theorist is in danger of forgetting. Father Bourdin, the author of the *Seventh Objection*, compares the philosophical edifice that Descartes has raised to Icarus. In his *Rules*, Descartes ridicules the good father's mixed metaphor, which attributes wings to architecure, and insists that he has built what he calls his church on sound foundations. But this rhetorical reply is not adequate. Maritain was to make essentially the same charge as Bourdin when he accused Descartes and his doctrine of a clear and distinct intuition of simple ideas of the sin of angelism, of mistaking human being for that of an angel, and criticized the pretension "in a flight of pure intellect, of rising to the place of pure intellect, without passing through the gate of the senses, the way fixed for us by nature."[49] Koyré had argued that Descartes drew his psychology from the angelology of St. Thomas, and Ehenne Gilson supported that suggestion.[50] There is indeed something angelic about the point of view claimed by the new science, a point of view that really is no longer such, for it claims to have left behind the perspectival distortions characteristic of points of view. Recall once more what I have termed the principle of perspective: to think a perspective as a perspective is to be in some sense already beyond its limitations. As old as philosophy is the thought that the search for the truth requires us to seek reality behind appearances. Inseparable from this thought is another—that reason is not imprisoned in perspectives, that it can transcend its initial limitations and arrive at a more objective understanding of what is. The idea of objectivity, as I am here using it, is tied to the idea of a knowing that is free from perspectival distortion, an angelic, divine, or ideal knowing. It is thus linked to the idea of a knower not imprisoned in the body and not bound by the senses, a pure subject. The idea of such a knower and that of objectivity belong together. If the idea of such a knower is illegitimate, so is that of objectivity. And with these ideas that of absolute truth also collapses. Such illegitimacy has been suggested by many recent thinkers. Heidegger, for example, in *Being and Time*, claims that in appealing to an idealized subject, to a pure ego, or to an ideal observer, we illegitimately read the traditional understanding of God into the human subject.[51] If this suggestion is accepted, the idea of scientific objectivity must be considered similarly illegitimate.

That there is both a historical and a systematic connection between the ideal or transcendental subject of philosophers and the idea of God cannot be denied. We also have to grant the connection between the understanding of reality and truth that guided the founders of modern science and such an ideal. To delegitimate the idea of transcendental a subject is indeed to delegitimate the very foundation of modern science.

But why should the connection between God and the ideal subject discredit the latter notion? We should ask rather: how was it ever possible for human beings to think God as an all-powerful, aperspectival knower? What reveals itself in even the possibility of that thought is a power of self-transcendence, self-elevation in reflection, that is inseparable from the life of reason. There is something profoundly right about the traditional view that makes an aperspectival knowing the measure of all perspectival knowing. Something similar is implicit already in our everyday understanding of truth as a correspondence of our thoughts or propositions to the facts. The truth is not bound to particular perspectives, is not mine or ours rather than yours or theirs. The ideal of objectivity, an ideal inseparable from our ordinary understanding of truth, has its foundation in the self-transcendence or self-elevation of the human spirit. That ideal has given and continues to give direction to our search for knowledge and more especially to our search for a knowledge of nature. It is inconceivable that science will retreat from its commitment to the ideal of objectivity, that it will cease to speak the language of mathematics, which, as already Plato knew, served such objectivity.

But though I cannot agree with Heidegger's suggestion that the connection between the idea of a pure or transcendental subject and that of the Christian God delegitimizes the former and with it the ideal of objective truth, we have to accept his claim that there is an intimate connection between these two ideas, that as a matter of fact meditations on the nature of God, on his omnipotence and omniscience, helped raise reflection to new heights. And such acceptance also means that the biblical idea of God deserves a central place in discussions of the development of the conditions that allowed modern science to develop. I shall develop this point in part 2 of this book.

Part Two

INFINITY AND TRUTH

1

In the introduction I claimed that our modern culture can only be understood as a post-Christian phenomenon. It assumes a particular understanding of the modern world as shaped by technology, of technology as shaped by science, of science as presupposing a particular understanding of reality. The preceding chapters explored some considerations that help define that understanding of reality. To review them briefly here:

1. The understanding of the modern world presupposes first of all the reflection on the perspectival character of appearance. Such reflection has to lead to a distinction between appearance and reality. Copernicus thus distinguishes the appearance of a daily revolution of the sun from the way things actually are. We saw that this reflection is as old as philosophy, and in this connection I turned repeatedly to book 10 of Plato's *Republic*.
2. Bound up with that reflection is the distinction between sensibility, tied to the body and thus to point of view and perspective—sight here provides the obvious paradigm—and reason, which is not so limited, and is therefore taken to provide a more adequate access to reality.
3. Such reflection is raised to a higher level when reason, too, is seen to be limited by its own mode of operation, to be governed by its own "point of view." This obstruction leads to the distinction between such reason and a

reason not so limited that is capable of grasping things as they are. To the Christian thinker, this difference presents itself as the difference between finite human reason and infinite divine reason. The thought of that theological difference is at the center of Cusanus's doctrine of learned ignorance.

4.   Reflection on this theological difference, more especially meditation on the infinity of God and his distance from finite human knowers, leads to a renunciation of the claim that the human being is capable of seizing the truth. Meditation on the infinite power of God thus readily leads to a certain cognitive resignation. A conceptual link joins thus late medieval nominalism and mysticism to Renaissance or Mannerist skepticism.

One casualty of meditations on the infinity and omnipotence of God has to be our confidence—not just in our ability to seize the truth, but more specifically in the truth of the Aristotelian view of nature. The destruction of Aristotle's astronomy and physics is a presupposition of the speculations of a Copernicus: had the authority of Aristotle not been undermined long before, Copernicus could hardly have formulated his hypotheses; and, had he done so, they would have fallen on deaf ears and been dismissed as fantastic speculations. But this shaking of the authority of the Aristotelian worldview, while necessary, is not sufficient to account for the possibility of a Copernicus. It also requires a renewed confidence in the human ability to seize or at least approximate the truth, a faith in our cognitive faculties that counteracts the cognitive resignation that issues from meditations on the infinity of God. The renewal of that faith contributes to the anthropocentric humanism of the Renaissance.[1] Both theological reflections on the infinity of God and humanist reflections on the dignity of man are indispensable foundations of the achievement of Copernicus and more generally of the new science.

This chapter is concerned primarily with the theological reflections. The condemnation of 219 supposedly erroneous propositions issued in Paris on March 7, 1277, by Bishop Tempier and certain doctors of theology—Pierre Duhem went so far as to call this condemnation "the birth certificate of modern physics"—provides strong support and a convenient focus: to cite Duhem once more, "By the condemnation that they brought forth in 1277, the theologians of the Sorbonne traced out a path to the system of Copernicus."[2]

TRUTH AS THE PROPERTY OF GOD

Of course, the authors of the condemnation had a quite different concern—primarily the new worldliness that seemed to surround them, a
wordliness that still touches us today in works such as the *Roman de la Rose,*
Carmina Burana, and the sculptures of Nicola Pisano or the Master of
Naumburg. All-too-worldly pleasures and intellectual pursuits seemed to
matter more to the hordes of students gathered in Paris than the kind of life
exemplified by the stigmatized St. Francis. That the university by then had
gained a considerable degree of autonomy from the Church (represented by
the bishop) must have seemed to many a conservative churchman a sad sign
of decline and decay. And they could hardly have been reassured to see that
it was in the pagan and very worldly Aristotle, especially as interpreted by
the Arab Averroës, that this Gothic naturalism had found its philosopher. At
the University of Paris Aristotle was then brilliantly represented by Thomas
Aquinas (1225–1274) and Siger of Brabant (ca. 1240–1284),[3] the former
more interested in philosophical and theological topics, the latter more in
the philosophy of nature. In 1255 study of all the known works of Aristotle
was made obligatory in the arts faculty of the University of Paris.[4] To be a
philosopher had come to mean to immerse oneself in the works of Aristotle
and of his Arab commentators. Conservatives, to be sure, many of them
Franciscans led by the great Bonaventure, continued to invoke the authority of Augustine. Others, including Thomas Aquinas, sought to appropriate
Aristotle for a distinctly Christian worldview, striving for a genuine synthe-
sis. Many students, however, seem to have found Siger's insistence on the
autonomy and independence of philosophy—that is, of research and reflection—more attractive. Small wonder then that he, together with Boethius
of Dacia, another leading representative of secular Aristotelianism, should
have been especially targeted by the condemnation.

Already in 1270 Bishop Tempier had condemned thirteen Averroistic
theses that in the name of reason denied the freedom of the will, a presupposition of the Christian understanding of sin; proclaimed the eternity of
the world, thus challenging the biblical account of creation; and insisted on
the unity of the human spirit in all human beings, thus denying an individual, immortal soul. But this rebuke had not put an end to the popularity of
"Siger the Great," as he was called.[5] The tenor of his philosophizing makes
it easy to understand the Church's objections to what he taught. Consider

his answer to the question "whether the human species had a beginning in time." Appealing to Aristotle, Siger denies such a beginning, insisting that "the human species always exists and that it did not begin to be after previous nonexistence."[6] And just as "man does not begin to be when he had in no way existed before," "neither does time." He points to the evident impossibility of the Christian creation account. From the fact that the prime mover is always moving, it is said to follow "that no species of being proceeds to actuality, but that it has proceeded before, so that the same species which were, return in a cycle; and so also opinions and laws and religions and all other things so that the lower circle around from the circling of the higher, although because of the antiquity there is no memory of the cycle of these."[7] Such a cyclical view of nature is clearly incompatible with the Christian understanding of history, and it is therefore not surprising to discover that Siger immediately hedges: "We say these things as the opinion of the Philosopher, although not asserting them as true." The truth claimed by philosophy may not be identified with *the* truth. Siger presents himself here as a representative of what has been called the double theory of truth, which would cut the bond between philosophy and theology: but if nominally the truth of philosophy here remained subordinated to the revealed truth of religion, there is also the suggestion that the latter must be considered unreasonable. The obvious theological rejoinder is that the philosopher must not forget that human reason and reality are finally incommensurable. But those who want to use their own God-given minds are invited to forget theology.

Speculations such as these could be expected to provoke the guardians of the faith. The Condemnation of 1277—both Thomas and Bonaventure had died in 1274—is a key document of their response, representing a victory of mostly Franciscan neo-Augustinians over the often Dominican Aristotelians. On January 16 of that year Pope John XXI, worried about the possible effect of speculation that would free philosophy from the tutelage of theology, had asked Étienne Tempier, the bishop of Paris, to investigate the matter. The bishop responded with the condemnations of March 7 and only eleven days later the archbishop of Canterbury followed suit. The pope would seem to have had reason to be pleased with the zeal of his bishops.

This brief account may suggest another case of the Church's unwillingness to accept intellectual progress, represented here by the rediscovery of Aris-

TRUTH AS THE PROPERTY OF GOD

totle, and thus another sad chapter in the suppression of free thought—a precursor perhaps of the later trials of Bruno and Galileo. And yet, strange as it may seem, precisely by challenging the authority of Aristotle in the name of theology, the conservatives helped prepare the way for an understanding of nature that was to issue in the new science. Paradoxically, these Christian conservatives opened up the way for what was truly progressive. As I have suggested a number of times, if Aristotle's philosophy of nature had not been shaken and challenged long before Copernicus, its authority would have blocked his achievement and its reception. Aristotelian physics, which depends on a geocentric cosmology, and the Copernican revolution cannot be reconciled. But Aristotle's physics also can not be reconciled with the Christian conception of God and creation, the condemnation insists. A very Christian reaction to Aristotelian ideas thus helped create the space that made Copernicus possible.

But let us take a closer look at the condemnation. As we might expect, many of its propositions, at least half of them, concern Aristotle's philosophy of nature. Some of these address the difficulty of reconciling that philosophy with the freedom of God's creative will. Here is one example: Aristotle thought that the world included all matter that could possibly exist, that the world therefore could not be any larger than it is, and that there could not be any other worlds. Someone convinced of God's omnipotence would dispute such claims, which subject God to natural necessity. The authors of the condemnation want to make sure that the faithful not limit God's freedom by subjecting it to supposed laws of nature. Consider number 27 of the condemned propositions:

Quod prima causa non potest plures mundos facere.

That the first cause cannot make more than one world.

Given God's infinite power, how can there be a limit to the number of worlds he could have created, had he chosen to do so? But to deny such a limit is also to admit the possibility of infinite magnitude.[8]

Another set of propositions seeks to safeguard the freedom of the human will against an Aristotelianism that at that time often tended toward an astral determinism. It is indeed easy to see how astrology might be justified, given a generally Aristotelian framework. The condemnation thus presents itself to us as a defense of both divine and human freedom. In chapter 9 I shall examine in more detail the close connection between these two freedoms.

Of particular interest in this connection are the propositions dealing with God's will. Propositions 16, 17, 20, and 23 are especially relevant. Consider 16:

Quod prima causa est causa omnium remotissima.—Error, si intelligatur ita, quod non propinquissima.

That the first cause is the most remote cause of all things.—This is erroneous if it is so understood as to mean that it is not the most proximate.

The condemned proposition suggests that the first cause acts by means of intermediaries, thereby presupposing a hierarchy of causes, through which power is delegated or transmitted. But, the rejoinder insists, God does not delegate power in this way. He is both the most remote and the most proximate cause.

Or take 17:

Quod impossibile simpliciter not potest fieri a Deo, vel ab agente alio.—Error si de impossibili secundam naturam intelligatur.

That what is impossible absolutely speaking cannot be brought about by God or by another agent.—This is erroneous if we mean what is impossible by nature.

The condemned proposition insists on the distinction between *impossibile simpliciter* and *impossibile secundam naturam*, between logical and natural impossibility. Even God cannot make a contradiction be true, nor can God commit suicide, which would violate his own being. But he can of course create miracles. The following proposition must therefore be rejected:

23. *Quod Deus non potest irregulariter, id est, alio modo quam moveto movere aliquid, quia in eo non est diversitate voluntatis.*

That God cannot move anything irregularly, that is in a manner other than in which He does, because there is no diversity of will in Him.

TRUTH AS THE PROPERTY OF GOD

The condemned proposition insists on absolute regularity, which would rule out miracles. Obviously, a Christian thinker should want to reject such a proposition. This thought inevitably leads to the conclusion that the world cannot be just as Aristotle describes it: God's freedom can not be imprisoned in Aristotle's philosophy.

20. *Quod Deum necesse est facere quidquid immediate fit ab ipso.—Error, sive intelligatur de necessitate coactionis, quia tollit libertatem, sive de necessitate immutabilitatis, quia ponit impotentiam aliter faciendi.*

That God of necessity makes whatever comes immediately from Him.—This is erroneous, whether we are speaking of the necessity of coercion, which destroys liberty, or of the necessity of immutability, which implies the inability to do otherwise.

Once more the point is to safeguard the free will of God. And in saving the free will of God, the authors of the condemnation also create room for human freedom. Is it not evident that in his omnipotence God could have created quite a different world or even worlds?—a thought that invites speculation on possible worlds.

Quite a number of the condemned propositions presuppose a view of nature as a hierarchical order, and I would like to underscore both "hierarchical" and "order." They attempt to subordinate the freedom of God to the regularity suggested by Aristotle's *Physics*. To save the omnipotence and freedom of God, the Condemnation of 1277 challenges both hierarchy and order. The condemnation of proposition 16 thus insists on God's omnipresence, which finds such striking expression in the metaphor of the infinite sphere. But with such insistence on God's omnipresence, the hierarchical conception of the cosmos threatens to collapse, a collapse that prepares the way for the more homogeneous conception of the cosmos that we meet almost two hundred years later in Cusanus and that was to triumph with the new science.

2

Particularly important to us are those propositions that suggest that God cannot produce an effect without the mediation of other causes. Consider 69 (as well as 67, 68, and 36):

Quod Deus non potest in effectum causae secundariae sine ipsa causa secundaria.

That God cannot produce the effect of a secondary cause without the secondary cause itself.

Even God, on the condemned view, cannot bring about effects here on earth without the medium of the causes that naturally bring about such effects.

On the Aristotelian view there can be no *actio in distans:* either a thing seeks its own proper place or it is acted on, whether pushed or pulled, carried or twirled. This is indeed a view of motion that experience readily suggests, and thus it has an initial plausibility. Like so much of Aristotle's *Physics* it is read off the way we experience things first of all and most of the time. But given this account, it is difficult to explain what Aristotle considered violent motions. Take the motion of a thrown stone. Aristotle had suggested that the air, set in motion by the thrower, pulls the stone along with it. To us, as already to Jean Buridan in the fourteenth century, that theory seems quite implausible. But we should keep in mind that in the Middle Ages it was subjected to serious questioning only when the difficulty of reconciling Aristotle's philosophy of nature with the requirements of faith had become evident. In this connection it is interesting to note that the impetus theory, which appeals to the momentum of the moving object, first appears in a discussion of the effectiveness of the Holy Sacraments—in a *Commentary on the Sentences of Peter Lombard* by Franciscus de Marchia, in 1320.[9] It may seem odd that a theory apparently belonging to physics should be developed in the context of a theological treatise. The sacraments were understood as instruments of divine grace. In the fourteenth century much thought was given to the question of whether the effectiveness of the sacrament derives immediately from God or is somehow a power inherent in the sacrament itself (*virtus inherens*). Franciscus de Marchia defends the latter view. And to make his case more plausible he offers the analogy of a thrown object, say a stone. The question raised is whether the impetus of such a stone is received directly from the thrower or is somehow inherent in the object thrown. The obvious fact of the distance separating the projectile and the thrower would seem to argue against saying that the impetus derives immediately from the thrower. De Marchia suggests that the thrower in a sense deposits the power of motion in the stone (*virtus derelicta ab ipso primo motore*).

The difference between this and the Aristotelian conception is obvious. Now one no longer needs to assume a vortex of air moving along with the stone. The thrower imparts an impetus and that impetus accounts for the motion of the stone. In defense of his interpretation Franciscus appeals to the principle of economy. What happens happens in the simplest possible way— *Quia frustra fit per plura quod potest fieri per paucior.*[10] We should keep in mind the context of the discussion: we can assume that what Franciscus de Marchia's real interest was in showing that God deposited in the sacraments a certain power. Administering the sacraments, priests became the custodians and administrators of that power. Transcendence was deposited in the immanent.

Yet if to the theory of motion that has here been advanced is at all plausible, there is no longer any reason to assume with Aristotle that the heavenly spheres are continuously pushed around by prime movers, out of which the Middle Ages had made angels. The angels lose at least one of their functions, though they are still needed to give the first push. Moreover, since Franciscus de Marchia thought that impetus weakened over time, he saw the angels as necessary to renew that motion.[11]

More important, the sublunar paradigm of the thrown stone here provides the starting point for a new interpretation of the motion of the heavens. That extension presupposes that the qualitative difference between the sublunar and superlunar realms on which Aristotle had insisted was no longer binding. Thus the paradigm challenges what we can call the cosmological difference fundamental to Aristotelian science.

We may well wonder why Franciscus de Marchia did not retain the Aristotelian view that there is no tiring in the superlunar realm and give his spheres an unending ceaseless motion. The answer is simply that he clung to the Aristotelian, or rather medieval, view that the spheres were moved by angels. Being finite creatures, he thought, they could not produce an infinite effect. Change was thus admitted into the superlunar realm. And to reassure his readers, who might find this admission worrying, he appeals to the traditional view that the blessed are supposed to converse in heaven; surely such conversation had to rely on words, which would have to come into being and again disappear.[12]

What we are likely to consider naïveté and extraordinary subtlety mingle in many of these medieval texts. I want to underscore as important in this context the breakdown of what I have named the cosmological difference, the difference between the superlunar and the sublunar realm. Behind that breakdown stands the recognition of the incompatibility of the hierarchical cosmology of Aristotle and the omnipotence of a God who is both the most remote and the most proximate cause of all that is.

De Marchia's willingness to introduce change into the superlunar world does nevertheless seem startling. One is thus not surprised to discover the Parisian nominalist Buridan returning to the cosmological difference, but without giving up the impetus theory. Buridan is indeed an articulate spokesman for such a theory, which he expounds after rejecting other theories, including Aristotle's. He argues as follows in his *Questions on the Eighth Book of Aristotle's "Physics"*:

And so it seems to me that what should be said is that the mover in moving what is moved impresses upon it a certain impetus or force that moves the moved thing in the direction the mover moved it, whether up or down, laterally or in a circle. And the more swiftly the mover moved the moved thing, the stronger the impetus it impresses on it. The stone is moved by that impetus after the projector ceases to move, but the impetus is continuously diminished by the resisting air and by the gravity of the stone inclining it against the direction the impetus inherently moves it. Hence the motion of that stone is made continuously slower, and finally the impetus is so diminished or corrupted that the gravity of the stone prevails over it and moves the stone down to its natural place.[13]

He applies the same analysis to a falling object:

And from this also appears the cause whereby the natural downward motion of a heavy thing is continuously speeded up, for at first only gravity moved it and so it moved more slowly; but in moving, impetus is impressed on that heavy thing, which impetus then moves it along with the gravity. Hence the motion becomes swift, and the swifter it goes, the more intense the impetus becomes.[14]

But as Buridan hints by speaking of "the natural downward motion of a heavy thing," the falling object is for Aristotle an example of a natural movement, not a violent one. This blurring of the distinction between the two kinds of motion is of crucial importance.[15]

Buridan thus does not hesitate to follow Franciscus de Marchia and apply the impetus theory to the heavens, though he upholds a version of the cosmological difference by insisting that in the heavenly sphere impetus once imparted does not tire. The impetus of the heavenly spheres thus remains constant. But on this amount we no longer need angels to keep the heavenly spheres moving, and they lose that function:

Also, since it does not appear from the Bible that there are intelligences to whom it pertains to move the heavenly bodies, one could say that there seems no need to posit such intelligences. For it might be said that when God created the world He moved each of the celestial orbs however He pleased; and in moving them He impressed an impetus which moves them without His moving them any more, except in the way of the general influence, just as He concurs in co-acting in everything which is done.[16]

Let me return once more to the distinction between natural and violent motions. Natural motions, according to Aristotle, tend toward their natural place. Why do things fall to the earth when dropped? Because they seek their proper place. Teleological interpretations are appropriate to natural motions. Violent motions, in contrast have their end outside themselves. Why did you throw that stone? That question is irrelevant to the physicist's account of its motion. Similarly, although God gave a particular impetus to each particular heavenly sphere, we do not know why. All we can do is try to understand the nature of the impetus imparted. The impetus theory enabled one to treat the movements of nature without reference to the desired end. And given the difference between the human and the divine intellect, how could human beings pretend to know for what end God created the heavens and their motions? The impetus theory thus suggests the possibility of a science of nature no longer in need of teleological explanations. The renunciation of such explanations, a renunciation central to Descartes's science of nature and to the science that issued from it, has its origin in a view of nature that first makes God its author and then makes that God infinite and declares that we cannot hope to know his ends. We have to be content with explanations that give us the efficient causes of things (though the ghost of the old teleological thinking continues to haunt the phenomenon of gravity).

Buridan concludes his discussion of impetus with a modest remark: "This is what I have to say on this question, and I would rejoice if anyone should find a more probable way with it."[17] Such a spirit of reflective experimentation seems representative of the thinkers of that period. Buridan himself tried to hold on to the cosmological difference in some fashion, arguing on the one hand that in the celestial realm, impetus once imparted does not tire and diminish, and on the other hand that in the sublunar realm, things tend toward rest. This view led him to reject the thought that the earth might rotate. Apart from this, he considered the possibility of earthly motion equivalent to another position, which ascribed the corresponding motion to the firmament. But Buridan's understanding of the heavenly bodies as *quasi per se mobilia*, moving as if by their own power, heralds the progressive banishment of God from nature.

While Franciscus de Marchia and Jean Buridan read a terrestrial paradigm into the heavenly sphere, another nominalist, Nicole Oresme, did the reverse and argued that in the sublunar world, too, circular motion alone is natural. This claim led him to conclude that the earth had to move. The details of these accounts do not matter here, though Oresme, with his thesis of the rotation of the earth, is often mentioned as a forerunner of Copernicus. More important is the gradual erosion and final rejection of the Aristotelian, medieval view of nature as a hierarchical order and of the cosmological difference that goes along with that conception. Discarded along with it is the idea of natural place, and with that goes the distinction between natural and violent motion as Aristotle had drawn it: that is to say, Aristotle's physics and the kind of teleological thinking appropriate to it are also rejected.

For one last example of the challenge divine omnipotence posed to Aristotle's philosophy of nature, I return once more to the Condemnation of 1277:

66. *Quod Deus non possit movere caelum motu recto. Et ratio est quia tunc relinqueret vacuum.*

That God could not move the heaven in a straight line, the reason being that he would then leave a vacuum.

Again we have an attempt to make room for God's infinite freedom and power in the face of Aristotle's *Physics*. To be sure, as Duhem points out, the reason given in support of the condemned proposition is one that Aristotle himself would have dismissed, for he would have insisted that outside the world there can be no space, and therefore also no vacuum.[18] The condemnation departs further from Aristotle's understanding of space by insisting that God could have moved the heaven had he so chosen. For that possibility to make sense, space can not be bound to or be imprisoned in the firmament, as it is in Aristotle's physics. And even if Aristotle was more or less right about the way things are, does this mean that God could not create a space outside the world, should he so choose? This is how Richard of Middleton bends together Aristotle and Tempier.[19] At any rate, the condemnation presupposes the ability to think of space as not occupied by any body, to think space as transcending place.[20] Underlying such thought experiments is a rejection of the Aristotelian attempt to think space in terms of place.

Important here is the liberating power of the Christian conception of God. It encouraged, even forced thinkers to engage in thought experiments that had to challenge the authority of Aristotle in order to safeguard divine freedom and omnipotence and thus to satisfy what the Condemnation of 1277 had made official doctrine. More specifically, it invited speculation at odds with the then still generally prevailing Aristotelian image of the cosmos. It invited, we can say, possible world speculations. Such speculations rendered what were believed to be necessary laws of nature contingent. There is no good reason for those laws being the way they are. They could be other than they are, certainly could be other than Aristotle thought they were. From such speculations the step claiming that they are actually other than Aristotelian is not very great.

3

The connection between Osiander's preface to Copernicus's *De Revolutionibus* and the Condemnation of 1277 should by this point be clear. Osiander claims that absolute truth is denied to the astronomer or more generally to human beings, except as a gift of grace. No science will be able to claim absolute truth for its accounts: it never offers more than models, hypotheses. All that we can demand of these models is that they be adequate to the observed appearances—that is, that they allow us to make predictions that accord with what we then later observe. This cognitive resignation is a consequence of the gap that separates God and his infinite wisdom from all merely human knowledge. But such resignation has its positive side: it makes science freer, more playful. It encourages the thinker to entertain and explore different hypotheses, different models.

The authors of the Condemnation of 1277, too, take the infinity of God's wisdom for granted. And they take for granted the authority of Scripture. But Aristotle, they are convinced, should not be granted a comparable authority: his works are after all but products of human reason. Those writings offer one, perhaps plausible, account of nature; but such an account should not be invested with the authority of absolute truth. Aristotle, too, was fallible. And where there are conflicts between revealed truth and such human accounts, it is clear which side will have to yield.

Still, the hold Aristotle had on those who speculated about nature was immense. To weaken that hold, the philosophers and theologians of the fourteenth and fifteenth centuries loved to engage in speculations, which often became rather wild. Think of the cosmological speculations in Cusanus's *On Learned Ignorance*. Or take this thought experiment of Nicole Oresme, one of many designed to test the Aristotelian view of nature. Presupposing the general validity of the Aristotelian cosmos, Oresme imagines

the case of a tile or copper pipe or other material so long that it reaches from the center of the earth to the upper region of the elements, that is up to heaven itself.

I say that, if this tile were filled with fire except for a small amount of air at the very top, the air would drop down to the center of the earth for the reason that the less light descends beneath the lighter body.[21]

The thought experiment is designed to call into question the Aristotelian doctrine of proper place, which is the foundation of his physics. Natural place becomes a relative notion. But if so, the Aristotelian account of natural movement must be abandoned. And Oresme does not hesitate to offer his own alternative: "the natural law concerning heavy and light bodies . . . is that all the heavy bodies as far as possible are located in the middle of the light bodies *without setting up for them any other motionless [or natural] place*."[22] As Duhem points out, with his theory of motion Oresme opens the possibility of viewing each planet as composed of a heavy earth surrounded by the other elements, a possibility that, as we saw, was eagerly seized by Cusanus.[23]

In the wake of the Condemnation of 1277, such thought experiments were above all meant to show us that God could have created a rather different world than the world Aristotelians were insisting was the only one possible. What Aristotle had thought to be necessary was shown to be just another all-too-human construction—as should perhaps have been evident to careful readers of the *Timaeus*, which hints at an alternative to Aristotle's theory of natural movement.[24] But more important is something else: insistence on the theological difference necessarily calls the cosmological difference into question. Human knowers are unable to understand why God created this world with this makeup and these laws, and why and how he chooses to preserve it. That mystery we cannot fathom. Nominalist emphasis on the primacy of God's will is thus part of the attempt to bring human beings to an understanding of the difference between the human and the divine. Implicit in such appreciation is a certain cognitive humility, even resignation.

But the other side of such resignation—and this point needs to be underscored—is the liberation of the human imagination from the weight of its historical, in this case Aristotelian, inheritance. The thought experiments of Oresme and Cusanus are expressions of that freedom. And the other side of such resignation is also a willingness to settle for something less than absolute truth. Since we cannot hope to fathom the reasons God had in creating the world, we have to be content with the models we make ourselves of the workings of nature. Of these models we can demand that they be adequate to observed appearances and also that they be as easy as possible to understand—as Descartes might have put it, as clear and distinct as possible. And so Cusanus argues, as we have seen, that our investigations, be they directed toward God or toward nature, ought to make use of mathematical symbols. Cusanus's reason is not that God wrote the book of nature in the language of mathematics, as Galileo later was to assert and Descartes attempted to prove, but that the human mind is dealing here with its own creations. Of the models we construct, we can demand that they be as clear as possible. We can also demand of them that they dispense with appeals to divine purpose: is that purpose not so infinitely beyond us as to be useless to the human knower? Once again: we understand things to the extent that we can reconstruct them, whether in thought or in fact. This is why Descartes turned to mechanical models.

4

Thoughts of the infinity of God had to invite a recasting of natural philosophy in the direction of what was to become our modern science of nature. To be sure, the authors of the Condemnation of 1277 and those thinkers who found themselves in fundamental agreement with its stance sought a quite different outcome: they wanted to oppose the arrogance of philosophers who, appealing to Aristotle, claimed independence from the tutelage of the Church. In opposing Aristotelian philosophy, they opposed an expression of what they considered the sin of pride. And should we not extend that condemnation to all theory that claims to pursue the truth not for the sake of salvation, nor even for the sake of practice, but just in order to know? The challenge is thus likely to extend to that peculiar desire and wonder in which philosophy has been said to have its origin. In the first words of the *Metaphysics* Aristotle speaks to us of that desire:

All men by nature desire to know. An indication of this is the delight we take in our senses; for even apart from their usefulness they are loved for themselves; and above all others the sense of sight. For not only with a view to action, but even when we are not going to do anything, we prefer sight to almost everything else. The reason is that this, most of all the senses, makes us know and brings to light many differences between things.[25]

Or consider his account of the origin of philosophy:

For it is owing to their wonder that men both now begin and at first began to philosophize; they wondered originally at the obvious difficulties, then advanced little by little and stated difficulties about the greater matters, e.g. about the phenomena of the moon and those of the sun and the stars, and about the genesis of the universe. And a man who is puzzled and wonders thinks himself ignorant (whence even the lover of myth is in a sense a lover of wisdom, for myth is composed of wonders); therefore, since they philosophized in order to escape from ignorance, evidently they were pursuing science in order to know, and not for any utilitarian end. (*Metaphysics* 1.2, 982b12–22)

Is Cusanus then, when teaching us to become learned about our ignorance, also recalling us to that state of wonder in which philosophy here is said to have its origin, a strangely ambiguous state that can lead to an attempt to stay with this wonder or to an attempt to act on it by finding answers? But let me return to Aristotle:

And this is confirmed by the facts; for it was when almost all the necessities of life and the things that make for comfort and recreation were present, that such knowledge began to be sought. Evidently, then, we do not seek it for any other advantage; but as the man is free, we say, who exists for himself and not for another, so we pursue this as the only free science, for it alone exists for itself. (*Metaphysics* 1.2, 982b22–26)

How can a Christian admit such a free science? Is not the conception of such self-sufficient freedom born of pride? Is not Aristotle's wisdom the fruit of sin?

The Christian suspicion of theory is only one form of a more widely held suspicion directed against all those who would speculate for the sake of speculation. Consider the anecdote Plato tells us in the *Theaetetus* about Thales, the traditional founder of philosophy. Socrates here is speaking not only of Thales but also of himself, indeed of all true philosophers: they all have little interest in the city and its affairs.

He is not even aware that he knows nothing of all this, for if he holds aloof, it is not for reputation's sake, but because it is really his body that sojourns in his city, while his thought, disdaining all such things as worthless, takes wings, as Pindar says, "beyond the sky, beneath the earth," searching the heavens and measuring the plains, everywhere seeking the true nature of everything as a whole, never sinking to what lies close at hand.[26]

The philosopher is seen here as someone who dislocates himself, like Daedalus, whom Socrates claims for a forebear, or Icarus, who takes wings, flying all over. That is to say, the philosopher is trying to use his imagination and thought to free himself from the place in which he happens to find himself. Such dislocation and loss of place are essential to his search for the truth. Recall what was said in the previous chapter about the relation between truth, objectivity, and the idea of a pure, transcendental subject. There I connected them to of the self-elevation of the human spirit.

But to return to the *Theaetetus:* when Socrates is asked by Theodorus to explain his meaning, he replies by telling the story of "the Thracian maidservant who exercised her wit at the expense of Thales, when he was looking up to study the stars and tumbled down a well. She scoffed at him for being so eager to know what was happening in the sky that he could not see what lay at his feet. Anyone who gives his life to philosophy is open to such mockery" (174a).

The question is whether the theoretical impulse deflects the human being from his true vocation or allows him to fulfill that vocation—whether that theoretical curiosity in which philosophy has its origin is legitimate.[27] Once again Aristotle set the stage for subsequent discussion:

Hence the possession of it [genuine knowledge, absolute truth] might be justly regarded as beyond human power; for in many ways human knowledge is in bondage, so that according to Simonides "God alone can have this privilege," and it is unfitting that man should not be content to seek the knowledge that is suited to him. If, then, there is something in what the poets say, and jealousy is natural to the divine power, it would probably occur in this case above all, and all who excelled in this knowledge would be unfortunate. (*Metaphysics* 1.2, 982b29–983a2)

It is easy to imagine a Christian theologian reading this with approval. Man's present condition is subject to the fall and its consequences. These consequences include the epistemological: our sight and intellect are no longer those possessed by Adam in paradise. And even in Adam's case it was a presumptuous self-elevation that let him listen to the snake's promise, *eritis sicut Deus,* that human beings might know as only God knows; the specification that the claim is to a knowledge of good and evil hints that such knowledge must be distinguished from knowledge of what is the case, hints at the importance of attending to that distinction.

Aristotle, however, raises the question of the legitimacy of theory only to dismiss it:

But the divine power cannot be jealous (indeed, according to the proverb, "bards tell many a lie"), nor should any other science be thought more honourable than one of this sort. For the most divine science is also the most honourable; and this science alone must be, in two ways, most divine. For the science which it would be most meet for God to have is a divine science; and so is any science that deals with divine objects. (*Metaphyscis* 1.2, 983a2–8)

In late atiquity we meet more and more often with voices that see in this desire for knowledge just another desire that must meet with disappointment. Epicurus and Lucretius thus would rid us of such an exaggerated demand for knowledge. Cognitive resignation is seen as a precondition of happiness.

   More important in this context is Augustine's critique of the desire to know. A key text is book 10 of the *Confessions;* we should keep in mind that the authors of the Condemnation of 1277 followed Augustine.

To this is added another form of temptation more manifoldly dangerous. For besides the concupiscence of the flesh which consisteth in the delight of all senses and pleasures, wherein its slaves, who go far from Thee, waste and perish, the soul hath, through the same senses of the body, a certain vain and curious desire, veiled under the title of knowledge and learning, not of delighting in the flesh, but of making experiments through the flesh. The seat whereof being in the appetite of knowledge, and sight being the sense chiefly used for attaining knowledge, it is in Divine language called The lust of the eyes.[28]

Here we have the Christian counter to the Aristotelian position: all men by nature desire to know, desire to know just for the sake of knowing, just because they are curious. Augustine might add, perhaps, but if so, then their desire arises only because nature has been corrupted by the Fall, by sin: "From this disease of curiosity are all those strange sights exhibited in the theater. Hence men go out to search out the hidden powers of nature (which is besides our end), which to know profits not, and wherein men desire nothing but to know."[29] Such sentiments lead easily to a celebration of the person who remains simple, free of the false learning of the philosophers. The claim to truth has thus been understood again and again as the illegitimate appropriation of something that belongs to God. He who claims to know for himself delegitimates himself by just that claim. It is in this context that we have to understand Descartes's attempt to interpret his method as a divine gift.

This Christian suspicion of theory could and often did claim Socrates for a pagan precursor. Had not Socrates renounced his youthful excursions into the philosophy of nature and regretted such thinking that neglected the needs of the soul (see *Phaedo* 99d)? When Cusanus celebrates ignorance and calls the Socratic main figure of several of his dialogues an *idiota*, an untutored, unread layperson, he follows that theme. But for him this is only one theme. Equally prominent is another that, following Aristotle, makes the desire to know constitutive of man and then goes on to legitimate that desire by saying that since God instilled in us such a desire, it cannot be vain. It must be capable of finding the knowledge that will satisfy it. Human beings should not renounce scientific inquiry, even if it can only approximate and never seize divine truth. We are here on the threshold of Renaissance humanism, although looking back one might also say that Cusanus is attempting to reconcile Augustine and Thomas Aquinas, according to whom (translating Aristotle into a Christian context) *omnis scientia bona est*, all science is good.

I have tried to show something of the ambivalence of meditations on the gap separating God's infinite from our finite knowledge. One consequence of that gap seems to be that we cannot gain truth relying on our own strength: the human knower can receive it only by divine grace, as a gift. On this understanding the very attempt to seize the truth is readily interpreted as a manifestation of sin. But if one result of the reflecting on the gap separating the human knower and God is cognitive resignation, another is the discovery of the godlike extent of the human spirit. For how could human beings even think the tension between God's infinite power and Aristotelian cosmology if their thinking were limited by that cosmology, if there were not something infinite about the human knower?

1

Earlier chapters linked the turn to an infinite universe characteristic of the emergence of the modern world-understanding to reflections on perspective and the power of point of view. In that connection I explored what I called the principle of perspective: to understand a perspective as a perspective, to understand perspectival appearance as perspectival appearance, is to be, in thought at least, already beyond these perspectival limitations—to oppose, as Copernicus put is, perspectival appearance to actuality. Similarly, to think human beings as limited in what they are able to understand by their finite nature is to think reality as transcending what can thus be understood. So understood, the principle of perspective grounds Kant's distinction between appearances and things-in-themselves. And again: to think the finite as the finite is already to have some understanding of the infinite. But this is to say that we human beings are not totally imprisoned in the finite: we could not think the infinity of the infinite if the infinite, an openness to what transcends the reach of our finite understanding, were not somehow part of our own essence. Meditation on the infinity of God or the infinity of the world of which we are part thus presupposes and awakens the human knower to the infinite within himself.

That human beings discover that they transcend the finite by contemplating the infinity of the cosmos or of nature is of course a quite traditional point. We have become used to speaking of such experiences in terms of the sublime. In this we are the heirs of the aesthetic sensibility of the 18th century. A passage from Addison's *Spectator* Nr. 412 brings out some of the features of such experience.

Our imagination loves to be filled with an Object, or to grasp at any thing that is too big for its capacity. We are flung into a pleasing astonishment at such unbounded views, and feel a delightful stillness and amazement in the soul at the apprehension of them. The Mind of Man naturally hates everything that looks like a restraint upon it, and is apt to fancy itself under a sort of confinement when the sight is pent up in a narrow compass, and shortened on every side by the neighborhood of walls and mountains. On the contrary, a spacious horizon is an image of liberty, where the eye has room to range abroad, to expatiate at large on the immensity of its views, and to lose itself amidst the variety of objects that offer themselves to its Observations.[1]

Addison did not yet use the word "sublime," which became popular only later in the eighteenth century, at a time when the Alps came to be considered the paradigmatically sublime landscape. That the aesthetic category of the sublime now comes to take its place as at least an equal beside the category of the beautiful has symptomatic significance: it helps mark the epochal threshold occupied by the Enlightenment. But if there is a connection between this emerging interest in the sublime and the Enlightenment, just what is the link?

In the *Critique of Judgment* (1790) Kant hints at the answer: what we find beautiful presents itself to us—on his and not only his interpretation—as if it were made to be appreciated by us. In beautiful nature we feel at home. There seems to be a marvelous attunement between the beautiful and the human being and his or her faculties. This is one implication of Kant's understanding of the beautiful as purposive appearance, even though we are unable to determine its purpose. Beautiful nature therefore invites thoughts of a higher purpose behind appearance, thoughts of a creator who cares for us and created this world so that we might feel at home in it: it invites, in other words, thoughts of the world as a well-ordered whole, as a cosmos.

Sublime nature leads to very different thoughts. Snow-covered mountain peaks, polar wastes, and the raging ocean, all paradigms of the sublime, are by no means experienced as homelike. Sublime nature seems indifferent to our needs. In it we are strangers, facing an immensity that threatens to reduce our little selves to insignificance. And yet it is precisely this threatening aspect that, if Kant is right, we enjoy aesthetically, although such enjoyment must be distinguished from the pleasure we take in the beautiful.

Natural beauty (which is independent) brings with it a purposiveness in its form by which the object seems to be, as it were, preadapted to our judgment, and thus constitutes in itself an object of satisfaction. On the other hand, that which excites in us, without any reasoning about it, but in the mere apprehension of it, the feeling of the sublime may appear, as regards its form, to violate purpose in respect of the judgment, to be unsuited to our presentative faculty, and as it were to do violence to the imagination, and yet it is judged to be only the more sublime.[2]

Sublime nature seems to transcend our ability to cope with it. Vainly does the imagination struggle to take it in as if it were a beautiful picture. The sublime knows no such closure; it floods every frame. But precisely this inadequacy awakens us to something in us that is not bound to the finite and comprehensible, awakens us, as Addison recognized, to our freedom. As the *zōon logon echon*, the *animal rationale*, the human being is the animal able to raise itself above all that is merely animal, all that is merely natural. Beyond the world, beyond all that is the case, reflection opens up the infinite realm of all that might be, an unbounded realm of possibilities that is the realm of freedom. Sublime nature figures that realm. In the sublimity of nature human beings recognize their own sublimity, recognize that within that allows them to transcend all that is finite and thus puts them in touch with the infinite.

We should not expect to find a receptivity to the sublime where reflection is developed only weakly or not at all. Kant gives the example of the peasant in the Alps who considers all those foreigners who come to visit in order to admire the mountains' sublimity mere fools who have no idea of what it really means to live in such an inhospitable environment.

In the indications of the dominion of nature in destruction, and in the great scale of its might, in comparison with which his own is a vanishing quantity, he will only see the misery, danger, and distress which surround the man who is exposed to it. So the good, and indeed intelligent Savoyard peasant (as Herr von Saussure relates) unhesitatingly called all lovers of snow-mountains fools. And who knows whether he would have been so completely wrong if Saussure had undertaken the danger to which he exposed himself merely, as most travelers do, from amateur curiosity, or that he might be able to give a pathetic account of them? But his design was the instruction of men, and this excellent man gave the reader of his travels soul-stirring sensations such as he himself had, into the bargain.[3]

Kant here takes care to distinguish the edifying experience of the sublime from the ordinary tourist's "amateur curiosity." Such curiosity, too, is marked by what may be called freedom: freedom primarily from the routines and cares of the everyday that normally bind us. But curiosity is extroverted; it enjoys aesthetically the novel and unexpected, bracketing in such enjoyment the misery, danger, and distress that are part of human existence. Freedom here is not the freedom of the moral agent; the sublime presents itself instead as a species of the interesting. The experience of the sublime becomes edifying only when it is tied to a recognition of the way freedom binds us, binds all human beings into the ideal community of rational agents ruled by the moral law. In the moral realm an enlightened humanity finds its true home.

But what matters here is above Kant's insistence that in the experience of the sublime the individual discovers himself to be more than just a being of nature. The immensity of nature awakens the human being to that power which belongs to him as a free, rational agent, raising him above all that is merely actual. To be sure, as Kant is well aware, as long as human beings are preoccupied just with how to survive, they cannot be expected to show sensitivity to the sublime. Such sensitivity presupposes also an openness to the demands made on us by our own freedom. An interest in the sublime and the French Revolution belong together.

2

It was Horace Benedict de Saussure, praised by Kant for having visited the Alps not just out of amateur curiosity but to instruct his fellow human beings, who in 1760 offered prize money for the first ascent of Mont Blanc. In 1786 the money was claimed by Michel-Gabriel Piccard, a doctor from Chamonix. Before that time there would seem to have been only scattered efforts to climb mountains. Among these Petrarch's ascent of Mont Ventoux is the most often cited. Not that he was the first to climb even that mountain: Buridan in fact had climbed it, just a few years before Petrarch, to make scientific observations.[4]

But to return to Petrarch. How justified is the comparison of him to a modern mountain climber?[5] How justified is my decision to begin this chapter with a brief and all-too-sketchy discussion of Kant and the sublime? How justified was Jacob Burckhardt's characterization of "that clear soul" Petrarch as "one of the first truly modern men"?[6] Petrarch himself invites us to understand what led him to climb this rather modest mountain, 1,912 meters high, not far from Avignon, as an early example of that amateur curiosity, that interest in the interesting, attributed by Kant to most tourists. In the very beginning of his account Petrarch thus tells us: "Nothing but the desire to see its conspicuous height was the reason for this undertaking."[7] This, to be sure, was hardly his reason for writing down an account of the climb. Like Saussure, by Kant's description, Petrarch is interested in the instruction of men. And such instruction begins with the admission that the ascent was prompted by what Augustine had criticized as curiosity. This confession of his initial motive should thus be read against the background of its explicit condemnation by Augustine: "And men go abroad to admire the heights of mountains, the mighty billows of the sea, the broad tides of the rivers, the compass of the ocean, and the circuit of the stars, and pass themselves by."[8] The young Petrarch attempted to excuse his curiosity with an appeal to an ancient precursor:

It happened while I was reading Roman history again in Livy that I hit upon the passage where Philip, the king of Macedon—the Philip who waged war against the Roman people—"ascends Mount Haemus in Thessaly, since he believed the rumor that you can see two seas from the top: the Adriatic and the Black Sea." Whether he was right or wrong I cannot make out because the mountain is far from our region, and the disagreement among authors renders the matter uncertain.

Petrarch suggests that were he in a position to make that climb, he would not leave the matter in doubt for very long. Nor did the young Petrarch see much wrong with thus giving in to such curiosity:

It seemed to me that a young man who holds no public office [*in iuvene privato*] might be excused for doing what an old king is not blamed for.[9]

He chooses his younger brother for a companion, and the two set out, attended by two servants. They meet an old shepherd, who tries to dissuade them. He tells them that as a young man he too had once climbed the mountain and brought home only regrets, pains, and torn clothing. As is to be expected, such well-meant advice is disregarded by the two young men; indeed, it serves only to spur them on. But very soon they begin to tire. The brother suggests that they take the most direct route, following a ridge. Petrarch chooses what he takes to be an easier way, only to discover that he has to do extra work. Frustrated and tired, he sits down and addresses himself as follows:

What you have so often experienced today while climbing this mountain happens to you, you must know, and to many others who are making their way toward the blessed life. This is not easily understood by us men, because the motions of the body lie open, while those of the mind are invisible and hidden. The life we call blessed is located on a high peak. "A narrow way" [Matt. 7:14—Sermon on the Mount] they say, leads up to it. Many hill tops intervene, and we must proceed from virtue to virtue with exalted steps. (pp. 39–40)

The reader, too, is invited to understand Petrarch's climb as an allegory.[10] Is not man's ascent to the life of the blessed like climbing a mountain? And are we not tempted again and again to choose the easier, more comfortable path, even though it does not lead where we should be going?

What is it, then, that keeps you back? Evidently nothing but the smoother way that leads through the meanest earthly pleasures and looks easier at first sight. However, having strayed far in error, you must either ascend to the summit of the blessed life under the heavy burden of hard striving, ill deferred, or lie prostrate in your slothfulness in the valleys of your sins. If "darkness and the shadow of death" find you there—I shudder while I pronounce these ominous words—you must pass the eternal night in incessant torments. (p. 40)

More and more, Petrarch's journey up the windy mountain presents itself to the reader as an allegory: "our ascent to the life of the blessed is like climbing a mountain." Nature is experienced as a book in which we human beings can read if we learn but to look beyond or through what is visible to what it signifies, to the invisible, spiritual significance of things. But to understand this significance presupposes the ability and a willingness to leap in "winged thoughts from things corporeal to what is incorporeal (p. 39).

Such edifying thoughts of the transcendence of the mind over the body give the weary hiker new strength:

You cannot imagine how much comfort this thought brought my mind and body for what lay still ahead of me. Would that I might achieve with my mind the journey for which I am longing day and night as I achieved with the feet of my body my journey today after overcoming all obstacles. And I wonder whether it ought not to be much easier to accomplish what can be done by means of an agile and immortal mind without any local motion "in the twinkling of the trembling eye" [I Cor 15] than what is to be performed in the succession of time by the service of the frail body that is doomed to die and under the heavy load of the limbs. (pp. 40–41)

When Petrarch finally reaches the top, he is overwhelmed by the sublime spectacle spread out before and beneath him.

At first I stood there almost benumbed, overwhelmed by a gale such as I had never felt before and by the unusually open and wide view. I looked around me: clouds were gathering below my feet, and Athos and Olympus grew less incredible, since I saw on a mountain of lesser fame what I had heard and read about them. From there I turned my eyes in the direction of Italy, for which my mind was so fervently yearning. The Alps were frozen stiff and covered with snow—those mountains through which that ferocious enemy of the Roman name once passed, blasting his way through the rocks with vinegar if we may believe tradition. They looked as if they were quite near me, though they are far, far away.

The distant Alps are here associated with Hannibal, "that ferocious enemy of the Roman name," just as before Mt. Haemus had been associated with "the Philip who waged war against the Roman people." Mountains are linked here with hostility to all that Rome stands for. And it is to Rome that Petrarch's thoughts turn, as he stands on his mountain: "I was longing, I must confess, for Italian air, which appeared rather to my mind than my eyes. An incredibly strong desire seized me to see my friend and native land again" (pp. 41–42). Far as the eye can reach, it is outdistanced by the imagination and by longing. The longing is said to be for his friend Giacomo Colonna, bishop of Lombez, who had gone to Rome, and for his native land, and although we know whom Petrarch had in mind, and although the native land is of course Italy, here, too, we should keep in mind the figural character of this trip up the mountain: "native land" also means "true home."

What matters in this context is how the vast expanse observed from the top of the mountain becomes a figure of an even vaster interior space. Spatial extension becomes a metaphor for the boundless extension of the spirit, which leaves behind not only every *here* but also every *now*.

Then another thought took possession of my mind, leading it from the contemplation of space to that of time, and I said to myself: "This day marks the completion of the tenth year since you gave up the studies of your boyhood and left Bologna. O immortal God, O Immutable Wisdom! How many and how great were the changes you have had to undergo in your moral habits since then." I will not speak of what is still left undone, for I am not yet in port that I might think in security of the storms I have had to endure. The time will perhaps come when I can review all this in the order in which it happened, using as a prologue that passage of your favorite Augustine: "Let me remember my past mean acts and the carnal corruption of my soul, not that I love them, but that I may love Thee, my God. (p. 42)

Memory attests to the spirit's power to transcend time, just as the imagination attests to its power to transcend space. But memory appears here also, as already with Augustine, as opposed to curiosity. Curiosity lets us explore and lose ourselves to many things. In this sense it scatters us. Memory, by contrast, gathers the soul unto what is essential, a return of the soul to its true essence that is at the same time a turn to God. The constant references to Augustine make clear that what Petrarch is here relating is a kind of conversion experience.

Musings about how to better himself follow: should he, by overcoming his proud old will, not reach a point where he can meet death with equanimity and genuine hope? He is called out of such reflections, back to reality, by his brother, who tells him that it is getting late, that he better use the time to look around a bit more.

Like a man aroused from sleep, I turned back and looked toward the west. The boundary wall between France and Spain, the ridge of the Pyrenees is not visible from there, though there is no obstacle of which I knew, and nothing but the weakness of the mortal eye is the cause. However, one could see most distinctly the mountains of the province of Lyons to the right and, to the left, the sea near Marseilles as well as the waves that break against Aigues Mortes, although it takes several days to travel to this city. The Rhone River was directly under our eyes. (pp. 43–44)

We should note that Petrarch is now looking west. And the West, given the medieval sense of space, has negative overtones. Isn't it the East that daily gives birth to light, while the West daily is devouring light? *Ex oriente lux.* Petrarch's home, both literally and figuratively, lies in the East.

Petrarch describes himself as having been in a kind of intoxication, a highly pleasurable aesthetico-religious state in which earthly and spiritual enjoyment mingle. To heighten that enjoyment he reaches for a copy of Augustine's *Confessions* that he had been given by the person who had first introduced him to St. Augustine, the Augustinian hermit Dionigi di Borgo San Sepolcro, then a professor of theology in Paris and the intended recipient of the letter. The book opens to a page that has to strike Petrarch as a rebuke. It is the same passage I quoted in the beginning of this chapter: "And men go abroad to admire the heights of mountains, the mighty billows of the sea, the broad tides of rivers, the compass of the ocean, and the circuits of the stars, and pass themselves by." In the *Confessions* this passage is preceded by sentences extolling the unmeasurable capacity of human memory, more wondrous by far than all the sublime sights of world around us.

Great is this force of memory, excessive great, O my God; a large and boundless chamber! who ever sounded the bottom thereof? yet is this a power of mine, and belongs unto my nature; nor do I myself comprehend all that I am. Therefore is the mind too strait to contain itself. And where should that be, which it containeth not of itself? Is it without it, and not within? how then doth it not comprehend itself? A wonderful admiration surprises me, amazement seizes me upon this.[11]

Small wonder then that Petrarch should understand these lines as a personal rebuke.

I was stunned, I confess. I bade my brother, who wanted to hear more, not to molest me, and closed the book, angry with myself that I still admired earthly things. Long since I ought to have learned, even from Pagan philosophers, that "nothing is admirable besides the mind; compared to its greatness nothing is great."[12] (p. 44)

The conversion, which has to be at the same time also an introversion, apparently had not been complete. Extroverted curiosity continued to have the upper hand in what had remained at bottom an aesthetic rather than a religious experience. Even the interest in Augustine had had an aesthetic significance, as Petrarch had reached for the *Confessions* to heighten the experience.

At this point there is a significant shift from the sights of nature to the written word. That he opened the *Confessions* to just this place is felt to have been no accident. Petrarch calls our attention to a similar experience that had long ago transformed St. Augustine. In book 8 of the *Confessions* Augustine indeed speaks of two such reading experiences. In his nineteenth year he read Cicero's *Hortensius*, which is said to have stirred in him an earnest love of wisdom. But this love was not sufficient to cure lust and curiosity, and the result was deepening despair. When this despair reached its worst, when, in Augustine's words, "a deep consideration had from the secret bottom of my soul drawn together and heaped up all my misery in the sight of my heart," he hears "from a neighboring house a voice, as of boy or girl I know not, chanting, and oft repeating, 'Take up and read! Take up and read!'" He returned to Paul's *Letter to the Romans* which he had been reading, and hit on these words: "Not in rioting and drunkenness, not in chambering and wantonness, not in strife and envying; but put ye on the Lord Jesus Christ, and make not provision for the flesh, in concupiscence."[13] And Augustine in turn had a precursor in St. Anthony, who had turned to a passage in Matthew.

Petrarch thus presents himself to us in this artfully composed letter as repeating what St. Augustine had done before him, who in turn repeated what St. Anthony had done, although "had done" is not quite right, because in each case the real agent is taken to be God, not man. Crucially, in each case we have a turn away from the sights of the world to a text, from the eye to the ear. St. Augustine plays the part for Petrarch that the Apostle Paul had played for Augustine and Matthew for St. Anthony. Important also is that in each case there is not much that needs to be read. As Augustine puts it: "No further would I read; nor needed I: for instantly at the end of this sentence, by a light as it were of serenity infused into my heart, all the darkness of doubt vanished away."[14] Petrarch follows his example. Reading issues quickly in a silence that is the proper language of the soul's return to itself:

Silently I thought over how greatly mortal men lack counsel who, neglecting the noblest part of themselves in empty parading, look without for what can be found within. I admired the nobility of the mind, had it not voluntarily degenerated and strayed from the primordial state of its origin, converting into disgrace what God had given to be its honor. (p. 45)

Compared to the height gained by this inner movement of the soul, the actual height of the mountain fades into insignificance: "It seemed to me hardly higher than a cubit compared to the height of human contemplation, were the latter not plunged into the filth of earthly sordidness" (p. 45). As he returns, the conquest of the mountain becomes a figure of the spirit's conquest of the flesh, the mountain itself a figure of the passions puffed up by worldly instincts that must be subdued.

We have to wonder about the plausability of Petrarch's claim that what we are reading is a letter he wrote to his friend, Francesco Dionigi de Roberti. What we have is a carefully constructed whole, aimed especially at recalling the Augustinian paradigm. We should note the date of the ascent: though it is supposed to have taken place on April 26, 1336, that date has been shown to be false.[15] Its choice is part of the poet's self-representation; Petrarch would have been then in his thirty-second year, just the age of Augustine when he converted. Easter was celebrated that year on March 31. The day chosen for this ascent was thus a Friday, though this is not mentioned in the account. Friday is the day of the crucifixion. Is the journey up the mountain then like the journey up the mountain on which Christ died? The crosses come to mind that still greet us on so many Alpine peaks, still make every peak a figure of that mountain on which Christ died, every climb a figure of the walk up to Golgatha. Note, too, that the reading of a pagan writer, Livy, is said to have been the incentive for this climb. Livy arouses Petrarch's curiosity, just as Cicero aroused in Augustine a desire to know. Livy is to *curiositas* as Augustine is to that *memoria* that allows the soul to find

itself, to return home, by turning inward and to God. We should also remember that Mt. Haemus, the mountain in Thrace (not Thessaly) of which
Livy speaks, was thought sacred to the Muses. Mont Ventoux is like that
mountain, but it is also like the mountain on which Christ died. It thus presents itself to us as a profoundly ambiguous image. The tension between Livy
and St. Augustine repeats the tension between Cicero and St. Paul in Augustine's *Confessions*. The reading of the former is opposed to the reading of
the latter, which heals the dispersal that always attends curiosity.

3

In the beginning of this chapter I raised a question: how close is the experience described by Petrarch to what later came to be described as the experience of the sublime? The sublime, I suggested, answers to the human
power of self-transcendence, to freedom. Such self-transcendence is part of
curiosity, which is drawn away from home by the promise of new sights and
pleasures. The climb up the mountain thus not only leads to a recognition
of the human power of self-transcendence, but at the same time fills Petrarch with a profound sense of homelessness. Curiosity and homelessness
belong together. And so it is not surprising that just when he had scaled the
mountain, achieved what his curiosity had bid him do, and been rewarded
with a godlike, extraordinarily "open and wide view," "an incredibly strong
desire" to return home should have seized him—home to Italy, but Italy is
here only a figure of his true home with God. To gain that home the individual has to turn to God. And that turn depends on the individual's recep-
tiveness to divine grace, a grace mediated here by a text or by texts. It
presupposes a turn away from the centrifugal desire to see and toward a centripetal desire to read and listen. Finally, it is the divine word that alone can
bind that freedom that finds expression in curiosity.

1

Petrarch invites us to understand the inward turn occasioned by sublime nature not only as a movement of self-elevation, but at the same time as a
movement that opens the soul to God. The first turn, it would seem, is not
an essentially religious one; the second of course is. The first, as Petrarch
describes it, reveals the power of the mind to transcend the here and now,
the limits imposed on us by the body, by the senses, which bind us into the
world and tie us to a particular point of view and perspective. But the mind,
in what Petrarch calls its agility, is not so limited: vast as is the expanse that
Petrarch could survey from his mountain, the soul leaps further to what lies
beyond the Alps, to Italy, to the Pyrenees, which are too far to be seen; and
the soul leaps further still, leaps beyond the present to the past and future.
The soul transcends whatever place and time the body would assign it.

It is such emphasis on the human power of self-transcendence that links
Petrarch to a mystic like Meister Eckhart (1260–ca. 1328), and links both to
St. Augustine. Eckhart's sermon "Adolescens, tibi dico, surge!" calls explic-
itly for such a movement of self-elevation:

Yesterday as I sat yonder I said something that sounds incredible: "Jerusalem is as
near to my soul as this place is." Indeed a point a thousand miles beyond Jerusalem

is as near to my soul as my body is, and I am as sure of this as I am of being human, and it is easy to understand for learned priests.[1]

Strange as at first may seem the claim that Jerusalem is as close to me as my body, what allows Eckhart to say this is nonetheless easy to understand. When I think of Jerusalem and Rome, is one city closer to my thinking than the other? Closer in what sense? Is there not a sense in which all objects of thought are equally close to the thinking self? Not only is Jerusalem as close to the thinker as her body is, but so is a place a thousand miles beyond, so indeed is every place. Following Plato and Plotinus, anticipating Descartes, Augustine had thus insisted that the soul knows itself to be a thinking being, and as such a spiritual substance essentially different from body and place.[2] How could such a substance, grasped in its essence only in a movement of introversion, be said to be nearer one place than another? Meister Eckhart appears to be quite in agreement with the philosophical tradition when he speaks of the soul as exempt from the limitations imposed on us by our embodied existence: no matter how distant some place may be, the soul can leap to it and beyond. Had Plato not already attributed wings to thought?

To be sure, the embodied self will have difficulty identifying with Eckhart's soul. As long as I understand myself concretely, as this individual, I understand myself as cast into the world, subject to place and time. Thus placed, I also know that my vision and understanding remain bound by perspective. Only to disembodied thought, only to a pure "I," would all things be equally close. I cannot recognize myself in that "I," an inability that could be used to give phenomenological support to the Averroist position that as this unique person I am bound to space and time and will perish with my body. To be sure, whenever I seize some truth I transcend myself as thus bound. The agent intellect, according to Averroës (commenting on Aristotle), does not belong to one individual more than another, but is one for all humanity. Christian readers of Averroës would find it difficult not to recognize in his "agent intellect" an aspect of their own God. As the light of the sun makes a body visible, so this transcendent logos must illuminate my intellect if it is to function at all. But such illumination presupposes a certain receptivity to the divine light. Once more interpreting Aristotle, Averroës ties such receptivity to the possible intellect; it too, according to him, is one and the same for all humanity. Were I locked up in my body, shut up in the here and now, no agent intellect could illuminate my sensations. To arrive at, say, the concept "tree," human beings had to experience trees as standing in a significant relation to other possible trees, as members of the same set; humans had to project what they actually experienced into a space of possibilities. The concept "tree" establishes a coordinate in that space. Such establishment would be arbitrary, were it not in response not just to particular trees but to what invites me to group just these objects together, to understand them as members of the same set—we can say, were it not in response to a transcendent logos—making a Christian of the Middle Ages think of the creative Word of God. But such establishment would be altogether impossible were the self not open to this infinite space of possibilities, an openness inseparable from human freedom.

As the twofold ground of my understanding, this twofold self-transcendence haunts my being: can I not turn inward in reflection, as Petrarch did on his mountain, away from the world of the senses, transcend my embodied self, and seize the freedom that is my birthright as a human being, thereby becoming a clear mirror for the divine light? Despite Averroës' teaching that, like the agent intellect, the possible intellect belongs to all mankind, not to the individual, can I not rise beyond myself, leave my old self behind so that I actually become that possible intellect of which Averroës speaks? *Adolescens, surge!* In this sense Eckhart maintains that to the soul all things are equally close. And nothing can limit the reach of the soul, for in thinking such limits I am already beyond them.[3] Thoughts are free, and such freedom has no limits. We are back with the metaphor of the infinite sphere.

And once again that metaphor invites not only a spatial reading; it can be understood temporally as well. Can the soul be located in time? Is there not a sense in which events that happened ten years ago may be as close to you as what happened only yesterday? And so Eckhart continues: "My soul is as young as the day it was created; yes, and much younger. I tell you, I should be ashamed if it were not younger tomorrow than it is today."[4] Temporal predicates no more fit Eckhart's soul than do spatial predicates. But what then does Eckhart mean when he tells his listeners that he "should be ashamed" if his soul "were not younger tomorrow than it is today"? Obviously the word "young" has changed its usual meaning. When we say of someone that he is young we mean that not much time has passed since he was born. Eckhart means by "young" proximity to one's origin, where this origin is no longer thought as a temporal beginning but considered more essentially, as an ontological ground.[5] To say that I should be ashamed if my soul were not younger tomorrow than it is today is to say that I should be ashamed if my soul had not come closer to that reality which is its origin and true home. It is possible to read this pronouncement as an appropriation of the Platonic understanding of the philosopher as a practitioner of the art of dying (see Phacedo, especially 61b–c): had Plato not already insisted that the soul's being is not like that of the things in space and time, that it belongs rather with the Forms, sharing the same home, an intelligible world beyond time and space? Must its homecoming then not be understood as a leave-taking from the world? Eckhart points toward such a interpretation with the word *abegescheidenheit*, suggesting a departure from the world.

But to return to the statement that Jerusalem is as close to me as my body is: Eckhart knows of course that I do not possess eyes with which I could now actually see either the earthly or the heavenly Jerusalem. Although I can conceive or imagine it, I do not in fact see it. Such conceptions or imaginings cannot give me information concerning how the city actually looks. Only to the disembodied soul are all things equally close; only it invites the figure of the infinite sphere. But the possibility of a self-elevation reaching for what this figure names haunts human beings: can I not turn inward, forsake the world of the senses and whatever binds me to it, transcend this desiring, embodied self in thought?

2

While the metaphor of the infinite sphere suggests itself when speaks of the ground of the soul, it also suggests itself when speaks of God. In Eckhart's sermon "Scitote, quia prope est regnum dei," we thus read: "God is equally near to all creatures." Implied once again is the image of a sphere or a circle:

To walk through the fields and say your prayers, and see God, or to sit in a church and recognize him, and to know God better because the place is peaceful: this is due to man's defective nature and not to God. For God is equally near to everything and every place and is equally ready to give himself, so far as in him lies, and therefore a person shall know him aright who knows how to see him the same, under all circumstances.[6]

As long as we think of God as closer to one thing than to another we have not understood his essence. As we have already seen, this thought can be developed to reject the Aristotelian hierarchical conception of the cosmos. Eckhart, to be sure, is not at all interested in this direction: it is to do justice to the divine essence that we must recognize the equivalence of place. But such recognition presupposes that power of self-transcendence that lets Jerusalem be as close or as far as my own body is. There is thus a connection between such mystical introversion and the new science: both rest on a discovery of the infinite self-transcendence of the human mind. In the experience of the divine ground of our existence, we become equidistant from all creatures, as demanded by another passage from the same sermon:

So, too, heaven is equidistant from earth at all places. Likewise the soul, too, ought to be equidistant from every earthly thing, so that it is not nearer to one than to the other and behaves the same in love or suffering, or having, or forbearance; toward whatever it may be, the soul should be as dead, or dispassionate, or superior to it.[7]

Heaven here figures the soul, equidistance a state of equanimity. Center and circumference merge to suggest the figure of the infinite sphere.

But, as we have already seen, that same figure can also be put to very different use. The idea of a pure "I" to which all things are equally close can be uncovered and made the measure of what we see. Measured by this idea, what presents itself to our senses, governed as it is by point of view and perspective, will seem defective. To overcome this deficiency, we have to redescribe the world in such a way that all aspects that presuppose a particular point of view, assigned to us by our body, drop out. The same self-transcendence that is the foundation of the mysticism of Meister Eckhart, which seeks to return to the soul's core to discover there its divine ground, is also presupposed by the ideal of objectivity that was to govern the new science. This ideal cannot be divorced from the idea of a pure subject, a subject from which, in Eckhart's words, all places are equidistant. Recall

Maritain's charge that Descartes is guilty of the sin of angelism, a charge supported by both Koyré and Gilson.

Some believe that to thus link the idea of objectivity that is one of the presuppositions of modern science to theological speculation is somehow to call objectivity into question and delegitimate it: Heidegger, as I pointed out in chapter 6, suggests something of the sort. But to grant that there is indeed such a connection is in no way to discredit the idea of a pure subject and the idea of objectivity bound up with it. Both ideas have their foundation in the self-awareness of concretely existing human beings, who—although situated by their bodies in inevitably particular places and times, bound to inevitably limited perspectives—in reflection are able to transcend and think beyond these limitations. That possibility, given authoritative expression by Augustine, is anchored in human freedom and rationality. Our perspectival understanding has its measure in the ideal of a nonperspectival understanding, an ideal of reason. The traditional understanding of God as the all-knowing creator of the world includes this ideal. But, to repeat, in thinking God as such an ideal knower human beings show themselves capable of thinking such an ideal knowledge in which knowing and being coincide. Thus, even while meditations on God's divine transcendence helped awaken human beings to their own power of self-transcendence, even though it is possible to tie such speculations to particular places and periods, something else is more important: the possibility of such self-transcendence in reflection is inseparable from our own being. Even if there is no God, the human being is sufficiently godlike to think beyond the limitations of perspective, to think of God, and to measure himself by that idea. In Eckhart's transference of the metaphor of the infinite sphere from the creator to the soul this power finds striking expression. *Adolescens, surge!*

3

I mentioned how the way such speculations can be tied to particular places and periods and so, before I return to Meister Eckhart and to his understanding of the self, a few remarks about his life and times are in order. For Europe the second half of the thirteenth and the first half of the fourteenth century were a time of unrest and upheaval. Both emperor and pope had lost much of their authority, a loss was made visible to all by the interregnum

(1254–1273), this "terrible time" when there was no emperor to bind the centrifugal forces that were emerging everywhere, and by the papacy's "Babylonian Captivity" (1309–1377) in Avignon. Leaders of the Church, too, proved human, all too human, power hungry and full of greed. Resistance to the Church and its taxes was especially apparent in the flourishing cities, many of which had learned to live with papal bans that denied them, often for decades, the consolation of the sacraments. And town after town was torn apart by struggles that pitted bishops and princes, patricians and artisans, haves and have-nots against one another.

It was into this age of upheavals that Eckhart was born in 1260, in Hochheim in Thuringia—five years before Dante, six years before Duns Scotus; Thomas Aquinas died when he was fourteen. His parents belonged to the lower nobility. As was not at all unusual for a young man of his class, Eckhart joined the Dominican order. Unusual, however, was his rapid advancement. After studying in Erfurt and in Cologne, where Albertus Magnus may still have been teaching, he became vicar of the Dominicans in Thuringia. Later he was sent to Paris to both study and teach. Here he received his master's degree in 1302, hence the epithet "Meister." His great gifts did not go unrecognized. In 1303 he was made provincial or head of all the Dominicans in eastern and northern Germany, and in 1310 he was also elected provincial of the Dominicans in southern Germany, although the nomination was not confirmed: one senses growing ecclesiastic opposition. Eckhart was sent back to Paris, where the rivalry between Dominicans and Franciscans was heating up. After that we find him in Strassburg—many of his sermons appear to have been written down by nuns of that city. Some time after 1320 he was called to a professorship in Cologne, where his teaching and especially his preaching were soon found to be threatening. At the court of the archbishop of Cologne, Heinrich von Virneburg, charges of heresy were raised against him in 1326. Eckhart wrote a long defense of his views and asked that the case be transferred to the pope's court at Avignon. He appears to have died before word could reach him that Pope John XXII considered him to have been "deceived by the father of lies who often appears as an angel of light" into "sowing thorns and thistles among the faithful and even the simple folk."[8] The same pope had just condemned Marsilius of Padua and William of Ockham (1328).

In this connection we should note that the kind of sermon of which Eckhart became the unsurpassed master belongs to a genre that became popular at this time. We know that the development of this genre was pushed especially by the Dominicans to address a quite specific social problem that had emerged:[9] at that time, especially in the upper classes, there were significantly more women than men. Privileged males no doubt lived more dangerously, engaged as they so often were in seemingly unending feuds; the Church, too, attracted many to a celibate life. The question was then what to do with young women who now could find no suitable husbands or whose husbands had died.[10] One obvious answer was to ship them off to some convent, or at least to affiliate them in some other way with the Church. But who should guide and direct passions and energies that were denied a natural outlet? And so the provincial of the Dominican order, Hermann von Minden, charged his *fratres docti* to minister to these women. According to Friedrich Heer, "Such instruction has rightly been called the 'birth hour' of German mysticism."[11] A new spirituality is born of this encounter of learned monks, unsettled by issues such as the ones that found expression in the Condemnation of 1277, and women, quite a number of them belonging to the highest nobility, forced to turn inward by circumstances that denied them what they most deeply desired. Eckhart's sermons were meant to offer consolation to such women and to help channel pent-up energies in a direction acceptable to the Church and the establishment. Often, to be sure, these energies were set free in ways the Church found impossible to control. We therefore have a deliberate attempt to encourage a movement of introversion: the spiritual realm was to compensate these women for the kind of life that the world denied them. Since most of them had not been taught Latin, the sermons had to be in the vernacular. A full account of the emergence of this new spirituality and of a new sense of freedom, centered on the convents of such cities as Cologne and Strassburg, remains to be written.[12]

The significance as well as the danger of such efforts is underscored by the readiness of many of these women to embrace heresies such as that of the Free Spirit. To understand the archbishop's fears, we have to place Eckhart's teaching activity into its social context. Until the end of the Middle Ages and beyond, Europe remained very much a peasant society and the paradigmatic life was that of the peasant; but the High Middle Ages saw the emergence of cities as major centers of wealth and therefore of power. With the emergence of a flourishing urban culture, this peasant society gained a new outside. In the cities a new wealth displayed itself that provoked denunciations of property and of the power and privilege it bought as temptations of the devil. The more pronounced the split between between haves and have-nots, the more meritorious a life of voluntary poverty, such as that lived in exemplary fashion by St. Francis, had to seem to those revolted by a material culture that threatened to drown all genuine spirituality. And if for the peasants life continued pretty much as it had for centuries, the move from country to city inevitably meant a profound dislocation, bringing not only new opportunities, a new freedom, but also a new disorientation and insecurity. In the cities we thus find not only artisans and merchants; they also attracted a new, rootless, often unemployed segment of society, especially drop-outs from the establishment, including the merchant class, the aristocracy, and the priesthood.

Norman Cohn describes these "Beghards" as "an ill-defined and restless fraternity—running about the world, we are told, like vagabond monks. . . . These self-appointed 'holy beggars' were full of contempt for the easygoing monks and friars, fond of interrupting church services, impatient of ecclesiastical discipline. They preached much, without authorization, but with considerable popular success,"[13] especially to women. It is among these displaced persons that we find a new sense of freedom emerging, a freedom that in the heresy of the Free Spirit was to become "so reckless and unqualified that it amounted to a total denial of every kind of restraint and limitation."[14] At the center of this heresy, as at the center of orthodox mysticism, we find the desire for an immediate apprehension of God and communion with him; here, however, the wish raises itself to the conviction that such communion could actually be achieved, rendering the adept incapable of sin. From this inability to sin, these self-styled perfect men drew the conclusion that it was all right for them to do what was ordinarily forbidden— that it was all right for them not only to eat on fast days, but to satisfy all the body's desires, to lie, steal, deceive, and even kill. Spiritual freedom came to mean freedom from all the tales of devil, hell, and purgatory with which priests sought to frighten an unenlightened humanity, leading even to claims that the truly enlightened no longer had a need for God.[15] And again and again we meet with demands for a transformed attitude to the body. Refusing to accept that spiritual freedom must be purchased at the price of the world and all its pleasures, the Free Spirit insisted that true freedom must embrace the whole human being and manifest itself in the world.[16] This led among other things to an eroticism that saw in free love a sign of a spiritual emancipation that restored to humanity the innocence of Adam and Eve, whose lovemaking knew nothing of shame.[17]

The heresy, which went at least to the twelfth century, began to spread rapidly toward the end of the thirteenth century, flourishing especially among the unofficial lay counterparts to the established mendicant orders, the so-called beghards and beguines. The Rhineland, which was just then undergoing rapid change proved fertile ground: Cologne had grown to be the largest city in all of Germany. Here a group of such heretical beghards, living off alms, had formed a house of voluntary poverty.[18] We hear of priests struggling desperately to keep up with the subtlety of people who, with little to do, loved to argue. In 1307 and 1322 the archbishop called synods to deal with their increasing propaganda. Heinrich von Virneburg had proved particularly zealous in his persecution of these beghards. Sometime in the mid-twenties their leader, the Dutchman Walter, was caught, tortured, and, unwilling to recant or betray his followers, burned.[19] At the same time a burgher of Cologne who had come to suspect his wife's doings disguised himself and followed her to witness and participate in a clandestine meeting that ended in an orgy. The authorities responded by burning and drowning more than fifty of these perceived heretics.[20] But although forced underground, the movement continued to flourish, especially in the urban centers along the Rhine. Some of the details resonate with our own experience of urban rebels: we know, for example, that members of the brotherhood liked to sew patches of colored fabrics on their garments, even if they did not need patching. Such patches seem to have become something like a uniform.

The archbishop of Cologne saw the Dominicans and Franciscans as abetting a spirituality that threatened to leave the Church behind altogether.[21] And such suspicion, which found just one expression in the charges brought against Meister Eckhart, would indeed seem to have been well founded. In *The Pursuit of the Millennium* Norman Cohn quotes a number of texts that make it easy to understand why the church authorities were made nervous by what Meister Eckhart had to teach. Consider a statement from a heretical treatise found in a hermit's cell near the Rhine:

The divine essence is my essence and my essence is the divine essence. . . . From eternity man was God in God. . . . From eternity the soul of man was in God and is God. . . . Man was not begotten, but from eternity was wholly unbegettable; and he could not be begotten, so he is wholly immortal.[22]

The essence of the individual is here equated with the essence of God: in its essence the soul is nothing other than God. The human power of self-transcendence is thought to allow the individual to achieve unity with God. And here is a statement attributed to an unnamed woman associated with the order of the Free Spirit: "The soul is so vast that all the saints and angels would not fill it."[23] This is to say that everything finite, everything God has created, including saints and angels, is infinitely small compared to the vastness of the human soul. Little separates this claim from Petrarch's observation that the mountain he had climbed seemed to him "hardly higher than a cubit compared to the height of human contemplation, were the latter not plunged into the filth of earthly sordidness."[24] The brothers of the Free Spirit, to be sure, thought themselves able to raise themselves above such sordidness, able to shed the burden of original sin, and not just occasionally but for good. Such hubris is attributed by the mystic Johannes Ruysbroeck to his heretical counterpart:

When I dwelt in my original being and in my eternal essence there was no God for me. What I was I wished to be, and what I wished to be I was. It was by my own free will that I have emerged and become what I am. If I wished I need not have become anything and I would not now be a creature. For God can know, wish, do nothing without me. With God I have created all things and it is my hand that supports heaven and earth and all creatures. . . . Without me nothing exists.[25]

Here, too, we find the human power of self-transcendence pushed to a point where the boundary separating God and the human being has to evaporate. To a modern reader the passage is likely to have an idealistic tinge: what is asserted is that human being is the ground of all other being. Take away human being and all other beings, too, must disappear.

As Cohn points out, Ruysbroeck attributes these lines to a heretic. But if so, Ruysbroeck must have considered Meister Eckhart that heretic, though these two mystics are often associated. Eckhart's sermon "Beati pauperes spiritu, quia ipsorum est regnum coelorum" is clearly the source on which Ruysbroeck relies:

When I stood in my first cause, I had no God and was cause of myself. I did not will or desire anything, for I was pure being, a knower of myself by divine truth. Then I wanted myself and nothing else. And what I wanted I was and what I was I wanted, and thus existed untrammelled by god or anything else. But when I parted from my free will and received my created being, then I had a god. For before there were no creatures, God was not god, but rather he was what he was. When creatures came to be and took on creaturely being, then God was no longer God as he is in himself, but god as he is with creatures.

Now we say that God, in so far as he is only God, is not the highest goal of creation, nor is his fullness of being as great as that of the least of his creatures, themselves in God. And if a fly could have the intelligence by which to search the eternal abyss of divine being out of which it came, we should say that God, together with all that God is, could not give satisfaction to that fly. Therefore, we beg God that we may be rid of God, and take the truth and enjoy it eternally, where the highest angels and the fly and the soul are equal, there where I stood and was what I wanted. And so we say: if a person is to be poor in will, he must will and want as little as when he not yet was. This is how a person is poor, who wills nothing.[26]

Consider the self-understanding that speaks to us out of this passage. An original state is contrasted with another: human being has parted from its origin. In the latter state, a person understands him- or herself as a creature and thinks God from this creaturely perspective. But God thus thought depends on human being. He has no independent reality. God as he is can be found only when we transcend the entire dimension of the finite, of time, and of creatures. To free myself from my creaturely existence in this manner I also have to free myself from my creaturely needs and desires. It is easy to see why Schopenhauer should have had such high praise for Eckhart.

The experience out of which such texts are written blurs the distinction between human and divine being. The human being identifies with her essential self, with the ground of her being, the womb from which she came, which radically transcends her time- and space-bound creaturely self. A clear distinction between this essential self and God is no longer possible. That origin from which we are said to have emerged is an infinite abyss that we may call God or the free will from which we departed when we assumed our creaturely being. But turning to this infinite ground does not help us find our place in the world. Indeed, concern for that place would appear to be incompatible with the kind of poverty of which Eckhart is here speaking. The enlightened individual, it seems, does not need to worry about what the world thinks important and values, about the standards by which it judges: does he or she not stand above that world's measure and law? To prove to himself his own enlightenment such an individual might even turn against the established order. Small wonder that such guardians of the establishment as the archbishop of Cologne were worried. Eckhart did attempt to distance himself from the brothers and sisters of the Free Spirit, but his sermons do not allow us to draw a sharp distinction between his teachings and their "wild" mysticism.[27]

There is the obvious objection that these sermons are not a reliable guide to what Eckhart actually thought: did not Eckhart himself suggest in his "Defense" that they distorted what he taught, "since now and then, even frequently, the clergy, students and learned men report incompletely and falsely what they hear"?[28] We can assume that those who preserved these sermons distorted what they heard. But what matters to me here is to recover not "the real Eckhart" but a pattern of thought that speaks to us more directly in these sermons than in academic scholastic treatises precisely because, coauthored in varying degrees by those who preserved Eckhart's message, it belongs not to some particular individual but to us all. It is a seductive, disturbing pattern. Freedom of thought here threatens every established order.

4

I have tried to show that the power of self-elevation presupposed by the pursuit of objectivity that rules the new science also makes possible the kind of

· · ·

plate 1

Holy Women at the Sepulchre Confronted by the Angel of the
Resurrection. From *King Henry II's Book of Pericopes*
(1002–1014).
Bayerische Staatsbibliothek.

. . .

plate 2

(opposite, top)

Ambrogio Lorenzetti, *Annunciation* (1344).

Pinacoteca Nazionale, Siena.

. . .

plate 3

(opposite, bottom)

Workshop of the Master of the Life of the Virgin,

***Conversion of St. Hubert* (ca. 1480–1485).**

National Gallery, London.

. . .

plate 4

Rogier van der Weyden, *St. Luke Sketching the Virgin* (1485).

Museum of Fine Arts, Boston.

. . .

plate 5

Hans Holbein the Younger, *The French Ambassadors of King Henri II at the court of the English King Henry VIII* (1533). National Gallery, London.

Erich Lessing/Art Resource, N.Y.

. . .

plate 6

Pieter Brueghel the Elder, *Landscape with the Fall of Icarus* (1588).
Museum of Fine Arts, Brussels.
Scala/Art Resource, N.Y.

mysticism that finds voice in the sermons of Meister Eckhart: both spring from the same root, which we can trace back to St. Augustine and beyond. The soul, Eckhart insists, is not imprisoned in the body. To be sure, insofar as we are finite creatures, bound to a particular place in space and time, our understanding, too, is finite and bound to particular perspectives. But this is only the shell, not the kernel: we are more than such finite creatures. Had not Augustine already insisted that God must illuminate the soul if it to understand anything? Just as we need light to see, so we need this divine light if we are to know. We possess a spirit that is open to the infinite. Within himself the human being discovers the infinite, an infinity that merges with the infinity of God—not God as creatures conceive him, but God as he is in himself.

The human being is given here a twofold being. The human being is described as having left or fallen from his infinite origin, or his infinite freedom, into space, into time, into the finite. But this fall does not mean that our origin has been covered up altogether. It is experienced as a reality that beckons us to turn inward in order to raise ourselves beyond our merely finite being. By their very nature human beings are finite creatures called by the infinite. That nature suggests that we can distinguish in human beings two very different modes of knowledge: one that belongs to us insofar as we are creatures, the other insofar as we transcend ourselves as creatures and reach up to the infinite. That distinction is indeed a recurrent theme in Meister Eckhart.

Consider once more the sermon in which Eckhart claims that Jerusalem is as near to his soul as is his body and states that he should be ashamed if his soul were not younger tomorrow than it is today. The paragraph following the passage quoted above develops the presupposed understanding of the soul:

The soul has two powers that have nothing to do with the body and these are intellect (*vernünfticheit*) and will: they function above time. Oh—if only the soul's eyes were opened so that it might clearly see the truth! Believe me, it would then be as easy for one to give up everything as it would be to give up peas and lentils and nothing. Yes—by my soul—all things would be as nothing to such a person.[29]

Eckhart here draws a distinction between faculties tied to the body and faculties independent of the body and thus also of time. He names two such higher faculties: intellect and will. Both presuppose that power of self-transcendence on which I have been focusing. To be free is to transcend one-self as what one is; it is the only way I can oppose to what I am what I might be, project myself and all I encounter into a boundless space of possibilities. This power of self-transcendence is inseparable from our humanity, from our freedom. That power makes possible also an inward turn, where the will wills a withdrawal from the world, wills a return to its own self.

The distinction between two modes of knowing returns again and again in Eckhart's sermons. Consider a passage from the sermon "Dum medium silentium tenerent omnia et nox in suo cursu medium iter haberet . . . ," to which a disciple gave the title: "This is Meister Eckhart from whom God hid nothing."

Whatever the soul effects, it effects with her powers. What she understands, she understands with the intellect. What she remembers, she does with memory; if she would love, she does that with the will, and thus she works with her powers and not with her essence. Every external act is linked with some *means*. The power of sight works only through the eyes; otherwise it can neither employ nor bestow vision, and so it is with all the other senses. The soul's every external act is effected by some means.[30]

In this respect the active soul resembles the Aristotelian God, who also depends on intermediaries to become effective, but in his essence transcends time.

But in the soul's essence there is no activity, for the powers she works with emanate from the ground of being. Yet in that ground is the silent "middle": here nothing but rest and celebration for this birth, this act, that God the Father may speak His word there, for *this* part is by nature receptive to nothing save only the divine essence, without mediation.[31]

First of all and most of the time our vision is mediated, and here Eckhart does not hesitate to invoke the language of Platonic (see especially *Timaeus* 31–35) and Aristotelian philosophy:

For whenever the powers of the soul make contact with a creature, they set to work and make an image and likeness of the creature, which they absorb. That is how they know the creature. No creature can come closer to the soul than this, and the soul never approaches a creature without having first voluntarily taken an image of it into herself. Through this presented image, the soul approaches creatures—an image being something that the soul makes of (external) objects with her own powers. Whether it is a stone, a horse, a man or anything else that she wants to know, she gets out the image of it that she has already taken in, and is thus enabled to unite herself with it.

Eckhart thus thinks of our knowledge of things as a matter of first conceiving and then appropriating ideas or pictures of things. Such knowledge therefore never gets at things as they are in themselves. It is never more than a knowledge of appearances, subject to our human mode of knowing.

But for a man to receive an idea in this way, it must of necessity enter from without through the senses. In consequence, there is nothing so unknown to the soul as herself. Accordingly, one master says that the soul can neither create nor obtain an image of herself. Therefore she has no way of knowing herself, for images all enter through the senses, and hence she can have no image of herself. And so she knows all other things, but not herself. Of nothing does she know so little as of herself, for want of mediation.

And you must know too that inwardly the soul is free and void of all means and all images—which is *why* God can freely unite with her without form or likeness.[32]

What we call knowledge presupposes images. But such images, Eckhart insists, always come from experience. Given our normal mode of understanding, the soul must be considered not anything—in this sense nothing. The absence of any definite content is inseparable from the soul's freedom. And yet, if the soul is in a sense, nothing, it is also true that without this "nothing" there could be no knowledge. As especially Sartre, following Heidegger, was to insist much later, this nothing is a presupposition of all understanding, of all knowledge. It would seem that the road to mysticism, at least to the kind of mysticism represented by Meister Eckhart, is open to human beings simply insofar as they are human beings. Key here is a movement of introversion, a return to what Eckhart calls the soul's "central silence." The call of that silence may be likened to what Heidegger calls the call of conscience; Eckhart, however, understands that silence as one that prepares one for the advent of God's word, a divine word that calls as a silent discourse. That it will be difficult to separate these two silences, the silence of the soul and the silence of the divine advent, that these two silences should tend to fuse, is to be expected.[33]

This understanding of two modes of understanding enables Eckhart to anticipate Cusanus's doctrine of learned ignorance. Consider this passage, still from the same sermon:

> For all the truth learnt by all the masters by their own intellect and understanding, or ever to be learnt till Doomsday, they never had the slightest inkling of this knowledge and this ground. Though it may be called ignorance, an unknowing, yet there is in it more than in all knowing and understanding without it, for this unknowing lures and draws you away from all understood things, and from yourself as well. This is what Christ meant when he said: "Whoever will not deny himself and will not leave his father and mother, and is not estranged from all these, is not worthy of me" (Matt. 10:37).[34]

"Himself" here means of course his worldly self.

In the sermon "Ubi est qui natus est rex Judaeorum," Eckhart's doctrine of learned ignorance becomes more explicit:

> Another question arises. You might say: "Sir, you place all our salvation in ignorance. That sounds like a lack. God made man to know, as the prophet says: 'Lord, make them know!' (Tob. 13:4). Where there is ignorance there is a lack, something is missing, a man is brutish, an ape, a fool, and remains so long as he is ignorant." Ah, but here we must come to a *transformed* knowledge, and this unknowing must not come from ignorance, but rather from *knowing* we must get to this unknowing. Then we shall become knowing with divine knowing, and our unknowing will be ennobled and adorned with supernatural knowing. And through holding ourselves passive in this, we are more perfect than if we were active.[35]

The main point is obvious enough: again there is the thought that by becoming learned about our ignorance we shall prepare that place in the soul which allows for the advent of the divine. To give some account of this advent, Eckhart sometimes uses the language of Aristotelian psychology as in the following passage from the sermon "In his, quae Patris mei sunt, oportet me esse":

We spoke just now of an active intellect and a passive intellect. The active intellect abstracts images from outward things, stripping them of matter and of accidents, and introduces them to passive intellect, begetting their mental image therein. And the passive intellect, made pregnant by the active in this way, cherishes and knows these things with the aid of the active intellect. Even then, the passive intellect cannot keep on knowing these things unless the active intellect illumines them afresh. Now observe: what the active intellect does for the natural man, that and far more God does for one with detachment. He *takes away* the active intellect from him and, installing Himself in its stead, He Himself undertakes all that the active intellect ought to be doing.[36]

Eckhart relies on a then familiar view: from the sensible, the agent intellect draws purified forms; these forms are then received by the possible intellect; the result of such reception is actual cognition. In the mystic experience the mind ceases to be active. It is quieted and becomes, so to speak, a clear mirror. This mirror then reflects God's light. And yet, it should also be clear that such an account is too obviously metaphorical, too obviously tied to creature knowledge, to be taken literally. Important here is that the mystic experience, as Eckhart understands it—and this point should distinguish what he had in mind from its heretical counterpart—is not a narcissistic withdrawal into one's own self, but implies a radical openness to the divine light: what mattered to Eckhart was the advent of the divine logos in the soul.

Cusanus had said that between the finite and the infinite there is no proportion: that is, an understanding that remains tied to the finite can never reach God. This is already Eckhart's view: "So in truth, no creaturely skill, nor your own wisdom, nor all your knowledge, can enable you to know God divinely. For you to know God in God's way, your knowing must become a pure unknowing, and a forgetting of yourself and all creatures."[37] Elsewhere the idea of creature knowledge or creature science is tied to a knowledge of this and that. The theologians are thus said to have tried to speak of God by seeing him in the image of familiar things:

It is natural to teach—and yet, it seems to me unsuitable—that man must demonstrate God by analogy, with this and that. For after all, God is neither this nor that and nothing satisfies the Father but the return to what is first and innermost, the ground and kernel of His Fatherhood, where He enjoys himself, the father the father in the onefold unity.

A little bit later Eckhart continues:

I have been thinking tonight that each analogy [of things spiritual] is like an outer gate. I cannot see anything unless it bears some likeness to myself, nor can I understand anything unless it is analogous to me. In a way hidden from us, God possesses all things in Himself, but not this as opposed to that, but as one in unity.[38]

We know things, and even God, in the image of things with which we are familiar, above all in our own image. But as long as we do, we remain inevitably caught up in a multiplicity of appearances. First of all and most of the time we exist, having dispersed ourselves in the world, doing many things, knowing many things.

The preceding chapter tied such dispersal to *curiositas*. And to *curiositas* it opposed Augustine's and Petrarch's *memoria*, which lets the soul return to itself. Eckhart's views are related, if more radical. The place of *curiositas* is taken by our everyday concern with this and that. Challenging its centrifugal claims, Eckhart would recall us to that central unity which is the origin of human being. "Humanity and the human being," Eckhart teaches, "are not the same thing." The distinction being drawn here is not between the universal and the particular, but between the essential humanity within each one of us and our usual mode of being:

Essentially, humanity ranks so high that, at its highest, it is equal to the angels and is kin to the Godhead. The greatest unity that Christ had with his Father is something I can gain—if I could put off "this and that" and seize myself as humanity. Whatever therefore, God gave to his only begotten Son, He has given to me in equal measure and not less.[39]

The difference between these two modes of knowing can also be understood as a difference between an understanding of what something is, this and not that, and an understanding that does not ask for what something is, but simply opens itself to the mystery of its being. Consider this passage from the sermon "In occisione gladui mortui sunt":

To know the least important thing as being in God, to know for example, just one flower, how it has its being in God, is more perfect knowledge than any other. To know the least of creatures as one of God's beings, is better than knowing an angel.[40]

Eckhart challenges thinking that would arrange creatures in a hierarchy and then place God at the top of this ladder. We know God best when we open ourselves to the material presencing of even the most insignificant things. A dung heap can become an epiphany of the divine. What Duns Scotus calls the thisness (*haecceitas*) of things, the thing in its material concreteness, here comes to be seen positively.[41]

5

The distinction between two modes of knowing is echoed by the distinction Eckhart often draws between God and the Godhead, the essential God beyond God. In the sermon "Dum medium silentium tenerunt omnia," Eckhart has this to say:

Dionysius exhorted his pupil Timothy in this sense saying: "Dear son Timothy, do you with untroubled mind soar above yourself and all your powers, above ratiocination and reasoning, above works, above all modes and existence, into the secret still darkness, that you may come to the knowledge of the unknown super-divine God. There must be a withdrawal from all things. God scorns to work through images."[42]

More radical is this statement from the sermon "Qui audit me, non confudetur":

Man's last and highest parting occurs when, for God's sake, he takes leave of God. St. Paul took leave of God for God's sake. He gave up all that he might get from God, as well as all that God might give him, together with all he might conceive of God. In parting with these he parted with God for God's sake and yet God remained to him as God is in himself—not as he is conceived by anyone to be—nor yet as something to be won—but as God is in Himself.[43]

And yet another such passage from a sermon that has been attributed to Eckhart:

God *becomes* as phenomena express him. When I existed in the core, the soil, the river, the source of the Godhead, no one asked me where I was going or what I was doing. There was no one there to ask me, but the moment I emerged, the world of creatures began to shout: "God!" If someone were to ask me: "Brother Eckhart, when did you leave home?"—that would indicate that I must have been at home sometime. I was there just now. Thus creatures speak of God—but why do they not mention the Godhead? Because there is only unity in the Godhead and there is nothing to talk about. God acts. The Godhead does not. It has nothing to do and there is nothing going on in it. It never is on the lookout for something to do. The difference between God and Godhead is the difference between action and nonaction.[44]

Once more we have the difference between two modes of knowing, which appears also as the ontological difference between the one and the many. The one is the origin of the many, but not in the sense of giving way to the many; rather, the one is present in the many things of the world as the mystery of their being.

The Eckhart of the sermon continues:

When I return to God, I shall be without form and thus my reentry will be far more exalted than my setting out. I alone lift creatures out of their separate principles into my own, so that in me they are one. When I return to the core, the soil, the river, the source which is the Godhead, no one will ask me whence I came or where I have been. No one will have missed me—for even God passes away.

If anyone has understood this sermon I wish him well! If no one had come to listen, I should have had to preach it to the offering box.[45]

6

The mystical movement these passages hint at is not so very different from what Kierkegaard called a movement of infinite resignation.[46] And as Kierkegaard also points out, such a movement inevitably leads to what he terms a teleological suspension of the ethical. It must have been just such a suspension that the Church authorities feared. It is difficult to imagine them unconcerned by this passage from the sermon "In hoc apparuit caritas Dei in nobis":

For if Life were questioned a thousand years and asked: "Why live?" and if there were to be an answer, it could be no more than this: "I live only to live!" And that is because Life is its own ground for being, springs from its own Source. That is why it lives without a "why," lives just to live. Thus if you ask a true human being, that is one who acts from his own ground: "Why are you doing what you are doing?"—the right answer could only be: "I do it because I do it."[47]

To live well, Eckhart seems to be telling us, we should not ask for the point of life, for justifications of it; we should not ask "why?" but simply open our-selves to and accept the mystery of life. And the same holds for the actions that make up our life: they will be done spontaneously, from the heart. Such a person will not act the way he does because there is some commandment or law, he will follow his heart and for the sake of his heart suspend the claims the world makes on him. Freedom here becomes spontaneity.

This view of the genuine person may have suggested, indeed probably did suggest to some of Eckhart's followers, that one way of proving oneself such a genuine person would be to violate the established order. Mysticism here invites a political and a moral anarchism. Eckhart directly addresses such an appropriation of his teaching in the sermon "Convescens praecepit eis, ab Ierosolymis ne discrederent, etc.":

There are people, who say: "If I have God and God's love, I may do whatever I want to do." They misunderstand this word. As long as you are capable of acting contrary to the will of God and His commandments, the love of God is not in you, however you may deceive the world. The person who stands in God's will and in God's love, takes his pleasure in whatever God loves and refrains from any act contrary to His wishes, finding it impossible to omit what God wants done, and impossible to do something that goes against God. He is like a man whose legs are tied together: just as such a man cannot walk, so it is impossible for a man who lives in God's love to do evil. Someone has said: "Even if God should command me to do evil and shun virtue, still I could not do what is wrong." For no one loves virtue but who is virtuous. The person who has denied himself and all else, who seeks his own advantage in nothing, and who loves without assigned reasons, acting solely from loving-kindness, is one who is dead to the world and alive in God and God is alive in him.[48]

The good life is here understood as lived in such a way that the individual feels that she has no choice. In such a life there is no tension between how one lives and how one ought to live. Such a person would no longer experience the tension between inclination and duty.

But this is a very formal characterization of virtue. Could one not imagine such a person committing acts we would consider profoundly evil? The problem with Eckhart's mysticism is that it makes it difficult to use the idea of God as the measure of our human being. Eckhart is too ready to leap beyond creatures and creature knowledge. A more orthodox Christian might perhaps put such concerns this way: Eckhart does not take the Incarnation, the second person of the Trinity, seriously enough; and what prevents him from doing so is the sin of pride.

The threatened loss of the ethical dimension is particularly apparent in the following text by the Rhenish mystic Heinrich Seuse (Suso), who had studied with Eckhart in Cologne and courageously defended his master against the charges that had been brought against him, even when such a defense had become impolitic. Seuse tells us of a disciple who, lost in meditation on a bright Sunday, sees an incorporeal image:

> He began to ask: Where do you come from?
>
> It said: I did not come from anywhere.
>
> He said: Tell me, what are you?
>
> It said: I am nothing.
>
> He said: What do you will?
>
> It answered and said: I do not will.
>
> He, however, said: This is a miracle! What are you called?
>
> It said: I am called the wild that has no name (*daz namelos wilde*).
>
> The disciple said: You may rightly be called the wild, for your words and answers are indeed wild. Answer me now one question: What is the goal of your insight?
>
> It said: Unbound freedom.
>
> The disciple said: what do you call unbound freedom?

It said: When a man lives entirely according to his own will, without anything other (*sunder anderheit*), without looking to before or after.[49]

To be sure, it is not *daz namelos wilde* but the disciple who speaks for Seuse in chapter 7 of *The Book of Truth*. This dialogue there bears the title "What Those Men Lack, Who Live False Freedom," and it ends with the disciple insisting that the person who becomes one with Christ yet remains distinct from him, and with an assertion of the importance of making proper distinctions. But as Loris Sturlese has shown, *daz namelos wilde*, which here represents the brotherhood of the Free Spirit, is able to appeal to some of Eckhart's theses that had been condemned by the bull of John XXII; and because of this proximity to the herectics, Seuse found it necessary to challenge the condemnation, to defend his master against what he considers a misinterpretation.[50] But such action acknowledges that a strand in Eckhart's thought invites such misinterpretation.

I began by suggesting that modernity has one origin in an understanding of God that places special emphasis on his infinity. That understanding opens an abyss: as all definite content is recognized to be profoundly incompatible with the divine, the divine comes to be thought of as "the wild that has no name." But a God who has become so indefinite threatens to evaporate altogether. God is transformed into an empty transcendence that cannot provide human beings with a measure. Experience of such a God cannot be distinguished from the experience of a freedom that, acknowledging no measure, has to degenerate into license.

An integral part of this development is a movement of introversion. The individual is cast back into himself. The movement I have described has to give a new significance to the individual even as it invites the individual to lose her individuality to the abyss within. In medieval spirituality we have one root of a very modern subjectivism. The representative of the Free Spirit in Suso's little dialogue is thus strangely close to the position of Sartre: already in the fourteenth century we find a conception of freedom as radical as anything the existentialists were going to come up with much later.

1

Trying to understand God in the image of creatures, the theologians, according to Meister Eckhart, had to fail to do justice to the divine essence. To be sure, it is only natural to proceed in this manner, only natural because "I cannot see anything unless it bears some likeness to myself, nor can I understand anything unless it is analogous to me."[1] We know things, and even God, in the image of those things with which we are familiar, above all in our own image. But though only natural, Eckhart yet thinks it unsuitable to demonstrate God by this or that analogy to creatures, for by so doing we remain caught up in a realm of appearances, governed by the perspective of our own finite understanding. If we are to approach God in a manner more adequate to his essence, we have to learn to transcend that perspective.

Eckhart recognizes that there is a sense in which the human being is the measure of all he or she can see and understand. From this it follows that there is a sense in which we cannot see or understand God: is not God separated from creatures and all creature knowledge as the infinite is separated from all that is finite? But as the distance between creatures as they are present to our understanding—Kant might say "phenomena"—and God becomes infinite, God no longer functions for us as their measure. The only measure we can now point to, it would seem, is supplied by the human knower. With this we are back with Protagoras.

Chapter 4 called attention to the remarkable appeal to Protagoras, a philosopher maligned by both Plato and Aristotle, that we find in both Alberti and Cusanus. Recall Alberti's statement: "Since man is the thing best known to man, perhaps Protagoras, by saying that man is the mode and measure of all things, meant that all the accidents of things are known through comparison to the accidents of man."[2] Alberti had preceded this remark with the statement that "all things are known by comparison": compared to ordinary mortals, Aeneas was tall; "next to Polyphemus he seemed a dwarf. . . . Among the Spanish many young girls appear fair who among the Germans are dusky and dark. Ivory and silver are white; placed next to the swan and the snow they would seem pallid." Usually we compare things with or measure them by what we are already familiar with. But we are most familiar with our own body. It thus provides us with something like a natural measure—think of the *braccio*, an arm's length—although this of course is not an absolute measure, dependent as it is on the accidental makeup of human beings. Similarly it seems natural for human beings to place themselves at the center of the world they live in. And the space constructed by the painter, too, has its center in the human observer's point of view. The art of perspective shows how the decentering into which the human being is led by the power of reflection is met by a recentering that places him once more at the center, but without allowing him to claim that what has thus been gained is an absolute center.

Let me restate this point: the power of self-elevation that finds such striking expression in Eckhart's mysticism has to lead to a denial of any absolute center or measure in the realm of creatures. In the previous chapter I pointed out the anarchic tendencies of such reflection. As the ethical reflections that concluded that chapter suggest, such decentering poses a problem: inevitably it leads to the demand for a new center, a new measure. And Eckhart already recognizes where this center will be found: it is natural for human beings to understand things in their own image. Here already we are given a hint as to how the decentering that is a consequence of thoughts of the infinity of God invites a humanist recentering. That a thinker like Nicolaus Cusanus should owe a debt to both Meister Eckhart and Alberti, to Rhenish mysticism and to Italian humanism, is not at all surprising. The anthropocentrism of the Renaissance offers a response to the decentering power of reflection on the infinity of God. The Christocentrism of the fifteenth century, so pronounced in book 3 of Cusanus's *On Learned Ignorance*, belongs in this same context. So does Alberti's rehabilitation of Protagoras, to which I now would like to return. Not that such rehabilitation was based on much more than the implications of the much-quoted line that man is the measure of all things. Alberti could not have known a great deal about the Greek sophist: at the time he wrote *On Painting*, Protagoras was known primarily through Aristotle's critique in the *Metaphysics*, though he was also mentioned and quoted by such Roman writers as Cicero and Seneca. But neither Plato's *Protagoras* nor his *Theaetetus* were available to Alberti, for they were translated only by Marsilio Ficino some thirty years later.[3] That one line was all Alberti needed.

In chapter 4 I also pointed out that we find a similar and more developed rehabilitation of Protagoras in Cusanus, in his 1458 dialogue *De Beryllo*, written thus quite some time after Alberti's *On Painting*. Was it the younger Alberti who led Cusanus to invoke Protagoras? We know that Cusanus owned Alberti's *Elementa Picturae*.[4] There are at any rate striking similarities between the way Alberti and Cusanus appeal to Protagoras. Here is Cusanus:

Thirdly, note the saying of Protagoras that man is the measure of things. With the sense man measures perceptible things, with the intellect he measures intelligible things, and he attains unto supra-intelligible things transcendently. Man does this measuring in accordance with the aforementioned [cognitive modes]. For when he knows that the cognizing soul is the goal of things knowable, he knows on the basis of the perceptive power that perceptible things are supposed to be such as can be perceived. And, likewise, [he knows] regarding intelligible things that [they are supposed to be such] as can be understood, and [he knows] that transcendent things [are to be such] as can transcend. Hence, man finds in himself, as in a measuring scale, all created things.[5]

To the extent that we can know things at all, they must be capable of entering our consciousness—either as objects of sense, or as objects of thought, or as mysteries that transcend the power of reason; and to enter our consciousness we must be able to take their measure. Just as the painter's representation of the world has its center in the perceiving eye, so the world as we know it has its foundation in the knowing subject. And if this suggestion that the human being is the foundation of things known ascribes a quasi-divine creativity to man, we should not be too surprised, given the biblical tradition that God created man in his own image. Cusanus understands the character of this image primarily in terms of man's ability to create a second world, the world of concepts, which allows us to measure what we experience. This second world, we can say, provides the linguistic or logical space in which what we perceive has to take its place if it is to be understood at all. Cusanus therefore continues:

> Fourthly, note that Hermes Trismegistus states that man is a second god. For just as God is the Creator of real beings and of natural forms, so man is the creator of conceptual beings and of artificial forms that are only likenesses of his intellect, even as God's creatures are likenesses of the Divine intellect.[6]

Like Alberti, Cusanus thus insists on the godlike character of man. Just as God's creative reason unfolds itself in creation, so the human intellect unfolds itself in whatever it knows. And just as creation has its center in God, so the known world has its center in the human subject. In this respect it is very much like the world created by Alberti's painter.

Later in *De Beryllo* Cusanus returns to Protagoras:

> There still remains one thing: viz., to see how it is that man is the measure of all things. Aristotle says that by means of this [expression] Protagoras stated nothing profound. Nevertheless, Protagoras seems to me to have expressed [herein] especially important [truths]. First of all, I consider Aristotle rightly to have stated, at the outset of his *Metaphysics*, that all men by nature desire to know. He makes this statement with regard to the sense of sight, which a man possesses not simply for the sake of working; rather, we love sight because sight manifests to us many differences. If, then, man has senses and reason not only to use them for preserving his life, but also in order to know, then perceptible objects have to nourish man for two purposes: viz., in order that he may live and in order that he may know. But knowing is more excellent and more noble, because it has a higher and more incorruptible goal. Earlier on, we presupposed that the Divine Intellect created all things in order to manifest itself;

likewise, the Apostle Paul, writing to the Romans, says that the invisible God is known in and through the visible things of the world.[7]

This, to be sure, hardly sounds like a critique of Aristotle. Quite the opposite: Cusanus sounds like a humanist Aristotelian when he here, and not only here, embraces the visible things of the world in all their variety as an epiphany of the divine. Charles Trinkaus is right to link this passage to Alberti's invocation of *la più grassa Minerva* to suggest a new emphasis on visible form.[8] But what does all this have to do with a rehabilitation of Protagoras? What impresses Cusanus here is not just the wealth of the visible but the way that all we see is dependent on our possession of eyes: Aristotle is said to have seen "this very point: viz., that if perceptual cognition is removed, perceptible objects are removed. For he says in the *Metaphysics*: 'If there were not things that are enlivened, there would not be either senses or perceptible objects.'"[9] The same holds for the objects of our knowledge. Thus Protagoras appears right when he "stated that man is the measure of things. Because man knows—by reference to the nature of his perceptual [cognition]—that perceptible objects exist for the sake of that cognition, he measures perceptible objects in order to apprehend, perceptually, the glory of the Divine Intellect."[10] The being of things as we first perceive and then know them is a being relative to the human perceiver and knower. Cusanus charges Aristotle with having failed to pay sufficient attention to such relativity and as a consequence having failed to do justice to Protagoras.

To understand how remarkable this rehabilitation of Protagoras is, consider once more Aristotle's critique of Protagoras, a critique that itself may have encouraged humanists who had come to associate the Stagirite with the scholasticism they rejected to give the maligned sophist a kinder reception.[11]

Knowledge also, and perception, we call the measure of things, for the same reason, because we come to know something by them,—while as a matter of fact they are measured rather than measure other things. But it is with us as if someone else measured us and we came to know how big we are by seeing that he applied the cubit-measure a certain number of times to us. But Protagoras says man is the measure of all things, meaning really the man who knows or the man who perceives, and these because they have respectively knowledge and perception, which we say are the measures of objects. They are saying nothing, then, while appearing to be saying something remarkable.[12]

Aristotle insists that more fundamentally our knowledge of things has its measure in these things. They are, as it were, the natural measures of knowledge. It is as if we were handed a yardstick and decided by that how tall we were.

For Cusanus too our knowledge begins with perception. But perception does not give us unmediated access to God's creation. Even the yardstick example invites more questions than may at first appear. Does our understanding of the length of a "yard" not presuppose an understanding of its relationship to our body? That relationship becomes explicit when we say, "A yard is three feet." Perception already imposes a human measure on whatever presents itself to our senses. And this dependence on the subject is compounded by the way perception is entangled in understanding. Thus, when I call an object an oak tree, Aristotle would insist that the proposition's truth or falsity is decided by the tree's being either an oak tree or not. Cusanus, however, might ask whether, when I see this object as an oak tree, such seeing does not itself depend on the humanly created concept "oak tree," as it depends on the makeup of our eyes. From the very beginning we have subjected appearance to our human measures.

One could, to be sure, challenge Protagoras by invoking Cusanus's own doctrine of learned ignorance: indeed as Aristotle himself recognized, there is a sense in which knowledge and perception must be said to measure things. But do we not lose the distinction between appearance and reality when we make man the measure of all things? Was Cusanus's teaching of learned ignorance not meant to block precisely such an undue self-elevation of the human knower by reminding us that the final measure of all human knowing is God?[13] Consider Plato's remark on Protagoras in the *Theaetetus*, a remark Cusanus is unlikely to have known, since Ficino had not yet finished his translation of that dialogue. "He says, you will remember, that 'man is the measure of all things—alike of the being of things that are and of the non-being of things that are not.' . . . He puts it in this sort of way, doesn't he, that any given thing 'is to me such as it appears to me and is to you as it appears to you,' you and I being men?"[14] Plato already accuses

Protagoras of confusing appearance and reality, or of confusing perceiving and knowing.

But for Cusanus the seeming obviousness of this distinction is called into question by a higher-order reflection: does not the knower, too, give to what he claims to know his human measures, subjecting them to a humanly constructed linguistic or conceptual space? It is precisely for this reason that Cusanus, like Alberti, calls man a second God, a creator of conceptual forms in which he mirrors or unfolds himself and by means of which he reconstructs or re-creates in his own image the manifold presented to his senses.

2

In his *Idiota de Mente*, Cusanus has his layman conjecture (*conicere*) "that mind [*mens*] takes its name from measuring [*mensurare*]."[15] Elsewhere Cusanus appeals to Albertus Magnus, who, relying on a false etymology, had tied the word *mens* to *metior* (to measure); he could also have appealed to Thomas Aquinas.[16] The important point here is not the etymology but the view that the proper activity of the *mens* is *mensurare*. But if so, where does such measuring find the proper measures? According to Cusanus we find the most fundamental measure within ourselves—and he is thinking primarily not of the body, but of the mind itself.

Plato already had understood thought as a process seeking unity:

If simple unity could be adequately perceived by the sight or by any other sense, then, as we were saying in the case of the finger, there would be nothing to attract towards being; but when there is some contradiction always present and one is the reverse of one and involves the conception of plurality, the thought begins to be aroused in us, and the soul perplexed and wanting to arrive at a decision asks "What is absolute unity?" This is the way in which the study of the one has the power of drawing and converting the mind to the contemplation of true being.[17]

Sight, as we have noted, furnishes us only ever different aspects of things. What then are these things in truth? The demand is for an understanding of the being of the thing in question that would allow us to gather those different aspects into a unity. Quite in the spirit of Plato,[18] Cusanus, too, understands the human intellect as essentially in between that unity that draws it and the manifold of the world to which it is tied by the body and its senses and desires. In this respect, what Cusanus experienced in Basel mirrored what he could now experience in his own self. This lived tension between the one and the many demands resolution. The human being demands unity and is yet prevented from seizing that unity by the manifold in which "some contradiction [is] always present." The manifold must therefore be brought under a unity. In seeking the unity that is its own measure, the intellect can succeed only to the degree to which it succeeds in applying this measure to the manifold.[19]

The nature of this unfolding is made more explicit in the very beginning of the first of the *Idiota* dialogues, *Idiota de Sapientia (The Layman on Wisdom).*[20] A learned, university-trained orator and an untutored layman meet. Two modes of knowing clash: a knowing in pride and a knowing in humility and charity. The orator is convinced that you can gain firm possession of the truth and then write down what you have thus come to possess in books, so that others later can add to this storehouse of knowledge. To such learning that insists on an additive approach, the layman opposes his insight into how the human being is cut off from the truth in an argument that recalls not only Cusanus's doctrine of learned ignorance but also Eckhart's distinction between two modes of knowing. The layman, too, insists on the infinite gap that separates human re-creative from divine creative knowledge. A corollary is the gap between being and human knowing. Never shall we know more than appearances. Ours will always be the limited creature knowledge of which Eckhart speaks.

But what then is the human knower's mode of operation? Having proclaimed, citing Scripture, that wisdom cries out in the streets, the layman points to the activities that take place in the marketplace. They see money being counted, oil being measured, produce being weighed. In each case a unit measure is applied to what is to be measured. And can we not observe something of the sort wherever there is understanding? The activities observed in the marketplace invite the thought that insofar as he is the being who measures, the human being transcends the beast. *Animal rationale* comes to be understood above all as *animal mensurans.*

How then do we measure? The layman notes that we always measure by means of some unit—that is to say, by means of the one. Therefore, the paradigm of all knowing is counting. The basic thought would seem to be quite traditional. In Thomas Aquinas, Cusanus could read that "*One* implies the idea of a primary measure; and number is *multitude* measured by *one*."[21] The proposition derives from Aristotle: "Evidently then, being one in the strictest sense, if we define it according to the meaning of the word, is a measure, and especially of quantity, and secondly of quality" (*Metaphysics* 10.1, 1053b4). However, for both Aquinas and Aristotle, as we have seen, man is more fundamentally measured than measure. And something of the kind must be true if we are not to confuse reality and fiction—as Cusanus indeed presupposes when he suggests that we seek to see and understand in order to better appreciate the glory of the Divine Intellect. As a Christian thinker, he never loses sight of the importance of the distinction between God's creative knowledge and human re-creative knowledge. The human knower may be likened to Alberti's painter, but we should not forget that this is a painter who paints creation in order to lead himself and others to greater appreciation of the work of the creator. God's creation remains the measure of the artist's re-creation.

All this implies, as is indeed obvious, that even if counting is constitutive of measuring, the latter nevertheless cannot be reduced to the former. Counting is not yet measuring. Thus if unity is the primary measure, that primary measure must be incarnated in some concrete unit measure if there are to be activities such as weighing flour or measuring the length of a piece of cloth. And these concrete measures are not given to us by the human mind: they must be established by human beings. The *braccio* that plays such an important part in Alberti's perspective construction provides a good example. That measure, an arm's length, is read off the human body. In that sense it has its foundation in nature—more precisely, in human practice embedded in nature. Not that a different unit of length might not have been chosen instead, which reminds us that such measures are created by humans but not ex nihilo: they also have their basis in nature, especially in the active nature of the human body. That just this measure is chosen has to do with the way the arm offers itself quite naturally when we measure cloth. Other activities might have suggested that we choose the foot or the digit of a finger. And does not something similar hold for our words or concepts? They too are, to use one of Cusanus's favorite terms, conjectures—a Latin term in which, Gandillac suggests, Cusanus hears the German *Mut-massung* it translates, implying a measuring with the mind. We can call such conjectures fictions, provided that we keep in mind that like *braccio* and "foot," they are created not ex nihilo but in response to certain experiences.

The difficulty is, of course, that we have no way of understanding God's creation as he understands it. It is thus not available to us in its truth. In the end everything real transcends our conceptual grasp: we have to interpret what the senses give us in confusing profusion. And even that has already been subjected to our human point of view. The world is therefore not simply given to human beings. As soon as there is experience, there is also the interpreting activity of the human mind. Constitutive of whatever we experience is our way of understanding it. This Cusanus takes to be the profound insight of Protagoras.

To repeat: in trying to understand understanding, we should not overlook the contribution made by human creativity. The human being himself provides the measures by which he knows. Cusanus thus invites consideration as a precursor of Vico. But when Cusanus understands the mind as an unfolding unity in search of unity, he is more obviously following Plato. Cusanus, too, understands the search for knowledge as an unending attempt to subject what presents itself to us to unity, to reduce what is many to one. In this connection he puts great stress on the way counting provides human knowing with a paradigm; and mathematics, as we have already seen, provides the form for our best conjectures. Cusanus, too, recognizes the tension between the human demand for unity and our often chaotic perceptions.

Because we are finite knowers, cast into a seeming chaos, this search for unity has to express itself in unending attempts to subject the manifold of the world to unity, to discover the same in what at first seems different, to reduce what is many to one. If there is thus a sense in which the human mind can be called a living unity that unfolds itself in measure and number, such an unfolding must realize itself in the world if it is not to substitute arbitrary invention for understanding. The unity we seek, which draws us toward a contemplation of true being, demands that we confront an often labyrinthine world of which we are not the authors, demands that our unfolding of the living unity that we are be at the same time a discovery of unity in that world.

THE REDISCOVERY OF PROTAGORAS

There is tension between this understanding of the mind as an unfolding unity and the demand that such an unfolding not lose touch with reality, lest the human knower lose touch with her own reality.

Whatever presents itself to our senses must already bear the traces of order and be illuminated by logos, if our intellect is to subject it to its own measures, if our mind is to unfold itself in that reality into which it has been cast.[22] I shall have to return to this point in a later chapter. Here I would like to focus on Cusanus's understanding of the mind as an unfolding unity, which recalls the Albertian artist who, godlike, creates a second world that has its unifying center in the position of the eye. But for Cusanus it is no longer the eye that furnishes our representation of the world with its center, no longer the human body that provides it with a measure: the human mind both provides our representation of the world with its unifying center and applies to whatever we perceives that measure of unity it carries within itself. This measure, however, is too formal and abstract to be immediately applicable to what is given. Just as in his perspective construction Alberti turns to the makeup of the body to furnish him with measures to mediate between the eye's point of view and what is to be represented, so Cusanus does not rest content with the abstract unity furnished by the mind but recognizes the need for measures with greater content to mediate between the abstract one and what is to be represented. Here, too, successful representation of the world in which we find ourselves requires that we furnish ourselves with the measures that will best allow us to take the measure of what is to be represented. But are we not handed such measures by the makeup of our mind, by its modus operandi, unity unfolding itself in number, just as Alberti's artist is handed his measure by the makeup of his body?

As has already been pointed out, counting, while the form of measuring, must not be confused with it. That form, however, does provide us with something like a measure of our measures. Cusanus thus insists that such measures be as transparent as possible: "Now, when we conduct an inquiry on the basis of an image, it is necessary that there be no doubt regarding the image, by means of whose symbolical comparative relation we are investigating what is unknown. For the pathway to the uncertain can be only through what is presupposed and certain." Whatever we perceive is too unstable and confused to provide us with the kind of measure demanded:

But all perceptible things are in a state of continual instability because of the material possibility abounding in them. In our considering of objects, we see that those which are more abstract than perceptible things, viz., mathematicals, (not that they are altogether free of material associations, without which they cannot be imagined, not that they are at all subject to the possibility of changing) are very fixed and very certain to us. Therefore, in mathematicals the wise wisely sought illustrations of things that were to be searched out by the intellect.[23]

To do justice to the requirements of our understanding, we should turn to mathematics. The world of mathematics is so transparent because we ourselves have constituted it. "And if the Pythagoreans, and whatever others, had reflected in this same way, they would have seen clearly that mathematical entities and numbers (which proceed from our mind and which exist in the way we conceive them) are not substances or beginnings of perceptible things, but are only the beginning of rational entities of which we are the creators."[24] It is therefore only to be expected that when looking for a form of representation that would do justice to the workings of their own mind, human beings should have turned to mathematics. That holds especially for our attempts to understand the workings of nature. But we should remember that according to Cusanus, the comparative transparency of the image of the world thus drawn by science has its foundation not in what is represented but in the form of representation—raising the question whether here, as with *costruzione legittima*, the power of the chosen form of representation is not purchased at the price of significant dimensions of our being-in-the-world.

As the fourth and last of his *Idiota* dialogues, *Idiota de Staticis Experimentis*, shows, there is a sense in which Cusanus, too, called for a mathematical treatment of nature.[25] That he should have done so may be understood as just another corollary of his Platonism. But this Platonism takes a very practical turn, as Cusanus throws out numerous suggestions for putting such insight into the power of mathematical measures to actual use: "It seems to me that by reference to differences of weight we can more truly attain unto the hidden aspects of things and can know many things by means of more plausible surmises."[26] Gesturing toward possible applications of the approach he is advocating, Cusanus's layman points to the invention of thermometer and barometer. More suggestive are the implications of this approach for under-standing the makeup of different substances. Convinced that there is much to be learned from a comparison of the different weights of things, Cusanus's layman thus calls for tables of the specific gravity of different substances, something he thinks might prove particularly useful in medicine. He calls on doctors not just to rely on secondary qualities, such as the color of urine, to diagnose a certain illness, but to weigh and record the specific gravity of the urine or blood of sick and healthy individuals. By using this quantitative ap-proach, doctors might gain a clearer understanding of exactly how much of a certain medicine to prescribe. Such a careful measuring of the specific grav-ity of different substances would also enable us to understand "how greatly the adultered products of alchemy veered from the real thing."[27]

And just as careful use of the balance scale will show how much or little the alchemists can accomplish, so an insistence on grounding the pro-nouncements of science in what can be observed, measured, and compre-hended lets Cusanus's layman be suspicious of astrology. Not that all its predictions can simply be dismissed—he himself claims to have had some success in foretelling the future. But when astrology appears successful, he suggests, such success rests on no science, it probably has less to do with the stars than with attention to some individual's "countenance, his clothes, his eye-movements, to the form of his words and their weightiness, to the state of things that I requested him to make known to me."[28] The supposed sci-ence of astrology here masks an intuitive psychological understanding. Not all our understanding is well-grounded. But while Cusanus is unwilling to deny the success of such an intuitive understanding and might thus have been willing to grant doctors and astrologers who relied on Renaissance magic a measure of success, he also is profoundly suspicious of their ap-proach, precisely because it does not rest on anything that deserves to be called science. And so he has his *idiota* say: "I know that I have often fore-told many things, according as my spirit brought [them] to mind; and yet, I did not at all know the basis for [my prediction]. In the end, it seemed to me not to be permitted to a serious man to speak without a basis, and I thence-forth kept silent."[29] Cusanus here presents himself to us as more modern than Ficino, Pico, Bruno, or Campanella, who all remained committed to a premodern, magical worldview.

What matters here are not the details but the general direction in which Cusanus would have us proceed: number gives us the key to how to represent and to learn more about the workings of nature. Like ruler and clock, the weight-scale helps us redescribe nature in a way that makes it more commensurable with our mind's mode of operation. Implicit in such calls for a mathematization of the science of nature is a shift from the heterogeneity of the immediately experienced world to the homogeneity of a world subjected to the measure of number. With Cusanus this privileging of mathematics does not have its foundation in the nature of things; instead, as he points out in *De Possest*, it relates to the nature of human understanding. We can imagine a being who knows what is by means of genetic definitions, somewhat in the way that the definition of a circle gives us a rule for its construction. But we do not construct the world we experience. In this respect, a tree is very different from a circle. What we construct is never more than a similitude, an enigma, an image or picture. By their form such pictures should conform to the nature of the human spirit. They should thus be as comprehensible as possible. But they should not be confused with the things pictured: these we shall never adequately comprehend.

That being said, it does not follow that Koyré is right when he claims that "in deep opposition to the fundamental inspiration of the founders of modern science and the modern world-view, who, rightly or wrongly, tried to assert the panarchy of mathematics, [Cusanus] denies the very possibility of the mathematical treatment of nature."[30] Far from it: as his *Idiota de Staticis Experimentis* shows, there is a sense in which Cusanus, too, called for just such a mathematical treatment. What separates Cusanus from the new science is thus not, as Koyré claims, that he denies the possibility of the mathematical treatment of nature; rather, he lacks the faith or confidence that human reason, thus relying on mathematics, is able to penetrate the secrets of nature, that God wrote the book of nature in the language of our mathematics. And yet at least some analogy between God's creative understanding and the unfolding of the human mind as it seeks to comprehend God's creation is presupposed by Cusanus's conviction that mathematics will lead us to ever more adequate conjectures—just as by inscribing polygons with ever more sides into a given circle, we come closer and closer to that circle, until finally we can no longer see a difference.

Cassirer suggested that Cusanus's call for a mathematical approach to nature may be understood as just another corollary of his Platonism.[31] There certainly are a great many and usually very favorable references to Plato scattered throughout Cusanus's writings, and the Renaissance's appropriation of Plato owes a great deal to Cicero's reading of Plato (see especially *De officiis*) and to St. Augustine. But once this has been said, it is necessary to add that Cusanus does not hesitate to criticize Plato when he thinks it necessary, and his critique brings out the profound distance that separates the two thinkers. Again I quote from *De Beryllo:*

Know, too, that I have found, as it seems to me, a certain additional failing on the part of [those] seekers of truth. For Plato said (1) that a circle can be considered insofar as it is named or defined—insofar as it is mentally depicted or mentally conceived—and (2) that from these [considerations] the nature of the circle is not known, but (3) that the circle's quiddity (which is simple and incorruptible and free of all contraries) is seen by the intellect alone. Indeed, Plato made similar statements regarding all [such things].[32]

Cusanus here is challenging the Platonic claim that we have an intellectual vision of mathematicals and of the other Forms as independent realities. Christian emphasis on the transcendence of God had to widen the gap between human and divine reason; as a result of this widening, a new weight comes to be placed on human creativity. Such creativity turns out to be a necessary condition of the very possibility of human knowing. There is thus a sense in which there is a poetic component to all human knowledge,[33] a sense in which all our concepts, embodied in our language, are human creations. Not that they are therefore creations *ex nihilo.* To give us insight into the world, such measures must be drawn in some sense from that same world, just as Alberti found his measure in nature, in the nature of the human body. But to say that these measures must in some sense be drawn from the world we experience is to recognize that such experience may not be reduced to a mere reception of sensibilia. The discovery/invention of such measures requires more than a perception of particulars: it requires what, with reference to Wittgenstein, we can call a perception of family resemblances. Cusanus, to be sure, would have chosen a different language. He might have spoken of the conjectural quality of perception.

But let me return to Cusanus's Plato critique: "For if Plato had considered that [claim], assuredly he would have found that our mind, which constructs mathematical entities, has these mathematical entities, which are in its power, more truly present with itself than as they exist outside the mind." The a priori character of mathematics is thus explained in proto-Kantian fashion by appealing to the power of the human mind. Mathematics has its foundation in the unfolding of the human mind:

For example, man knows the mechanical art, and he has the forms of this art more truly in his mental concept than as they are formable outside his mind—just as a house, which is made by means of an art, has a truer form in the mind than in the pieces of wood. For the form that comes to characterize the wood is the mental form, idea, or exemplar.[34]

But unlike Plato, Cusanus sees no reason to reify the idea of the house and to give it an independent reality. As he recognizes, all such things have their origin not in nature but in the human spirit. Plato's Forms, just like mathematicals, are thus understood as human creations. For Cusanus already, as later for Descartes, there is a sense in which we understand things precisely to the extent that we can make them.

1

The 1438 Council of Ferrara, later transferred to Florence, was less important for achieving a fleeting union of the Eastern and Western Church than
for occasioning the arrival in Italy of a host of Byzantine scholars, including Gemistus Pletho. In his dedication of his Plotinus commentaries to
Lorenzo de' Medici, Marsilio Ficino tells of the impetus this event gave to
Greek studies, an impetus that proved decisive for his own life and helped
direct science for almost two centuries away from the supposedly pedantic
and bookish Aristotelians toward a magical empiricism of the sort Cusanus
had thought unworthy of "a serious man."[1]

Ficino was born in Figline near Florence in 1433. He is thus quite a bit
younger than Alberti and Cusanus, belonging to the next generation. After
training in Latin language and literature, he studied Aristotelian philosophy
and medicine, probably in Florence. Thomas Aquinas and especially Augustine helped alert him to the importance of Plato; and it was in order to
be able to read Plato in the original that he took up the study of Greek.[2] In
Cosimo de' Medici he found the patron willing to provide him with the time
he needed for his work, and it was Cosimo who in 1462 gave him a villa at
Careggi—Ficino called it his Academia—and furnished him with manuscripts so that he could translate, interpret, and teach the works of Plato and
the Platonists: this was the beginning of what has come to be called the Pla-

tonic Academy of Florence. Ordination as a priest in 1473 and a number of benefices brought Ficino financial security.

Ficino devoted much of his life to the translation of Plato and such Platonists as Plotinus, Proclus, and Pseudo-Dionysius. As already mentioned, it is to Ficino that we owe the first translation of all Plato's works into Latin or indeed any Western language. In his own thinking he attempted to synthesize Platonic and Christian themes, as suggested by the title of his principal philosophical work, the *Theologia Platonica* (1469–1474). But before Ficino could begin his translation of the works of the Divine Plato and his successors, he had to translate for his dying patron the *Corpus Hermeticum*, a copy of which—more precisely, a copy of whose first fourteen discourses—had just been brought to Florence by one of Cosimo's agents.[3] Not that Ficino did not welcome this diversion: did not these texts, believed ever since Lactantius and Augustine to date back perhaps even to the time of Moses, promise access to the Egyptian *archē* of both theology and Greek philosophy? As Heidegger sought the origin of philosophy with the pre-Socratics, so Ficino, in the words of Paul Kristeller, believed he had found in Hermes or Mercurius Trismegistus, thrice great as philosopher, priest, and king, "the *fons et origo* of a wisdom tradition which led in an unbroken chain to Plato."[4] With good reason, Ficino thought, was this supposed Egyptian called "the first author of theology." For Hermes, he believed, "was succeeded by Orpheus, who came second amongst ancient theologians: Aglaophemus, who had been initiated into the sacred teaching of Orpheus, was succeeded in theology by Pythagoras, whose disciple was Philolaus, the teacher of our Divine Plato. Hence there is one ancient theology (*Prisca theologia*) . . . taking its origin in Mercurius and culminating in the Divine Plato."[5] The recovery of this origin promised a renaissance of true theology and philosophy, and more: did it not also promise a reformation of the political order? Did Europe not need such a wise ruler, a new Hermes who would rescue it from the strife that was tearing it apart?

With such importance attributed to the treatises collected in the *Corpus Hermeticum*, we are not surprised to learn that more manuscripts exist of this translation than of any other of Ficino's works.[6] Ficino called it *Pimander*, giving the whole the title of the first treatise. The significance of such popularity becomes apparent when we think of Augustine's already-mentioned critique

THE DIGNITY OF MAN

of Hermes Trismegistus, directed especially against the *Asclepius*. Augustine's authority, to be sure, could be countered with that of the church father Lactantius, who had understood Hermes Trismegistus as a pagan prophet who foresaw the triumph of Christianity. And throughout the Middle Ages there are thinkers who speak of the legendary Hermes with respect, including the Dominicans Albertus Magnus and Thomas Aquinas, as well as Nicolaus Cusanus. Still, the Augustinian association of the *Asclepius* with diabolic magic had to cast a heavy shadow on those tempted to turn to the Hermetic tradition to find there the key that would unlock the secrets of nature. Ficino's *Pimander* helped lift that shadow, not by reinforcing the old understanding of Hermes Trismegistus as someone who foresaw the Christian message, but by connecting him to Plato in a way that aided a fusion of Platonic metaphysics and cosmology with the magical lore condemned so vehemently by Augustine—the lore about which, Cusanus thought, a serious man ought to keep silent.[7] Ficino's Platonism invited even serious men to break that silence and thus helped make Renaissance magic respectable: could not such magic help a needy humanity make this earth a bit more homelike?

In chapter 5 I pointed out that the association of painting with magic shadows Alberti's treatise. Ficino enabled the painters of his day to reinterpret this shadow as in truth a light. Consider once more Alberti's reference to the *Asclepius*, with its talk of an art of making gods, of creating "animated statues full of *sensus* and *spiritus* who can accomplish many things." Whereas in the *Republic* Plato had criticized the art of the painter for being concerned only with representations of appearances, and as such thrice removed from reality, Ficino could counter such a critique with passages from Plotinus that opened the way to a much more elevated understanding of the art of the painter and invited a very different understanding of Plato's simile likening the painter to a magician.

To be sure, we find in Plotinus a critique of material beauty that may make him seem even more hostile to painting than the Socrates of the *Republic*. Consider this passage where, in the manner of the *Symposium*, Plotinus describes our experience of beauty as a kind of mystical experience:

How come to vision of the inaccessible Beauty, dwelling as if in consecrated precincts, apart from the common ways where all may see, even the profane?

He that has the strength, let him arise and withdraw into himself, foregoing all that is known by the eyes, turning away for ever from the material beauty that once made his joy. When he perceives those shapes of grace that shown in body, let him not pursue: he must know them for copies, vestiges, shadows, and hasten away towards That they tell of. For if anyone follow what is, like a beautiful shape playing over water—is there not a myth telling in symbol of such a dupe, how he sank into the depth of the current and was swept away to nothingness? So, too, one that is held by material beauty and will not break free shall be precipitated, not in body but in Soul, down to the dark depths loathed of the Intellective-Being, where, blind even in the Lower-World, he shall have commerce only with shadows, there as here.[8]

The allusion to the Narcissus myth suggests that we should understand Alberti's use of the same myth, discussed earlier, as a self-conscious refusal to heed the Plotinian warning.

But while Plotinus's dismissal of material beauty seems here at least as decisive as Plato's, he also presents us with a defense of art against the critique of the *Republic:*

Still the arts are not to be slighted on the ground that they create by imitation of natural objects; for, to begin with, these natural objects are themselves imitations; then, we must recognize that they give no bare reproduction of the thing seen, but go back to the Reason-Principles from which Nature itself derives, and, furthermore, that much of their work is all their own; they are holders of beauty and add where nature is lacking. Thus Pheidias wrought the Zeus upon no model among things of sense but by apprehending what form Zeus must take if he chose to become manifest to sight. (*Enneads* 5.8.1)

The artist here is said to be able to reach "back to the Reason-Principles from which Nature itself derives," thereby creating works in which these principles are more fully present. The beauty of such a work is thus said to be like the beauty of the appearing God. And surely this helps us understand

that those ancient sages, who sought to secure the presence of divine beings by the erection of shrines and statues, showed insight into the nature of the All; they perceived that, though this Soul (of the world) is everywhere tractable, its presence will

THE DIGNITY OF MAN

be secured all the more readily when an appropriate receptacle is elaborated, a place especially capable of receiving some portion or phase of it, something reproducing it and serving like a mirror to catch an image of it.

It belongs to the nature of the All to make its entire content reproduce, most felicitously, the Reason-Principles in which it participates; every particular thing is the image within matter of a Reason-Principle which itself images a pre-material Reason-Principle: thus every particular entity is linked to that Divine Being in whose likeness it is made. . . .[9] (*Enneads* 4.3.11)

Frances A. Yates points out that Ficino's commentary on this passage in *De Vita Coelitus Comparanda*—Ficino assumes Plotinus's dependence on the *Asclepius* of Hermes Trismegistus—draws from it a defense of Hermetic magic.[10] Does not art show us that it is indeed possible to create works able to secure the descent of the spiritual into the visible, incarnations of spirit that will reveal divinity more clearly than do natural objects? His insight into the forces of nature will enable the expert to channel them into particular objects, to create, say, potions with magical properties. And like Augustine, Ficino is convinced not only that demons have a certain influence on us humans, but that it is possible to obtain their help through ritual—a possibility that he, too, condemns as incompatible with Christianity, though demons may be exorcized. All this suggests the possibility of transfiguring the reality that is our lot in ways that will make it more truly our home. So understood, art points the way to a magical science of nature.

2

That it is possible to reach "back to the Reason-Principles from which Nature itself derives" and create works in which these principles are more fully present is also suggested by Ficino's introduction to his "Five Questions Concerning the Mind" (1476). Here he is thinking not of art but of philosophy. Once again we encounter the by now familiar mountain metaphor:

Wisdom, sprung from the crown of the head of Jove, creator of all, warns her philosophical lovers that if they truly desire ever to gain possession of their beloved, they should always seek the highest summits of things rather than the lowest places; for Pallas, the divine offspring sent down from the high heavens, herself frequents the high citadels which she has established. She shows, furthermore, that we cannot reach the highest summits of things unless, first, taking less account of the inferior parts of the soul, we ascend to the highest part, the mind. She promises, finally, that if we have concentrated our powers in this most fruitful part of the soul, then without doubt, by means of this highest part itself, that is by means of mind, we shall ourselves have the power of creating mind, mind, which, I say, is the companion of Minerva herself and foster-child of highest Jove. So then, O best of my fellow philosophers, not long ago on Monte Cellano, I may perhaps have created, in a night's work, a mind of this kind, by means of mind.[11]

Ficino tells us that he wrote this brief work, which followed his much lengthier *Platonic Theology on the Immortality of the Soul*, in just one night on a mountain, both literally and figuratively. To work through the night is to have left behind the everyday and its concerns, while to work on a mountain is to have left behind this embodied self—an ascent that, we are told, must be made if we are to gain wisdom. The pursuit of truth demands self-transcendence, demands a more open vision than that allowed by our space- and time-bound senses, demands freedom.

But as important as this by now familiar emphasis on the mind's self-elevation and freedom is the emphasis on creativity. Ficino's talk of a work creating mind by means of mind once more recalls the *Asclepius:* is not what he has written like one of those animated statues that incarnate spirit in a sensible material and are able to accomplish many things? We are also reminded of the *Symposium*, where Diotima tells young Socrates that for us humans the best life is not one spent in contemplation of the form of beauty; it is lived rather by the man who, having mounted "the heavenly ladder, stepping from rung to rung—that is, from one to two, from two to every lovely body, from bodily beauty to the beauty of institutions, from institutions to learning, and from learning in general to the special love that pertains to nothing but the beautiful itself"—having come "to know what beauty is," returns to take his place in the world. Quickened now with the true, quickened by "virtue's self," not "virtue's semblance," he is able to bring forth and rear perfect virtue.[12] A contemplative eros here yields first place to a creative or rather procreative eros: the noblest thing we can give birth to is spirit. And so Ficino is quite in the spirit of Plato in insisting that having ascended his mountain, he was able to create spirit, that is to say, to conceive and write down what he has conceived in a philosophical work that will communicate truth.

Ficino's brief essay shows once again that despite all that Renaissance humanism owed to Plato and the Platonic tradition, it remained very much a Christian humanism. What Christian humanists could find in Plato was what so many Christian thinkers before them had found: a pagan philosopher who could furnish them the means of gaining a clearer understanding of the mysteries of their faith—even as the very power of those means carried the threat that pagan philosophy might push into the background the Christian contents it was to serve. And what the Christian could most obviously find in Plato was an interpretation of the soul as transcending this mortal body, having its true home beyond this perishable world and being for that reason immortal. Ficino's "Five Questions" thus links the theory of knowledge to an investigation into the immortality of the soul in a way that has to recall Plato's *Phaedo*. Key in Plato's dialogue is the emphasis placed on the human power of self-transcendence. This emphasis leads to two further thoughts: by transcending himself as an embodied self and thereby returning to his true essence, to what we can call the soul, the human being discovers within himself the source of knowledge. As Plato puts it: to gain knowledge, we have to recollect the Forms, the reason-principles of all things. Such recollection also means a homecoming of the self, a return to the essential self. Yet here this essential self is thought not, as in Eckhart, as an infinite abyss but as belonging with the Forms, in which nature, too, has its ground and measure. In its essence the soul is thus attuned to the essence and ground of nature. Such attunement is the foundation of the very possibility of pursuing knowledge. The soul's homecoming is also a homecoming to the logos dwelling in things. To a Christian it must have seemed evident that with his doctrine of Forms, the pagan Plato was giving philosophical expression to God's creative Word.

In its ability to recollect the Forms, the soul exhibits its immortality. For surely "what we recollect now we must have learned at some time before, which is impossible unless our souls existed somewhere before they entered this human shape." The Socrates of the *Phaedo* goes on to explain the doctrine: "Suppose that when you see something you say to yourself, This thing which I can see has a tendency to be like something else, but it falls short and cannot be really like it, only a poor imitation. Don't you agree with me that anyone who receives that impression must in fact have previous knowledge of that thing which he says the other resembles, but inadequately?" But if so, must we not "have had some previous knowledge of equality before the time when we first saw equal things and realized that they were striving after equality, but fell short of it"? And such knowledge must have been acquired "before our birth, and lost at the moment of birth." What we call learning is the recovery of that lost knowledge. But if any of this is to make sense, our souls must have had a previous existence, before taking on this human shape.[13]

We have knowledge, Plato's Socrates argues, that cannot be derived from experience. An example of such knowledge is the knowledge of equality. The fact of such a priori knowledge presupposes that the soul in some manner transcends sense experience and the body. Plato expresses this fact of transcendence by claiming that the soul's being is not to be identified with the embodied self, which comes into being at birth and passes away with death. The soul is not similarly touched by time; it preexisted the embodied self and will not die when the body dies. We have to ask ourselves whether such talk of preexistence can be more than a metaphor for the intellect's transcendence of and irreducibility to the body: it is not at all certain that this implies, or that Plato in the *Phaedo* even wanted to argue for, something like personal immortality. But of primary importance to the argument of this book is the claim that human beings transcend themselves as embodied selves; that, transcending themselves, they discover within themselves a ground of reason that is also the ground of nature; and that having gained this ground, they can also hope to gain at least some measure of control over those natural forces to which they are subject.

All these thoughts are important to the Plato reception of Renaissance humanism, though we should note that someone like Cusanus would have had particular difficulty endorsing the second claim. There is indeed a profound difference between the Platonism of Ficino, based on a much better understanding of the Platonic texts, and that of Cusanus: we sense here what separates the two generations. Consider once more Cusanus's claim, challenging the Pythagoreans, that "mathematical entities and numbers (which proceed from our mind and which exist in the way in which we conceive them) are not substances or beginnings of perceptible things, but are only the beginning of rational entities of which we are the creators."[14] With this

Ficino could not have agreed: mathematicals entities, he would have protested, can indeed provide a key to the spirit dwelling in nature and thus to ways of channeling its forces so that they would foster health and happiness. Ficino was therefore convinced that the stars had a bearing on human destiny and himself embarked on what Yates calls "a mild form of astral magic, attempting to alter, to escape from, his Saturnian horoscope by capturing, guiding towards himself, more fortunate astral influences."[15] Such magic relies on mathematics in a way Cusanus would have considered baseless. Cusanus's appropriation of Plato has to be understood in light of his turn from Pythagoras to Protagoras, a turn that makes it difficult to take horoscopes seriously. To be sure, as we saw in the previous chapter, Cusanus is willing to grant that the astrologer casting a horoscope may possess a psychological understanding of some individual that enables him to make true predictions, which he may then ornament with mathematical calculations and talk of the planets and their influences. But whatever understanding such an astrologer may in fact possess is intuitive and in this sense baseless, not worthy of a "serious man." And although our everyday dealings with our fellow humans presuppose such an intuitive understanding, it should be distrusted by anyone seeking a better-grounded understanding of the workings of nature. Such inquiry requires a different sort of check. Learned ignorance teaches us that we are incapable of divining the souls of things or the forces innate in nature. Cusanus therefore counsels us to count and measure, demands that we redescribe nature in a way that makes it more commensurable with our mind's mode of operation, without claiming that such redescription will grant us insight into the essence of things.

To Ficino, however, the Platonic theory of recollection promised precisely such an intuitive understanding of the forces governing things. Convinced of the attunement of our souls and the souls of things, he no longer shares Cusanus's suspicion of the occult sciences. By making the marriage of Platonism and magic seem philosophically respectable, he helped lay the foundation for the Renaissance philosophy of nature.[16]

3

Ficino's emphasis on human creativity raises the question: what binds such creativity? Where is the human being to find her proper place and measure?

An answer is hinted at by the way Ficino begins his "Five Questions" with a quite traditional discussion of motion, where by "motion" he means not only locomotion but also growth and decay. All such motion, he points out, proceeds in an orderly manner, possessing a definite direction and advancing from some definite origin to some certain end.[17] Quite in the spirit of Aristotle, Ficino, too, binds motion between origin and end. And he does not hesitate to extend his thought to the universe as a whole: "In this common order of the whole, all things, no matter how diverse, are brought back to unity according to a single determined harmony and rational plan. Therefore we conclude that all things are led by one certain orderer who is most full of reason" (p. 195). Ficino here gives us the barest sketch of an argument from design, narrowing the gap between divine and human reason insisted on by Eckhart and Cusanus. Ficino does not think his God as quite so radically transcendent as they do. His Platonic-Hermetic philosophy makes the world more homelike. Is not divine reason visible in the cosmos? Does not our own reason allow us to participate in God's reason? As Plato taught, the same divine logos alive in us manifests itself in nature. And because it is present in both, the rational plan of the whole can present itself to the human knower. Potentially anarchic freedom can bind itself by insight into the divine order.

How indebted to the tradition Ficino remains is shown by his account of the proper motions of the elements, of plants, and of animals: elements are said to seek their proper places; the life of plants is discussed in terms of nutrition, generation, and reproduction; and the life of the animals is described in terms of the fulfillment of natural needs. But if all things tend toward an end, what is the proper end of the human mind?

Mind, I say, must be directed in a far greater degree to some ordered end in which it is perfected according to its earnest desire. Just as the single parts of life [of man], that is, deliberations, choices, and abilities, refer to single ends (for any one of these looks towards its own end, as it were, its own good); so in like manner the whole life [of man] looks towards the universal end and good. Now, since the parts of anything serve the whole, it follows that the order which is inherent in them in relation to each other is subordinate to their order in relation to the whole. It follows further that their order in relation to particular ends depend upon a certain common order of the whole—an order which especially contributes to the common end of the whole. (p. 197)

Once again we meet with the Platonic emphasis on unity: the human mind is understood as essentially desire, and, as also in Cusanus, this desire is first of all a desire for unity, for the whole. A striving for integration is the consequence: the different ends of life are to be gathered together into one major end. Platonic, too, is the additional claim "that the mind, because it knows rest and judges rest to be more excellent than change, and because it naturally desires rest beyond motion, desires and finally attains its end and good in a certain condition of rest rather than of motion" (p. 198). Desire presupposes a lack of satisfaction. To be satisfied is to be at one with oneself, that is, to be at rest. But we cannot be at one with ourselves as long as we remain caught up in this temporal world. Our deepest desire bids us transcend our temporal condition, to ascend to a higher reality not tarnished by time.

We begin to approach this higher reality whenever we occupy ourselves with subject matter not subject to time—for example, when we do mathematics.

The familiar objects of the mind are the eternal reasons of things, not the changeable passions of matter; just as the characteristic power or excellence of life, namely, intelligence and will, proceeds beyond the ends of mobile things to those things which are stable and eternal, so life itself certainly reaches up beyond any temporal change to its end and good in eternity; indeed the soul could never pass beyond the limits of mobile things, either by understanding or by willing, unless it could transcend them by living [a formulation that may seem self-contradictory]; finally, motion is always incomplete and strives towards something else, while the nature of an end, especially the highest, is above all that it is neither imperfect nor proceeds toward some other thing. (pp. 198–199)

To be human is to be restless, to long for a satisfaction that our temporal condition denies us. Ever since Plato, such an ethics of satisfaction has played an important part in ethical thought, threatening to transform the art of living and loving into the art of dying, and privileging contemplation over creation. This returns us to that tension between a contemplative and a procreative eros so important in the *Symposium*.

The cognitive expression of this desire for the plenitude of being is the desire for truth, and like Aristotle Ficino is confident that the human being is capable of grasping the truth.

The intellect divides being into ten most universal genera, and these ten by degrees into as many subordinate genera as possible. It then arranges ultimate species under the subordinate genera; and, finally, it places single things, without end, as it were, under the species in the manner we have described. If the intellect can comprehend being itself as a definite whole, and, as it were, divide it by degrees into all its members, diligently comparing these members in turn both to the other and to the whole, then who would deny that by nature it is able to grasp universal Being itself. (pp. 199–200)

Here we have an expression of a renewed faith in the human ability to seize the essential, a confidence that is both humanist and Christian, but that also underlies Renaissance magic. The human knower and nature are commensurable, a commensurability that has its origin in God, who created us in his own image. It is the same confidence with which we meet later also in Copernicus, although there barely tinged by the Hermetic tradition.

The following passage is revealing:

For this reason, Aristotle says: just as matter, which is the lowest of natural things, can put on all corporeal forms and by this means become all corporeal things, so the intellect, which is, as it were, the lowest of all supernatural things and the highest of natural things, can take on the spiritual forms of all things and become all. In this manner the universe, under the concept of being and truth, is the object of the intellect; and similarly, under the concept of goodness, it is the object of the will. What, then, does the intellect seek if not to transform all things into itself by depicting all things in the intellect according to the nature of the intellect? And what does the will strive to do if not to transform itself into all things by enjoying all things according to the nature of each? The former strives to bring about that the universe, in a certain manner, should become intellect; the latter, that the will should become the universe. In both respects therefore, with regard to the intellect and with regard to the will, the effort of the soul is directed (as it is said in the metaphysics of Avicenna) toward this end: that the soul in its own way will become the whole universe. Thus we see that by a natural instinct every soul strives in a continuous effort both to know all truths by the intellect and to enjoy all good things by the will. (pp. 200–201)

The intellect is thought here in the image of Aristotelian matter: just as matter can put on all corporeal forms, so the intellect can take on the spiritual forms of all that actually is and could possibly be. Our intellect is open to boundless possibilities. As beings of reason, we thus experience the seductive pull of the possible. The familiar Platonic eros here generates a new dynamism. Before, we met with the soul's desire to transcend its temporal condition; now eros manifests itself as a desire to appropriate the universe, and not only intellectually, in the pursuit of knowledge, but in a stronger sense: the universe comes to be seen as material for human enjoyment. To be sure, our technological ethos is still far away, but we begin to see a connection.

Ficino, too, ties the intellect to infinity and takes its desire to be such that no finite thing will finally satisfy it. We seek always the unconditioned, the absolute. But every finite thing is conditioned. "It is indeed necessary to remember that the universe which we say is the end of the soul, is entirely infinite. We reckon to be peculiar and proper to each thing an end for which that thing characteristically feels a very strong desire" (p. 201). Given the human spirit's openness to the infinite, only what is infinite can finally satisfy it. "For this reason the inquiry of the intellect never ceases until it finds that cause of which nothing is the cause but which is itself the cause of causes. This cause is nothing other than the boundless God." The final end of human beings can only be God: "Nowhere can you rest except in boundless truth and goodness, nor find an end except in the infinite" (p. 201). Not only does the human being possess the power of self-transcendence, but a transcending of all that is finite is also what is most deeply desired, making it impossible for us to make our peace with our finite condition: "the rational soul in a certain manner possesses the excellence of infinity and eternity. If this were not the case, it would never characteristically incline toward the infinite. Undoubtedly this is the reason that there are none among men who live contentedly on earth and are satisfied with merely temporal possessions" (p. 202). The pathos of the infinite here threatens to undercut the work of the magus to make the universe more homelike.

But does it follow from the fact that we seek this infinite end that we can therefore also attain it? In the *Symposium* Aristophanes' circle-men, desiring a plenitude denied to them, are led by this impossible desire to lay claim to the place of the gods, only to be punished for such hubris by being cut in two, becoming less than they were in the beginning. And is this not also the lesson of the Christian story of the Fall? For a modern variation on what is essentially the same theme we can turn to Sartre, who, though a self-proclaimed atheist, yet takes the end of human existence to be God thought as the coincidence of freedom and being. But according to him nothing corresponds, nothing can correspond, to that idea: the idea of God, argues Sartre, is self-contradictory. Chasing after this oxymoron—the fundamental project of human beings, our deepest passion—is therefore vain. Not so, however, for Ficino, who, like every good Christian, is convinced that our desire for God is a natural desire, itself the gift of God—so convinced in fact that every such natural desire will find its satisfaction, that he does not feel he needs to offer an argument in support of such conviction.

Bound up with the recognition of the human power of self-transcendence is the recognition that we are not at the mercy of our inclinations. Our reason raises us above our passions, above the animals, makes us free and lets us use language. "Reason is certainly peculiar to us. God has not bestowed it upon the beasts, otherwise he would have given them discourse which is, as it were, the messenger of reason. [He also would have given them] the hand, the minister and instrument of reason. [If the beasts possessed reason] we would also have seen in them some indications of deliberation and versatility" (p. 206). To be sure, as we have already seen, this gift of reason is not unambiguous: the same power of self-transcendence that elevates us above the beasts has to make us restless and unhappy. Thus we are bored when all the desires of the senses have finally been satisfied.

We know by experience that the beast in us, that is, sense, most often attains its end and good. . . . [But] when sense itself, in the greatest delights of the body, is as much satisfied as is possible to it, reason is still violently agitated and agitates sense. If it chooses to obey the senses, it always makes conjectures about something; it invents new delights; it continually seeks something further, I know not what. If, on the other hand, it strives to resist the senses, it renders life laborious. Therefore, in both cases reason not only is unhappy but also entirely disturbs the happiness of sense itself. (p. 207)

A shadow falls over Ficino's worldview as he is forced to recognize that the human ability to ascend to the highest peaks, the freedom that gives us humans our dignity, is also a source of profound unhappiness. Is not everyone the unfortunate Prometheus?—whose only remedy, Ficino tells us, is to return to that place from which he received his fire, that is, to God. As Sartre recognized, there is no magic strong enough to heal the breach between nature and freedom. Ficino held on to the hope for this deeply longed-for reconciliation, but he also recognized that left to its own resources, human reason must leave such hope unsatisfied. And so he, too, turned from philosophy to religion: only the Law of Moses will solve the conflict for us. In Ficino, too, we thus discover a dark side, countered by Christian hope:

Now, in the body the soul is truly far more miserable, both because of the weakness and infirmity of the body itself and its want of all things and because of the continual anxiety of the mind: therefore, the more laborious it is for the celestial and immortal soul continually to follow its happiness, while fallen into an intemperate earthly destructible body, the more easily it obtains it when it is either free from the body or in a temperate immortal celestial body. (p. 211)

And if, as Ficino believes, no natural desire will go unfulfilled, we can be sure that we will acquire such a body: "The condition of the everlasting soul which seems to be in the highest degree natural is that it should continue to live in its own body made everlasting" (p. 211). Important in this context, especially when compared with Plato, is the emphasis Ficino places here on the body. Such emphasis invites that rehabilitation of the eye so prominent in Alberti, and present also in Cusanus. For the Christian such a rehabilitation is demanded by the Incarnation and the promised Resurrection.

Ficino concludes his essay on the soul with a vision of blessedness: "Therefore, at that place [shall be found] eternal life and the brightest light of knowledge, rest without change, a positive condition free from privation, tranquil and secure possession of all good, and everywhere perfect joy" (p. 212). What sense can he, can we make of such a state? Is it not the wooden iron Schopenhauer and Sartre took it to be? Can it be distinguished from death? Does Ficino follow his great model, the Divine Plato in this, too, that he also ends up transforming the *ars amandi*, the art of loving, into the *ars moriendi*, the art of dying?

4

The human power of self-transcendence and the freedom that it grants was given even greater emphasis by Ficino's younger friend, the precocious Pico della Mirandola.[18] Pico was born in 1463, the year before Cusanus died. He is thus a generation younger than Ficino and just ten years older than Copernicus. His father was prince of a small territory near Ferrara, well enough connected to see to it that his son was given his first ecclesiastical appointment at the age of ten—which meant in his case, as we have seen so often, above all a source of income. The father made sure that his gifted son received a good education in Latin and Greek literature and philosophy. Pico studied law in Bologna, the humanities in Ferrara, and Aristotelean philosophy in Padua. He then went to Paris to become more familiar with the medieval philosophical tradition, and it was there that he conceived the idea of summarizing all knowledge then available. No longer willing to invoke just the Greeks and the Romans, he found truths in all traditions. Indeed, Pico had learned Hebrew, Aramaic, and Arabic.

To his contemporaries Pico seemed a wonder of learning. And the young man, it seems, found himself very much in agreement with such a judgment. He possessed, at any rate, a self-confidence that matched his learning: in December 1486—Pico was then only twenty-three and in Rome—he published and planned to defend 900 theses he had drawn from a vast variety of sources, including also Hermetic texts. Was he really expecting the Church to welcome such a discussion, as his "Oration" proclaims? "For my part, reverend Fathers, I was not unaware that this very disputation of mine would be as grateful and pleasing to you who favor all good sciences, and have been willing to honor it with your most august presence, as it would be offensive and annoying to many others."[19] But instead of his labors gaining the support of Pope Innocent VIII, as Pico had hoped, the pope appears to have been disgusted with the young man's arrogance. A commission was appointed to examine his theses. Three were considered heretical, ten suspect, and the debate was forbidden. One of the condemned propositions invites the Church to embrace magic and cabala: "Nulla est scientia que nos magis certificet de divinitate Christi quam magia et cabala."[20] Such an elevation of magic and cabala had to be found unacceptable by the Church. Pico made things worse when he defended the condemned theses in an *Apologia*, which he published with part of the "Oration." Forced to retract his theses, he fled to Paris, where he was arrested at the behest of the papal legate and imprisoned for a time in Vincennes, outside that city. Friends arranged for the well-connected young man's return to Florence, where Lorenzo de' Medici and the Florentine Academy, especially Ficino, welcomed him with open arms. And when the Borgia pope Alexander VI, himself interested in magic, succeeded Innocent VIII in 1492, the absolution Lorenzo had sought for Pico was soon granted: the orthodoxy of his attempt to wed Christianity to magic and cabala was certified by the pope on June 18, 1493.

Published only after his death by his nephew Gian Francesco, the famous "Oration on the Dignity of Man" was meant to introduce the great disputation. It begins with an expression of wonder at the greatness of the human being, in which Pico shows his colors by choosing to cite neither a Christian nor a Greek thinker: "I have read in the record of the Arabians, reverend Fathers, that Abdala the Saracen, when questioned as to what on this stage of the world, as it were, could be seen most worthy of wonder, replied: 'There is nothing to be seen more wonderful than man.' In agreement with this opinion is the saying of Hermes Trismegistus: 'A great miracle, Asclepius, is man.'"[21] Ficino had already cited the latter passage.[22]

To a modern reader this beginning is likely to recall the choral hymn of Sophocles' *Antigone* on which Heidegger bases so much of his *Introduction to Metaphysics* (1953):

Wonders are many, and none is more wonderful than man; the power that crosses the white sea, driven by the stormy south-wind, making a path under surges that threaten to engulf him; and Earth, the oldest of the gods, the immortal, the unwearied, doth he wear, turning the soil with the offspring of horses, as the ploughs go to and fro from year to year.

And the light-hearted race of birds, and the tribes of savage beasts, and the sea-brood of the deep, he snares in the meshes of his woven toils, he leads captive, man excellent in wit. And he masters by his arts the beasts whose lair is in the wilds, who roams the hills; he tames the horse of shaggy mane, he puts the yoke upon its neck, he tames the tireless mountain bull.

And speech, and wind-swift thought, and all the moods that mould a state, hath he taught himself; and how to flee the arrows of the frost, when 'tis hard lodging under the clear sky, and the arrows of the rushing rain; yea, he hath resource for all; without resource he meets nothing that must come; only against Death shall he call for aid in vain; but from baffling maladies he hath devised escapes.

Cunning, beyond fancy's dream is the fertile skill which brings him, now to evil, now to good. When he honours the laws of the land, and that justice which he hath sworn by the gods to uphold, proudly stands his city: no city hath he who, for his rashness, dwells with sin. Never may he share my hearth, never think my thoughts, who doth these things![23]

What makes the human being wondrous is what lets him oppose himself to nature, what enables him to confront and meet the neediness of his natural state with his resourcefulness. But the same power that lets him raise himself above and oppose himself to nature, only to assert himself as its master, also threatens him with a loss of way. Both the promise of mastery, now to be raised to a higher level by magical science, and the threat of monstrous evil attend Pico's "Oration" as well.

The second authority referred to by Pico deserves to be cited at greater length, for it shows how squarely Pico places himself in the Hermetic tradition:

All species reproduce their individuals, whether demons, men, birds, animals, and so on. The individuals of the human race are diverse; having come down from on high where they had commerce with the race of demons they contract links with all other species. That man is near to the gods who, thanks to the spirit that relates him to the gods, has united himself to them with a religion inspired by heaven.

And so, O Asclepius, man is a *magnum miraculum*, a being worthy of reverence and honour. For he goes into the nature of a god as though he were himself a god; he has familiarity with the race of demons, knowing that he is of the same origin; he despises that part of his nature that is only human for he has put his hope in the divinity of the other part.[24]

THE DIGNITY OF MAN

In his "Oration" Pico considers a number of answers that have been proposed to explain the greatness of man, only to reject them all: man has been
said to be

intermediary between creatures
the intimate of the gods
the king of the lower beings
the interpreter of nature
the interval between fixed eternity and fleeting time
the bond, or the marriage song of the world, a little lower than the angels

Such answers, Pico suggests, are inadequate in that they do not explain why
angels should not be ranked above human beings and be considered more
wondrous. These answers are unsatisfactory because they assign the human
being a definite place in the cosmos. But the human being is the being who
has no such place. The cosmos does not need the human being to form a
perfect whole. Given its perfection, human being seems excessive. Much
more sharply than Ficino had done, Pico opposes human freedom to the architecture of the cosmos.

God the Father, the supreme Architect, had already built this cosmic home we behold,
the most sacred temple of his godhead, by the laws of His mysterious wisdom. The
region above the heavens He had adorned with Intelligences, the heavenly spheres He
had quickened with eternal souls, and the excrementary and filthy parts of the lower
world He had filled with a multitude of animals of every kind. But when the work was
finished, the Craftsman kept wishing that there were someone to ponder the plan of
so great a work, to love its beauty, and to wonder at its vastness. (p. 224)

Once again Pico's source is the *Asclepius:*

But there had to be another being which could contemplate what God had made and
so he created man. Seeing that man could not regulate all things unless he gave him
a material envelope he gave him a body. Thus man was formed from a double origin,
so that he could both admire and adore celestial things and take care of terrestrial
things and govern them.[25]

The human being is said by Pico to have been created to ponder, somewhat like the Aristotelian god, God's creation, "to love its beauty, and to wonder at its vastness." But this is to say that human beings must have been created with capacities that allow them to understand that plan. Faith in the human ability to know expresses itself in this statement. Vast as it is, the cosmos can be understood by the human mind. If we are to love the beauty of creation, we must be able to grasp what we should thus love. To wonder at the world's vastness the human mind must itself be wondrously vast.

The human being is understood by Pico as a divine afterthought. God had already distributed everything: like a perfect work of art, creation was already a perfect whole. The new being is thus inevitably a being that falls out of the cosmic order. It is therefore defined as the being who transcends the cosmos and precisely because of such transcendence is fitted to be its admirer.

At last the best of all artisans ordained that that creature to whom He had been able to given nothing proper to himself should have joint possession of whatever had been peculiar to each of the different kinds of being. He therefore took man as a creature of indeterminate nature and, assigning him a place in the middle of the world, addressed him thus: "Neither a fixed abode nor a form that is thine alone nor any function peculiar to thyself have we given thee, Adam, to the end that according to thy longing and according to thy judgment thou mayest have and possess what abode, what form, and what functions thou thyself shalt desire. The nature of all other beings is limited and constrained within the bounds of laws prescribed by Us. Thou, constrained by no limits, in accordance with thy own free will, in whose hand We have placed thee, shalt ordain for thyself the limits of thy nature." (pp. 224–225)

Bound by no laws, constrained by no limits, the human being is the being who has to choose or create his nature. In essentially the same spirit the existentialists were later going to proclaim that existence precedes essence. With good reason one might thus call Pico an early existentialist—and, in passing, I would like to call attention to the telling fact that the first English translation of Pico's "Oration" was published in a number of issues of the surrealist magazine *View*,[26] and it appears to have been widely discussed in the artistic circles in which Jackson Pollock moved.

THE DIGNITY OF MAN

That we have been created to be our own lawgivers, to be in that sense autonomous, is our dignity. The human being's freedom and lack of essence belong together. Pico, too, to be sure, again and again invokes the chain of being and its associated valuations. God is said to have assigned the human being a place "in the middle of the world." All the same, it would seem that we can locate ourselves anywhere on this chain: we can rise to the level of the angels or fall to that of the beasts. Pico thus likens the human being to Proteus and to a chameleon: "Who would not admire this our chameleon? Or who could more greatly admire aught else whatever? It is man who Asclepius of Athens, arguing from his mutability of character and from his self-transforming nature, on just grounds says was symbolized by Proteus in the mysteries" (p. 255). Among the possibilities that Pico holds open is that of a mystic flight beyond all things in the manner of Meister Eckhart: "Whatever seeds each man cultivates will grow to maturity and bear in him their own fruit. If they be vegetative, he will be like a plant. If sensitive, he will become brutish. If rational, he will grow into a heavenly being. If intellectual, he will be an angel and the son of God. And if, happy in the lot of no created thing, he withdraws into the center of his own unity, his spirit, made one with God, in the solitary darkness of God, who is set above all things, shall surpass them all" (p. 225).

This Protean character has to face the human being with a question: what am I to do? The traditional image of the great chain of being suggests an answer to that question: be still and keep your place! Nor does Pico have any doubt concerning the meaning of up and down: the life of the spirit is surely better than that of the senses. And it seems obvious that we should measure ourselves by the highest beings God created, by the seraphim and their love, by the cherubim and their intelligence, by the thrones and their steadfast judgment. Indeed, best of all would be to withdraw into that solitary darkness where that God who is set above all things is one with the center of our own being. But is that obvious? There is tension between Pico's understanding of "the solitary darkness of God" and his placement of the dignity of man in man's freedom, on the one hand, and his appeal to the great chain of being and the traditional valorization of up and down, on the other. How do these go together?

There is another related question: what should our attitude be toward our senses? Should the human being negate the senses and the body in an ascent to God, which here comes to be indistinguishable from an inward turn into the infinite core of her own being? A suggestive but also question-provoking answer is given by Pico's use of the image of Jacob's ladder, which extends from the lowest earth to the highest heaven, the Lord seated at the top, angels ascending and descending. We should be like that ladder.

If this is what we must practice in our aspiration to the angelic way of life, I ask: "Who will touch the ladder of the Lord either with fouled foot or with unclean hands?" As the sacred mysteries have it, it is impious for the impure to touch the pure. But what are these feet? What these hands? Surely the foot of the soul is that most contemptible part by which the soul rests on matter as on the soil of the earth, I mean the nourishing and feeding power, the tinder of lust, and the teacher of pleasurable weakness. Why should we not call the hands of the soul its irascible power, which struggles on its behalf as the champion of desire and as plunderer seizes in the dust and sun what desire will devour slumbering in the shade? These hands, these feet, that is, all the sentient part whereon resides the attraction of the body which, as they say, by wrenching the neck holds the soul in check, lest we be hurled down from the ladder as impious and unclean, let us bathe in moral philosophy as in a living river. Yet this will not be enough if we wish to be companions of the angels going up and down on Jacob's ladder, unless we have first been well fitted and instructed to be promoted duly from step to step, to stray nowhere from the stairway, and to engage in alternate comings and goings. Once we have achieved this by the art of discourse and reasoning, then inspired by the Cherubic spirit, using philosophy through the steps of the ladder, that is of nature, and penetrating all things from center to center, we shall sometimes descend, with titanic force rending the unity like Osiris into many parts, and we shall sometimes ascend, with the force of Phoebus collecting the parts like the limbs of Osiris into a unity, until, resting at last in the bosom of the Father who is above the ladder, we shall be made perfect with the felicity of theology. (pp. 229–230)

There is tension in this image. One view suggests that to live the complete life we must know both descent and ascent, both Osiris and Phoebus; must sometimes rend unity into countless pieces and then again collect these pieces into unity; to use Nietzsche's terms, must know both Dionysus and Apollo. Another view would subordinate down to up, descent to ascent, multiplicity to unity, movement on the ladder to rest in the bosom of the Father. Similarly there is tension in Pico's thinking between philosophy and theology, although in the end it is theology that wins out—perhaps not too surprisingly, given the way freedom pushed this far has to give new urgency to the question "What should I be doing?"

Pico's introductory statement on the dignity of man leads to a brief discussion of the present conditions of philosophy, which he describes as a state of war between its different factions, and to a defense of his undertaking, which he presents as serving theology, the study that alone can grant the peace we long for. For himself he claims a freedom from the different schools and their doctrines that resembles the freedom from the order of the cosmos he claims for every human being. Contrasting his own position with that of followers of Aquinas or Scotus, he writes: "I, on the other hand, have so prepared myself that, pledged to the doctrines of no man, I have ranged through all the masters of philosophy, investigated all books, and come to know all schools" (p. 242). And he goes on to sketch how far he has ranged, from Christian to Arab, Greek, Hebrew, Persian, and Babylonian thinkers. From all these traditions he proposes to cull certain true propositions, demonstrating that not only Plato and Aristotle but all these different traditions are joined in a higher harmony. Pico takes special pride in having added to the tenets held in common by these traditions "many teachings taken from the ancient theology of Hermes Trismegistus, many from the doctrines of the Chaldeans and of Pythagoras, and many from the occult mysteries of the Hebrews" (p. 245).

And in a manner that may seem to anticipate Descartes, but in fact belongs with that magical science of nature Descartes sought to replace, he speaks of "another method of philosophizing through numbers, which I have introduced as new, but which is in fact old, and was observed by the earliest theologians, principally by Pythagoras, by Aglaophamos, Philolaus, and Plato, and by the first Platonists, but which in this present era, like many other illustrious things, has perished through the carelessness of posterity, so that hardly any traces of it can be found." Whereas Cusanus found wisdom crying out in the marketplace, in the counting and measuring of merchants, Pico invokes Plato, who is said to have warned us "with raised voice not to think that this divine arithmetic is the arithmetic of traders" (p. 246).

Pico claims to have recovered this long-lost divine mathematics with its insight into the occult powers of certain numbers and figures and to have shown its importance for physics and metaphysics. And it is only to be expected that he should follow this claim with a discussion of the importance of magic—a good magic, to be sure, that is said to be the highest wisdom and that must not be confused with the monstrous magic, rightly condemned by the Church, that depends on the authority of demons and "makes us the bound slaves of wicked powers." While bad magic leads us to lose our freedom to these demonic powers, good magic, which he calls nothing other than "the utter perfection of natural philosophy," makes us their ruler and lord (pp. 246–248).

Again and again we meet in Pico this concern for freedom, which led him to reject an astrology that would subject our fates to the stars. And that same concern for freedom supports his method of eclecticism. Pico is proud not to be bound to any school. Is such eclecticism not itself an expression of the dignity of man? But his grand project of gathering truths from so many different positions presupposes that in the end freedom of thought will not leave us adrift, at sea in an ocean of conflicting opinions. In all the many traditions there are truths to be discovered, truths that converge in that truth to which only Christian theology can finally guide us, but which had also found expression in the *prisca theologia* of Hermes Trismegistus, available now only in fragments, refracted and diluted in the clashing philosophies and religions. Still, like a rainbow, the dream of that truth rises over the strife of philosophers as the dream of a return of Hermetic kingship rises over the strife that divides humanity.

With Pico, too, this dream is shadowed by a gnostic world-weariness that made him vulnerable to the ascetic preachings of Savonarola, who was trying to convince the ailing Pico that he should enter the convent of San Marco. Pico was only thirty-one when he died in 1494. His mentor Ficino died in 1499.

Part Three

THE LOSS OF THE EARTH

1

With his phony preface to Copernicus's *De Revolutionibus* (1543) Andreas Osiander, as we have seen,[1] had hoped to disarm hostility that the revolutionary hypotheses might arouse by insisting that what the book advances are just that, only hypotheses, that no claim is made by the author that things are in truth as they are described. As Osiander put it: "These hypotheses need not be true or even probable; if they provide a calculus consistent with the observations that alone is sufficient."[2] Osiander here shares what we can call the astronomical resignation of the medievals. Had not Aristotle admitted that the astronomer had to settle for less than absolute truth, suggesting that the number of spheres necessary to explain the phenomena could reasonably be assumed to be forty-nine or perhaps fifty-five? "The assertion of *necessity* must be left to more powerful thinkers."[3] And had not Ptolemy been forced to grant that the order of the spheres of sun, moon, and the five planets could not be definitively established and that his all-too-often ad hoc constructions of the motions of the planets could be reasonably challenged by other hypotheses?[4] In the same spirit Thomas Aquinas had pointed out that constructions using eccentrics and epicycles were not sufficient to establish truth, since other explanations are also able to save the phenomena.[5] Supported by such authorities, scholars of the Middle Ages were pretty much convinced that astronomers had to settle for less than the truth, had to be content to save the phenomena, a phrase that goes back to Plato (see *Timaeus* 29b–d). And so Tiedemann Giese, bishop of Kulm, could warn Copernicus not to aspire to outdo Ptolemy, king of astronomers: had Averroës not been right to insist that epicycles and eccentrics had no place in God's creation, that Ptolemy's astronomy was useful only for calculation and could in no way claim to describe how things were in truth?[6]

Copernicus did claim more: except for the suspicious preface, the reader of *De Revolutionibus* was given no sense of cognitive resignation, as is shown by the certainty with which Bruno, without knowing the real author of the preface, declared that it could not have been by Copernicus. He called its real author an "ignorant and conceited ass," while Kepler termed the preface a *fabula absurdissima*, a most absurd tale.[7] In Copernicus we do indeed meet with a renewed confidence in the human ability to seize the truth.

Having read the preface, the reader unaware of its real author must have been surprised by what followed: a letter by Cardinal Schönberg of Capua and Copernicus's dedication to Pope Paul III, which amounts to a second preface. In that dedication Copernicus tells of his reluctance to publish the treatise, of his fear concerning how he and his work would be received. He describes how Cardinal Schönberg and a bishop encouraged him to publish it and tells the pope that it was nothing but the lack of agreement among astronomers that led him to rethink the geocentric hypothesis. Cardinal, bishop, and pope are thus invoked to underscore the Church's support for this undertaking. Copernicus goes on to insist that the geocentric worldview is based on the authority of Greek science and philosophy, not on scriptural authority. He points out that he first read in Cicero, later in Plutarch, that even antiquity knew of thinkers (such as Hicetas, Philolaus, Heraclides of Pontos, and Ecphantus) who thought that the earth moved.[8] Copernicus does not appeal to new observations. As he himself stresses, it was primarily long-familiar problems and conflicts within the astronomical tradition that had led him to advance his new hypothesis. Too many ad hoc hypotheses had been advanced. The solution he was proposing seemed to him to work. But in his dedication already Copernicus makes quite clear that he meant to claim truth for his heliocentric view. Astronomy should offer us more than a calculus consistent with observations. Even if it might fall short of the mark, it should at least seek to describe reality. This assumption presupposes that we are not cut off from the truth.

COPERNICAN ANTHROPOCENTRISM

In support of this presupposition Copernicus appeals both to the Bible and to Plato. Would the Psalmist have sung for joy at the greatness of God's works (Psalm 92:4–5), had he thought human beings incapable of gaining insight into their divine order? And did not Plato in the *Laws*, not only stress the importance of astronomy for "the grouping of days into monthly periods, and months into the year in such fashion that the seasons with their sacrifices and feasts may fit into the true natural order and receive their several proper celebrations, and the city thus be kept alive and alert"[9]—a remark whose continued relevance a Church concerned with calendar reform could not help but recognize—but also insist that no one could either become or be called godlike who had not mastered astronomy, this "divine rather than human science"?[10] To be sure, in Plutarch Copernicus could read that the Greeks should have condemned Aristarchus of godlessness because to save the phenomena he made the earth move, (*De facie in orbe lunae* 923a), a warning that may have reinforced his own doubts about the wisdom of publishing his convictions. But as Aristotle had dismissed the claim of Simonides that the truth belongs only to God, Copernicus did not connect the claim to truth with godlessness. Would God have created us in his image, if not to have us strive to become ever more godlike? And so Copernicus laments that after so many centuries astronomers had failed to give a convincing account of the motions of this *machina mundi*, which had been created *propter nos*, for our sake, by the best and most exacting of all craftsmen.[11]

But how, if we human beings are capable of the truth, do we know that we have indeed gotten hold of it? What is the test of truth?—assuming that the meaning of truth is correspondence. What are the conditions that allow us to understand the propositions of astronomy as serious claimants to truth? According to Copernicus there are two. First of all, the propositions must "save the appearances," that is, they must agree with the best available observations.[12] This, of course, was commonly taken for granted and would not distinguish Copernicus from Osiander. But Copernicus, following Ptolemy, also makes a second demand: the hypotheses advanced by science have to be arrived at by following a method based on principles that are certain (*certa principia*)[13] certain because supported by insight into the very essence of nature. Ptolemy had included among these principles the sphericity of the heavens and the central position of the earth. And from the sphericity of the heavens seemed to follow the principle of circular motion, familiar from the *Timaeus*, where we learn that having created the world a perfect globe, the demiurge gave it the movement appropriate to its perfection: "But the movement suited to his [referring to 'the animal which was to comprehend all animals,' i.e., the cosmos] spherical form was assigned to him, being of all the seven that which is most appropriate to mind and intelligence, and he was made to move in the same manner and on the same spot, within his own limits revolving in a circle."[14] To be considered at all plausible, Ptolemy thought, the hypotheses of the astronomers had to obey these principles. They determine what Ptolemy took to be the only proper form of representation to be used in astronomy. Copernicus, while no longer willing to include the geocentric thesis among his principles, holds on to the Platonic axiom. Thus he had begun the presumably much earlier *Commentariolus* by pointing out that this axiom had been granted by all his precursors. And it is the axiom that the motion of the heavenly bodies is circular and uniform, or composed of such motions, that is the title of chapter 4 of *De Revolutionibus: Quod motus corporum caelestium sit aequalis ac circularis perpetuus vel ex circularibus compositus.* Copernicus remained convinced that this axiom expressed an insight into the being of nature that the astronomer had to accept. Kepler soon was to recognize the untenability of this supposed axiom and came to understand the elliptical paths of the planets as indirect representations of the circle's perfection, which he, too, took for granted.[15] Copernicus, however, presupposes the validity of the Platonic axiom when he criticizes the speculations of his predecessors for not having been either "sufficiently absolute" (*satis absoluta*) or "sufficiently in agreement with reason" (*rationi satis concinna*).[16] The Ptolemaic system is rejected by him in part because it violated the requirement of uniformity.

What I want to emphasize here, however, is something else: Copernicus's faith in the human ability to get at the truth. He hedges a bit when he writes: "The philosopher endeavors in all matters to seek the truth, to the extent permitted to human reason by God. With the favor of God, without whom we can accomplish nothing, I shall attempt to press further the inquiry into these questions."[17] Copernicus does not claim here to have seized the truth, once and for all. But he leaves no doubt concerning his goal: to describe, as best he could, *mundi formam*, the true form of the world.[18]

The dedicatory letter to Paul III, the same humanist pope for whom Michelangelo painted his *Last Judgment*, brings to mind Alberti's celebration of the godlike artist, who with that fresco triumphed in a way that threatens to relegate the sacred content to second place. It was Paul III who called the Council of Trent, which resulted in the Counter-Reformation and laid the foundation for the culture of the Catholic Baroque, including an art that sought to place the mastery of perspective in the service of faith (fig. 8). Only two generations later a reformed Catholic Church was to recognize in the new science and the human self-assertion that supported it enemies more to be feared than Luther or Calvin.

Copernicus's main work appeared in the very year in which the council had been convoked. The conjunction is surprising: Copernicus, one of the heroic founding figures of modernity, and the pope, associated with the Counter-Reformation and thus with traditionalist reaction to modernity. Or is there perhaps a more intimate connection between the two, between a science that in the face of theological reservations had regained confidence in the human ability to know and a Church that, confronted with challenges to its authority, had reformed itself? We should, at any rate, keep in mind that it was only in 1616—seventy-three years after its appearance—that the Church placed *De Revolutionibus* on the Index, where it remained until 1822. At first, opposition came more from the Protestant camp, including from Luther himself.

I have emphasized the liberating power of the thought of an omnipotent, all-powerful God. In thinking through the implications of the infinite power of God, the Christian thinker is brought to the recognition that the world does not have to be as Aristotle declared. Inseparable from the thought of God so understood is the thought of the contingency of creation: God could have created a different world or perhaps no world at all. To us finite knowers, the world has to present itself as just happening to be the way it is. We have no insight into the why of things. To claim such insight is to presuppose a proximity of divine and human reason that may not be presupposed. But this very inability to explain the world necessarily liberated the imagination. The thought experiments of Oresme and Buridan are an expression of this freedom.

Copernicus, too, explicitly claimed such freedom of thought for himself. Why should he not be given the freedom of investigation that his pagan predecessors enjoyed, he asks.[19] The pursuit of truth requires freedom. But there is a decisive difference between the speculations of a Buridan and an

Oresme and those of Copernicus: the nominalists' freedom of imagination went along with the kind of cognitive resignation that we also find in Osiander. Their freedom was purchased at the price of surrendering the claim to truth, which they were quite willing to leave to God. As Osiander admonished the readers of Copernicus: "So far as hypotheses are concerned, let no one expect anything certain from astronomy which cannot furnish it, lest he accept as the truth ideas conceived for another purpose, and depart from this study a greater fool than when he entered it."[20] The astronomer should content himself with models that enable him to calculate the motion of the stars with the greatest possible simplicity. The effectiveness of the model has its measure in the human intellect not the divine. And on this point, as we have seen, Osiander had a right to feel himself supported by the tradition.

Copernicus, however, was unwilling to renounce the claim to truth, as he states very clearly in the dedicatory letter to Pope Paul III. Here it is interesting to note that Copernicus makes a point of telling his readers that this work was written *in hoc remotissimo angulo terrae*, in this most remote corner of the earth. He is referring, of course, to the fact that he was working and writing in Frauenburg, far away from such centers of learning and power as Padua, Florence, or Rome. But he also knows that his eccentric location does not deny him access to the truth: reason triumphs over eccentricity. Later thinkers such as Schopenhauer and especially Nietzsche were to claim that Copernicus's rejection of geocentrism necessarily had to lead also to a rejection of anthropocentrism, a point to which I shall have to return. But the idea does not seem to have occurred to Copernicus himself: he disassociated anthropocentrism and geocentrism. And we should keep in mind that such a dissociation had its solid foundation in the Christian understanding of the dignity of man: Thomas Aquinas had already insisted that by virtue of his soul the human being stands higher than the heavenly bodies (*Summa Theologica* 1.70, art. 2 ad 4). Here already we find the recognition that was to become so important to Pico: the place assigned to the human being by the body cannot really place her. The spirit is free.

2

Copernicus's confidence in the astronomer's ability to lay claim to truth seems to have its foundation in humanism. Born in 1473 in Torun (Thorn) on the Vistula, where he also received his early training, Copernicus studied at the University of Cracow (1491–1495); in 1496 he left Poland for Italy, to study the liberal arts, medicine, and law at Bologna; Ferrara, where in 1503 he earned his doctor of law; and Padua. These are the same universities to which Pico had been sent by his father not long before. This humanism joined Pope Paul III and Copernicus, a humanism that fused pagan philosophy, represented above all by Cicero, with Christian themes and the Hermetic tradition. Faith in the attunement of human reason to reality triumphs here over the skepticism that is the result of the theocentric conception of truth.

Petrarch already presents himself to us as such a humanist. In a passage from his little book *On His Own Ignorance and That of Many Others*, quoting from Cicero's *De natura deorum*, he tells of a rude shepherd who sees the ship on which the Argonauts were sailing to Colchis: "When the shepherd saw this ship from a distant mountain, he was stupefied and terrified by the novelty of the miracle and made various conjectures: whether a mountain or rock thrown out from the bowels of the earth was driven along by the winds and hurled over the sea, or whether 'black whirlwinds were conglutinated by a collision of the waves,' or something of this kind."[21] Stupor, terror, and wonder fade when he sees the heroes on the boat and begins to understand the phenomenon. Cicero draws from this the following lesson:

This man believed at first sight he was beholding an inanimate object devoid of sense. Then he began to suspect from clearer indications what it was about which he was in doubt. In such a manner the philosophers may perhaps have been confused when they first beheld the world. However, as soon as they saw that its motions are finite and equable and every single one organized in a precisely calculated order and in immutable consistency, they were compelled to understand that there is someone in this heavenly and divine mansion who is not merely an inmate but a ruler and supervisor and, as it were, the architect of this huge work and monument.[22]

God is like an architect in that his work, like that of a human craftsman, is governed by reason. Cicero (and we could of course go back to Plato, especially to the *Timaeus*) already provides us with the analogy between divine and human craft that was to become so important to Descartes. The following passage from Cicero, quoted by Petrarch, especially seems to anticipate Descartes:

We see something moved by machinery, for instance, a sphere, a clock, and a great many other things. Are we not convinced by such a sight that they are works contrived by reason? When we see the moving impulse of the sky rotating around and revolving with admirable swiftness, most constantly producing the annual alterations for the most perfect welfare of everything, do we then doubt that all this comes to be not merely by reason but by some outstanding and Divine Reason? For we may now put aside all subtle discussion and behold to a certain degree with our eyes the beauty of everything of which we say that it has been brought into existence by Divine Providence.[23]

These sentiments prompt Petrarch to add that Cicero speaks here not like a pagan philosopher but like an Apostle—namely Paul, who in his *Letter to the Romans* wrote: "God has made it manifest unto them. For the invisible things of Him since the creation of the world are understood and clearly seen by the things that are made, even His everlasting power and divinity."[24] Petrarch thinks that Cicero leads us to the conclusion that "Whatever we behold with our eyes or perceive with our intellect is made by God for the well-being of man and governed by divine providence and counsel."[25] Because God created the world for us humans, our desire to understand creation is not in vain. But we understand nature by applying to it the measure provided by human craft.

Recall Ficino's claim that by diligently studying the world around us, comparing and classifying, the human intellect is able to grasp "universal Being itself." The soul seeks to appropriate the cosmos: more particularly, the soul seeks to appropriate the cosmos by knowing it. And Ficino assures his readers that this desire is not in vain. Similarly Pico suggests that God created the human being so that there might be someone to admire the work of the divine craftsman. Copernicus, too, expresses an evidently Christian sentiment when he writes: "With the favor of God, without whom we can accomplish nothing, I shall attempt to press further the inquiry into these questions." And yet this pledge also recalls Cicero's claim : "Without divine inspiration no one ever was a great man."[26] Petrarch adds the gloss that by inspiration a pious person could understand nothing but the Holy Ghost. Christian humanism would seem to be a presupposition of the new science. Without such a humanist faith Copernicus could hardly have persevered as he did.

3

Copernicus tells us in his prefatory letter to Paul III that nothing brought him to his revolution other than the inability of the mathematicians—that is, the astronomers—to agree on one account of the motions of the heavenly bodies. Fundamentally, the problem is the plurality of hypotheses noted by Osiander. Recall a passage I cited already in chapter 6: "Now when from time to time there are offered for one and the same motion different hypotheses (as eccentricity and an epicycle for the sun's motion) the astronomer will accept above all others the one which is easiest to grasp. The philosopher will perhaps rather seek the semblance of truth. But neither of them will understand or state anything certain, unless it has been divinely revealed to them."[27] Osiander's position here is not very different from that of Thomas Aquinas, who, following Simplicius, points out that in astronomy we often lack sufficient reasons to decide between competing hypotheses.[28] According to Ptolemy one problem astronomy alone could not solve had to do with the order of the planets. Should the sequence be

moon, Mercury, Venus—Sun—Mars, Jupiter, Saturn;

or

moon—Sun—Mercury, Venus, Mars, Jupiter, Saturn.

The question whether Mercury and Venus have their place below or above the sun could not be given a definite answer, although Ptolemy found "the order assumed by the older [astronomers]," which placed the sun in the middle of the planets, more plausible.[29] But because either hypothesis would explain the observed phenomena equally well, the astronomer could claim truth for neither. Copernicus appears to have found such uncertainty intolerable.[30] To him it seems to have suggested the thought that the planets had no independent orbits around the earth, instead orbiting around the sun. But with this shift, the sun lost its central position among the planets.

In arguing for his ordering of the planets, Ptolemy had used the time a planet needed to complete its orbit. Copernicus kept this criterion, though he left the moon to rotate around the earth. Given these premises, there is no good reason to include the earth among the planets: Tycho's solution, which leaves the earth motionless at the center of the stellar sphere but has the planets move around the moving sun, is adequate. But two reasons, in particular, Hans Blumenberg suggests, prevented Copernicus from stopping there:[31] the assumed realism of the spheres and his *horror vacui.* For once the planets had all been related to the sun as their center, a large empty space appeared between the outer surface of the sphere of Venus and the inner surface of the sphere of Mars. Only by assuming the earth to be a planet, orbited by the moon, could this space be filled. This, to be sure, ascribed to the moon an embarrassingly unique role, difficult to reconcile with the assumption of cosmic homogeneity. It became the great exception, remaining an obstacle to acceptance of the Copernican system until Galileo discovered the moons of Jupiter.

Duhem, as we saw, faulted Copernicus for his realism. Copernicus, he suggested, should have been content with mere hypotheses. But if Copernicus had been such a fictionalist, he would scarcely have arrived at his cosmology. Indebted to Ptolemy and to the Hermetic tradition, which held that intellectual intuition can give us insight into the reason-principles governing nature, his reasoning depends on assumptions about how the world is in fact, on his understanding of what he took to be the "certain principles" or axioms of physics. Copernicus's faith in the truth of his cosmological model was bound up with an understanding of the essence of nature that was surpassed as the science that he helped to inaugurate made further progress. But its failure is instructive. Consider once more Copernicus's two requirements for a description of the cosmos to claim truth: it must be faithful to observation and it must be in accord with what we take to be the essence of nature. Science on this view requires a determination of that essence; it is in need of something like an ontology of nature, which in turn prescribes a certain form of description. A commitment to such a form of description is inseparably linked to the scientists' claim to truth. With his determination a century later of the being of nature as *res extensa,* Descartes hoped to secure such an ontology and thus the proper form of description for science, thereby securing the claim of science to truth in a way that would dispense with the Hermetic wisdom that still played an important part in Copernicus's and Kepler's thinking.

4

A legend about Alfonso the Wise, the thirteenth-century king of Castile and Leon, tells that he blasphemously suggested that God would have created a better world if he, Alfonso, could have been there to advise him.[32] The name of this king is associated with the Alfonsine tables, which recorded the observed positions of the heavenly bodies and remained authoritative through many centuries. Copernicus continued to rely on them. The king's supposed claim makes us think of the messiness of the heavenly mechanism on the Ptolemaic account, with its proliferation of eccentrics, epicycles, and the like. The Alfonsine tables, so it seemed, could be used to demonstrate the inelegance of God's creation. The thought of giving advice to God is of course blasphemous, and according to legend the king paid the price: he was struck by lightning and quickly descended into hell.

Many years later Leibniz defended the wise Alfonso and said that his misfortune was only that he was born so long before Copernicus,[33] who had proved the marvelous simplicity and beauty of creation. Copernicus is thus understood by Leibniz as someone who, by exhibiting the simple order of the cosmos, absolved God from the charge that he created a messy universe. He serves to justify God's action in creating the universe. Such a belief presupposes that God's ways are justifiable by man, that a theodicy is possible. In other words, it presupposes the conviction that human reason is capable of understanding the order of the cosmos, that it can judge the wisdom of God, that human and divine knowledge are commensurable.

This, however, was not how conservative readers of Copernicus tended to react to his achievement. To them what Copernicus had to say seemed counterintuitive. In his *Dialogue* on the world systems Galileo suggests that the naive person thinks that if the world were rotating and moving through space at terrific speed—as it must, according to Copernicus—the centrifugal force would have to throw earth, stones, animals, and human beings up to the firmament.[34] The Salviati of the dialogue replies that this belief presupposes that the earth once stood still, that animals and human beings came into being on the unmoving earth, and then something happened to set the earth into motion. Galileo himself believed the circular motion of the earth on its axis and around the sun to be natural and, thought that no natural motion could have destructive consequences.

On the naive view the cosmological reformer is transformed into a quasi-divine actor—someone who actually set the earth in motion and bid the sun stand still. It is surprising how often we meet with this description of Copernicus. Thus on his grave monument we find the inscription *Terrae Motor Solis Caelique Stator,* "mover of the earth and stayer of the sun and the firmament."[35] This, to be sure, was a monument set up by an admirer: it was raised in the nineteenth century by the king of Prussia. But the phrase ascribes to the theorist an activity that to a more conservative Europe was likely to seem blasphemous; in the proceedings against Galileo one of the accusers, the Jesuit Melchior Inchofer, calls the Copernicans *terrae motores et solis statores.*[36] The inscription on the monument seems deliberately to refer to the earlier condemnation.

Copernicus himself was quite aware that his theory he contradicted common sense. He himself uses just those words in his preface to *De Revolution-ibus,* addressing Pope Paul III, declaring that he is going *contra communem sensum.* Nor should one criticize common sense by opposing to it the consensus of the experts. As Copernicus points out, there is no such consensus, regardless of the validity of the appeal to such a consensus. Did not even some of the ancients advance the heliocentric hypothesis? Reason therefore must refuse to rely on either common sense or the consensus of the experts. In a way that anticipates Descartes, the authority of both common sense and of the past is put into question. One should compare this approach with the much more conservative view of Copernicus's contemporary Machiavelli, who writes in the *Discorsi* that we should imitate the ancients in law, in medicine, and in politics, on the grounds that nature does not change.[37] Those who think such imitation anachronistic should logically also think that the heavens, the sun, the elements, and human beings, their order and their power, were different in antiquity than they are today.

We might raise an obvious question: must theory remain constant just because nature does? But we should also keep in mind how reassuring people find the belief in constancy, both in human nature and in theory. It is this comfort that Copernicus threatened to take away. But is this a particularly Christian comfort, or in fact of pagan origin?

In his dialogue Galileo ascribes a view rather like that of Copernicus to Pythagoras. He represents Aristotle and Ptolemy as theoreticians who displayed a quite understandable emotional resistance to what was then a new theory.[38] The resistance with which Copernicus is now meeting is thus interpreted as an emotional response to a truth that one finds painful. It seems that the world has become less our home. But again: is the earlier understanding specifically Christian?

To be sure, some argued that Copernicus's writings were obviously incompatible with the authority of the Bible, although it is difficult to find many biblical passages in support such a claim. Perhaps the most famous is one that Luther used against Copernicus and that later figures prominently in the proceedings against Galileo: Joshua 10:12–14, which tells of how Joshua bade the sun stand still and of how, following his invocation, God did let the sun stand still. Joshua is thus called a *stator caeli*, although it is of course God who really deserves the credit. But does the story not presuppose that the sun did in fact move before Joshua bade it stand still until the battle had been completely won?[39]

As a matter of fact, this miracle is also incompatible with the Aristotelian view of nature. Only a nominalist who insists on the omnipotence of God would have little difficulty with these verses. Oresme thus cites them with approval.[40] But such approval presupposes a theocentrism that Copernicus rejects. His humanist anthropocentrism insists once again that nature be understood as an order. Hostility to the very idea of a miracle is part of such an anthropocentrism. Kepler had already suggested that the account not be taken literally: to Joshua, caught up in the Israelites' pursuit of the enemy, it seemed as if the sun stood still. That the text should be understood metaphorically seemed obvious to the Enlightenment.

5

In an early biography (1627), Simon Starowalski gives a mythical account of the deed of Copernicus that recalls the myth related by Aristophanes in Plato's *Symposium:* Aristophanes tells of the circle-men who, like the giants of myth, sought to displace the Olympians. To punish their pride Zeus split these circle-men in two; and now he threatens to split us fragmentary humans once again so that we would have to hop on one foot, thereby reminding us of our place. Starowalski has his Jupiter observe Copernicus defying the laws of nature by stopping the revolving heavens and putting the earth in motion. Fearfully he remembers the battle with the giants who wanted to storm the Olympian heaven and wonders whether in Copernicus one of these giants might have survived, threatening once more the rule of the gods.[41] That not only Jupiter had reason to be concerned is suggested by Nietzsche, who sees Copernicus as responsible for putting us on an inclined plane, letting us roll into nothing. Copernican self-assertion is taken to have issued in nihilism.

It is only to be expected that in discussions of Copernicus as the one who succeeded in moving the earth, we should find mention of Archimedes, who said that he would move the earth if only given a firm place outside it to plant his lever. Did Copernicus not find this firm place in human reason? Consider this statement by one of the main exponents of the Enlightenment in Germany, Johann Christoph Gottsched:

One heard the news that on the tower of his church, from which he used to observe the heavens, Copernicus found that firm place outside the earth, which Archimedes asked for in order to move with a lever the entire earth from its place. One heard that with bold hand he had shattered the crystal orbs of the heavens in order to clear a path on which the planets could move freely through the thin air of the heavens. One heard that he had freed the sun from the path she had run for thousands of years, that he had, so to speak, anchored her and brought her to rest. One heard that he had transformed the earth into a spinning top which, surrounded by the wandering planets, should hurl itself around the sun once a year. The entire learned world heard with terror this talk of a canon, who was supposed to have made the dwelling place of man, which once was securely and firmly established, insecure and unsteady.[42]

This conception of Copernicus as a revolutionary who transformed a system that was widely believed to have been firmly established and in accord with common sense is part of our understanding of Copernicus and of Copernican revolutions.

COPERNICAN ANTHROPOCENTRISM

Copernicus himself, as we have seen, calls our attention to his science being at odds with common sense. Indeed, if common sense is the measure of reality, Aristotle and Ptolemy fared much better than Copernicus and the new science. The latter presuppose a radical leave-taking from common sense, a willingness to assume what seems an eccentric position. Copernicus thus makes a point of telling his readers that he is thinking his thoughts in a place far away from the centers of learning. And Gottsched has Copernicus climb a tower to gain the vantage point that lets him become the mover of the earth. This tower differs little in metaphorical significance from that mountain Ficino climbed to write his "Five Questions" or from Petrarch's mountain. We moderns are mountain climbers, literally and metaphorically.

That leave-taking from common sense is also a leave-taking from appearances. The measure of reality is given not by the senses but by the spirit. In other words, reality, as it is, cannot be seen: it can only be thought. What we see is never more than appearance. This claim implies a downgrading of the senses. Nietzsche is right: we have no organ for the truth. Reality, as it is, is invisible. Such a downgrading of the senses is part of the modern understanding of reality, as grasped only by the spirit. But the spirit does not see. We have no spiritual eyes. In this respect modernity has sided with Cusanus against Plato and the Hermetic tradition. Reality gives itself to us as it is only in our own spirit's reconstructions. This, too, is part of our Copernican inheritance. By now this inheritance has become questionable enough to us moderns that many dream of a step beyond modernity, dream of a postmodern world. Such dreamers may well want to side with Osiander's attempt to present the Copernican achievement in a way that takes away the challenge to the old theocentric conception, undoing the anthropocentric turn that it implies.

It may seem odd that a Lutheran minister should have engaged himself so energetically on behalf of Copernicus, even if he misrepresented the intentions of the author. But is it really so surprising? The Reformation insisted on the profound gap between the natural order and the order of salvation. The human being on this view was spiritually lost in this world. Faith and grace alone could give the human being a true center. Perhaps such conviction attracted Osiander to Copernicus, who had presented, so he thought, a hypothesis that deserved to be placed beside the Ptolemaic, thus putting into question the confidence so many still had in Aristotelian science. Osiander may have felt that the new science could further a cognitive resignation that could open an individual to divine grace. But this position required that he reject the claim of Copernicus to have described the way things really are. Luther, therefore, when he hears the first rumors concerning what Copernicus had done, insists that only a fool would attempt to revolutionize the art of astronomy.[43] The very attempt to offer a new cosmological model seemed to him suspect. According to Luther, too, no human reason can comprehend God's creation. In this respect he shares Osiander's position, which is essentially that of medieval nominalism.

In opposition to such resignation, Christian humanists such as Ficino and Pico, and also Copernicus, insisted that God created the world so that it could be known by us humans. He created it for our sake, *propter nos*.[44] But this conviction is difficult to reconcile with another: if the world had really been created for us human beings, why did Christ have to die on the cross, also *propter nos*? Is that dignity of human being claimed by Pico not denied to fallen humanity, to be regained only through Christ? As Philipp Melanchthon put it, "For all things that are said of the dignity of man are to be said only of Christ, in whom we have recovered that dignity lost by Adam. It is a great thing therefore to believe that Christ is Lord and master and to believe that all things are subject to us."[45] The term *dignitas hominis* appears in a very different light here than in Pico's "Oration." The dignity of man does not derive from the fact that he was created in order to know the world; rather it is the dignity of Adam to whom all things were subjected, who was created the master and possessor of nature. That dignity, to be sure, humanity lost with the Fall. But according to the reformer, faith in Christ can restore to us—that is, can restore to us Christians—that dominion over all things held by Adam (see Genesis 1:28). This interpretation leads to a much more aggressive stance toward nature, a more exploitative attitude toward nature and more generally, than that of the humanists, although as I pointed out, this attitude is foreshadowed by Ficino. But we should keep in mind that our technological world, which looks at nature primarily as a source of materials, has one root in a line in the first chapter of Genesis.

1

More than any other of his works, *The Ash Wednesday Supper* established Giordano Bruno's reputation as a leading Copernican. The title already suggests that this will be a difficult and puzzling book: why should a work so often cited as a defense of the Copernican system be given a title that invites us to think of Communion? And the content of the work makes it quite clear that Bruno here is indeed as concerned with the Lord's supper, which he parodies, as with Copernicus. But what is the connection?

Once vilified as an abominable atheist—Descartes's friend Marin Mersenne condemned Bruno as "un de plus méchans hommes que la terre porta jamais,"[1] a charge repeated by Pierre Bayle in his *Dictionnaire* (1697)[2]—Bruno is now, following the restoration of his reputation by Joachim Jacobi in his "Letter on Spinoza's Philosophy" (1785), usually seen as perhaps the first martyr that the Copernican revolution produced. Because of his denial of geocentrism and his teachings about the infinity of the cosmos, Bruno is supposed to have been tried for heresy by the Inquisition and burned at the stake in 1600. So understood he appears as a precursor of Galileo, whose less extreme fate will occupy us later. To be sure, by this point in the argument such an edifying interpretation of his gruesome end has become difficult to reconcile with the available facts. As we saw, it took the Church quite some time to place Copernicus's *De Revolutionibus* on the Index, and there were many other Copernicans in the Church who did not meet with Bruno's fate. There must have been other reasons that led the Church to single him out.

Consider once more the vehemence of Mersenne's condemnation of Bruno. As Frances A. Yates points out, Mersenne "devoted his energies to dethroning the Renaissance Magus from his seat and to attacking the efflorescence of base magics of all kind which the long prevalent Hermetism and Cabalism had brought in their train." At stake in this attack on Renaissance magic, most fundamentally, are ontological issues: an animistic understanding of nature that was supposed to allow the magus to practice his art by "guiding the influx of *spiritus* into *materia*."[3] For someone like Mersenne the real enemy of Christianity was not the just-emerging new science but rather a magical worldview that promised to the initiated an intuitive grasp of the inner workings of nature. In an age that saw the old religious worldview in ruins, Renaissance magic promised a true renaissance—a return not to the worn-out wisdom of Aristotle and his Christian followers but to that older wisdom, supposed to have come down to us, if only in fragments, in the Hermetic treatises.

Bruno, too, was convinced of the superiority of the ancient religion of the Egyptians over Christianity, of the wisdom of Hermes over the teachings of Aristotle, and was certain that, as the Lament from the *Asclepius* had foretold, the Hermetic sun that had set so long ago was about to rise once again. And one has only to recall the threefold role of Hermes Trismegistus as philosopher, priest, and king to recognize that such expectation also held political implications bound to worry defenders of the establishment. They had to resist those who proclaimed that "The marvelous magical religion of the Egyptians will return," that "their moral laws will replace the chaos of the present age," and that "the prophecy of the Lament will be fulfilled."[4]

Even a cursory reading of *The Ash Wednesday Supper* suggests that any interpretation of Bruno as the first martyr of the Copernican cause fails to do justice to the complexity of his life and thought.[5] Such an interpretation also fails to do justice to the manner of his death. Bruno was executed on February 17, 1600, the day after Ash Wednesday, on the Campo di Fiore in Rome.[6] He was then fifty-two. Early that morning he was led from the dungeon by the Friars of the Company of St. John the Beheaded, men "dedicated to the comfort and conversion of condemned prisoners."[7] Bruno, however, unrepentant, made a point of ridiculing his executioners, averting his eyes from the crucifix offered to him. His tongue was spiked and the heretic was burned at the stake. By now it is generally granted that the motives of the Church were mostly political: Bruno, it would seem, died not so much for his views concerning the cosmos but to serve as a warning example to all those who, with Tommaso Campanella, then in a Naples prison, had hoped that the year 1600 would bring about the long-dreamed-of Golden Age.[8] The execution was to demonstrate the vanity of such dreams. As I shall try to show, there is indeed a sense in which Bruno's death may be said to have ushered in a new age, and I shall sketch some of its contours—whether it is a golden age is quite another question. But first we must return to the execution.

In an announcement published on February 19, 1600, in the *Avvisi Romani* we find an account of what occurred. We read there that this "eretico obstinatissimo, ed avendo di suo capriccio formati diversi dogmi contro nostra fede, ed in particolare contro la SS. Vergine ed i Santi, volse obstinatamente morite in quelli lo scelerato." Surrendering to his capricious fantasy, the obstinate heretic refused to renounce the dogmas he had formed against the Catholic faith, particularly against the Virgin and the saints. The report also says that he wanted to die a martyr for his conviction: "e deciva che moriva martire e volentiere."[9] If we are to believe this contemporary account, what was found most offensive was Bruno's rejection of central doctrines of the Church, doctrines that at first blush appear to have little to do with the Copernican revolution.

By that time Bruno had been imprisoned for eight years. He was first jailed in Venice on May 23, 1592. Just previously the ever restless Bruno had been in Germany, where he received and accepted an invitation from the Venetian patrician Giovanni Mocenigo to come to Italy.[10] Venice was then known for its liberal attitude; Bruno was looking once again for a regular university position, and the chair of mathematics at the University of Padua had just become vacant. He went to that city, lecturing to German students. But the coveted chair was offered not to him but to Galileo. So he went back to Venice, where he joined a circle of aristocrats interested in philosophical discussion. And since there seemed to be no real future for him in Italy, he decided to go back to Frankfurt, ostensibly to oversee the printing of some of his books. It was at this point that Mocenigo—disappointed perhaps in the private lessons that he had been receiving from Bruno in the art of memory, more likely feeling cheated that he had not been initiated into the magical arts in which he thought Bruno a master, and certainly angered by Bruno's decision to return to Germany—denounced him to the Inquisition, accusing him of a host of heretical views. Among other things, the Venetian charged that Bruno claimed that the miracles Christ performed were only apparent, that Christ was in fact a magus, who initiated the apostles into his art.[11] Mocenigo had made good on his threat to keep Bruno in Venice one way or another.

Shortly after Bruno's arrest, the Inquisition began its interrogations; these continued in Rome, where he was moved in January 1593, the Venetian authorities caving in to papal demands. The transcript of the Venice interrogation has survived. We also have a report on the entire course of the interrogation: altogether there were seventeen sessions.[12] It is difficult to explain why Bruno, who for seven years appeared to recognize and to repent ever more decisively the errors of his ways, and who in April 1599 actually acknowledged his guilt, by September 16 should have fallen back into his old errors, which he defended with increasing conviction to the very end.[13] The main charges concerned key dogmas: cosmological issues were given much less weight by his judges, and there is hardly any mention of Copernicus in the record. To be sure, among the condemned theses is that of the eternity of the world; but, as we have seen, this is not a particularly Copernican view: an Aristotelian would be at least as likely to hold it. The Copernican issue is raised by Bruno, not by his interrogators, when he declares that in *Ash Wednesday Supper* he wanted to ridicule the geocentric views of some doctors.[14] The interrogators seem quite uninterested, responding with a question that leads in a quite different direction: have you ever praised heretical princes? As we know, there were good reasons for this question: in *The Ash Wednesday Supper* Bruno had celebrated Queen Elizabeth as the ideal monarch who would realize his political vision of a unified Europe and overcome the division between Protestants and Catholics that was tearing it apart, granting religious freedom to all. "There is no room here to speak of that earthly divinity, of that singular and most exceptional

Lady who, from this cold sky near the Arctic parallel serves as a beacon to the whole terrestrial globe: I mean Elizabeth, who in her title and royal dignity is not inferior to any king in the world; in judgment, wisdom, counsel and rule, she is second to no one who holds the sceptre on earth" (p. 119). Elizabeth is celebrated as a light that illuminates the globe. And in this respect she may well be likened to the Copernican sun.

Bruno had earlier celebrated the French king Henry III as a peace-loving prince, who, not at all "pleased with the noisy uproar of martial instruments," with his justice and sanctity would reconcile Protestants and Catholics.[15] And after he became disenchanted with Queen Elizabeth, he expected that transformation of the Catholic faith of which he dreamed from the Calvinist king of Navarre, who had just converted to Catholicism in order to ascend to the French throne but who stood for religious freedom. Mocenigo had indeed reported to the Inquisition that Bruno hoped for his labors to be rewarded by this king with honors and riches, that he expected to become a *capitano*—fulfilling a dream of becoming a philosopher-king in the image of the thrice-great Hermes?[16] That the Inquisition should have shown a great deal of interest in Mocenigo's report is hardly surprising. The king of Navarre was then engaged in a religious war that was to end only in 1598, when the king issued the Edict of Nantes granting freedom of worship to Protestants, the same freedom Bruno claimed for himself. In the interrogation, to be sure, Bruno points out that he never met the king, nor any of his ministers; that his praise was not for the heretic, but for someone who promised to bring peace. He dismisses the suggestion that he hoped to become a *capitano*, a soldier: he was content with his chosen profession, philosophy.[17]

In an earlier session Bruno had offered the inquisitors a summary of his understanding of nature, underscoring his conviction that the universe was infinite: the inevitable outpouring of the infinite divine power had to express itself in an infinite space, in which could be found worlds without number, similar to our earth.[18] We still sense something of the enthusiasm with which Bruno seized on this topic even in these dire circumstances, citing the Wisdom of Solomon, Virgil's *Aeneid*, and *Ecclesiastes*. The inquisitors showed little interest; they wanted to know about his denial of the Trinity. That there is in fact an intimate connection between these cosmological and religious themes is demonstrated by *The Ash Wednesday Supper*.

2

One of Bruno's targets in these dialogues is the sacrament of the Eucharist, which is caricatured in the work and reduced to a disgusting ceremony. The celebration of the Eucharist was one of the issues that then divided Catholics and Protestants and soon was to help precipitate the Thirty Years' War, with the Protestants insisting on communion in both kinds, bread and wine, the Catholics on bread alone. Bruno's caricature had to put any good Christian on edge:

Then, thank God, the ceremony of the cup did not take place. Usually the goblet or chalice passes from hand to hand all round the table, from top to bottom, from left to right, and in all directions with no order but that dictated by rough politeness and courtesy. After the leader of this dance has detached his lips, leaving a layer of grease which could easily be used as glue, another drinks and leaves a crumb of bread, another drinks and leaves a bit of meat on the rim, still another drinks and deposits a hair of his beard and, in this way, with a great mess, no one is so ill mannered, tasting the drink, as to omit leaving you some favor of the relics stuck to his moustache. If one does not want to drink, either because he has not the stomach or because he considers himself above it, he need merely touch the cup to his mouth so that he too can imprint on it the morsels of his lips. The meaning of all this is that, since all of them come together to make themselves into a flesh-eating wolf, to eat as with one body the lamb or kid or Grunnio Corocotta.[19] (pp. 126–127)

The suggestion is that only the most superficial kind of community is achieved by such a ceremony: the more essential, universal community of which Bruno dreamed and for which he lived and died has been totally missed. The argument between Protestants and Catholics, whether the communicant should partake of both bread and wine, or just of the bread, had to seem to him silly. Cusanus's call on all believers to rise above the perspectives that divided them is given a more radical, no longer Christian turn by Bruno's Hermetic humanism. But to continue with the caricature: "By applying each one his mouth to the selfsame tankard, they come to form themselves into one selfsame leech, in token of one community, one brotherhood, one plague, one heart, one stomach, one gullet and one mouth" (p. 127).

In the prefatory epistle Bruno had promised his readers that his Ash Wednesday Supper would not be a banquet of "leeches for a trifle" (p. 67): "You may well ask me: what symposium, what banquet is this? It is a supper. What supper? Of ashes. What does 'supper of ashes' mean? Has it perhaps taken place before? Can one properly say at this point: *cinerem tamquam panem manducabam?* No, but it is a banquet which begins after sunset on the first day of Lent, which our priests call *dies cinerum* and, sometimes, day of memento" (p. 68). The Latin words cite a line from Psalm 102, which are spoken by one whose "days pass away like smoke," who "eats ashes like bread, and mingles tears with my drink because of thy indignation and anger," yet looks forward to the day when the Lord will appear in his glory and build up Zion. But while Bruno, too, harbors similar expectations, he does not expect their fulfillment from the biblical God. His is a different deity.

When in his preface Bruno suggests that he is preparing for us with this work a higher supper, Plato's *Symposium* comes to mind, though Bruno says quite explicitly that this is not going to be the supper of Plato for philosophy. He has in mind a different kind of audience than Plato's symposiasts. In the positive description of his banquet Bruno makes a point of joining opposites: "This is a banquet so great and small, so professorial and student-like, so sacrilegious and religious, so joyous and choleric, so cruel and pleasant, so Florentine for its leanness and Bolognese for its fatness, so cynical and Sardanapalian, so trifling and serious, so grave and waggish, so tragic and comic that I surely believe there will be no few occasions for you to become heroic and humble; master and disciple; believer and unbeliever. . . ." (p. 67). Sacrilegious and religious this banquet certainly is— small wonder the Inquisition was concerned. Bruno's play with oppositions invites us to think of this as a banquet for those who have been impressed by Cusanus's doctrine of learned ignorance and the coincidence of opposites; and together with Copernicus, Cusanus (the divine Cusanus, as Bruno calls him) is one of the persons for whom he expresses great admiration.[20]

3

But just how are Bruno's Copernicanism and his attack on traditional dogmas related? What kind of a Copernican was Bruno? In the Third Dialogue Bruno has Nundinio, one of the derided Oxford academicians, take a position rather like Osiander's: "We must believe that Copernicus was not of the opinion that the earth moves, since this is unseemly and impossible, but that he attributed a motion to it rather than to the eighth heaven, for ease in calculations" (p. 136). Bruno's stand-in, the philosopher Teofilo, replies "that Doctor Torquato gave birth to this assertion; . . . because he was not ignorant of grammar he understood a certain prefatory epistle which was added by I know not what ignorant and conceited ass. [The latter] (as if he wanted to support the author by excusing him, or for the benefit of other asses who, finding grass and small fruit, would not put down the book without having eaten) gives this advice to them before they begin reading and considering its opinions" (p. 137). Bruno follows this with a long quote from Osiander's preface. As we have already seen, Gosselin and Lerner's claim that Bruno was probably the first to have realized that the preface was not by Copernicus cannot be accepted: those closer to Copernicus, such as Rheticus, knew right away that the preface was not his. A number of early owners of that work had indeed written Osiander's name into their copy of the book. This is how Kepler came to know the name of the real author. But Bruno had only the text, and in refutation of the authenticity of the preface he cites the dedication to the pope to which I referred earlier: "For Copernicus it did not suffice to say that the earth moves, but he also affirmed and asserted it in his dedicatory letter to the Pope. In this he wrote that the opinions of philosophers are very far from those of the common mob [whose opinions] are unworthy of being followed and most worthy of being avoided, since they are contrary to truth and to right thinking" (p. 138). We have here the turn away from common sense that was to become characteristic of the understanding of truth and reality that was to guide the new science.

Bruno, however, is eager to disclaim any authority, even that of Copernicus:

But in truth it signified little for the Nolan that the aforesaid [motion of the earth] had been stated, taught, and confirmed before him by Copernicus, Niceta Syracusus the Pythagorean, Philolaus, Heraclitus of Pontus, Hecphantus the Pythagorean, Plato in the *Timaeus* (where the author states his theory timidly and inconstantly, since he held it more by faith than by knowledge), and the divine Cusanus in the second book of *On Learned Ignorance*, and others in all sorts of first-rate discourses. For he [the Nolan] holds [the mobility of the earth] on other, more solid grounds of his own. On this basis, not by authority, but through keen perception and reason, he holds it just as certain as anything else of which he can have certainty. (p. 139)

What are these more solid grounds to which Bruno appeals? On closer inspection, some are already familiar; in other places his reasoning seems rather confused. Among the familiar reasons is the reflection on perspective, which for Bruno, too, leads the way to insight into the infinite. Here Cusanus is the obvious precursor:

Now, if we come to an understanding which is sufficiently wise and enlightened, so that we recognize that this apparent motion of the universe derives from the rotation of the earth, and if we consider, moreover, that the constitution of all the other bodies in the firmament is similar to that of this body [the principle of cosmic homogeneity], we will be able first to believe, and then to conclude rigorously, the contrary of that dream, that fantasy, that basic mistake which has given and will give rise to innumerable others. This error arises thus. From the center of [our] horizon, turning our eyes to all sides, we can reckon the magnitude of the distance from, between, and within those things which are fairly close to us; but, beyond a certain limit, all things appear equally distant. In the same way, if we look at the stars in the firmament, we will be able to distinguish the differences in motions and distances of some of the closer stars, but those which are farther or very far away will appear immobile and equally distant and far away as to distance. (pp. 203–204)

The supposed firmament of fixed stars is but a perspectival illusion. Bruno here, too, appeals to the traditional example of the moving ship, although he makes a different use of it:

This may be seen in the example of a very distant ship which, having covered a distance of thirty of forty yards, nonetheless appears to be stationary, as if it had not moved at all. Thus it is in proportion, considering greater distances, and the largest and most luminous bodies (of which it is possible that innumerable others are as large and luminous as the sun, and even more so). Their circles and motions, though very great, are not visible. Thus, even if it happens that some of these stars make some sort of approach [to the earth], we do not see it, except through the lengthiest observations; these have not been undertaken, not pursued, because no one has believed in, or looked for, or presupposed such motions; and we know that the beginning of inquiry is the knowledge and the understanding that the thing exists, or is possible and fitting, and that one may draw profit from [the inquiry]. (pp. 204–206)

Following Cusanus, Bruno explodes the much-enlarged but still finite cosmos of Copernicus. He not only explains why, on his understanding of the cosmos, appearances are as they are. He also offers an account of why we should not expect empirical evidence for the view he supports. Such evidence would come only from observations extending over a long period of time. But since no one had believed that such observations would yield anything interesting, there seemed to be no reason to make them. Before such evidence can be expected there has to be a thinker who shows that what is sought is plausible or possible. In this Bruno sees the significance of someone like himself; and we should note that the principle of cosmic homogeneity functions here as an axiom supported by an intellectual intuition that guides rather than follows scientific observation.

As a matter of fact, Bruno was rather cavalier about the details of his observations. This carelessness gets him into trouble when he tries to criticize Osiander:

That idiot, who so mightily feared that one could be driven mad by the teaching of Copernicus! I cannot imagine how he could have raised more absurdities than by stating with such solemnity and persuasive conviction that those who believe that [the earth moves] are grossly ignorant of optics and geometry. I would like to know what optics and geometry that beast means, [which] show only how excessively ignorant he himself and his teachers are of true optics and geometry. I would like to know how it is possible to deduce the reckoning of the propinquity and remoteness of luminous bodies from their size, and conversely, how it is possible to deduce the proportional variation of size of like bodies from their distance and propinquity. (pp. 139–140)

Bruno is referring to the following passage from Osiander's preface:

Perhaps there is someone who is so ignorant of geometry and optics that he regards the epicycle of Venus as probable, or thinks that it is the reason why Venus sometimes

THE CRIME OF BRUNO

precedes and sometimes follows the sun by forty degrees and even more. Is there any-one who is not aware that from this assumption it necessarily follows that the diameter of the planet in its perigee should appear more than four times, and the body of the planet more than sixteen times, as great as in the apogee, a result contradicted by the experience of every age? In this study there are other no less important absurdities.[21]

Osiander here advances an argument against those who would take Coper-nicus (and for that matter Ptolemy) too seriously. The supposed fact that Venus apparently retains pretty much the same size and brightness is taken to be incompatible with a consequence of the Copernican theory that would have the distance of Venus from the earth vary in such a way that we should expect significant variations in its apparent size and brightness.[22] Bruno takes for granted that there is no variation in the apparent brightness of Venus. But he denies that a variation in distance is necessarily related to a variation in apparent brightness. As a matter of fact, while the diameter of Venus and variations in that diameter cannot be detected by the naked eye, there is significant variation in the apparent brightness of Venus (which Os-iander seems to have overlooked, too). Furthermore, this change in the ap-parent brightness of Venus, known already to the ancients, is something predicted by the Ptolemaic system as well as the Copernican.

Bruno demonstrates here his disdain for mathematics. "Reflected and straight rays, acute and obtuse angles, perpendicular, incident, and plane lines, larger or smaller arcs: aspects such as these are mathematical circum-stances and not natural causes. It is one thing to play with geometry and another to verify with nature" (p. 208). Mathematics he considered too insignificant to occupy a mature thinker, and so he reproached Euclid and Archimedes for having wasted their time in intellectual games, when more important matters demanded their attention.[23] That Bruno dedicated to Emperor Rudolf a book bearing the provocative title *Articuli adversus Mathematicos* speaks for itself.[24] To be sure, the work was illustrated with geometrical figures—interspersed with alchemical symbols. To the mathe-matics of the mathematicians he opposed his Hermetic mathesis.[25]

As his so often confused and confusing argumentation in *The Ash Wednes-day Supper* shows, Bruno was not very careful with his reasoning; he was hardly a scientist in the mold of Copernicus or Galileo. The certainty with which he holds the Copernican position seems to have little to do with scientific evidence. His cosmological speculations supported by an intellectual intuition appear to put Bruno closer to Cusanus than to Copernicus. Indeed, with his view of the infinity of the cosmos he takes a decisive step beyond Cusanus, for Cusanus thought that God alone deserved to be called infinite in the full sense of the term. The cosmos was understood by him as only a created or finite infinite, unlimited rather than truly infinite. Bruno no longer has such reservations; the universe is infinite in the full sense of the term, as ancient wisdom already recognized: "Now, Heraclitus, Epicurus, Parmenides, and Melissus understood this point concerning bodies in the ethereal region, as the fragments we possess make manifest to us. In [these fragments] one can see that they recognized an infinite space, an infinite region, infinite matter, and infinite capacity for innumerable worlds similar to this one, rounding their circles as the earth rounds its own" (p. 206). We should note the dynamism suggested by this conception of the cosmos as a process creating infinite worlds over and over again.

But just what is the relation between this cosmology and the charges that the Inquisition was raising against Bruno—that he was a heretic who disclaimed central tenets of the Catholic faith, and that he was a political troublemaker who threatened the established order? Consider once more one obvious consequence of the cosmology that has been advanced: according to it there are no privileged places in the cosmos. Certainly the earth is not such a privileged place. But what sense can we then make of the Incarnation? Denial of the Incarnation was one of the key charges raised against Bruno. And just as there are no geographically privileged places for Bruno, so, it would seem, there are no historically privileged places. Does it make any more sense to speak of a beginning or end of history than it does to speak of a beginning or end of space? Again the question arises: what sense can we then make of the Incarnation and Crucifixion? Here we come to the heart of what must have troubled the authorities about Bruno. It would appear that in Bruno's mind his rejection of Christianity and his espousal of the Copernican system, which he expanded into the infinite cosmos, were inseparably bound together.

4

As we have seen, the often-repeated description of Bruno as the first martyr of the Copernican revolution is difficult to defend. I have already discussed some aspects of Bruno's trial and death. In hindsight both seem to provide his restless life with a tragic but strangely fitting conclusion. Bruno was born the son of a soldier in 1548 in Nola near Naples—hence he calls himself with pride and affection the Nolan.[26] In 1563 he entered the convent of San Domenico Maggiore in Naples, the same convent where Thomas Aquinas had once lectured and is buried, and assumed the name Giordano. No doubt he made good use of the convent's impressive library, as Campanella was to do a quarter century later. Already at this early stage he appears to have been suspected of heresy. Still, he was ordained a priest in 1572 and became a doctor of theology in 1575—not that he was ever happy in that role. Further study in theology convinced him of the sterility of much theological speculation. He read forbidden authors such as Erasmus, whose works he is said to have hid in his privy, and, a far more serious charge, he is said to have shown sympathy for the Arian heresy that denied the divinity of Christ.[27] Heretical thoughts would thus seem to have antedated his cosmological interests.

When a trial on charges of heresy was being prepared against him, he shed his monk's habit and fled to Rome, where he soon was accused of murder. The charge was apparently unfounded, but facing yet another examination he fled Rome after just two months, in April 1576. He started his long wandering, passing through a number of northern Italian towns. After a brief foray into France, he ended up in Geneva, where he was converted to Calvinism—only to make himself unpopular by attacking Antoine de la Faye, a leading Calvinist professor. Once again he was arrested, excommunicated, and rehabilitated when he retracted. But by then he had had enough of Geneva: he decided to leave that city, and the city fathers, probably relieved, let him go. He then journeyed through France, hoping to be received back into the Catholic Church, without success. But first in Toulouse and later in Paris he finally found a congenial climate and was given a minor position at the court of Henry III, who was himself trying to steer a difficult course between the Catholic and Protestant factions that were threatening to tear France (indeed Europe) apart. While in Paris, he published works on the art of memory and a comedy indicting Neapolitan society *(Il Candelaio)*. In 1583 he went to England, with an introductory letter from Henry III to Michel Castelnau, marquis de Mauvissière and the French ambassador at Queen Elizabeth's court. Bruno himself was to hint at having been entrusted with a secret mission.

Bruno arrived in time to participate at Oxford in a debate on Copernicus that had been ordered by the queen in honor of the visiting Polish prince Albert Laski.[28] But Bruno, the Copernican enthusiast, did not distinguish himself; he was in fact accused by his opponents of not knowing his Copernicus. Soon he was to avenge himself for that hostile reception with his vitriolic caricature of Oxford scholars in *The Ash Wednesday Supper*. Whatever hopes he may have had of securing for himself a professorship were dashed, though for a time at least he did find in the household of the French ambassador as much of a home and security as he would ever enjoy. While it lasted, Bruno was amazingly productive: this period saw the publication of not just *The Ash Wednesday Supper* but a considerable number of works on astronomy, morals, religion, and other topics. But Bruno's good fortune did not last long. In the fall of 1585 the ambassador was recalled to France and there was no one to take his place. So Bruno returned to Paris.

By then the climate in the French capital had changed. The king had abrogated his policy of accepting and living in peace with the Protestants, and Bruno soon made himself unpopular by attacking some of the figures on the Catholic side. So he left for Germany, where we find him lecturing and publishing a number of pamphlets, including his *One Hundred Sixty Articles*, in which (once more following in the footsteps of Cusanus?) he pleads for the peaceful coexistence of all religions and for free and reciprocal discussion— ever on the lookout for a university appointment that would give him the freedom to teach and publish what he thought needed to be heard. And so we find him passing through Marburg on his way to Wittenberg, where he met at first with a friendly reception and stayed for twenty months, before the Calvinists, who by then had gained the upper hand over the Lutherans, caused him to leave in March 1588. He looked for greener pastures in the Prague of Emperor Rudolph II, patron of so many magi. But here, too, he found it impossible to secure a more permanent position; and on he went to Helmstedt, where he once again managed to offend the academic establishment. This time it was the Lutherans who excommunicated him, although he found a protector in Heinrich Julius, duke of Brunswick. In Helmstedt he wrote Latin poems, developing his atomic theory of matter. After a year and a half the restless Bruno went to Frankfurt to publish them. The senate of the city denied his request for permission to stay, but he found refuge in a Carmelite convent, even though, as the prior said of Bruno, he did not possess a trace of faith.[29] He was in Frankfurt when Giovanni Mocenigo's fateful invitation to come to Venice reached him.

Bruno thus lived the unruly life of an intellectual drifter; and in a way, that life was in keeping with his understanding of space, which denies that there are any privileged places. Like so many at the time, Bruno felt that an age was coming to an end, that a new and much better age was about to begin. The heliocentrism of Copernicus was understood by Bruno as a figure of the dawn of a new age.

> Please tell me, what opinion you have of Copernicus?
>
> Teo [filo]: He was a man of deep, developed, diligent, and mature genius; a man not second to any astronomer before him except in order of succession and time; a man who, in regard to innate intellect was greatly superior to Ptolemy, Hipparchus, Eudoxus, and all others who followed in their footsteps. . . . Who then, will be so rude and discourteous toward the labors of this man as to forget how much he accomplished, and not consider that he was ordained by the gods to be the dawn which must precede the rising of the sun of the ancient and true philosophy, for so many centuries entombed in the dark caverns of blind, spiteful, arrogant, and envious ignorance? (pp. 86–87)

The self-understanding expressed in this praise of Copernicus is characteristic of the start of modernity: a new age is beginning. The night of the Middle Ages is coming to an end. We are witnessing a new dawn. Recall that the term "Middle Ages" was first used by Giovanni de Bussi in his eulogy for Cusanus, given shortly after the cardinal's death. Particularly, important in the passage by Bruno are the cyclical implications of the sun metaphor. The metaphor itself is Platonic, but heliocentrism is given a Hermetic turn by Bruno: had Copernicus himself not invoked the authority of Hermes Trismegistus? Frances A. Yates thus takes Bruno to have been "an intense religious Hermetist, a believer in the magical religion of the Egyptians as described in the *Asclepius*, the imminent return of which he prophesied in England, taking the Copernican sun as a portent in the sky of this imminent return."[30] Bruno does not hesitate to give the Copernican revolution a figural reading: is he not himself the new sun?

The quoted text thus leads to a self-congratulatory passage in which Bruno compares his own achievement with that of Columbus and other explorers:

[If these men are so praised,] how shall we honor this man [the Nolan] who has found the way to ascend to the sky, compass the circumference of the stars, and leave at his back the convex surface of the firmament? The helmsmen of explorations have discovered how to disturb everybody else's peace, [how to] violate the native spirits of the [diverse] regions, [how to] mingle together that which provident nature had kept separate; [how] by intercourse to redouble defects and to add to old vices the new vices of other peoples, with violence to propagate new follies and to plant unheard-of inanities where they did not before exist, so that he who is strongest comes to conclude that he is wisest. They showed new ways, instruments, and arts for tyrannizing and murdering each other. The time will come when, in consequence of all this, those men, having learned at their own expense (through the way things turn out), will know how to and will be able to return to us similar and worse fruits of such pernicious inventions. (pp. 88–89)

We meet here with the premonition of a time when Europe will no longer be able to assert its hegemony over the world, when all the mischief it has wrought will be revisited on it. Bruno describes his own achievement in very different terms:

The Nolan, in order to cause completely opposite effects, has freed the human mind and the knowledge which were shut up in the strait prison of the turbulent air. Hardly could the mind gaze at the most distant stars as if through some few peepholes, and its wings were clipped so that it could not soar and pierce the veil of the clouds to see what was actually there. . . . By approving and confirming the misty darkness of the sophists and blockheads, they extinguished the light which made the minds of our ancient fathers divine and heroic. Therefore human reason, so long oppressed, now and

again in a lucid interval laments her base condition to the divine and provident Mind
that ever whispers in her inner ear, responding in suchlike measures:

> Who will mount for me, O Madonna, to the sky,
>
> And bring back thence my lost wisdom?
>
> [*Orlando Furioso*]

Now behold, the man [the Nolan] who has surmounted the air, penetrated the sky,
wandered among the stars, passed beyond the borders of the world, [who has] ef-
faced the imaginary walls of the first, eighth, tenth spheres, and the many more you
could add according to the tattlings of empty mathematicians and the blind vision of
vulgar philosophers. (pp. 89–90)

The Nolan's achievement is supposed to bring about a completely different
effect from that produced by the explorers, who showed no respect for diversity; in their greed clothed in orthodoxy they did violence to other cul-
tures, other beliefs. We meet here with a much more radical version of that
concordantia catholica, or *pax fidei*, which Cusanus had earlier struggled to realize. In both cases there is an intimate connection between a cosmological
vision and the plans for pacifying of warring factions.

5

I have emphasized the theme of liberation: the new age whose dawn Copernicus is taken to figure is an age of enlightenment and, by the same token,
of freedom. Human relations will be based no longer on power but on free
discussion, born of respect for the differences that inevitably divide persons
and nations insofar as they find themselves in different situations.[31] Bruno's
vision is one of unity in diversity.

We should keep in mind the ambivalence of such a post-Copernican
vision. As I pointed out in the introductory chapter, while there were those
who, like Bruno, rejoiced in the way the cosmos seemed to have opened up,
who felt that they had been released from a prison, many more felt that they
had been cast out into an inhospitable expanse. And this ambivalence extends to Bruno's vision of history. A cyclical view of history is implied by
Bruno's use of the sun metaphor: history is like an endless succession of
nights and days. As he wrote in the album of the University of Wittenberg
in 1586 under the title *Salomon et Pythagoras*:

Quid est quod est?

    Ipsum quod fuit.

Quid est quod fuit?

    Ipsum quod est.

Nihil sub sole novum.[32]

As already pointed out, it is impossible to reconcile such insistence—that what is is what was, that what was is what is, that there is nothing new under the sun—with the Christian understanding of history, which to Bruno must have been subject to the same blindness that prevented geocentrists from recognizing the achievement of Copernicus. But we must also keep in mind that Bruno claims to be beyond Copernicus: Copernicus, after all, represents only the dawn, while Bruno belongs to the day. And in astronomy the shift from dawn to day would seem to mean the shift from a heliocentric cosmos to one that knows no center and therefore generates a tolerance for infinitely many centers. Bruno's cosmos is not a system. If one wants to understand it as a political metaphor, then the politics appropriate to it would have to do away with the absolutist state. Bruno's cosmological paradigm calls for a withering away of the state.

Such an understanding of space and time also makes it difficult to speak of the age whose coming Bruno awaited so impatiently as the millennium. Millennial thinking conceives of a succession of ages culminating in a final and golden age in which history reaches its fulfillment and comes to an end, an age in which the historical process is so to speak redeemed. Such millennial ideas were common in the Middle Ages. Joachim of Fiore thus thought history in terms of three ages—the age of the Father, the Son, and the Holy Spirit—marking the progressive descent of the divine into the human. Mediated by Lessing, Hegel's understanding of the progress of history still owes a great deal to this millennial schema, as does the thinking of Marx.

In the past millennium such eschatological ideas have resurfaced again and again.[33] They flourished especially in the years just preceding 1600, thought to "be particularly important," as Yates points out, "owing to the numerological significance of nine and seven, the sum of which is sixteen. In the coming dispensation there will be established a better religious cult and better moral laws, both based on nature and natural religion."[34] Tomaso

Campanella saw himself as the Messiah of this new age, and his dreams of a democratic, God-centered republic inspired Calabrian peasants to revolt against the Spanish authorities in 1598 and 1599.[35] As Yates suggests, it is difficult not to see a connection between Campanella's imprisonment and torture in Naples and his fellow Dominican's execution in Rome.

Bruno's thinking, however, is more pagan (he might have said, more truly Hermetic) than that of Campanella. Bruno does not anticipate Hegel, who would have us understand Descartes as the sailor who finally reaches terra firma. According to Bruno there can be no terra firma. That is true of the cosmos, and it remains true when the thought is extended to history. With this declaration, however, the promise of a final golden age is put into question; and just as there is something terrifying about the infinite cosmos, so there is something terrifying about this vision of history, which knows only the unending and therefore finally pointless succession of dark and light.

Bruno's rejection of terra firma also suggests that we should think perspectival illusion not just with respect to particular places, but also with respect to particular times. We can thus speak of the Copernican revolution being raised to a higher level, or perhaps being transposed into a different key. This transposition holds true not just for the vision of the cosmos that Bruno gives us, but also for the historical vision of which we get glimpses. We can say: just as the eye is subjected to its spatial location, so reason is subjected to its temporal location. Bruno invites us to struggle against both.

Bruno's world is rather like that of Cusanus, yet there is a decisive difference, as we have seen: according to Cusanus the infinity of the cosmos is not infinity in the full sense of the word. From the absolute infinity of God the created infinity of the cosmos remains infinitely distant. Behind that insistence lies the thought that God is unable to create anything equal to himself, just as he is not capable of doing away with himself. According to this traditional view, God's creativity does not exhaust itself in what he creates. God could have created many things that he did not will to create. Creation, on that view, is radically contingent. Bruno challenges such views and relies instead on what Arthur Lovejoy in *The Great Chain of Being* calls the principle of plenitude.[36] On this view creation is the full manifestation of the infinite divine essence. In keeping with that infinity, creation had to be itself infinite. All that God could create he did create. A voluntarist conception of an all-powerful deity is here rejected. Rejected, too, is the idea of the contingency of the world: creation could not have been other than it is. The universe comes to be understood as the fully adequate self-reproduction of God. Creation is thus the necessary unfolding of the infinite divine essence. There is no place in this vision for a personal creator. Nor is there a need or even a place for the Incarnation, as Bruno was ready to tell the inquisitors.[37]

According to Cusanus the Incarnation provides the human being with a measure, as it provides history with its center and fulcrum. Bruno's intuition of an infinite cosmos, thought as the completely adequate unfolding of the divine essence, so adequate indeed that the difference between God and the cosmos all but disappears, cannot be accepted by such a religion. And we should not think that only Christianity finds the thesis of infinite worlds incompatible with its beliefs. In this connection Blumenberg quotes the Jewish scholar Franz Rosenzweig, who insists on the absolute incompatibility of such a view and all revealed religion, arguing that the difference between pagan thought and any revealed religion is "that for pagan thinking there are many worlds and possibilities, reasons and accidents, for [revealed religion] everything is given only in one exemplar. For revelation founds an up and a down, a Europe and an Asia, as it founds an earlier and a later, a past and a future. The infinite descends to earth and from the place of its descent it draws boundaries in the ocean of space and in the river of time."[38] It was precisely his insight into the necessity of such a descent that led Cusanus to place such emphasis on his Christology. Bruno returns to what Rosenzweig considers a pagan view, although his pathos of infinity cannot be understood without the prehistory of Christian speculation on the infinity of God.

The following passage underscores the Hermetic animism bound up with Bruno's vision of the cosmos:

I take it as understood that not otherwise than in animals which we recognize as such, its parts [of the universe] are always in continuous alteration and movement and have a certain ebb and flow, always absorbing something from the exterior and emanating something from the interior: just as the nails grow, the fur, wool and hair feed, skins mend and hides harden; so, in the same way, the earth receives the efflux and influx of the parts through which many living beings (manifest to us as such) show us their life in a different way. Thus it is more than plausible that, since everything participates in life, many and innumerable beings live not only within us but also in all composite things; and when we see something which is said to die, we must not believe that that thing dies but rather that it changes and terminates its accidental composition and unity, since the things which we see incurring death always remain immortal. This is even more true of the so-called spiritual entities than of the so-called material and corporeal ones, as we will show at some other time.[39] (pp. 156–157)

Such a view of the cosmos, which has one root in Plato's *Timaeus*, makes it difficult to take the individual, and therefore to take death and the need for salvation, very seriously. In proto-Nietzschean fashion, Bruno overcomes the sense of contingency and the nihilism associated with it precisely by denying the existence of a personal God. The other side of this denial is the deification of the cosmos, which is described with adjectives once reserved for God: it is now said to be necessary. But along with this necessity goes an understanding of the cosmos as a dynamic state that knows no final satisfaction. The life of the individual is but an accidental configuration of simpler substances, a superficial phenomenon, transitory and quite insignificant.

6

It should have become clear just how this vision of the cosmos and Bruno's denial of central dogmas are tied together. Consider once more the dogma of the Incarnation that Bruno had challenged already as a young monk and that was at issue in his final condemnation. We should keep in mind what dignity that dogma could give to man: recall the passage from the reformer Melanchthon that I cited in the previous chapter. Christian humanism draws on this doctrine. Bruno's vision of the cosmos threatens to undercut not only the doctrine of the Incarnation but every anthropocentrism. But with this the Copernican revolution has to call itself into question, for it depends on the cognitive confidence that is inseparable from an anthropocentric bias. In this respect, too, we are reminded of Nietzsche and of the tale that introduces "On Truth and Lie in an Extra-Moral Sense," which deserves repetition in this context:

Once upon a time, in some out of the way corner of that universe which is dispersed into numberless twinkling solar systems, there was a star upon which clever beasts invented knowing. That was the most arrogant and mendacious minute of "world history," but nevertheless, it was only a minute. After nature had drawn a few breaths, the star cooled and congealed, and the clever beasts had to die.[40]

Bruno might have added that this gives still much too much significance and uniqueness to the event. The tale would have been better told had Nietzsche spoken not of the most arrogant and mendacious minute, in the pathetic superlative, but of a happening that repeats itself over and over again.

1

In chapter 12 I asked: what are the conditions that according to Copernicus allow one to claim truth for a theory in astronomy? I pointed to two such conditions:

1. It must "save the appearances"; that is, it must be supported by observation.

2. It must be in accord with what is understood to be the essence of nature. In Copernicus's language: it must be in accord with the axioms or principles that are accepted as certain because based on an understanding of that essence. That is, science must be given its foundation in a metaphysics of nature.

When we judge Copernicus's theory by his own criteria, it obviously does not fare very well. His understanding of the essence of nature, with its insistence on uniform, circular motion, was soon rejected; and the available observations, too, did not argue strongly for his system rather than the Ptolemaic. The fundamental insight of Copernicus continued to lack anything like adequate observational support until the discoveries of Galileo; and only with the development of physics, culminating in Newton's work, was there a determination of the essence of nature that provided something approximating the sort of foundation that Copernicus demanded.

But to return to the question of observational support, we see some as early as the observations of Tycho Brahe. Thus his observation of a new star showed that there was change in the superlunar realm, dealing a severe blow to the Aristotelian theory of nature. Of similar significance was his demonstration that the comets had to break through the shells of the old cosmology, although this demonstration was not always accepted. Indeed we find Galileo still defending with unwarranted vehemence the sublunar character of the comets. Still, it was Galileo who, more than anyone else, provided the Copernican theory with observational support when his discovery of the moons of Jupiter seemed to offer a miniature model of the solar system.[1]

2

But here I want to focus less on Galileo than on the telescope, and more generally on the extent to which the development of modern science depended on instruments. Think of the clock, the scale, the thermometer, and the like. The potential importance of quantification and therefore of such instruments had already been recognized by Cusanus in his little dialogue *De Staticis Experimentis*. The development of these instruments serves the demand for ever more precise quantification. The conviction that such quantification helps us get closer to the truth presupposes a determination of the essence of nature such as the famous one that Galileo gives us in *The Assayer* (1623):

Philosophy is written in this grand book, the universe, which stands continually open to our gaze. But the book cannot be understood unless one first learns to comprehend such language and read the letters in which it is composed. It is written in the language of mathematics and its characters are triangles, circles, and other geometric figures without which it is humanly impossible to understand a single word of it; without these, one wanders about in a dark labyrinth.[2]

Note once more the anthropocentrism of this view. God wrote the book of nature in such a way that we human beings might understand it: mathematics provides us with proper access to nature.

I have mentioned the clock and scale. The telescope and microscope are instruments of quite another sort: they promise to extend the power of human vision, to remedy its natural deficiency. They answer to a hope that human beings might actually see the real makeup of the cosmos. That such hope is not vain is suggested by Galileo in *The Starry Messenger* (1610):

Here we have a fine and elegant argument for quieting the doubts of those who, while accepting with tranquil mind the revolutions of the planets about the sun in the Copernican system, are mightily disturbed to have the moon alone revolve about the earth and accompany it in an annual rotation about the sun. Some have believed that this structure of the universe should be rejected as impossible. But now we have not just one planet rotating about another while both run through a great orbit around the sun; our own eyes show us four stars which wander around Jupiter as does the moon around the earth, while all together trace out a grand revolution about the sun in the space of twelve years.[3]

Galileo's hope to actually see the makeup of the cosmos is common in this period. Remember Joseph Glanvill's suggestion in *The Vanity of Dogmatizing* (1661) that Adam was able to see the truth of the heliocentric position; that he "needed no spectacles . . . '[T]is not unlikely that he had a clear perception of the earths motion, as we think we have of its quiescence."[4] Adam was a natural Copernican. He is thought to have seen what we must recover with our art. But note also that our technology has given us eyes that are in an important way better than Adam's: with the aid of instruments, we moderns see more. The Fall has been undone by technological invention. "Galilaeus without a crime out-saw all Antiquity; and was not afraid to believe his eyes, in spite of the Opticks of Ptolemy and Aristotle."[5] We should note that Glanvill recognizes the possibility of transgression, but he also declares there was no crime. That Galileo, too, was worried about such a construction of his achievement is clear from that passage in *The Starry Messenger* where he speaks of his invention:

But what surpasses all wonders by far, and what particularly moves us to seek the attention of all astronomers and philosophers, is the discovery of four wandering stars not known or observed by any man before us. Like Venus and Mercury, which have their own periods around the sun, these have theirs about a certain star that is conspicuous among those already known, which they sometimes precede and sometimes follow, without ever departing from it beyond certain limits. All these facts were discovered and observed by me not many days ago with the aid of a spyglass which I devised, after first being illuminated by divine grace.[6]

Galileo is thus eager to present his "discovery" of the telescope as a divine gift. We should recall that Descartes, too, thought it important to present his method as such a gift. As a matter of fact, as Galileo continues to tell his readers, his discovery of the telescope was really a rediscovery: "About ten months ago a report reached my ears that a certain Fleming had constructed a spyglass by means of which visible objects, though very distant from the eye of the observer, were distinctly seen as if nearby."[7] Galileo goes on to describe how he then took a pipe of lead, at the ends of which he fixed a convex and concave lens. He perfected this first telescope until he achieved a magnification of more than thirty times.

What then did the tube show? How did it transform popular opinion? Let me quote from *The Vanity of Dogmatizing*.

That the Heavens are void of corruption is Aristotle's supposal: But the Tube hath betray'd their impurity; and Neoterick Astronomy has found spots in the Sun. The discoveries made in Venus, and the Moon, disprove the Antique Quintessence; and evidence them as coarse materials, as the Globe we belong to. The Perspicil, as well as the Needle, hath enlarged the habitable World; and that the Moon is an Earth, is no improbable conjecture.[8]

The hope here is that the telescope is part of the story of mankind's coming of age—recall Bruno's praise of Copernicus as the dawn of a new day. It is a thought Glanvill shares with Descartes and Bacon. The telescope is to free us from the limitations imposed on us by our spatial location coupled with the weakness of our vision.

As a matter of fact, the telescope could not fulfill such expectations. As distances were overcome, new and much greater distances opened up; instead of granting a new security, the instrument added to the sense of insecurity. Descartes was thus to insist that only the turn back to the self can give us a true terra firma, a true center. Osiander would no doubt have thought this an expression of pride: true security is to be found only in God, who is the true center of the cosmos and of our existence.

3

In the invention of instruments like the telescope the early modern period saw, quite rightly, one way in which the moderns had outdone the ancients. The question of why the ancients did not invent the telescope is indeed interesting. Its inventor had to suspect the fundamental inadequacy of the human eye. Suppose you were convinced of the adequacy of your sight: there would be no reason to improve it. Or suppose you were convinced of the inadequacy of your eyes, but thought that condition to be a given, perhaps ordained as part of the punishment for Adam's fall. Again attempts to improve human vision would be unlikely, in this case because they would suggest pride. The invention of the telescope thus presupposes an awareness of the imperfection of our eyes; an awareness of what, given our present condition, escapes our vision; an awareness that the now visible is only a small part of the potentially visible—and also a conviction that the eyes' present condition is corrigible.

Skepticism and the telescope are thus linked. In the "Apology for Raymond Sebond," Montaigne considers whether we might be missing senses. Would we, for example, know that we lacked a sense of sight, if all of us had been born without it? Is the human being placed in a particularly favorable position to observe the universe? Are our sense organs particularly adequate? And what about human reason? The very fact that the Copernican system could effectively challenge the Ptolemaic, that Luther could challenge the traditional faith, that a Paracelsus could offer a new science of medicine intended to overthrow that of the ancients, shows to Montaigne the lack of clear, compelling evidence to settle such matters. Crucial to such skepticism is a thought he shares with Copernicus: the insight into the eccentric position of the human observer and knower. But, as I pointed out, part of the humanist faith of Copernicus is the confidence that this place is not a prison. And to this confidence Galileo adds another certainty, that the inadequacy of our senses need not be accepted as a natural condition: we can take steps to improve ourselves. The thought of the corrigibility of human nature is thus closely linked to the idea of real progress, and this faith in progress has helped shape the modern world.

The Aristotelian and Ptolemaic view of the cosmos had presupposed that the eye is able to reach the very limits of the cosmos, the firmament that enclosed all. The boundaries of the visible world were also the boundary of the real. But should one not look at the firmament as a perspectival illusion, as Bruno suggests, following Cusanus? The traditional cosmology had a ready answer to such questions: the firmament was needed to impart its motion to the subordinate spheres. But the Copernican revolution in astronomy also implies a rejection of the Aristotelian theory of motion. The firmament is no longer necessary. Thomas Digges thus extends the Copernican universe and makes it infinite.

Galileo could pity Copernicus because he did not live long enough to see the proof of his system. And yet, if the universe is infinite, do we ever get closer to grasping it as a totality? Will we ever escape from perspectival appearance? Is reality not in its very essence invisible, something to be grasped by the spirit and not by the eye? Galileo's confidence in the eye is thus suspect, and such suspicion could voice arguments as old as Plato. And, as I pointed out in chapter 6, attempts to improve the eye—to construct glasses, let alone instruments like microscopes and telescopes—had to seem to many an arrogant transgression of what God himself had ordained. In *The Starry Messenger* Galileo dismisses such doubts.

4

But what did Galileo see with his telescope?

First, he greatly increased the number of fixed stars, thereby showing that what is visible for us does not exhaust the limits of the potentially visible. The visible becomes an island in the potentially visible. And perhaps even the potentially visible is but an island in a reality whose greatest part may remain forever invisible. We have here an important contribution to that progressive dissociation of the real and the visible that I suggested is part of our modern understanding of reality.

Second, Galileo showed the moon to have an earthlike surface, with mountains and plains. This discovery provided empirical support for the belief in cosmic homogeneity already prominent in Cusanus's *On Learned Ignorance*. Consider this statement from *The Starry Messenger:* "Hence if anyone wished to revive the old Pythagorean opinion that the moon is like another earth, its brighter part might very fitly represent the surface of the land and its darker region that of water."[9] Clearly it is difficult to reconcile this thesis of cosmic homogeneity with Scripture, as a letter Giovanni Ciampoli wrote to Galileo, reporting on a conversation he had just had with Cardinal Barberini, makes evident:

Your opinion regarding the phenomena of light and shadow in the bright and dark spots of the moon creates some analogy between the lunar globe and the earth; someone expands on this and says that you place human inhabitants on the moon; the next fellow starts to dispute how these can be descended from Adam, or how they could have come of Noah's ark, and many other extravagances you never dreamed of.[10]

Among the dogmas difficult to square with the thesis of cosmic homogeneity is, as we have seen, that of the Incarnation. As Galileo understood cosmic homogeneity, it meant above all an upgrading of the earth from its former lowly position to the level of the stars.

Galileo says he will refute "those who argue that the earth must be excluded from the dancing whirl of stars for the specific reason that it is devoid of motion and of light. We shall prove the earth to be a wonderful body surpassing the moon in splendor, and not the sink of all dull refuse of the universe; this we shall support by an infinitude of arguments drawn from nature."[11] We should remember here that for a Christian Aristotelian, "up" meant better. The center of the system was also a place of evil, of the devil. There is a sense in which the medieval conception of the cosmos can be called diabolocentric. Galileo understands himself as arguing against such diabolocentrism.

A third discovery, less momentous in its implications, is the recognition that the Milky Way is just a conglomeration of stars. Galileo suggests that what had been called "nebulous stars" are a similar conglomeration. Again, better observation supports the thesis of cosmic homogeneity.

Finally, and what seems to Galileo by far the most important, is his discovery of the moons of Jupiter—or, as he called them in honor of his patron-to-be, the Medicean planets. In reporting on their discovery Galileo warned his readers that they would be able to duplicate his observations only if in possession of an instrument as good as his. A hostile reader might have taken this warning as an attempt to forestall criticism.

Kepler tells of his confused feelings when he receives the news that Galileo had discovered four new planets. He had argued in his *Mysterium Cosmographicum* that the spheres of the planets were separated by the five regular Euclidean bodies, which meant that there could be only six planets.[12] The young Kepler had indeed once toyed with the idea of other planets— one between Jupiter and Mars, another between Mercury and Venus—but had given up on the notion. Hearing a sketchy report about four new planets and relying on the principle of homogeneity, Kepler now jumps to the conclusion that every planet must have its own satellite, Mercury's being too small and close to the sun to be visible. On reading Galileo's text, he assumes that there must be other such moons and attempts to think up a principle that would account for their distribution. Here, too, scientific speculation is governed by certain assumptions concerning the makeup of the cosmos.

Kepler's response should be compared with that of the head of the department of philosophy at the University of Padua, the much-maligned Cesare Cremonini, who was in fact a friend of Galileo. In a letter of May 6, 1611, he wrote that he would not look through the telescope; it would only confuse him. Giulio Libri, Galileo's colleague both at Padua and Pisa, took the same position, declaring the observations impossible. After Libri's death Galileo expressed the hope that the philosopher who had refused to look at the newly discovered planets during his life would see them at least on his way to heaven.

But how justified is Galileo's appeal to the eye? Did he himself not have doubts about the eye's reliability? Consider once more Galileo's refusal to acknowledge that comets were, as Tycho Brahe had demonstrated them to be, superlunar phenomena, rather like planets. Galileo had no room for Kepler's ellipses. In *The Assayer* he thus attacks those who want to make comets into planets and accuses them of trying to create facts simply by the power of the word: "If their opinions and their voices have the power of calling into existence the things they name, then I beg them to do me the favor of naming a lot of hardware I have about my house 'gold.' But names aside, what attributes induced them to regard the comet as a quasi-planet for a time?"[13] Galileo's own view was that these objects arose from the earth, being produced by terrestrial vapors rising up into the sky, and finally dissolved at immense distances. What is interesting in this connection is that here Galileo himself argues against reliance on evidence presented to the senses:

Your Excellency will note the great confidence which Sarsi places in the sense of sight, deeming it impossible for us to be deceived by a spurious object whenever that may be placed besides a real one. I confess that I do not possess such a perfect faculty of discrimination. I am more like the monkey that firmly believed he saw another monkey in a mirror, and the image seemed so real and alive to him that he discovered his error only after running behind the glass to catch the other monkey.[14]

We see only images, appearances. Before we can claim truth for them, we need a theory that accounts for their appearing as they do. And yet in *The Starry Messenger* Galileo himself appeals above all to the eye, aided by an instrument, without supplying the theory that would explain the telescope's effectiveness, as Kepler was to do with his optics. What justified Galileo's trust in the telescope? There is tension in Galileo's attitude toward the eye.

5

It has become fashionable to speak of the Platonism of Galileo and of the new science. We owe this view especially to Ernst Cassirer,[15] and there certainly is something right about it: I suggested that one of the main obstacles standing in the way of modern science was Aristotle's philosophy of nature and it is also true that Plato with his emphasis on mathematics offered a more congenial approach. Recall that passage from Galileo's *Assayer* that claims that "philosophy is written in this grand book, the universe." To write this book God used the language of mathematics. Plato, to be sure, would have had some difficulty with this passage, which better fits Pythagoras. As Cassirer points out, Plato did not think that philosophy was written in nature; much of his philosophy seems in fact to circumvent nature. Think of his Socrates, who regretted the time he had spent studying the philosophy of nature with Anaxagoras. Plato's doctrine of recollection teaches that within itself the mind finds access to the invisible cosmos of the ideas. Implicit in Platonism is thus a tendency to downgrade the material world, which is of course informed by the Forms—as shown by the creation account in the *Timaeus*—but also always offers resistance to such formation.

In the material world the Forms are never completely victorious. Plato thinks in terms of the opposition of matter and form, an opposition that easily leads to a certain demonization of the material and sensuous, which is seen as a force that alienates us from our true spiritual home and drags us down into time.

On just this point there is a decisive difference between the Christian and the Platonic vision of nature. If God is omnipotent, if he is the creator of all that is, then there can be nothing outside and resisting his creative power. And thus if, as Plato thought, God is a geometer, must not matter too be geometrical in its very essence? So Kepler could insist that "Where there is matter, there is geometry."[16] Closely related to this claim is Galileo's understanding of nature as a book written in the language of mathematics. There is, however, an important difference: Kepler's God is not only a geometer but also a musician who created the universe as a harmonious whole.[17] To understand the cosmos we have to attend to its music. In Galileo's science such music had no place. Only careful observation and experiment could open the book of nature.

What was it that bothered the Inquisition about Galileo's views? We should keep in mind that Pope Urban VIII, before becoming pope, had known Galileo in Florence and had admired the man and his work. In the meantime, to be sure, Copernicus's *De Revolutionibus* had been put on the Index of forbidden books. According to Maurice Finocchiaro, the pope

interpreted the decree of the Index to mean that the earth's motion was a dangerous doctrine whose study and discussion required special care and vigilance. He thought the theory could never be proved to be necessarily true, and here it is interesting to mention his favorite argument for this skepticism, an argument based on the omnipotence of God: Urban liked to argue that since God is all-powerful, he could have created any one of a number of worlds, for example one in which the earth is motionless; therefore, regardless of how much evidence there is supporting the earth's motion, we can never assert that this must be so, for that would be to want to limit God's power to do otherwise.[18]

But even for this humanist pope, Galileo went too far in pushing the claims of truth. His transgression is communicated by the final sentence against him:

We say, pronounce, sentence, and declare that you, the above-mentioned Galileo, because of the things deduced in the trial and confessed by you as above, have rendered yourself according to this Holy Office vehemently suspected of heresy, namely of having held and believed a doctrine which is false and contrary to the divine and Holy Scripture: that the sun is the center of the world and does not move from east to west, and the earth moves and is not the center of the world, and that one may hold and defend as probable an opinion after it has been declared and defined contrary to Holy Scripture.[19]

As the quote from *The Assayer* demonstrates, Galileo was convinced that there is a certain similarity between divine and human knowledge. That similarity is greatest when knowledge turns to mathematics. When we think the truth of a mathematical proposition we participate in the thoughts of God. Human and divine mathematics are essentially the same, even if God knows infinitely more and intuits in a moment what may take us a lifetime to know. But there is no fundamental incapacity that prevents the human knower from reading the book of nature.

Once again, part of this humanist anthropocentrism is the claim to the truth. And access to the truth need not be mediated by a human institution such as the Church. But such a claim necessarily brought Galileo in conflict with the Inquisition. By that time it had recognized more clearly the threat the new astronomy posed to its authority. In this connection a letter that Cardinal Bellarmine wrote to Galileo's supporter Foscarini is of interest: "Your Reverence and Sig. Galileo did prudently to content yourselves with speaking hypothetically and not positively, as I have always believed Copernicus did. For to say that assuming the earth moves and the sun stands still saves the appearances better than eccentrics and epicycles is to speak well. This has no danger in it, and suffices for mathematicians."[20] Bellarmine is using here the strategy of Osiander: he renders the new astronomy ideologically acceptable and harmless by resisting its claim to truth. Galileo, although he sometimes showed himself a rather timid defender of the truth, could not accept this presentation of himself as a mere calculator who wanted only to save the appearances. Like Copernicus, he laid claim to truth. We should note that when he left his professorship of mathematics at the University of Padua to take up a position at the court of Cosimo Medici and a professorship at Pisa, he insisted that his title be mathematician and philosopher. And the censure of 1616 makes quite clear that it is a censure of Galileo the philosopher, not of Galileo the mathematician.

Galileo refuses Bellarmine's suggestion that he be content with the role of the mathematician. In a letter to Piero Dini from May 1615, he states very plainly what is at stake: "I should not like to have great men think that I endorse the position of Copernicus only as an astronomical hypothesis which is not really true. Taking me as one of those most addicted to this doctrine, they would believe all its other followers must agree, and that it is more likely erroneous than physically true. This, if I am not mistaken, would be an error."[21] Galileo is here concerned not only for the truth but also for his reputation as a defender of the truth. Given his investment in that image, it was difficult to avoid collision with a Church that since the days of Copernicus, let alone those of Cusanus, had grown ever more conservative. It could not be reassured by a statement such as the following from the same letter: "To me, the surest and swiftest way to prove that the position of Copernicus is not contrary to Scripture would be to give a host of proofs that it is true and that the contrary cannot be maintained at all; thus, since no two truths can contradict one another, this and the Bible must be perfectly harmonious."[22] Galileo was of course aware that the defender of the tradition would point to many apparent contradictions; the Bible does seem to assume a geocentric cosmology. If one accepts Galileo's position, then these "contradictions" must be considered only apparent. "As to rendering the Bible false, that is not and never will be the intention of Catholic astronomers such as I am; rather, our opinion is that the Scriptures accord perfectly with demonstrated physical truth. But let those theologians who are not astronomers guard against rendering Scripture false by trying to interpret against it propositions which may be true and might be proved so."[23] The implications of such an assertion for theology are clear: science is capable of the truth. As a Catholic astronomer, Galileo is also prepared to grant the truth of Scripture, but he is not willing to grant that its interpreters have grasped that truth. "It may be that we will have difficulties in expounding the Scriptures, and so on; but this is through our ignorance and not because there really are, or can be, insuperable difficulties in bringing them in accordance with demonstrated truth."[24]

INSIGHT AND BLINDNESS OF GALILEO

We should note the shift; while the theologians insisted that the truth claims of science be brought into accord with Scripture, Galileo reverses the direction: now our interpretation of Scripture has to accord with what science has to tell us. It is the natural philosopher rather than the theologian who has become the privileged custodian of truth. But this distinction between the real, though perhaps undiscovered, meaning of Scripture, which is taken to be in principle compatible with the new science, and its apparent meaning, which may well be incompatible, threatens to make Scripture an uncertain guide to truth. How can we be sure that we have gotten hold of the real meaning of the scriptural text and not just of an all-too-human and therefore fallible interpretation? Such questioning invites skepticism in matters of religion. Against such skepticism the Counter-Reformation insisted on the authority of the tradition. Once more I quote from Bellarmine's letter to Foscarini:

I say that, as you know, the Council [of Trent] would prohibit expounding the Bible contrary to the common agreement of the holy Fathers. And if your Reverence would read not only all their works, but the commentaries of modern writers on Genesis, Psalms, Ecclesiastes, and Joshua, you would find that all agree in expounding literally that the sun is in the heavens and travels swiftly around the earth, while the earth is far from the heavens and remains motionless in the center of the world. Now consider, whether, in all prudence, the Church could support the giving to Scripture of a sense contrary to the holy Fathers and all the Greek and Latin expositors.[25]

According to Bellarmine, this continuing tradition of interpretation must be considered the guardian of truth. Galileo has a very different conception: the truth, as he understands it, is open in principle to any unprejudiced observer. And all claimants to the truth—including theologians—must meet that new standard. The theocentric has yielded to an anthropocentric conception of truth.

The Church tried to force Galileo to acknowledge the priority of the former. When Galileo wanted to publish his *Dialogue Concerning the Two Chief World Systems*[26] the Roman censor thus insisted on a number of additions:

1. A preface, rather like Osiander's preface to Copernicus's *Revolutions*, should make clear that truth is not claimed for the Copernican system.

2. Galileo must add to his theory of the tides a remark that God's infinite power could have produced the same effects in a manner very different from that suggested by Galileo's Salviati.

3. The conclusion of the work was to be in keeping with this insistence on divine omnipotence.[27]

What Galileo was asked to surrender was thus his anthropocentric understanding of truth.

6

Why should Galileo's theory of the tides have been singled out for special attention? According to Galileo the tides are produced by the motion of the earth both around its axis and around the sun. That motion, he believed, caused a periodic sloshing of the water, just as we can observe when someone carries water in a basin. The tides, Galileo thought, offered an immediate and convincing interpretation of the motion of the earth. For the modern reader this theory is another instance of Galileo's blindness, for by that time Galileo knew of Kepler's essentially correct theory. Kepler had explained the tides in terms of his theory of gravity—that is, in terms of the mutual attraction of earth and moon. This argument, however, would have robbed Galileo of what he considered his strongest argument for the Copernican system. Kepler also posited an *actio in distans*, across the space separating the two bodies. To Galileo the very idea of such an occult force seemed impossible. Galileo therefore mentions Kepler's theory only to dismiss it. How much his own theory of the tides meant to Galileo is shown by his initial intention to call his dialogue *Dialogue on the Tides.*

The Church recognized its importance and therefore ordered that the title of the work not mention the tides, but refer only to mathematical representation of the motion of the earth. Barberini, now Pope Urban VIII, insisted on the nominalist thesis of the omnipotence of God. Human beings will never be able to explain how and why God created what he did, and thus science would never be able to state the laws of nature. Supposed laws of nature on this view are only human conjectures, which might have to be withdrawn at any moment. Miracles are always to be expected. Science can offer no cognitive security, and the very attempt to gain such security is vain.

With such insistence, Galileo thought, the Church was abusing its authority. In his "Letter to the Grand Duchess Christina" (1615) he had already written:

Let us grant that theology is conversant with the loftiest divine contemplation, and occupies the regal throne among sciences by dignity. But acquiring the highest authority in this way, if she does not descend to the lower and humbler speculations of the subordinate sciences and has no regard for them because they are not concerned with blessedness, then her professors should not arrogate to themselves the authority to decide on controversies in professions which they have neither studied nor practiced. Why, this would be as if an absolute despot, being neither a physician nor an architect, but knowing himself free to command, should undertake to administer medicines and erect buildings according to his whim—at grave peril of his poor patients' lives, and the speedy collapse of his edifices.[28]

The comparison of the Church to an ignorant absolute despot is telling. The letter amounts to a declaration of independence for the new science. It was written fifteen years after the death of Bruno, one year before the condemnation of Copernicus, and of course long before the trial of 1633, which forced Galileo to renounce his views and led to his imprisonment and house arrest. In the *Dialogue*, published only a year before the condemnation, he appears much more careful. Salviati, at the end of the dialogue, calls the doctrine of the omnipotence of God "An admirable and truly angelic doctrine." But, he continues, even if human fancy cannot limit divine power, we should yet be allowed "to argue about the constitution of the world" so that in this way we may come to admire the mystery of God's greatness. Is such an exercise not "granted and commanded to us by God"?[29] And does this not suggest that even if we shall never discover just how God constructed the world, it is yet possible to progress from a less to a more adequate formulation of the truth? That view is essentially the same as Cusanus's. What is at issue here is once more not so much the problem of a geocentric versus a heliocentric cosmology as the autonomy of scientific reason, a reason that has to acknowledge only the authority of what Galileo calls physical truth.

As a matter of fact, Galileo was himself not quite as free as his conception of science and of truth would demand. He, too, found it difficult to liberate himself from inherited preconceptions and from his often naive trust in the eye, as his relation to the other great astronomer of the age, Kepler, suggests. Already in 1597, years before the public knew Galileo to be a Copernican, Galileo had written Kepler on August 4, 1597, that he, Galileo, had long been a follower of Copernicus; he had found new arguments in support of the Copernican position, but he had not dared to publish them. In that letter he does not refer to Bruno, who was then in prison in Rome. He speaks rather of his fear that such a publication would meet with little positive response, would lead instead only to the derision of its author. Kepler replies on October 13 with an almost evangelical fervor: *Confide, Galilaee, et progredere*, "confess, Galileo, and progress."[30] The letters resume only in 1610, after the publication of *The Starry Messenger,* when Kepler writes him a long letter, expressing his appreciation and agreement. A year earlier Kepler had published his *Astronomia Nova*, which presented his revolutionary thesis of the elliptical orbits of the planets. Galileo was too committed to the Platonic axiom of circular movement to recognize the enormous importance of that work.

In his letter to Kepler of August 10, 1610, Galileo describes his colleagues at Padua, who, as he puts it, with the persistence of a snake, closed their eyes *contra veritatis lucem*, to the light of truth.[31] The evidence of the eyes becomes here the light of truth. It is surprising how quickly Galileo settles for that evidence. Thus he does not attempt to go beyond his observations of the moons of Jupiter to the formulation of the law that governed their motion. Had he done so he might have anticipated Kepler's third law of motion, which related the period of the planets to their mean distance from the sun. But at the time of *The Starry Messenger* Galileo appears to have had little interest in such theorizing. He was focused instead on demonstrating the truth of the Copernican system to the eye. And he still had the same aim when later he appealed to the evidence of the tides, rather uncritically drawing on the analogy between a basin with sloshing water and the oceans.

The same uncritical use of analogy is apparent in the challenge he mounts in his *Dialogue* to the axiom of the uniform circular motion of the heavenly bodies. We should remember that Kepler had broken with this axiom already in his *Astronomia Nova*, long before Galileo's dialogue appeared in 1632. But Galileo's theory was very different. Galileo's refusal to accept Kepler's theory of planetary motion may have been due in part to Kepler's failure to accompany it with an adequate theory of motion. To Galileo it had no basis in an adequate philosophy of nature, a philosophy that only Newton was to supply. But without such a basis, Kepler's theory, which was forced on him by the data he had inherited from Tycho Brahe, must have seemed to Galileo too much like the attempts of medieval astronomers to save the appearances by a purely mathematical calculation—that is, the theory was too mathematical, not philosophical enough. Galileo's own account relies once more on a familiar phenomenon, a swinging pendulum. Galileo had noted that the period of such a pendulum remains constant, increasing with the pendulum's length; he then applied this paradigm to the motion of the earth around the sun. He argues that the moon's motion around the earth means that the distance of the earth-moon system from the sun varies—shorter when the moon is closer to the sun, longer when the moon is more distant. Such variation, by analogy with the pendulum, leads one to expect a change in the speed with which the whole system travels around the sun. It should be greatest at the time of the new moon, significantly less at the time of the full moon. Galileo suggests that future observations will bear this hypothesis out.

The significant point here is that Galileo is prevented from being open to Kepler's new astronomy by his overly great trust in the eye and in analogies of heavenly to terrestrial phenomena. There is an interesting contrast between the near-sighted Kepler, who never was able to match the observations of a Tycho Brahe, and the clear-sighted Galileo, armed with his telescope, who for much of his life was too ready to rely on his eyes.

Eventually Galileo would lose his eyesight. And long before that happened, he had begun to reflect more critically on the authority of the eye. Remember that passage in *The Assayer* with which I began. There he recognizes clearly the role mathematics has to play in natural philosophy. And Galileo was right to be suspicious of speculation that, like Kepler's, lacked an adequate basis in physics. Kepler was too ready to trust in his mathematical imagination, too ready to give numbers and geometric figures an almost magical power. Galileo is much more down-to-earth in his thinking than Kepler—perhaps too much so. That was the source of his blindness. Husserl accused Galileo of replacing the real world, the world in which we live and perceive, with the world constructed by science.[32] This elision of the life-world (which in part entails that devaluation of the visible that has been a persistent theme in this book) is indeed characteristic of our modern understanding of reality, shaped as it is by science and technology. It is thus a mistake to oppose the positivism of the moderns to the idealism of the medievals. There is a sense in which Aristotelian medieval science remained closer to the life-world than our modern science and world-understanding. For the same reason it is difficult to make Galileo *the* founder of this modern worldview. He certainly contributed to this founding. But in many ways he remained still too tied to the life-world, was too ready to trust the evidence of the eye. In this respect Descartes is a better representative of the modern.

1

We have been taught to ridicule those critics of Galileo who refused to look
through his telescope, critics such as Giulio Libri or Galileo's celebrated colleague and friend at the University of Padua, Cesare Cremonini,[1] the leading
Aristotelian of the day, who thought it would only confuse him. History has
not been kind to Cremonini: once extravagantly praised as the first philosopher of the age, as *genius philosophiae*, as "genio d'Aristotele, e la Lucerna de'
Greci Interpreti," he was to become the exemplar of a backward-looking obstinacy that refused to acknowledge what should be evident to all willing
simply to open their eyes, caricatured by Bertold Brecht with the philosopher
in his *Life of Galileo* (1938).[2] In his study of Cremonini Heinrich C. Kuhn
goes so far as to claim that "if one were to look for the worst and least interesting philosopher" of all times and were to base one's judgment on the secondary literature, "hardly a doubt seems possible that the choice would fall
on Cesare Cremonini."[3] As if to support such an assessment, on the Internet
Joseph W. Newman today offers us Cremonini's refusal to look through
Galileo's tube as "a sterling example of 'intellectual dishonesty.'"[4]

Cremonini hardly deserves such censure. With justified pride he could
write in his will: *Ad philosophiam sum vocatus, in ea totius fui.*[5] And such love of
and service to the truth, as he understood it, had to bring this Aristotelian,
too, into conflict with the Inquisition,[6] which was troubled by the evident in-

compatibility between Aristotle's teaching concerning the eternity of the world, the inseparability of intellect and body, and God's self-contemplation, it was troubled also by Cremonini's willingness to criticize Thomas Aquinas in the name of Aristotle. Admonished to resist the temptation to appear as a great philosopher rather than as a good Catholic, Cremonini pretty much holds his ground. He grants that Aristotle, forced to think without the help of divine revelation, relying only on experience and reason, cannot be said to have been in possession of the truth, but knew truth only in a *modus diminutus & falax*, in a diminished and fallible mode. But was it not the task of philosophy to limit its claims to what could be supported by human reason, without the help of revelation?

Did Cremonini betray his own understanding of the philosopher's vocation when he refused to look through Galileo's telescope? Was he really so unreasonable? We say of someone who claims to see what we believe to be impossibilities, "He is seeing things." Many years ago someone offered me mescaline with the promise that it would open the gates of perception: was my refusal a mark of intellectual dishonesty? My understanding of reality has no room for the wondrous things the drug promised me. When Galileo claimed to see mountains on the moon, was he not just seeing things? Rather like Copernicus, who demanded more of the astronomer than ad hoc hypotheses to save the phenomena, requiring that the explanations he offered be in accord with the axioms of nature, and like Galileo himself who also claimed the mantle of the philosopher, Cremonini insisted that theses advanced by science deserved to be taken seriously only when in accord with the essence of nature. And his understanding of that essence included Aristotle's understanding of the elements. Through his tube, Galileo claimed that he could see that the moon was another earth—not at all a novel view, since Plutarch already had entertained something of the sort. But if the moon were indeed another earth, would it not have crashed down into this earth long ago? The incompatibility of what Galileo claimed to see with the tube and Cremonini's (as he himself admitted) *diminutus & falax* understanding of the essence of nature makes his refusal to look through Galileo's telescope much more than a mere irrational act.

Galileo appealed to the eye aided by an instrument. But how reliable was this instrument? When the archbishop of Cologne looked through a telescope

Galileo had sent him to advance his cause, he could not see anything; he passed it on to Kepler, who saw brightly colored squares.[7] And when Galileo presented his telescope on the evening of April 24, 1610, at the house of the mathematician Giovanni Antonio Magini to twenty-four professors at the University of Bologna, not one, we are told by one of Magini's students, was able to see Jupiter's satellites; dejected, Galileo stole away early the next morning.[8] A year later in Rome, those who used it during the day to look at terrestrial objects were enthusiastic, but those who peered through it at night could not agree on just what they were seeing.[9] In his *Dianoia Astronomica* of 1611, Francesco Sizi reminds Galileo of an evening they had spent, joined by other renowned scholars, studying Jupiter through the telescope with very uncertain results.[10] Such demonstrations could hardly convince a skeptic that Galileo's tube would allow one to see the truth.

There was a more fundamental objection: does it even make sense to claim that the truth is something that can actually be seen? As discussed in chapter 6, the authority of the eye had been questioned ever since Plato and optical instruments had long been associated with magic. Was Galileo's telescope more than a toy? Should the questionable evidence it offered outweigh what were thought to be the time-honored results of a science supported by the authority of Aristotle? Consider once more Sizi's *Dianoia Astronomica*, which appeared in Venice just a year after Galileo's *Starry Messenger*. Sizi was not so much concerned to save the Aristotelian worldview. What upset him was the claim that four new planets had been discovered. He was certain that there had to be seven. His conviction was based on analogies that link astronomy to sacred Scripture, science to theology.[11] And Sizi's reflections were not at all an oddity. As mentioned in the previous chapter, even Kepler questioned the news of Galileo's discovery of four new planets; at the time he was convinced that there could be only six planets, whose orbits were separated by the five regular Euclidean solids. The difficulty was removed when what he had already suspected turned out to be correct: the supposed new planets were not really planets at all but moons.

Unlike Cremonini or Sizi, Kepler did not really doubt the reliability of Galileo's observations. But were they so wrong to question the authority of the eye aided by an unfamiliar optical instrument? Galileo's confidence in the eye must have seemed just a bit naive to anyone who took Plato seriously.

Conversely, such confidence in the eye had to call into question the use of mathematics, not just by a Sizi but also by a Platonist such as Kepler. It is difficult to imagine Galileo impressed by the use Kepler made of the Platonic solids. Too much here would have reminded him of the reasoning relied on by Renaissance magic and its science of nature. He would have listened more sympathetically to Francis Bacon's condemnation of the natural philosophy of his time as "tainted and corrupted: in Aristotle's school by logic; in Plato's school by natural theology; in the second school of the Platonists, such as Proclus and others, by mathematics, which ought to give definiteness to natural philosophy, not to generate or give it birth."[12] In each case experience is not taken seriously enough. Think of the reasoning of Sizi. But Kepler, too, appears to be a good example of someone led astray by mathematics. And would we not have to include Copernicus and even Galileo himself in the list of those condemned by Bacon: what justified their insistence that the heavenly bodies move in circles?

Bacon's attempt to recall science to experience makes an important point. And yet, had his appeal been taken as seriously as Bacon had hoped, it would have forestalled the development of modern science, which relied not just on its greater empiricism but on mathematics being given a more important role than Bacon was willing to grant it. But that role had to be different from the one it was assigned, according to Bacon, by the Second School of Platonists, of which even Kepler may be taken as a late representative, a role gladly embraced by Renaissance magic. The new science had to steer a course between Bacon's empiricism and such a Platonism.[13]

2

A critique of Bacon could once more draw on that critique of the eye that appears as early as Plato. By now I have said more than enough about perspectival distortion. But recall the critique's central thesis: that to submit to the eye is to submit to appearance. Is Descartes not right to insist in the *Third Meditation*, of "things such as light, colors, sounds, scents, tastes, heat, cold, and other tactile qualities," that "they are thought by me with so much obscurity and confusion that I do not even know if they are true or false, i.e. whether the ideas which I form of these qualities are actually ideas of real objects or not (or whether they only represent chimeras which cannot exist in fact)"?[14] When we trust the eye, we are imprisoned, as Galileo put it, in a labyrinth of appearances. How are we to escape from this labyrinth?

In chapter 6 I pointed out how such magical creations as anamorphic compositions with their multiple perspectives and automata, whose beautiful exteriors conceal a hidden mechanism, suggested to Descartes the way out. In each case the magical appearance is understood as the product of human ingenuity. To the extent that we understand nature as if it were the product of human craft, we can unriddle its secrets. As *homo faber*, the human being carries the secrets of this craft within himself. The young Descartes therefore claims that within ourselves we bear the seeds of a science that will deliver us from deceptive appearance. Descartes thus shares and seeks to legitimate the humanist anthropocentrism of a Copernicus and a Galileo.

In the *Rules* Descartes, as we have seen, make's a first attempt to show in some detail how we might escape from the labyrinth of appearances. He there argues that we possess intuitions that are free from the distortions of perspective. Descartes ties such intuitions to an apprehension of simple natures. The intuition I have of my own being is said to be of that sort; so is my intuition of extension; or of equality. We should note that no matter what the examples, by their very simplicity such simple natures cannot leave us in doubt about what they are: we either grasp or fail to grasp them; we cannot grasp them falsely or partially. We should also note that the intuition by which we grasp them must be very different from sight: for whatever we see is always seen from a particular point of view—what we see is inevitably not seen as it is. Sight presents us only with one of many possible aspects, and the same is true of the other senses. By their very simplicity, Descartes's simple natures cannot be construed as sensibilia: they must be intelligibilia.

Descartes goes on to suggest that the way to escape from the labyrinth of perspective is to represent or reconstruct the seen in terms of these simple natures. The turn to simple natures thus implies a devaluation of ordinary sense-bound experience. It suggests that to gain proper access to reality we first have to transform ourselves into thinking subjects. This is not to say that we can dispense with experience; experience has to offer us our data. But what experience has to offer us needs to be redescribed in a language that by its form assures us that we are not victims of appearance. That language will attempt to eliminate words that presuppose our senses and their distortions. It will therefore have no room for secondary qualities, for sights or smells. Remember the extent to which Aristotle's physics depends on secondary qualities, on notions like dry and moist, hot and cold. Here is his table of elements:

	Dry	Moist
Hot	fire	air
Cold	earth	water

Aristotle also believed these elements to be categorized as heavier and lighter, a relation he considered of secondary importance. The new science will reverse that priority. Such secondary qualities as hot and cold, dry and moist, belong to the order of appearances, and a science that takes them too seriously will condemn itself to an only superficial understanding of reality. All I want to emphasize here is that the superiority of the new over the old science is based not so much on its particular insights but rather on a change in its form of description—and we may not forget the price at which such superiority is bought: it has to cover up what Husserl calls the life-world and bring with it an enormous reduction both of experience and of being, a reduction that leaves no room for meaning or value in the domain of scientific truths.

But the very hope of the new science to escape from the labyrinth of appearances by turning inward to simple ideas present in the human mind suggests the danger that this turn will lead to its losing touch with reality, that the world created by the new science will prove a mere fiction, having no more claim to truth than would a work of art. Such fictions would give us no power over the world we live in. Yet it is precisely such power that Descartes seeks and promises us in the *Discourse on Method*. What justifies his confidence that science does in fact provide us with more than fantastic fictions? A first answer is given by what one can call Descartes's pragmatic turn, which invites us to think the scientist in the image of the craftsman, whose know-how presupposes an insight into reality very different from that of the Renaissance magus. In the *Rules* Descartes thus admonishes us that science should not rest content with mathematical models but should progress to mechanical ones. We can understand reality only to the degree that we can re-create it, a re-creation not only in thought but in fact. Mathematics offers us indeed one approach, but our mathematical models of reality are not genuine re-creations of it: to understand reality, we have to know what causes bring about what effects. Nature can be understood to the extent that it can be represented by mechanical models,[15] and Descartes is convinced that such understanding will extend to biology. All the natural sciences are in principle reducible to mechanics—that is to say, to physics.

The rewards that Descartes expected his method to bring us are clearly stated in *The Discourse on Method:*

But as soon as I had acquired some general notions concerning Physics, and as, beginning to make use of them in various special difficulties, I observed to what point they might lead us, and how much they differ from the principles of which we have made use up to the present time, I believed that I could not keep them concealed without greatly sinning against the law which obliges us to procure, as much as in us lies, the general good of all mankind. For they caused me to see that it is possible to attain knowledge which is very useful in life, and that, instead of the speculative philosophy which is taught in the Schools, we may find a practical philosophy by means of which, knowing the force and the action of fire, water, air, the stars, heavens, and all other bodies that environ us, as distinctly as we know the different crafts of our artisans, we can in the same way employ them in all those uses to which they are adapted, and thus render ourselves the masters and possessors of nature.[16]

We will realize God's promise to Abraham (see Genesis 17).

What must nature be like to enable us to be confident that this promise will indeed be fulfilled? What are the necessary conditions that must be met if nature is to be grasped and possessed, if science is to be possible? For one, it must be sufficiently stable. If nature were an ever-changing chaos, we would never get hold of it. If, for example, the way gravitation worked constantly changed, neither Kepler nor Newton could have formulated their laws. But what reason is there to believe that nature and her laws will not change? Time is thus one source of cognitive dread, threatening to undermine Cartesian confidence in the reliability of the cosmos. Another condition is that nature cannot be infinitely complex. It must be possible to interpret it as a manifold built up from a manageable set of elements we can comprehend. In the *Rules* Descartes thus appeals to simple natures to show us the exit from the labyrinth of appearances.

But what if these so-called simple natures are our own inventions, fictions that exist only in our minds? What if the demand for such simplicity is one that reality does not meet, if the simple natures of Descartes are only logical atoms to which no real properties of things correspond? We know that while Descartes worked on the *Rules* he read Bacon's *Novum Organum*,[17] and what he read there must have struck him as a direct challenge to his program:

The human understanding is of its own nature prone to suppose the existence of more order and regularity in the world than it finds. And though there may be many things in nature which are singular and unmatched, yet (the understanding) devises for them parallels and conjugates and relatives which do not exist. Hence the fiction that all celestial bodies move in perfect circles.[18]

This is a denial of the thesis that God wrote the book of nature in the language of mathematics—a thesis that Descartes needed to defend.

Here is another passage that demands a response:

The human understanding is of its own nature prone to abstractions and gives a substance and reality to things which are fleeting. But to resolve nature into abstractions is less our purpose than to dissect her into parts, as did the school of Democritus which went further into nature than the rest. Matter rather than forms should be the object of our attention, its configurations and changes of configurations, and simple action, and laws of action or motion; for forms are figments of the human mind.[19]

And mathematics, too, is considered by Bacon a figment of the mind.

The human understanding is unquiet; it cannot stop or rest, and still presses onward, but in vain. Therefore it is that we cannot conceive of any end or limit to the world; but always as of necessity, it occurs to us that there is something beyond: Neither again can it be conceived how eternity has flowed into the present day: for that distinction which is commonly received of infinity in time past and in time to come can by no means hold; for it would follow that one infinity is greater than another, and that infinity is wasting away and tending to become finite. The like subtlety arises touching the finite divisibility of lines, from the same inability of thought to stop.[20]

THE REEF OF THE INFINITE

Descartes had hoped to appeal to mathematics to find the exit from the labyrinth of appearances, but here he reads Bacon's argument that makes mathematics itself but an idol of the tribe. The confidence that he had shared with Galileo, that God wrote the book of nature in the language of mathematics, was thus severely shaken.

The *Meditations* address that crisis of confidence. They were written to restore faith in the power of mathematics to reveal the structure of reality. To do so, Descartes must show that violence is not done to nature by such mathematization. He needs a metaphysics or an ontology of nature. Descartes hopes to provide this by showing that the being of nature is extended substance, justifying Kepler's conviction: *Ubi materia, ibi geometria.* We are said to possess a clear and distinct idea of the being of nature as extension. And is geometry not based on extension? If the being of nature can indeed be shown to be extended substance, there can be no question of the applicability of mathematics to nature. The trust in mathematics would be vindicated.

But what right does Descartes have to trust simple or clear and distinct ideas? Bacon warns that human nature is liable to mistake its own fictions for reality, and he quite expressly considers our intuition of infinitely divisible space—that is, that very idea which Descartes thought he held clearly and distinctly—such a fiction. To meet Bacon's challenge, Descartes has to show that whatever I perceive clearly and distinctly is as I perceive it. Here there can be no gap separating the idea and what the idea is about, between the logical and the ontological.

Consider the simple steps that are to secure Descartes's method against the critique implicit in Bacon:

1. In order to gain an indubitable, unshakable foundation, Descartes proposes to doubt everything he had up to then taken for granted.

2. In a way that recalls Augustine,[21] he establishes that foundation by reflecting on the *cogito:* I cannot doubt that I, a thinking thing, exist.

3. This certainty leads to the discovery of a criterion of what is necessary if I am to truly know something: I must possess a clear and distinct representation of it.

4. But doubts return: cannot even clear and distinct representations deceive?

It was to meet these returning doubts that Descartes thought he had to prove the existence of a God who is not a deceiver, to demonstrate that human thought is attuned to reality. Unfortunately, this whole chain of reasoning is not as strong as it would have to be to justify Descartes's faith that his method will make us the masters and possessors of nature. Thus we may well question the use he makes of the *cogito:* do we have a clear and distinct idea of ourselves as thinking substance? We may grant Descartes that we know with certainty *that* we are. But is this to say that we know also *what* we are? This criticism was pushed especially by Pierre Gassendi, the author of the most thoughtful set of objections. But if the *cogito* gives us no insight into what we are, it gives us no insight into reality and thus cannot function as the paradigm Descartes needs.

And even weaker is the attempt to prove the existence of a God who is not a deceiver. Such a God may well be demanded if we are to know with certainty that we are indeed capable of the truth. The proof that such a God exists would secure what I have called the cognitive anthropocentrism of the Renaissance. But how can I even attempt to prove that such a God exists, unless I already have the right to trust my own clear and distinct ideas? And is it not precisely this trust the desired outcome of the proof? That is to say: if I am already convinced of the reliability of my clear and distinct ideas, then I do not need God to shore up such conviction; but if I am not so convinced, I cannot be sure that the clear and distinct ideas that I need to prove the existence of God can be trusted.

Should Descartes's method then be dismissed? Should we say that Descartes is not Theseus to whom Ariadne, or rather the Virgin as the Christian Ariadne, gave the thread that enables him to find his way out of the labyrinth?[22] Should we say rather—as Father Bourdin, the author of the seventh set of objections, suggests—that he is Icarus? It is difficult to accept that conclusion—the method has proved too fruitful. Descartes's faith has in good measure been justified by the very real power and mastery that it has given us. That power is no fiction. Descartes did not lose himself in idle speculation, in good part because he recognized the importance of tying theory to practice—recall his promise of a practical philosophy. Repeatedly he invokes the craftsman, who shows that he possesses an understanding of what he is making simply by his ability to make it. Similarly, we have to demonstrate our understanding of nature by our ability to make or remake it: we will not really have understood the human

heart as long as we cannot make such a heart; until we can make a human being we have not fully understood human nature. This emphasis on making
presents Daedalus as a more suggestive persona for Descartes than either Theseus or Icarus. The identification is supported by the fascination with automata
that plays, as we saw, such an important role in Descartes's thinking. Even while
admitting its final failure to do full justice to nature and especially to human nature, we have to grant the power Cartesian method gave humanity.

3

Just because Descartes's promise to render us the masters and possessors
of nature was so much more than just another idle promise—has indeed
shaped our reality—it seems to me important to attempt to take a step back
from his *mathesis universalis*, his universal mathematics, to the *docta ignorantia*, the learned ignorance, of Cusanus.[23] Such an attempt demands a re-
thinking of the Cartesian project.

I know of only one reference by Descartes to the works of Cusanus. In a
letter to Chanut of June 16, 1647, Descartes defends his own understanding of the infinity of the cosmos by pointing out that "the Cardinal of Cusa
and many other Doctors have supposed the world to be infinite without ever
being censured by the Church," insisting that his own opinion "is not as difficult to accept as theirs, because I do not say that the world is infinite, but
only that it is indefinitely great. There is quite a notable difference between
the two: for we cannot say that something is infinite without an argument to
prove this such as we can give only in the case of God himself; but we can
say that a thing is indefinitely large, provided we have no argument to prove
that it has bounds."[24] Descartes returns to this distinction in the *Principles of
Philosophy*, where he admonishes us "that we must never discuss the infinite,
but must simply consider those things in which we notice no limits as indefinite: as, for instance, the extension of the world, the divisibility of parts
of matter, the number of stars, etc." He explains that

Thus we shall never be wearied by any debates concerning the infinite. For of course,
inasmuch as we are finite, it would be absurd for us to attempt to determine anything
concerning the infinite, and thus attempt as it were to prescribe limits to it and comprehend it. Therefore, we shall not bother to respond to those who ask whether half

of a given infinite line would also be infinite; or whether infinite number is even or odd, and such: because surely only those who judge their own mind to be infinite ought to think about such things."[25]

Descartes, so it seems, would have rejected Cusanus's speculations concerning the coincidence of opposites as refusing to honor the essential finitude of our understanding. To be sure, he would have agreed with Cusanus that it is "self-evident that there is no comparative relation of the infinite to the finite." But while Cusanus concludes from this that a finite intellect cannot "precisely attain the truth about things,"[26] Descartes denied that infinity is so constitutive of things that whenever we try to understand them we become entangled in what he would dismiss as wearying debates concerning the infinite. This dismissal covers up an abyss that lies beneath the supposedly secure realm of truth.

Let me return to the infinity of the cosmos. Like Cusanus and Bruno, Descartes, argues from the infinity of space to the homogeneity of the cosmos (II. 21). From the perceived identity of the ideas of extension and corporeal substance, he deduces "that the matter of the heaven does not differ from that of the earth; and that even if there were countless worlds in all it would be impossible for them not to all be of one and the same kind of matter" (II. 22, p. 49). Where Descartes differs from Cusanus is in the confidence with which he asserts that our inability to imagine a limit of space allows us to say that "in reality" space has no limit. Cusanus would have questioned the supposed commensurability of reality and imagination and would have insisted that the boundless cosmos opened up in reflection is itself but a human conjecture—"conjecture" here standing between a true representation and a hypothesis to save the appearances. Cusanus insists that absolute truth about reality belongs only to God. When we try to seize it we inevitably end up in antinomies and paradox. To sail past these pillars of Hercules is to lose all bearings. All we can know will bear the imprint of our human measure, our human perspective.

Descartes, too, recognizes how our supposedly clear and distinct perception of extension entangles us in the infinite. But on this reef of the infinite the Cartesian resolution—to make the human understanding the measure of reality, to accept only that as true which is completely known and incapable of being doubted—has to founder. Descartes is thus forced to conclude his *Principles of Philosophy* with the admission that in natural science absolute certainty is not to be had, that we have to settle for what is "morally certain," where this is defined as certain "to a degree which suffices for the needs of everyday life; although if compared to the absolute power of God, they are uncertain" (IV. 205, p. 287). Some suggested that this retreat from his earlier, stronger claim to truth is strategic only: that Descartes wanted to avoid the fate of Galileo, let alone Bruno. And there can be little doubt that Descartes was not eager to cast himself in the role of a martyr for science (one reason for his decision to leave France and to settle in more liberal Holland). But we must take Descartes at his word when he insists that "the works of God cannot be thought too great" and "that we must beware, lest, in thinking too highly of ourselves, we suppose that we understand for what ends God created the world" (III.1–2, p. 84). Descartes's conception of God remains close to that of the nominalists. But in that case, we have no reason to assume that God created the world so that we might gain an adequate understanding of it, that our understanding is indeed the measure of reality. Is not the physicist limited to constructing mechanical models of what he observes and using these to predict what is going to happen? Such ability to predict need not mean that the real causes have been understood. Indeed, given the infinite divisibility of matter, it is very unlikely that our finite models will ever enable us to precisely duplicate nature's processes:

For just as the same artisan can make two clocks which indicate the hours equally well and are exactly similar externally, but are internally composed of an entirely dissimilar combination of small wheels; so there is no doubt that the greatest Artificer of things could have made all those things which we see in many diverse ways. And indeed I most willingly concede this to be true, and will think that I have achieved enough if those things which I have written are only such that they correspond accurately to all the phenomena of nature. (IV.204, p. 286)

Descartes compares the scientist to someone who attempts to read a letter in code:

Thus, for example, if someone wishes to read a message written in Latin letters, to which however their true meaning has not been given and if, upon conjecturing that wherever there is an A in the message, a B must be read, and a C wherever there is a B, and that for each letter, the following must be substituted; he finds that by this means certain Latin words are formed by these letters: he will not doubt that the true meaning of that message is contained in these words, even if he knows this solely by conjecture, and even though it may perhaps be the case that the person who wrote the message did not put the immediately following letters but some others in the place of the true ones, and thus concealed some different meaning in the message. (IV.205, p. 287)

If we believe that God's power is infinite, or perhaps accept just the infinite divisibility of matter, there is no way for science to take the measure of nature.

All that Descartes can claim for most propositions of science, measured by his own conception of absolute truth, is that they are well-founded conjectures. Descartes, to be sure, modifies this claim by insisting that there are "even among natural things, some which we judge to be absolutely and more than morally certain." He mentions mathematical demonstrations, knowledge that material things exist, and indeed "all evident demonstrations which are made concerning material things." He goes on to suggest that despite his disclaimers, "These reasonings of ours will perhaps be included among the number of these absolutely certain things by those who consider how they have been deduced in a continuous series from the first and simplest principles of human knowledge" (IV.206, p. 287). But where in the *Principles* do evidence and deduction leave off and conjectures begin?

4

While the endless divisibility of space suggests the artificiality of Descartes's reconstruction of nature by means of mechanical models, its limitless extension makes it impossible to assert either absolute motion or rest. Descartes thus follows Cusanus with his relativistic conception of motion: "Movement, properly understood, concerns only the bodies contiguous to the body which is moving" (II.28, p. 52). In this sense someone who rests on the deck of an ocean liner can say rightly that she is not moving. And in the same sense Descartes can agree with Copernicus and yet say that properly speaking the earth does not move, since on his conception of a fluid heaven it is carried along by its vortex. Descartes knew that his insistence that the earth does not properly move but is carried around the sun was not likely to satisfy those critics of the Copernican system who not long ago had attempted to silence Galileo. As he himself points out, besides its own proper movement, a body "can also participate in innumerable other movements, in as much as it is a part of other bodies which have other movements" (II.31, p. 54). He asks us to imagine a sailor wearing a watch. Although each of the watch's wheels will have its own proper movement relative to the watchcase, it also participates in the movement of the sailor, the ship, the ocean, the earth—and, we can continue, the solar system, the galaxy. Is there a final, all-encompassing whole that would allow us to speak of the absolute motion of each wheel? Given Descartes's clear and distinct conception of extension, that question is as meaningless as the question of whether the infinite number is odd or even. Thus, too, someone who wants to hold on to his conviction that the earth is at rest cannot finally be refuted by astronomy:

Since the nature of the intellect is such that it perceives no limits to the universe and since, consequently, anyone who takes careful notice of the greatness of God and the weakness of our perception will judge that it is much more appropriate to believe that perhaps, beyond all the fixed Stars which we see, there are other bodies in relation to which we would have to say that the Earth is at rest and all the Stars move together, than to suppose that none such could exist. (III.29, p. 96)

No doubt the fate of Bruno, the incarceration of Campanella, the difficulties of Galileo with the guardians of the faith, and the Church's recent placement of Copernicus's *De Revolutionibus* on the Index of forbidden books figured in Descartes's refusal to simply proclaim the truth of the Copernican system. But we also have to recognize that he could not have reconciled such a proclamation with the infinity of the cosmos implied by what he took to be his clear and distinct perception of extended substance.

Cusanus, as we have seen, derives the infinity of the cosmos from our inability to think an absolute maximum. If the boundlessness of the cosmos is thus not grasped, it nevertheless shows itself in the knowledge that we are free to pass beyond any boundary (in thought or imagination, at least). Such knowledge, however, presupposes that we possess a faculty that reaches up to what will in the end always elude our grasp. While our ability to comprehend is finite, the freedom of thought is infinite. Descartes, too, recognizes that by its very essence human being, no less than extension, is entangled in the infinite.

For to take an example, if I consider the faculty of comprehension which I possess, I find that it is of very small extent and extremely limited, and at the same time I find the idea of another faculty much more ample and even infinite, and seeing that I can form the idea of it I recognize from this very fact that it pertains to the nature of God.[27]

Indeed, if we could not measure the reach of our faculty of comprehension by a "much more ample and even infinite" faculty, we could not recognize its finitude. In this case, too, the principle applies that to understand a perspective as such is to be already beyond it, at least in thought: to think the reach of our faculty of comprehension as essentially finite we have to in some sense transcend ourselves as finite knowers. Regardless of whether God exists, our ability to form some idea of God's infinite nature presupposes that the power of human self-transcendence reaches up to the infinite. Descartes points in this connection to the will:

It is free-will alone or liberty of choice which I find so great in me that I can conceive no other idea to be more great; it is indeed the case that it is for the most part this will that causes me to know that in some manner I bear the image and similitude of God. For although the power of will is incomparably greater in God than in me, both by reason of the knowledge and the power which, conjoined with it, render it stronger and more efficacious, and by reason of its object, inasmuch as in God it extends to a great many things; it nevertheless does not seem to me greater if I consider it formally and precisely in itself.[28]

In its manifestation as will, our mind transcends the finite understanding toward infinity. And just as the fact that I have a clear and distinct understanding of God does not mean that I comprehend him, so the fact that I have a clear and distinct idea of myself as thinking substance does not mean that I fully comprehend myself. The self transcends its own understanding. Every free action manifests human self-transcendence. All human behavior remains finally incomprehensible insofar as it is free.

THE REEF OF THE INFINITE

Descartes touches on this difficulty in *The Passions of the Soul*, where he suggests that

the machine of the body is so formed that from the simple fact that this [the pineal] gland is diversely moved by the soul, or by such other cause, whatever it is, it thrusts the spirits which surround it towards the pores of the brain, which conduct them by nerves into the muscles, by which means it causes them to move the limbs.[29]

This raises the question that had already troubled Gassendi: "how that union and apparent intermingling, or confusion, can be found in you, if you are incorporeal, unextended, and indivisible."[30] How, given the distinction between *res cogitans* and *res extensa*, can the soul be said to be the cause of bodily actions? What would "cause" mean here?

But perhaps we are given a hint of how to approach this problem in the response to Arnauld's question of what Descartes might possibly mean when he calls God his own efficient cause.[31] Descartes's answer, interestingly enough, depends on the symbolism Cusanus had advanced in *De Docta Ignorantia*—without mentioning Cusanus.

But in order to reply expressly to this, let me say that I think we must show that intermediate between *efficient cause* in the proper sense, and *no cause*, there is something else, viz. *the positive essence of a thing*, to which the concept of efficient cause can be extended in the way in which in Geometry we are wont to extend the concept of a circular line that is as long as possible to that of a straight line; or the concept of a rectilinear polygon with an indefinite number of sides to that of a circle.[32]

When Descartes calls God his own efficient cause, "efficient cause" is to be understood not literally but in an extended sense that presupposes a willingness to follow Cusanus in his infinite ascent to the *coincidentia oppositorum*.

I would like to suggest that if we are to understand Descartes's claim that the soul is the cause of bodily actions, "cause" must be given a similar extended meaning, which involves a movement to the infinite. We should note the change of scale when in his reconstruction of the machine of the body Descartes turns to the "animal spirits," which name "a certain very subtle air or wind" that courses through the nerves and the brain—and only the most subtle enter the cavities of the brain. These animal spirits are nothing but material bodies, and their one peculiarity is that they are bodies of "extreme minuteness."[33] The soul is said to exercise its functions only in a "certain very small gland" that is so situated "that the slightest movements which take place in it may alter very greatly the course of these spirits; and reciprocally that the smallest changes which occur in the course of the spirits may do much to change the movements of this gland."[34] Descartes's mechanics of the body proves incapable of giving a fully adequate account of human action. Because to do so it would have to model what is indefinitely small, it must remain indeterminate. This indeterminacy opens up the space that allows for what Gassendi considered the confusion of body and soul. Perhaps it would be better to follow Cusanus and speak of their coincidence.

5

Openness to transcendence is part of our encounter with reality. This means that our finite understanding will never fully master and possess nature as Descartes seemed to promise. The inadequacy of our concepts or words to reality has its foundation in the very nature of thought and language, which determines what something is by assigning it a place in a humanly established conceptual or linguistic space, thus measuring it by a measure that is not its own. Language—and this is not its fault, but its very point—is finally incommensurable with reality. But language would also lose its point if there were not some sense in which our propositions did not have their measure in *rerum veritas*, in the truth of things[35]—if our understanding lost its measure in a logos incarnated in the sensible things, of which we are not the author. The incomprehensible incarnation of logos in matter is a presupposition of responsible speech, taking "responsibility" here to mean the ability to respond to such a logos.

There is a sense in which we can know adequately only what we can create. Thus, according to Cusanus, there is adequate knowledge in mathematics. This claim also forces us to take seriously Descartes's suggestion that we understand nature precisely to the extent that we can reconstruct nature. But we also must be open to the limits that are set to such understanding. The Cartesian method invites reconsideration in the light of Cusanus's *docta ignorantia*.

THE REEF OF THE INFINITE

1

In *Truth and Method* (1960) Hans-Georg Gadamer calls the prejudice against prejudice the fundamental prejudice of the Enlightenment—a prejudice, he suggests, that must rob the tradition of its power.[1] It is this prejudice that already rules Copernicus's thinking, as it does that of Galileo and Descartes. And not just theirs: such prejudice is indeed a presupposition of the conviction that the truth is in principle available to any rational being. It finds particularly striking expression in the early modern period's celebration of the self-taught man. Thus, though prefigured by Socrates and by Cusanus's *idiota*, Descartes covers up how much he owes to the tradition. Hans Blumenberg has drawn our attention to another such example: it is taken from an anonymous biography of the eighteenth-century scientist and philosopher Johann Heinrich Lambert that appeared in Christoph Martin Wieland's *Deutscher Merkur* (1773).[2] Now pretty much forgotten, Lambert was once celebrated as one of the great thinkers of the day, placed by one writer beside Rousseau, Haller, and Voltaire. I mentioned Lambert once before, in chapter 4, when I pointed out that it was Lambert who, in his *Neues Organon*, introduced what he called "phenomenology" as one of the main branches of philosophy. By phenomenology Lambert meant "the theory of appearance (*Schein*) and its influence on the correctness or incorrectness of human knowledge,"[3] a study of the logic of appearance as a necessary part of the acquisition of knowledge. He called his phenomenology a "transcendent optics." His interest in such a phenomenology was closely related to his interest in the mathematics of perspective. Today Lambert is indeed more likely to be remembered by mathematicians than by philosophers; his modern translator declares, "His really lasting achievements were in pure mathematics and geometry, among them his proof of the irrationality of *e*, the basis of natural logarithm, and of π, the ratio of the circumference of a circle to its diameter. He came within striking distance of formulating a non-Euclidean geometry."[4]

In 1764 Lambert had been proposed for membership in Frederick the Great's Berlin Academy of Sciences. The enlightened monarch asked to see the famous scholar. "The scene could not have been more unusual. The candidate was seated and almost all the candles were extinguished shortly before the king entered."[5] Frederick the Great had been warned that neither Lambert's manners, nor his looks, nor his mode of dress would make a favorable impression. A portrait suggests that Lambert was indeed quite ugly; and as the son of a tailor he had little formal education. As befits a truly enlightened monarch, the king is reported to have replied that he wanted to meet the famous man in the dark. He did not want to see him; he wanted to hear what he had to say. The visible light is seen here as an obstacle to the spiritual light, the logos. That devaluation of the eye, which we encountered as early as Plato, is given particularly striking expression by this anecdote. Despite the king's precautions, he was not at all impressed.

"Would you do me the favor of telling me in what sciences you are specialized?" the king asked the visitor of whom he could see at best a dark silhouette. "In all of them," came the answer from the man in the dark. "Are you also a skilful mathematician?" the king asked again. "Yes," the visitor answered. "Which professor taught you mathematics?" the king pressed on. "I myself," went the reply as curt as before. "Are you therefore another Pascal?" "Yes, your majesty." At that the king turned aside for he could hardly hold his laughter, and returned to his private office. Later, at dinner, the king remarked that the greatest blockhead in the world had just been presented to him for membership in the Academy.[6]

Before a year had passed the king was to revise his judgment, spurred on, no doubt, when the Russian ambassador invited Lambert to become a member of the St. Petersburg academy. The king acknowledged that the learnedness of this "blockhead" seemed to have no bounds and granted him the unique privilege of reading papers in all the academy's divisions.[7]

Lambert is presented here in the Enlightenment's image of Socrates: ugly, not at all at home in polite society, the paradigm of the absent-minded philosopher. But along with such eccentricity goes a mind remarkably free from the burden imposed by tradition and its prejudices. Such rhetoric is part of the Copernican revolution. Did not Copernicus, too, live quite literally far away from the centers of the scientific culture of the sixteenth century? And along with the rhetoric of eccentricity goes the rhetoric of inwardness. Within themselves Copernicus and Descartes find the keys to the truth, and Lambert is also presented, with considerable justice, as self-taught. And just as Copernicus liberates his thinking by imagining possibilities and perspectives different from those generally taken for granted, so does Lambert. It is this freedom of imagination that enables Lambert to become one of the fathers of non-Euclidean geometry and of a new cosmology that extends the Copernican diagram from the solar system to the galaxy and beyond.

In his *Cosmological Letters* the reflection on perspective is crucial. In the "Twelfth Letter" the Milky Way is thus interpreted, as it was by Thomas Wright (1750) and Kant, as the perspectival appearance of a lenslike conglomeration of stars.[8] But Lambert extends the Copernican paradigm much further when he suggests that our solar system is itself but a small part of a much larger system, which in turn is but a part of our galaxy, which in turn is just one element of a supersystem whose dark central body keeps all its elements in orbit. In this form Lambert retains the idea of an immense, but centered, finite cosmos.

In this connection Lambert makes a revealing statement: We may well not yet have become sufficiently Copernican.[9] The Copernican revolution is here understood as having furnished a paradigm that awaits ever more adequate appropriation, presenting us, and especially scientists, with a still-continuing challenge. Part of this invitation is the suggestion that we still need to liberate ourselves from inherited perspectives and prejudices, a task that has not yet been completed. But the progress that is here envisioned has its telos in the not-yet-discovered dark center of the cosmos.

It cannot surprise us therefore to learn that Kant, even though he argued for an infinite universe, mentioned *The Cosmological Letters* in his essay "On the Only Possible Ground for Proving of the Existence of God"[10] and at one point thought of dedicating his *Critique of Pure Reason* to Lambert as the philosopher with whom, he felt, he had most in common. But Lambert's extension of the Copernican revolution at the same time has to put it into question: when is the analogical extension of the paradigm supplied by the solar system going to stop? Will it end at the dark body that Lambert envisioned? But why should this, too, not turn out to be just another preliminary determination of the center, responding to the needs of the intellect more than to the essence of reality? Will the idea of a cosmic center perhaps always elude us, as Bruno and Cusanus thought?

According to Lambert, too, all theory—that of Copernicus as well as the astronomy of his own time, the eighteenth century—is bound to a particular historical period. What Copernicus presented as the truth turned out to be not an escape from appearance altogether, but only a step toward a higher order appearance. Further reflection showed that the sun, too, could not be considered the cosmic center. The speculations on the Milky Way belong in this context. But such recognition of the way in which theory is inevitably bound to a particular historical situation, a particular historical perspective—of how what a particular period calls true, even its metaphysics of nature, is inevitably bound to its historical prejudices—is part of what we call the Enlightenment's growing disenchantment with Copernicus. Lambert thus asks not only if we will ever be sufficiently Copernican but also that other and in the end much more bothersome question: "should we" perhaps "never have become Copernican" in the first place?[11] That is to say, is the insistence on objectivity perhaps a mistake that fails to do justice to how human beings are always bound to particular points of view and encourages them to aspire in vain to God's truth—or, to get away from theological discourse, to true objectivity?

2

I am concerned here not with Lambert, though he is no doubt one of the most thoughtful representatives of the Enlightenment, but with his two questions:

1. Will we ever become sufficiently Copernican?

2. Should we perhaps never have become Copernican in the first place?

Consider the first. To ask, if we will ever become sufficiently Copernican is to suggest that Copernican revolutions will have to be repeated over and over again, that there will have to be a series of Copernican revolutions. The rhetoric has by now become quite common. In the history of philosophy the most famous "Copernican" revolution is of course Kant's.

What did Kant mean when he invoked Copernicus? Bertrand Russell raised an obvious objection to an interpretation of Kant's achievement as a Copernican revolution. Kant would have been more nearly right, he writes in *Human Knowledge*, had he spoken of a Ptolemaic counterrevolution, since he attempted to restore the human knower to that central place from which Copernicus had dethroned him.[12] As a matter of fact, Kant himself does not use the expression "Copernican revolution," though what he says certainly invites talk of his having effected one. But back to Russell: does he not have a point? If we understand the Copernican revolution and its successor revolutions, such as Darwin's and Freud's, as having undercut the special position of the human being at the center, then it does indeed seem difficult to consider Kant's philosophical revolution Copernican.

But, as we have seen, Copernicus himself had a very different understanding of what he had accomplished. And does his revolution not presuppose rather than challenge a cognitive anthropocentrism? The rejection of geocentrism should not be thought of as entailing the rejection of this anthropocentrism. Furthermore, Russell's statement rests on a misunderstanding of what Kant meant. Kant appeals to what he calls Copernicus's "first thought,"[13] which he took to be the thought of the daily rotation of the earth. Whereas Russell is thinking of the shift from geocentrism to heliocentrism, Kant suggests that we might do well to assume the apparent motion of the stars to be an illusion based on the actual motion of the terrestrial observer. Similarly, Kant invites his readers to consider whether what we attribute to the objects around us might not in fact be contributed by our faculty of knowledge. The reflection on perspective is thus raised to a higher level: man's faculty of knowledge is interpreted on the model of his faculty of sight. Could experience perhaps be so governed by the subject's point of

view that what is experienced can be no more than appearance? Just as objective reality, according to Kant, eludes the eye, so the thing-in-itself eludes cognition.

Kant did not think that Copernicus had proved his hypothesis. Something approaching such a proof, he thought, had been furnished only by the physics of Kepler and Newton. Similarly, in his preface Kant offers his own transcendental idealism as no more than a hypothesis. The *Critique of Pure Reason* as a whole, especially the discussion of the antinomies, is taken to provide the proof. If this proof succeeds, humanist anthropocentrism would arguably have been vindicated by Kant, who could then be said to have succeeded where Descartes failed—and yet this humanist anthropocentrism is at the same time severely challenged. A theoretical knowledge of things as they are in themselves is said to be impossible. Kant, too, settles for the equivalent of what Descartes called "moral truth." Thus the reality Copernicus sought to describe is shown to be only phenomenal reality, that is, a reality relative to the knower, understood not as the particular human subject—Kant does not hold a subjective idealism—but as any rational being. Kant did not draw from this argument the conclusion that objectivity was an idle dream. Quite to the contrary: as already in Descartes, the turn to the subject, more especially to a purified, transcendental subject from which the thinker excludes the accidents of his own person, place, and time, ensures a genuinely objective knowledge of nature. Within the limits imposed by his understanding, the human being, according to Kant, can escape from the tyranny of perspective and strive for objective knowledge. But again, the objects with which science is concerned are, if Kant is right, not the things-in-themselves.

3

There is an obvious objection to the Kantian enterprise: can human beings really transform themselves into pure knowing subjects as Kant demands? Will they not always remain stuck in the human, all too human? The question leads to another Copernican revolution. If we can call Kant's a second Copernican revolution, may be a third.[14] The thought is once again that the earlier revolution was insufficiently radical, insufficiently self-critical, leaving too many of its own prejudices unchallenged. Crucial to this third

Copernican revolution is the belief that Descartes's or Kant's idea of a pure knowing subject that can grasp objects free from all merely cultural or subjective distortions was mistaken. We always remain caught up in our own cultural situation, with its prejudice and perspective. We always remain caught up in historically conditioned language games. A central theme of what I have called the third Copernican revolution is thus a reflection on language and history. Language is not the obedient servant of thought but its ruler. And language can be rendered so pure as to be free of those perspectival distortions that are part of human experience. For a thinker like Roland Barthes, there can be no escape from subjective prejudice:

Every utterance implies its own subject, whether this subject be expressed in an apparently direct fashion, by the use of "I," or indirectly, by being referred to as "he," or avoided altogether by means of impersonal constructions. Those are purely grammatical decoys, which do no more than vary the ways in which the subject is constituted within the discourse, that is, the way he gives himself to others, theatrically or as a phantasm; they all refer to forms of the imaginary. The most specious of these is the privative, the very one normally practiced by scientific discourse, from which the scientist excludes himself because of his own concern for objectivity.[15]

Barthes's remark may be taken as representative of the radicalization of Kant's Copernican revolution that has shaped much of twentieth-century philosophy and has turned Kant against himself.

Barthes is hardly the only one to deplore what he calls the spectacular exclusion of the person and to insist that the objectivity it yields is fantastic or imaginary. In chapter 6 I made reference to this quote from Heidegger's *Being and Time:*

The ideas of a "pure 'I'" and of a "consciousness in general" are so far from including the *a priori* character of "actual" subjectivity that the ontological character of the human being is either passed over or not seen at all. . . . Both the contention that there are "eternal truths" and the jumbling together of man's phenomenally grounded "ideality" with an idealized subject belong to those residues of Christian theology within philosophical problematics that have not as yet been radically extruded.[16]

The charge is that in drawing on the idea of a pure subject, be it the transcendental subject of Kant or the thinking subject of Descartes, to ground the possibility of a knowledge of objects—that is, to ground the understanding of objectivity that guides science as we know it—philosophers have drawn illegitimately on their theological precursors. Our science presupposes theology even as it covers up this presupposition. Heidegger here calls for a thinking that has rid itself of this burden.

The general point is indeed an obvious one. It was made already in the eighteenth century by Herder, who in his "Meta-Critique of the *Critique of Pure Reason*" protested against Kant's elision of the person and of ordinary language.[17] Against Kant, Herder insisted that we think with words, not with abstract concepts, and that we cannot think in any language other than our own. Instead of a *Critique of Pure Reason* we need a physiology of human faculties and a study of language as it is. It is an argument that was to be repeated in different forms by Nietzsche, Heidegger, and Wittgenstein. What matters here is the claim that human beings will never be able to free themselves from the limitations imposed on them by their language. If correct, there can be no genuine objectivity. Language will never become pure or innocent.

All this suggests that if we succeed in becoming even more critical than Kant, if we free his crucial insight from the remaining remnants of the Christian understanding of truth as founded in the creative, aperspectival vision of God, we will be forced to recognize that we have to submerge both subject and logos in the world and thus subject both to time. This recognition leads to a temporalization of structures to which Kant had given transcendental status. Instead of the categories, which according to Kant are constitutive of all possible experience, we have the claim that it is concrete language that constitutes our experience. Nietzsche's now so popular fragment "On Truth and Lie in an Extra-Moral Sense" illustrates what I have called the third Copernican revolution and challenges all faith in the possibility of gaining a truly objective knowledge.

I quoted this fragment, which begins with an invocation of the disproportion between our claim to knowledge and our actual conditions, in the introduction to this book. Measured by the spatial and temporal immensity of the cosmos, the location and duration of human existence dwindles to insignificance. The universe was not made for human beings, nor was it made to be known by human beings. In secularized form we have here a return to Osiander's position and to his renunciation of the claim to truth. Modernity's cognitive anthropocentrism, as we have seen, is framed by skepticism. Nor, if Nietzsche is right, is it really truth that matters to human beings—it is their own welfare, which of course for Nietzsche has been separated from any idea of divine grace.

The various languages placed side by side show that with words it is never a question of truth, never a question of adequate expression; otherwise, there would not be so many languages. The "thing in itself" (which is precisely what the pure truth, apart from any of its consequences, would be) is likewise something quite incomprehensible to the creator of language and something not in the least worth striving for. This creator only designates the relations of things to men, and for expressing these relations, he lays hold of the boldest metaphors. To begin with, a nerve stimulus is transferred into an image: first metaphor. The image, in turn, is imitated in a sound: second metaphor. And each time there is a complete overleaping of one sphere, right into the middle of an entirely new and different one.[18]

When Nietzsche writes that pure truth would be the thing in itself, he still follows the traditional understanding of truth, according to which truth in the fullest sense is the privilege of God. God alone, on this view, has a fully adequate grasp of things because his creative knowledge permits no gap between thought and reality: for God, to know is to create. His thought of the thing is the thing itself. But to human beings such knowledge is denied, the thing in itself is not even given to us as a measure of our knowledge.

So far we have not really gone beyond Kant's second Copernican revolution. But according to Nietzsche the Kantian demand for objectivity, even if it is admitted that objective knowledge can never be more than a knowledge of phenomena, rests on the illusion that we can exit from the labyrinth of subjective appearance. Given the complete unavailability and indeed uselessness of such divine truth, what then is truth? Nietzsche's often-cited answer:

A movable host of metaphors, metonymies, and anthropomorphisms: in short, a sum of human relations which have been poetically and rhetorically intensified, transferred, and embellished, and which, after long usage, seem to a people to be fixed, canonical, and binding. Truths are illusions which we have forgotten are illusions; they are metaphors that have become worn out and have been drained of sensuous force, coins which have lost their embossing and are now considered as metal and no longer as coins.[19]

The shift from poetic metaphor to the abstractions of theory is here seen as an impoverishment. There is no literal speech.

4

If Kant raised the Copernican revolution to a higher power, then the turn to language and history that characterizes so much modern philosophy raised the reflection on perspective to a still higher level. But with this recent turn, reflection on perspective has to undermine the Copernican confidence that the human being is capable of the truth. In this sense I have suggested that modernity is framed by skepticism: modernity, born from the defeat of the still medieval skepticism of someone like Osiander, may be said to come to an end as its cognitive anthropocentrism is undermined and the claim to truth surrendered.

Today it has indeed become more and more fashionable to consider human beings incapable of the truth. One could point to developments in the philosophy of science, to what was called the New Philosophy of Science represented by Thomas Kuhn and Paul Feyerabend. Following Nietzsche, we have learned to appreciate the fictional character even of scientific texts. Richard Rorty, whose *Mirror of Nature* gives symptomatic expression to what I have called the third Copernican revolution, thus insists that today we no longer can call Cardinal Bellarmine's objections to the Copernican theory, on the grounds that it conflicted with the scriptural interpretation of the heavenly fabric, in any way "illogical or unscientific."[20] According to this post-Copernican, postmodern philosopher, we simply do not know how to draw a clear line between theological and scientific discourse. Let me repeat here the opposite claim, stated already in the introduction: philosophy today, if it is to be more than an aesthetic play, must be able to explain why we must reject Cardinal Bellarmine's reflections—not as illogical but as unscientific. What forces us to side with Galileo against Bellarmine is the commitment to objectivity that is a presupposition of being scientific. And this commitment is a presupposition not only of science but also of the world we live in, of our understanding of reality. As I have tried to show, the privilege that modernity has accorded to objectivity was won in a pattern of thought we can call Copernican reflection.

Let me recall its key features. Crucially, it entails reflection on how our access to things is above all governed by a point of view that is inseparable from our location in time and space and from the makeup of our sense organs: that is to say, first we know only appearances. But such reflection inevitably suggests the possibility of going beyond these appearances and of gaining better access to reality. This distinction between appearance and invisible reality was, as we have seen, drawn expressly by Copernicus himself. Inevitably, reflection on the phenomenon of perspective will generate again and again the distinction between appearance and reality, the former subjective and perspectival, the latter less dependent on the distortions of perspective and in this sense more objective. At the same time, such reflection has to lead to a dissociation of reality and visibility. Objects as they are in themselves are essentially invisible: reality does not present itself to us as it is. It is seized only in our reconstructions, which are provided by science.

This modern understanding of reality rests on a twofold reduction of experience, whose nature and cost we must keep in mind.

First of all and most of the time we find ourselves caught up in the world. The way we encounter things is tied to the activities in which we are engaged. Their mode of presentation is bound up with our mood and interest and the inevitable distortions to which they lead. A first reduction attempts to liberate thought from such all-too-personal interests and perspectives. The self is disengaged from the world and made into a disinterested observer of what is. Being comes to be understood as mute presence to such a subject. The world is transformed into a collection of necessarily mute, meaningless pictures. As Schopenhauer points out, lost is the real significance of things, that element "by virtue of which these pictures do not march past us, strange and meaningless, as they would otherwise inevitably do, but speak to us directly, are understood, and acquire an interest that engrosses our whole nature."[21] The price that has to be paid for this first reduction is the banishment of meaning from the world. The pursuit of truth, so understood, cannot be divorced from nihilism.

Whereas the first reduction dissociates the meaningful and the sensible, the second reduction dissociates the sensible and the real. Once again reflection on perspective provides the key. Is not the way we experience things subject to the accident of our spatial and temporal location? But the perspective assigned to us by our body is not a prison. We can demand descriptions and forms of description that are as free as possible from all that binds discourse to a particular perspective and point of view. Mathematics, as we have seen, offers the key to such descriptions.

One may object that if the eyes do not see things as they are, the disembodied spirit has even less success; indeed it does not see at all. Nietzsche thus suggests that we have no organ for the truth.[22] Similarly Osiander had insisted that truth is the privilege of God. To the religiously motivated skepticism of someone like Osiander, who wanted to preserve the infinite distance that separates human beings from God, corresponds the modern skepticism of someone like Nietzsche, who no longer knows anything of God or sin but insists once again that the hope to seize reality, as it is, is vain, as is the hope to secure a foundation on which we can confidently raise the edifice of knowledge (to use this Cartesian metaphor). But we should not forget that modern science begins with and is still supported by the confidence that we are not altogether cut off from the truth. Descartes tried to prove that we have a right to such confidence or faith.

Nietzsche might have replied that if Copernicus clung to such faith in our ability to grasp reality, his adherence just shows that he was not yet sufficiently Copernican. And must we not say the same thing of Descartes and Kant? We thereby push reflection on perspective to a point where it has to turn against every cognitive optimism. The third Copernican revolution turns Copernican reflection against Copernican faith in the human ability to grasp reality as it is. And if, as I have suggested, such faith lies at the origin of the modern world, and therefore also at the origin of its nihilism, such destruction seems to promise a humanism beyond nihilism—a postmodern humanism that, to quote Geoffrey Hartman, has "blown the cover of reified or superobjective thinking,"[23] freed itself from modern logocentrism, and rendered theory more playful, not so much work as fun.

5

Modern romantics have long dreamed of a postmodern paradise where theory turns poetic and the rift that separates the sciences and the humanities is healed in a higher play. Unfortunately the realities of the modern world, the world we actually live in, argue differently. We have only to think of the profoundly ambiguous achievement of our technology to be awakened from such dreams. To the extent that the humanities surrender themselves to such play, they render themselves peripheral and ineffective. They become part of an attempt to cover up and escape from a reality that is found lacking. We may find attractive such flight from our often frightening modern reality, a reality that pushes the humanities more and more onto the defensive, to the periphery; we can escape into dreams of the arts and the humanities conquering science. But these remain dreams. Those in the humanities must understand and respect the gap that separates discourse committed to an understanding of objective reality from discourse committed to the preservation of humanity. In other words, humanists need to understand the legitimacy of science and of modernity if they are to have a genuinely critical function. In claiming this I am presupposing that what I called the third Copernican revolution and its attack on objectivity have failed. But is this presupposition justified?

Consider once more what argues for that third Copernican revolution. The crucial claims are that reality will never present itself to us in a way that is uncontaminated by perspective, that there will never be descriptions free of all prejudice. Both must, I think, be granted: things will never present themselves as they are, but offer only perspectival appearances. But if so, how can we claim objective truth—that is, truth understood as a correspondence between our thoughts or propositions and the objects themselves? Although the idea of such objects is necessarily an idea that we have constructed and that is subject to our prejudices, it does *not* follow that we cannot demand objectivity and state criteria that enables us to distinguish the more from the less objective account. And if we can make such a distinction, then the Enlightenment's prejudice against prejudice was more than just another prejudice. It only reaffirmed a commitment that is inseparable from the life of reflection.

Consider once more Heidegger's claim in *Being and Time* that the appeal to an idealized or pure subject to ground objectivity relies illegitimately on the traditional understanding of God. Why should modern science be discredited because it is guided by an understanding of reality that rests on presuppositions inseparable from Christian theology? How was it ever possible for human beings to think God as Petrarch or Eckhart or Cusanus thought him, as an aperspectival knower? This possibility presupposes, as Descartes recognized, that human beings are not lost in the finite. The thought of God as an infinite knower was possible only because there is a sense in which human beings transcend themselves as finite knowers in reflection. Reflection on the infinity of God had to awaken human beings to the infinity within themselves. The third Copernican revolution—and it does not matter whether we choose Heidegger, Nietzsche, or someone else to represent it—does not take seriously enough the power of reflection. There is something profoundly right about the traditional view that makes an aperspectival knower the measure of the finite and perspectival human knower. The legitimacy of this view is established in a reflection on knowledge and truth that in its fundamental structure is as old as philosophy itself: think of Thales wondering what things are really made of. The ideal of objectivity that guides modern science may be said to have its foundation in the traditional understanding of truth as correspondence. It is inseparable from the self-transcendence and self-elevation of the human spirit.[24] The theological reflection of the Middle Ages only raised speculations familiar to philosophy—voiced, for example, by Plato—to a higher level.

This ideal of objectivity has given and continues to give knowledge and more especially our knowledge of nature its direction. We do not know what revolutions in science still lie ahead, but it is inconceivable that science will retreat from its commitment to objectivity, that it will cease to speak the language of mathematics. Precisely because Bellarmine's discourse does not subject itself to this ideal, it cannot be considered scientific—but it is not therefore rendered illogical. To say that it is inconceivable that science would retreat from objectivity is not to say that there might not be a retreat from science itself, or some natural or human catastrophe that would make science as we know it impossible. But simply by virtue of its form of description—that is, simply by virtue of its greater objectivity—modern science may be said to have progressed beyond the Aristotelian science that preceded it. And this is also to say that our modern culture is not just another culture that may now be coming to an end, that it is not just chauvinistic prejudice or blind power that has led modernity to interpret itself as the culture toward which all of history has been tending. Hegel was right to insist that there is a progress to reflection and that this progress has helped shape the course of history.

It is hardly an accident that the whole world is succumbing to Western culture, notwithstanding powerful fundamentalist reactions here and abroad. It is no accident that we are unable to point to some other culture that offers effective resistance, much as we might hope to find one, just as we might hope that attacks launched on objectivity from so many different quarters today were more effective than they are. The concern and seriousness behind such hopes must be honored. For as Nietzsche saw, the progress that celebrates its triumphs in modern science and technology is necessarily attended by the specter of nihilism. The price of pursuing objectivity appears to be the progressive loss of whatever gives significance to human existence. Small wonder that dreams of postmodernism have long been part of modernity, though of course sometimes named something else, such as romanticism.

But are not my remarks just another example of the pre-Copernican illusion that we are lucky or perhaps unfortunate enough to be standing at the center, a sign that we still have not become Copernican enough? Should not historical reflection have made such cultural chauvinism impossible by now? To be sure, in our attempt to ground our understanding of what is, we will always appeal to centers, seek the true elements, search for foundations that will support the edifice of knowledge. But has not the immensity of space and time denied us every center? Has not every supposed foundation given way under further reflection, forcing the search for the true elements to be renewed once again?

Even answering each question "yes" does not lead to the conclusion that the pursuit of objective reality has therefore been fruitless. It has liberated our understanding, has given us a freer if by no means a completely free access to what is, and has granted us an ever more adequate understanding of the workings of nature, "adequacy" being here tied to power. Technology demonstrates daily the actual power we have gained by pursuing objectivity. To be sure, we also see with ever clearer eyes the frightening dimensions of such power. But we abdicate our responsibility to meet that threat when we seek refuge in a rhetoric that suggests that our science is not really superior to all science that has gone before it, or that our technological way of life is just one among many. Technology is not a simple tool that leaves us fully in charge: it is a force that threatens to reduce all it touches, including human beings, to material to be organized by and subjected to technological planning. But this reductiveness is a tendency, not a fate to which we have to submit—a tendency supported by an ontology that makes the human ability to understand and master, and that is to say to remake things, the measure of our being. Reality comes increasingly to mean what science can capture in its constructions. A different and richer ontology is needed, if there is to be a responsible critique of technology; and by "ontology" here I mean primarily not something thought up by philosophers, but an understanding of being that expresses itself concretely in the way we concern ourselves with persons and things. Such a critique is needed if there is to be a recognition of humanity— the pursuit of objective truth necessarily loses sight of persons—and a way of responsibly meeting the threat of nihilism. And today nihilism, which, as I have described it, cannot know anything of the value of human life, constitutes a threat that is beginning to affect everyone's life in very concrete ways.

I do not mean that such a more-encompassing ontology should invite us to take leave from the technological world. To do so would be altogether irresponsible. There are still countless problems that await technological solutions, including problems produced by technology. But the idea of boundless technological progress must be questioned, as must an ontology that reduces reality to the objective reality pursued by science. In other words, we need to reappropriate the truth of Kant's distinction between objective phenomena and things-in-themselves, a "truth" that cannot mean objective truth. We have little choice but to attempt to put technology in its place: we must affirm it, even welcome it, but at the same time keep our distance from it—as Heisenberg recognized when in *Das Naturbild der heutigen Physik* he cites an old Chinese story that warns that working with machines will give us a machine heart.[25]

COPERNICAN REVOLUTIONS

But if technology today threatens to gain dominion even over human beings, it does so only because and to the extent that they, that we, want this, only because the power and security technology promises continue to be valued more than the threat they pose is feared. Life, however, loses its meaning when nature and human beings are reduced to mere material for the technological process. To recognize that there is meaning only where there is respect is to know also that we are faced today not simply with guiding technological progress but with the much more difficult task of determining where the boundaries of such progress should be. And to the extent that the shape of our modern world is determined by the Cartesian promise that our science will make us the masters and possessors of nature, even of our own nature, that task can be accomplished only if we find the strength to renounce that promise and learn to overcome the dread of insecurity and death that supports it. Such renunciation anticipates and calls for a new ontology. It presupposes an overcoming of what the tradition would have called the sin of pride. Pride bids us place ourselves in God's position; cognitive pride bids us replace ourselves with our own constructions. Human reason is made the measure of all that is.

Avoiding such a view is difficult for us. Characteristically, modernity tends to replace God with the ideal scientist—or better, the ideal community of scientific researchers. The very traditional concept of pride leads us to the source of the hold over us by an ontology that must reduce persons and things to material for scientific or technological reconstruction. This pride is the other side of our inability to accept that we are not masters of our own being, that we are vulnerable and mortal. But such an ontology that reduces being to objective reality must strip being of value. Pride is the origin of nihilism.

An ontology is needed that is not born of pride. Such an ontology will recognize that the pursuit of truth has its measure in an ideal that will always be denied to human beings, accepting that the pursuit of truth demands objectivity even though we shall never be able to be altogether objective. But this ontology will also recognize that when reality in its entirety is subjected to the pursuit of objective truth, such a pursuit must become a movement toward nihilism. For the pursuit of objectivity is inseparable from the twofold reduction I sketched above, where the first reduction robs the world of meaning and the second transforms it into a ghostly collection of facts. That is to say, such an ontology will recognize that theory, while legitimate within its limits, does not provide our only access to what is, as every lover knows. Theory alone will never overcome nihilism. That conquest presupposes respect, above all respect for the earth and its inhabitants. Notwithstanding the decentering power of Copernican reflection, there is a sense in which such respect will return the earth to that central position from which Copernicus had dethroned it.

1

The term "astronoetics" demands an explanation. I found it in Hans Blumenberg's *Die Vollzähligkeit der Sterne*, a posthumously published collection of texts written in the course of almost three decades, circling somewhat uncertainly around the concept of theory.[1] Ever since I first encountered the *Legitimität der Neuzeit* some time in the late 1960s, Blumenberg's thought has been with me, accompanying me in my own work like a good spirit, helping me find my own way.

I never met Hans Blumenberg. To be sure, many years ago I did make an attempt to get him to visit Yale University for a year or a semester. His was a voice, I was convinced, that needed to be heard. And at first everything went well. The Philosophy Department at Yale extended its invitation; his first response was positive. But as the date at which he would have had to leave Germany approached and as with every passing week the possibility of leaving home threatened ever more insistently to become reality, his brief communications became more discouraging. In the end he did not come at all. Were there health problems that interfered? I don't remember. But somehow this change of heart seemed to fit quite well the mental image I had already formed of him from his work: first the lure of the far away, the fascination with journeying, far away from Münster, from Westphalia, from Germany; in the end the decision to content himself with just thinking about such journeys and to stay at home. Here, too, centrifugal and centripetal forces were at odds. The centripetal forces won out. And something like that seems to me to hold also for his thinking. Expressed in hyperbolic terms: Blumenberg was always unwilling to trade astronoetics for astronautics. I share his unwillingness.

The very last section of *Die Vollzähligkeit der Sterne* bears the title "Was ist Astronoetik?" "What is astronoetics?" The title of a much earlier section—"Auch Lichtenberg ein Astronoetiker," "Lichtenberg, too, a practitioner of astronoetics"—gives the reader a first idea of what to expect. In that section Blumenberg quotes Lichtenberg's version of the often-told story of Newton and his apple. "The story is this: an old inspector at the mint in London guessed why the moon, unsupported by nail or rope, hangs up there, when we walk beneath it, when one day an apple, not bigger than a fist, fell from a tree hitting his nose" (p. 66). The apple's fall is the occasion that led Newton to formulate his laws.

It is not Newton, the scientist, but Lichtenberg, the story telling, astronomy-infatuated satirist, struck by the way a triviality may occasion something momentous, who is here said to be "auch ein Astronoetiker" and it is to Lichtenberg that Blumenberg likens himself when in the book's final section he claims for himself the establishment of astronoetics. Blumenberg begins that section by telling us that had he not lacked the taste for dedications, he would have dedicated his book to Wolfgang Bargmann, a well-known brain anatomist and busybody, good at writing grant proposals and endlessly urging his colleagues at the University of Kiel to do likewise. Those urgings reached new heights in 1958. The first sputnik had been launched the year before and was now merrily peeping as it circled the earth, generating widespread panic in the West at being left in terrestrial dust by the progress of Russian astronautics. Bargmann did his best to encourage his colleagues to help eliminate this *Forschungsrückstand*, this research lag—the German makes it sound even more ominous—by formulating and submitting research proposals. Blumenberg knew of course that pure thinking is a breadless art, notwithstanding the story about Thales cornering the olive market—a story meant no doubt to show that philosophers, too, can be quite practical and worldly, should they only wish to be so. Blumenberg did not quite respond like Thales when pressured to make his contribution to the effort to help the West catch up with the Russians. But he decided to do his bit by at least simulating his colleague's concern. And so he, too, wrote a grant proposal, requesting unspecified financial support for an investigation of the then still invisible backside of the moon by pure thought alone. The results were to be published in a journal to be called *Current Topics on Astronoetics*. Thus astronoetics received its name, though its prehistory goes back at least to Thales. Philosophy and astronoetics indeed have the same origin.

In 1958 no one suspected that it would not be very long until the backside of the moon would be photographed and astronauts would actually land on the moon. Astronautics would seem to have rendered astronoetics irrelevant, just as the progress of science may seem to have rendered philosophy irrelevant. Has philosophy not long claimed as its own the white spots left on the maps we are furnished by science, their whiteness an irresistible invitation to pure thinking and imagining to take flight? But, as Blumenberg reminds us, "'Astronoetics' is called so not as an alternative to 'astronautics'—to think of instead of actually traveling somewhere. 'Astronoetics' also names the thoughtful consideration of whether, and if so just what sense it would make, to travel there. It could be that even after a successful round-trip, the question whether the effort had been worthwhile could not be decided" (p. 320). Astronoetics so understood does not just precede but also follows astronautics. In Blumenberg's astronoetics, centrifugal curiosity is balanced by centripetal care for the earth. And so understood astronoetics may well deserve funding after all: by occasionally pouring cold water on projects that would take many millions to realize, it might make an important contribution to human welfare.

2

Like Lichtenberg, Blumenberg was another *Astronoetiker*—indeed, as one might expect from the author of the name, the leading *Astronoetiker* of our time. But in the age of astronautics, is there really a need for this questionable discipline, astronoetics, in which much of this book has also been engaged? Astronautics here is also a metaphor for technology, and thus the question raises another, closely related: in the age of technology and the science that supports it, is there still a need for philosophy? Confronted with the oh-so-serious work of the scientist, is not insistence on the breadless and all-too-often seemingly pointless art of pure thinking either, as Blumenberg himself put it, insolence or obstinacy, relying on irony and humor to keep a positivistic science at bay? But, to quote Blumenberg once more, "what else was left to those left at home by astronautics?" (p. 548).

Blumenberg understood himself, and invites us late moderns to understand ourselves, as left at home by astronautics and just because of this in need of astronoetics. Left at home—that may suggest left behind, as the Russian astronaut Yury Gagarin once seemed to have left the West in the dust. And have the practitioners of astronoetics not been left in earthly dust by the progress of astronautics? Not quite, for despite repeated trips to the moon, despite manned and unmanned satellites circling the earth, astronautics has left not only astronoetics but all us, and that includes Neil Armstrong and his fellow astronauts, at home here on earth, to wonder whether the effort was worth it.

It is more than a trivial platitude to point out that astronautics has left us at home. The observation is tinged by regret. Dreams of leaving home, that place assigned us by our nature, for some much more wonderful reality have long been part of dreams of freedom: gnostic dreams that invite us to look at this world into which we have been cast as a world that withholds what we most deeply want, as not really a home at all but a prison. And science appears finally to be enabling us to flee this prison. On the other side of the gnostic understanding of the world as a prison—and we find today a distinctively postmodern gnosticism—are dreams of redemption from this world, of a homecoming to the "other." Might this saving "other" not be found somewhere out there, perhaps in deep space? Blumenberg helps us avoid being seduced by such dreams of the other.

Long before astronautics became a reality, when it was still no more than a dream of astronoetics, of thinkers such as Cusanus and Bruno, Kepler and Kant, the progress of astronomy and of science more generally had already made this earth seem ever less homelike—as Blumenberg put it, "dieses Dasein wollte nicht gemütlicher werden" (p. 548), where "wollte nicht" ambiguously suggests both a progress in which we find ourselves caught up and something we ourselves will and for which we thus bear responsibility. This growing "Ungemütlichkeit" finds expression in Nietzsche's lament, cited in the introduction of this book, that ever since Copernicus we have been slipping ever faster and faster away from the center into nothingness. As Nietzsche understands it, the modern world is shadowed by this loss of the center, *Verlust der Mitte*,[2] and by nostalgia for what has been lost. Have we not all become displaced persons since Copernicus? But should we understand this simply as a loss? Is it not rather something that something in us wants? What homecoming could satisfy our freedom?

A tendency toward self-displacement, toward self-decentering, would seem to be inseparably bound up with human freedom. To show that connection has been one point of this book. It is precisely such a self-decentering that found its classical expression in the tale of Thales who, looking up to the stars, fell into a well only to be ridiculed by that pretty Thracian servant girl for whom he did not have any eyes—a tale to which the *Astronoetiker* Hans Blumenberg, who called it the *Urgeschichte der Theorie*, returned many times, no doubt himself familiar with such mocking laughter. What did the stars matter to Thales? What do they matter to any of us earthlings?

Perhaps Vitruvius was thinking also of the story of Thales when, in his account of what makes the still-brutish builders of his first house different from such shelter-building animals as ants and bees, swallows and badgers, he mentions first not their extraordinary ability to use their hands, nor their capacity to imitate, learn from, and improve on what they observe, but their verticality, their upright posture, which lets them rise up from the horizontal earth, raise their eyes up from the supporting ground, and "gaze upon the splendour of the starry firmament."[3] Did the sublime spectacle of the starry sky awaken the spirit sleeping in Vitruvius's proto-humans, somewhat as the snake's promise, "you will be like God," opened the eyes of Adam and Eve? Did it awaken them at the same time to their own time-bound existence, to their mortality, even as eye and spirit, open to the firmament's apparently unchanging order, let them dream of a more perfect, more genuinely humane dwelling, not subject to the terror of time?

Vitruvius's description of the human being as the being who looks up to the firmament is of a piece with the Greek understanding of the human being as *zōon logon echon*, which becomes the Latin *animal rationale*. As the animal that possesses reason, the human being is the intersection of horizontal temporality and a vertical linking time to eternity: the *erecti homines* are not bound to their particular place, as are the *prona animalia*. Standing up and gazing at the firmament, admiring its order, the human being transcends his or her natural place. In the *Phaedrus* Plato therefore attributes wings to the soul. Our winged soul enables us to dream of flying, dream of leaving behind this terrestrial prison. Balloons, airplanes, and now spaceships have thus offered themselves as potent figures of liberation, symbols of "a freedom that always had consisted of not being fettered to the earthly, even if that was thought as transmigration of souls or ascent to heaven" (p. 210).

Related to this verticality is the biblical understanding of humans as beings who, created in the image of God, look up to God and thus transcend themselves, measuring themselves by the idea of a timeless, eternal logos. As I have tried to show, every attempt to speak the truth is witness to such self-transcendence, for when I claim truth for my words, I am saying something more than an accurate description of how I now happen to see some matter: the truth I claim is in principle open to all. To be sure, from the very beginning the pursuit of truth has been shadowed by that warning of Simonides, cited by Aristotle, that the truth will ever elude us human knowers. But even if Simonides should prove right and absolute truth should prove to be the property of God alone, the mere attempt to speak the truth is sufficient to show that we do indeed look up to and measure ourselves by a timeless, placeless logos, belonging to no one or to all.

I referred to the biblical understanding of human being as created in the image of God. But this reference, and the snake's promise, implies a warning: by claiming a higher place, a permanence and plenitude denied to them, human beings, like the proud, globular proto-humans of Aristophanes in Plato's *Symposium*, run the danger of losing their proper perfection and place; instead of rising beyond their mortal condition, they will become less than they were. Consider once more Icarus, who, lured by the splendor of the sun, flew high above the earth only to fall and perish: *cadet impostor dum super astra vehit* is the inscription above Alciatus's Icarus emblem, which bears the title *In Astrologos, Wider die Sterngucker,* "against the stargazers." The Icarus emblem would have made a good cover image for Blumenberg's projected *Current Topics on Astronoetics* (pp. 49–51)

Could we add another possible translation of *In Astrologos: Wider die Astronoetiker,* "against the practitioners of astronoetics"? But the *Astronoetiker* is not someone who actually seeks to fly high above the earth, although he does delight in thinking about and in reading accounts of such flights, even when they end in disaster. Such flights do not tempt him to leave the earth; they rather let this earth appear more precious, a bit more homelike, just as a winter storm raging outside may make the warmth within seem even more comfortable.

3

I have spoken of a growing *Ungemütlichkeit* that has attended the progress of science, especially the progress of astronomy, which has threatened to transform the earth into a spaceship adrift in boundless space. In the introduction I quoted the beginning of the second volume of Schopenhauer's *World as Will and Representation* and Nietzsche's appropriation of the great pessimist's dismal if sublime vision in "On Truth and Lie in an Extra-Moral Sense": the universe does not present itself to us as made for man, nor as made to be known by man. It is this thought of cosmic indifference that leads to nihilism, as modernist nostalgia for the lost center must be opposed to postmodern refusals of all supposed centers, refusals haunted by the promise of an unheard-of freedom.

But with what right can one deduce from the various decenterings effected by science that the human being could or should no longer be the center of his or her own interest (p. 493)? As Blumenberg has pointed out, there is no logical connection between geocentrism and anthropocentrism—no logical connection between scientific decenterings on the one hand, and existential decenterings, on the other. He thereby teaches one important lesson of astronoetics, and in this sense my book too seeks to make a contribution to astronoetics. A whole series of Copernican revolutions may have called into question our position at the center of the cosmos, but that questioning has not robbed us of our home. There is a sense in which not just astronautics but science has left us behind, so far behind that it has lost sight of the whole human being; by the same token it has both left us at home and left us our home. In this double sense Blumenberg helps us understand and affirm ourselves ourselves as *die Daheimgebliebenen der Astronautik.*

Daheimgebliebenen der Astronautik: the phrase may seem to carry an aura of regret to those dreaming of journeys into some sublime beyond. Are we who were left at home not those who were left behind by the progress of astronautics? Many of us remember where we were when we saw the first televised images of the first human landing on the moon on July 20, 1969. Had we been left behind? I was in Maine at the time. My wife and I awakened the children so that they would not miss this momentous event. They were too sleepy to show much interest. Only our seven-year-old son kept staring at our then still black-and-white television screen and finally said, "Look at all those green people." We sent him back to bed. What we saw was of course not nearly as interesting. Did this demonstration of American technical know-how have more value than a giant military parade meant to intimidate the Russians and to reassure the West of the superiority of the democratic way of life, as the *Astronoetiker* Hans Blumenberg has suggested? Popular comparisons of what had just happened to the discovery of America were no more than wishful thinking: no new world opened itself to us; despite Neil Armstrong's famous words, humanity did not take a giant leap. What Armstrong and Buzz Aldrin had to tell us was not nearly as exciting as the stories brought home by a Columbus or even by explorers of the dark continent in the nineteenth century. Not only did the astronauts not see God out there, they did not even see little green men, only mute matter. As a result of the moon landings, space lost another part of the aura with which it has so long been invested—think of Stanley Kubrick's film *2001: A Space Odyssey*, released just a year before the first moon landing. As that film demonstrated once again, the aura of space had from the very beginning been supported by two contradictory desires: on the one hand the desire for the sublime, the longing for the excitement of encountering something totally other, an excitement born of a gnostic longing for a reality beyond this all-too-familiar world; on the other hand the desire for the beautiful, the longing to encounter out there intelligence much like our own, so that instead of feeling lost in space, we could once more feel at home in this now so greatly enlarged cosmos.

Looking up at the stars, Vitruvius's primitive builders experienced themselves as responding to a higher spirit. And the thought that spirit out there should answer to our own spirit did not die with Ptolemaic cosmology, nor did it die with the old God. Quite the opposite: astronoetic speculations about intelligent life, first on the moon, then on some planet, and if not there at least somewhere in this celestial desert, have attended the progress of astronomy and have been part of the Enlightenment; they seem to be warranted by the conviction that out of the cosmic soup had to emerge life and intelligence, that from the very beginning matter was bound to give birth to spirit. Is it more than an anthropocentric prejudice that insists that intelligence emerged only once, here on earth? The distances are growing, and with every astronomical and astronautical advance the suspicion that we are after all, certainly for all practical purposes, alone in the cosmos becomes ever more insistent: even if there were intelligent beings somewhere out there, curious or perhaps compassionate or stupid enough to want to engage us in conversation, the cosmic distances make it unlikely that we would ever have the time necessary to communicate with those unknown aliens we both dread and long for—and to whom on August 20, 1977, we sent an astronautical valentine of sorts. It was a copper record crammed with representative music and information about life here on earth, including greetings in sixty languages, carried by the space probe Voyager 2 into the unknown, complete with record player, needle, and easy-to-decipher instructions. In 1989 it passed Neptune (pp. 501–504).

As long as we do not experience in our world incarnations of spirit we cannot feel at home in it. Vitruvius thus has his primitive builders gaze at the starry firmament and build their houses in the image of the well-ordered cosmos to make them more homelike. An echo of such correspondence between above and below finds expression in some verses by Hans Carossa that Hans Blumenberg cites in the beginning of *Die Vollzähligkeit der Sterne:*

Finsternisse fallen dichter
Auf Gebirge, Stadt und Tal.

Doch schon flimmmern kleine Lichter
Tief aus Fenstern ohne Zahl.
Immer klarer, immer milder,
Längs des Stroms gebognen Lauf,
Blinken irdische Sternenbilder
Nun zu himmlischen herauf. (p. 33)

The constellations formed, as darkness falls over mountain, city, and valley, by the artificial lights of human habitations answer to the constellations above. But what are the latter to those living in a modern megalopolis with its overpresence of artificial light? "In what province," asks Blumenberg, "will those live, who can relate Hans Carossa's verses to their own experiences?" "Perhaps the poet wanted to speak of something that already then was no longer self-explanatory, because it gave expression to a trust in the world, that made it for the belated reader a dark text, let it become something no longer understood, under suspicion of a no-longer-permitted *Behaglichkeit*"—ill-translated as "comfort." "But," Blumenberg continues, "this, too, must be kept in mind: that the poet did not know and did not expect the consolation that was granted to those who came only a little later by seeing the earth from space, our own planet before the black darkness of the sky"—"this cosmic oasis on which the human being lives," as he had described it in *Die Genesis der kopernikanischen Welt:* "This miracle of an exception . . . in the midst of the celestial desert is no longer 'also a star,' but the only one that seems to deserve this name."[4]

Between these two experiences, that of the poet and that of the *Astronoetiker,* lies astronautics, both its promise and, for the *Astronoetiker* Blumenberg of even greater interest, also the disenchantment it has brought. This disenchantment opens up the way to a new geocentrism and a new anthropocentrism. From this perspective it seems to be more than mere coincidence that in 1962, when John Glenn became the first American to circle the earth, Rachel Carson launched the environmentalist movement in this country with the publication of *Silent Spring;* Blumenberg calls our attention to the fact that the year of the first moon landing is also the year the Germans coined the word *Umweltschutz* to name a department of the

Ministry of the Interior (p. 439). And not long ago Vice President Al Gore suggested that we send a satellite into space to beam back images of the earth, invoking Socrates who, according to Gore, 2,500 years ago said that "Man must rise above the earth to the top of the atmosphere and beyond, for only thus will he understand the earth in which he lives."[5] He might have cited the conclusion of *Die Genesis der kopernikanischen Welt:* "Only as the experience of a re-turn will it be accepted that for the human being there is no alternative to the earth, just as there are no alternatives of reason to human reason."[6] Out of such acceptance can grow a new responsibility.

4

The assertion that "there is no alternative to the earth, just as there are no alternatives of reason to human reason," invites us to consider what a philosophy would be like that took seriously the challenge of astronoetics. To claim that "there are no alternatives of reason to human reason" is to recognize that despite what is here asserted, we not only dream of a reason beyond that reason that happens to be our own—dream of a pure reason not contaminated by natural language and metaphor, of a philosophical homecoming—but also take steps to realize such dreams. Behind such steps lies the hope that by thus raising ourselves above the place assigned to us by nature and history, we will finally come home to ourselves. And Blumenberg knew very well that Descartes's promise of a practical philosophy that would render us the masters and possessors of nature, including our own nature, was not idle. That promise bears witness to the power of self-transcendence that not only lets us oppose to the place where we happen to find ourselves the idea of unbounded space, to the time allotted to us the idea of an endless time, but also to that language in which we happen to think the idea of a pure language no one has yet spoken, to the always-situated self we happen to be the idea of an absolute subject—which is also the idea of a mode of access to things that would reveal them as they really are. The attempt to actually seize what such self-transcendence promises must leave behind that world in which we first of all and still most of the time feel at home. But the pursuit of truth demands this attempt. Does it also promise to compensate us for the home left behind?

As we have seen, both Francis Bacon and Descartes thought that their new science would return to us that paradise lost because of Adam's pride. And in this expectation they were hardly alone: our leave-taking from what we first experience as home is haunted by the idea of a return to our unknown true home. How are we to think this home? That it would have to be altogether other than our terrestrial home stands to reason, as does our lacking words to name what here haunts us. Far easier to find metaphors to express the sense of homelessness that is a presupposition of such dreams.

One such metaphor, a metaphor Blumenberg has explored at length, is that of a ship at sea, under way, of uncertain origin and unknown destination.[7] In this connection he cites Paul Lorenzen's use of a ship at sea as a metaphor for our language, the language in which we dwell: "If there is no *terra firma* we can reach, the ship has to have been built by our ancestors. They must have been able to swim and built themselves—perhaps out of wood that was drifting around—some sort of raft, improved it over and over, so that today it has become a ship so comfortable that we have no longer the courage to jump into the water and start once again from the beginning."[8] But does this mean that the leap is impossible? Does it even mean that we should not leap? As Blumenberg points out, Lorenzen's parable makes it difficult to understand what should tempt those who have grown accustomed to life on their ship to want to leave it in order to start all over. He speaks also for himself when he suggests that the parable only "strengthens the conviction to remain on the comfortable ship," to watch from a safe distance those who possess and would like to spread the courage to jump into the water, perhaps convinced that it will always be possible to return to the still intact ship, "that preserve of a despised history."[9] We sense here what separates Blumenberg from those modernists who, like Descartes or, in a very different key, like the Heidegger of *The Origin of the Work of Art*, would replace the ship on which we happen to find ourselves with one we have built ourselves. Descartes wisely admonishes us not to allow revolutionary zeal, our demiurgic eagerness to construct a new world-home, to tear down that old home, in which we were after all quite comfortable, before the new one has been completed. But Blumenberg's response to Lorenzen's parable also makes clear what separates him even more profoundly from those postmodernists who, valuing sublimity over beauty, would have us leap into the water, not on the way to a new ship but because, infatuated with the swimmer's freedom, they would have us renounce the comforts of home—only in theory, to be sure, confident that there still will always be that original ship to which they can return when they tire of swimming.

When Blumenberg suggests that Lorenzen's parable only "strengthens the conviction to remain on the comfortable ship," he invites a question: what then tempts those who want to leave the ship, either to build themselves a new one or perhaps just to swim? Why did we travel to the moon? Is it too simple to answer, just because it is there and we now had the means to get there? Because of that curiosity, that desire to know just for the sake of knowing, that Aristotle makes constitutive of human being? If human beings by their very nature desire to know, then it is their own nature that calls them again and again beyond the points of view and perspectives assigned to them by whatever happens to be their place in the world, calls them away from what they once called home. The loss of paradise will be repeated over and over through human curiosity. The pursuit of truth demands objectivity, but, as Blumenberg also notes, such objectivity has to elide all that might let us take an interest in that world, has to transform it into a "sphere of indifference *toward all.*"[10] To this indifference of the world corresponds the loss of the knower's own subjectivity: both have their foundation in that self-transcendence of the mundane subject, which "completes itself by making the most difficult of all concessions that can be expected of it: to let its world become the world, to witness the transformation of its lifetime into one of many lifetimes, into world-time, and as such alienated from itself."[11] To the extent that the world we live in has in fact been shaped by this renunciation, it is anything but *gemütlich*, one reason why just today we need Blumenberg's *Astronoetik*, which, as he tells us, by opposing to the astronaut's centrifugal longing the centripetal desire to come home also aims at *Gemütlichkeit.*

In this connection Hans Blumenberg would have us remember that the earth, which once, because of its central position in a finite cosmos, was thought to provide human beings with a privileged place for the *theōria* of the cosmos, a place that allowed them to actually observe all that mattered, and which then came to be understood as just another among countless stars, "as a result of the technology of space travel has unexpectedly 'shown' us a property that extends to us something rather like grace: that it is possible to come back home to the earth, if one has been sufficiently curious and self-assertive to leave it. Odysseus—once more and dressed in the space suit of a figure of humanity: To return to Ithaca—this much has not changed—requires and rewards the widest detour" (p. 383). In the wake of astronautics, astronoetics invites an altogether new postpostmodern geocentrism.

Notes

1 Introduction: The Problem of the Modern

1. Suzi Gablik, *Has Modernism Failed?* (New York: Thames and Hudson, 1984), p. 114.

2. See Denis Hollier, *Against Architecture: The Writings of Georges Bataille*, trans. Betsy Wing (Cambridge, Mass.: MIT Press, 1989), p. xi.

3. Ibid., p. ix; quoting Georges Bataille, "Architecture," in *Oeuvres Complètes*, 12 vols. (Paris: Gallimard, 1971–1988), 1:171–172.

4. Ibid., p. xii.

5. Friedrich Nietzsche, *Zur Genealogie der Moral*, III, par. 25, in *Sämtliche Werke: Kritische Studienausgabe*, ed. Giorgio Colli and Mazzino Montinari (Munich: Deutscher Taschenbuch Verlag; Berlin: de Gruyter, 1980), 5:404 (this edition is abbreviated hereafter as KSA). Trans. Walter Kaufmann and R. J. Hollingdale as *On the Genealogy of Morals and Ecce Homo* (New York: Vintage, 1989), p. 155.

6. Arthur Schopenhauer. *The World as Will and Representation*, trans. E. F. J. Payne, 2 vols. (New York: Dover, 1966), p. 2:3.

7. Friedrich Nietzsche, "Über Wahrheit und Lüge im aussermoralischen Sinne," KSA 1:875. Trans. as "On Truth and Lie in an Unmoral Sense," in *Philosophy and Truth: Selections from Nietzsche's Notebooks of the Early 1870's*, trans. and ed. Daniel Breazeale (Atlantic Highlands, N.J.: Humanities Press, 1979), p. 79.

8. See Hans Blumenberg, *Lebenszeit und Weltzeit* (Frankfurt am Main: Suhrkamp, 1986).

9. Ivan Turgenev, *Fathers and Sons*, trans. Constance Garnett (New York: Modern Library, 1950), pp. 148–149.

10. Rainer Maria Rilke, *Die Aufzeichnungen des Malte Laurids Brigge*, in *Werke in drei Bänden* (Frankfurt am Main: Insel, 1966), 3:269. Trans. Walter Kaufmann in *Existentialism from Dostoevsky to Sartre* (New York: Meridian, 1956), p. 119.

11. Cf. Hans Blumenberg, *Schiffbruch mit Zuschauer: Paradigma einer Daseinsmetapher* (Frankfurt am Main: Suhrkamp, 1979).

12. Nietzsche, *Zur Genealogie der Moral*, III, par. 25, KSA 5:404; trans., *On the Genealogy of Morals*, p. 155.

13. Friedrich Nietzsche, *Die fröhliche Wissenschaft*, III, par. 125, KSA 3:480–481; trans. Walter Kaufmann, as *The Gay Science*, in *The Portable Nietzsche* (New York: Viking, 1959), pp. 95–96.

14. Karl Jaspers, *Der philosophische Glaube* (Frankfurt am Main: Fischer, 1958), p. 116. Except where specified otherwise, all translations are my own.

15. Turgenev, *Fathers and Sons*, p. ix. Cf. pp. 24 ff.

16. Consider the explanation of his mission given by Adolf Hitler to Hermann Rauschning: "Providence has predestined me to become the greatest liberator of humanity. I liberate human beings from the coercion of a spirit that has become its own end, from the dirty and demeaning self-lacerations of a chimera called conscience and morality, and from the demands of a freedom and personal autonomy, only very few are up to." Quoted in Joseph Wulf, *Die bildenden Künste im Dritten Reich: Eine Dokumentation* (Hamburg: Rowohlt, 1966), p. 12.

17. Hans Blumenberg, *Die Legitimität der Neuzeit* (Frankfurt am Main: Suhrkamp, 1966), trans. Robert M. Wallace as *The Legitimacy of the Modern Age* (Cambridge,

Mass.: MIT Press, 1983); and *Die Genesis der kopernikanischen Welt* (Frankfurt am Main: Suhrkamp, 1975), trans. Robert M. Wallace as *The Genesis of the Copernican World* (Cambridge, Mass.: MIT Press, 1987).

18. Alexander Koyré, *From the Closed World to the Infinite Universe* (New York: Harper Torchbook, 1958), p. 3.

19. Ibid., p. v.

20. Pierre Duhem, *Medieval Cosmology*, ed. and trans. Roger Ariew (Chicago: University of Chicago Press, 1985), p. 3.

21. Koyré, *From the Closed World to the Infinite Universe*, pp. v–vi, 3–4.

22. René Descartes, *Discourse on the Method VI*, in *The Philosophical Works*, trans. Elizabeth Haldane and G. R. T. Ross, 2 vols. (New York: Dover, 1955), 1:119; *Oeuvres de Descartes*, ed. Charles Adam and Paul Tannery, 8 vols. (Paris: J. Vrin, 1964), 6:62.

23. Leonardo Olschki, *Die Literatur der Technik und der angewandten Wissenschaften vom Mittelalter bis zur Renaissance* (Leipzig: Olschki, 1919), p. 59.

24. J. V. Field, *The Invention of Infinity: Mathematics and Art in the Renaissance* (Oxford: Oxford University Press, 1997), pp. 4–19. See also Richard Hadden, *On the Shoulders of Merchants: Exchange and the Mathematical Conception of Nature in Early Modern Europe* (Albany: State University of New York Press, 1994).

25. Nicolaus Copernicus, *De revolutionibus Orbium Caelestium* I.1, in *Das Neue Weltbild, Drei Texte: Commentariolus, Brief gegen Werner, De revolutionibus I*, Lateinisch-deutsch, trans., ed., and intro. Hans Günter Zekl (Hamburg: Meiner, 1990), p. 86; trans. in Koyré, *From the Closed World to the Infinite Universe*, p. 31.

26. Ibid., I.10, p. 136; trans., p. 33.

27. Cf. Frances A. Yates, *Giordano Bruno and the Hermetic Tradition* (Chicago: University of Chicago Press, 1979).

28. Koyré, *From the Closed World to the Infinite Universe*, p. 43.

29. John Donne, "An Anatomie of the World," "The first Anniversary," in *Poetical Works*, ed. J. L. Grierson (Oxford: Oxford University Press, 1971), pp. 212–213.

30. Blumenberg, *Legitimität*, pp. 11–74.

31. Donne, "An Anatomie of the World," pp. 215–216.

2   Perspective and the Infinity of the Universe

1. Alexander Koyré, *From the Closed World to the Infinite Universe*, (New York: Harper Torchbook, 1958), p. 5.

2. Ibid., p. 278 nn. 5, 6.

3. Ibid., p. 8.

4. Thomas P. McTighe, "Nicholas of Cusa's Theory of Science and its Metaphysical Background," in *Nicolò Cusano: Agli Inizi del Mondo Moderno*, Atti del Congraso internazionale in occasione del V centenario della morte di Nicolò Cusano, Bressanone, 6–10 settembre 1964 (Florence: Sansoni, 1970), p. 317. See also A. Richard Hunter, "What Did Nicholas of Cusa Contribute to Science?" in *Nicholas of Cusa: In Search of God and Wisdom*, ed. Gerald Christianson and Thomas M. Izbecki (Leiden: Brill, 1991), pp. 101–115.

5. See Günter Gawlick, "Zur Nachwirkung cusanischer Ideen im Siebzehnten und Achtzehnten Jahrhundert," in *Nicolò Cusano*, pp. 225–239.

6. Koyré, *From the Closed World to the Infinite Universe*, p. 18. See also Karsten Harries, "The Infinite Sphere: Comments on the History of a Metaphor," *Journal of the History of Philosophy* 13, no. 1 (1975), pp. 5–15. This and the following chapter develop the argument of my article.

7. See Edmond Vansteenberghe, *Le cardinal Nicolas de Cues (1401–1464), l'action, la pensée* (Frankfurt am Main: Minerva, 1963); Maurice de Gandillac, *La philosophie de Nicolas de Cues* (Paris: Aubier, 1942), and thoroughly rev. German ed., *Nikolaus von Cues: Studien zu seiner Philosophie und philosophischen Weltanschauung*, trans. Karl Fleischmann (Düsseldorf: Schwann, 1953); Erich Meuthen, *Nikolaus von Kues 1401–1464: Skizze einer Biographie*, 2nd rev. ed. (Münster: Aschendorff, 1992).

8. See Will-Erich Peuckert, *Die Große Wende: Das apokalyptische Saeculum und Martin Luther*, 2 vols. (Darmstadt: Wissenschaftliche Buchgesellschaft, 1948), 2:501–505.

9. See *Acta Cusana: Quellen zur Lebensgeschichte des Nikolaus von Kues*, ed. Erich Meuthen, Bd. I, 1 (Hamburg: Meiner, 1976), Nrs. 2–10, 13.

10. Gerd Heinz-Mohr, "Bemerkungen zur Spiritualität der Brüder vom gemeinsamen Leben," in *Nicolò Cusano*, p. 471.

11. See *Acta Cusana*, Nr. 11, pp. 3–4.

12. See Paul E. Sigmund, *Nicholas of Cusa and Medieval Political Thought* (Cambridge, Mass.: Harvard University Press, 1963), pp. 11–38.

13. Ibid., pp. 221, 227.

14. Ibid., p. 233.

15. Ibid., p. 224. Cf. Peuckert, *Die Große Wende*, 2:501–505.

16. Sigmund, *Nicholas of Cusa*, p. 229.

17. Ibid., p. 228.

18. Ibid., p. 225.

19. Erich Meuthen, *Die letzten Jahre des Nikolaus von Kues: Biographische Untersuchungen nach neuen Quellen* (Köln: Westdeutscher Verlag, 1958), p. 28.

20. Ibid., pp. 116–122.

21. Ibid., pp. 122–125.

22. *Vir ipse, quod rarum est in Germania, supra opinionem eloquens et Latinus, historias idem omnes non priscas modo, sed mediae tempestatis tum veteres, tum recentiores usque ad nostra tempora memoria retinebat.* Cited in Nikolaus von Cues, *Vom Nichtanderen*, trans. Paul Wilpert, (Hamburg: Meiner, 1952), p. 101 n. 1.

23. See Peuckert, *Die Große Wende*, 2:333–344.

24. On Hermes Trismegistus and the Hermetic tradition, see Frances A. Yates, *Giordano Bruno and the Hermetic Tradition* (Chicago: University of Chicago Press, 1979), pp. 1–19; see also p. 247 n. 2. That the author of the Hermetic texts could not have been the legendary Egyptian, but that they dated from early Christian times and were in fact dependent on Platonic and Christian texts, was shown by Isaac Casaubon in 1614 (pp. 398–403).

25. Jorge Luis Borges, "The Fearful Sphere of Pascal," in *Labyrinths: Selected Stories and Other Writings* (New York: New Directions, 1964), pp. 189–192.

26. Thomas S. Kuhn, *The Structure of Scientific Revolutions*, 2nd ed. (Chicago: University of Chicago Press, 1970), p. 117.

27. The best account of the history of the infinite sphere is Dietrich Mahnke, *Unendliche Sphäre und Allmittelpunkt* (Halle: Niemeyer, 1937). In tracing that history, Mahnke stresses the importance of Cusanus and shows that modern cosmology has at least one of its roots in mathematical mysticism. But his account leaves the philosophical significance of this connection somewhat obscure.

28. For a good discussion of "the speculative interpretation of the infinite sphere in Nicholas of Cusa's *On Learned Ignorance*," see Elizabeth Brient, "The Immanence of the Infinite: A Response to Blumenberg's Reading of Modernity," (Ph.D. diss., Yale University, 1995), pp. 228–313.

29. Nicholas of Cusa, *On Learned Ignorance*, trans. Jasper Hopkins (Minneapolis: Banning, 1981), II. 12, pp. 116–117. This edition is hereafter cited parenthetically in the text.

30. Nicolaus Copernicus, *De revolutionibus Orbium Celestium*, I, 8 in *Das neue Weltbild: Drei Texte: Commentariolus, Brief gegen Werner, De revolutionibus I*, Lateinisch-deutsch, trans., ed., and intro. Hans Günter Zekl (Hamburg: Meiner, 1990); trans. as "The Revolutions of the Celestial Spheres," in *The*

Portable Renaissance Reader, ed. James Bruce Ross and Mary Martin McLaughlin (New York: Viking, 1953), p. 591.

31. Tycho Brahe, *De Nova Stella,* trans. J. H. Walden as "The New Star" in Ross and McLaughlin, *The Portable Renaissance Reader,* pp. 593–.

32. See chapter 7, section 3.

33. See Günter Gawlick, "Zur Nachwirkung cusanischer Ideen," pp. 225–239.

34. Tommaso Campanella, *Apologia pro Galileo* (Frankfurt am Main: Tampach, 1622), p. 9; Gawlick, "Zur Nachwirkung cusanischer Ideen," p. 329.

35. Gawlick, "Zur Nachwirkung cusanischer Ideen," p. 232.

36. Hans Blumenberg, *Die Genesis der kopernikanischen Welt* (Frankfurt am Main: Suhrkamp, 1975), pp. 783–794.

37. "Close Encounters with Alien Beings Are Held Unlikely," *New York Times,* November 4, 1979, p. 12.

3 Learned Ignorance

1. Nicholas of Cusa, *On Learned Ignorance,* trans. Jasper Hopkins (Minneapolis: Banning, 1981), I.1; p. 50. This edition is hereafter cited parenthetically in the text.

2. Plato, *Republic* 10. 602 c–d, trans. Benjamin Jowett (New York: Random House, 1960).

3. Jasper Hopkins, preface to Nicholas of Cusa, *On Learned Ignorance,* p. vii.

4. See Karsten Harries, "The Philosopher at Sea," in *Nietzsche's New Seas: Explorations in Philosophy, Aesthetics, and Politics,* ed. Michael Allen Gillespie and Tracy B. Strong (Chicago: University of Chicago Press, 1988), pp. 21–44.

5. Ludwig Wittgenstein, *Philosophical Investigations,* trans. G. E. M. Anscombe (New York: Macmillan, 1959) par. 123; Aristotle, *Metaphysics* 1.2, 982b1, 11–17, trans. W. D. Ross in *The Complete Works of Aristotle: The Revised Oxford Translation,* ed. Jonathan Barnes, 2 vols. (Princeton: Princeton University Press, 1984), vol. 2; this translation is hereafter cited parenthetically in the text. Cf. p. 143.

6. Jasper Hopkins, *Nicholas of Cusa's Debate with John Wenck: A Translation and an Appraisal of "De Ignota Litteratura" and "Apologia Doctae Ignorantiae,"* 3rd ed. (Minneapolis: Banning, 1988), pp. 21–22.

7. Schopenhauer, where Wittgenstein could find the term "family resemblance" *(Familienähnlichkeit),* interpreted such a seeing as perceiving a Platonic Idea, with an eye not only on Plato but on Kant's understanding of the aesthetic idea. To see a Platonic Idea is to see in the particular the characteristic and essential.

Such seeing is a presupposition of concept formation. Cusanus would have us understand such seeing as openness to God's creative Word, which is nothing other than the thing, now understood not as a mute fact but as an incarnation of the divine logos.

8. See Hopkins's note in Nicholas of Cusa, *On Learned Ignorance*, pp. 184–185 n. 6.

9. Immanuel Kant, *The Critique of Pure Reason*, A 235–236/B 294–295, trans. Norman Kemp Smith (London: Macmillan, 1933).

10. Thomas Aquinas, *De veritatem*, qu. I, art. 1 and 2.

11. On the "truth of things," see Karsten Harries, "Truth and Freedom," in *Edmund Husserl and the Phenomenological Tradition*, ed. Robert Sokolowski (Washington, D.C.: Catholic University of America Press, 1988), pp. 136–139.

12. See pp. 81–82, especially note 7, above.

13. For a good discussion of this transference, see Elizabeth Brient, "The Immanence of the Infinite: A Response to Blumenberg's Reading of Modernity," (Ph.D. diss., Yale University, 1995), pp. 228–256.

14. See Dietrich Mahnke, *Unendliche Sphäre und Allmittelpunkt* (Halle: Niemeyer, 1937), pp. 76–106, 144–158, 169–176, and Herbert Wackerzapp, *Der Einfluß Meister Eckharts auf die ersten philosophischen Schriften des Nikolaus von Kues (1440–1450)* (Münster: Aschendorff, 1962), pp. 140–151.

15. Clemens Baeumker, "Das pseudo-hermetische 'Buch der 24 Meister' (Liber XXIV philosophorum): Ein Beitrag zur Geschichte des Neupythagoreismus und Neuplatonismus im Mittelalter," *Beiträge zur Geschichte der Philosophie und Theologie des Mittelalters* 25 (1928), p. 208, prop. 2: "Deus est sphaera infinita, cuius centrum est ubique, circumferentia nusquam." In Alan of Lille's *Regulae theologicae* we find the closely related and dependent formulation: "Deus est sphaera intelligibilis, cuius centrum ubique, circumferentia nusquam." It is thus possible to distinguish two strands in the history of the sphere, one having "infinite" where the other has "intelligible." Eckhart and Cusanus are familiar with both versions. Cf. Mahnke, *Unendliche Sphäre und Allmittelpunkt*, pp. 171–174; Wackerzapp, *Der Eintluß Meister Eckharts*, pp. 141–144.

16. Edward J. Butterworth suggests that "one must take issue with Karsten Harries who sees a gradual transition (and one which he deems necessary) from the infinite sphere as a metaphor for God to a metaphor for the created cosmos. I do not find evidence for such an evolution, since it seems that as early as Alan of Lille, the world as sphere is treated as a reflection of God as Sphere. Cusanus appears to be placing himself solidly within this tradition in which the geometry of the sphere represents that which is most perfect in the cosmos and which, therefore, is best suited to re-

vealing the presence of God in the cosmos." See "Form and Significance of the Sphere in Nicholas of Cusa's *De Ludo Globi*," in *Nicholas of Cusa: In Search of God and Wisdom*, ed. Gerald Christianson and Thomas M. Izbecki (Leiden: Brill, 1991), p. 99; see also pp. 89 n. 4, 91 n. 10. While I find the term "gradual" misleading, it seems to me impossible to deny that there is indeed a transition: Alan of Lille's use of the metaphor is clearly not that of Cusanus, let alone that of Giordano Bruno. Butterworth's focus on Alan of Lille's *intelligibilis* rather than on the *infinitus* of the *Liber XXIV philosophorum*, on Cusanus's meditation on perfect *rotunditas* in *De Ludo Globi* rather than on his conjectures concerning the infinity of the universe in *De Docta Ignorantia*, helps him place Cusanus in a familiar tradition, but fails to do justice to the way his use of the infinite sphere looks forward to Bruno.

17. See chapter 9.

18. Hopkins, *Nicholas of Cusa's Debate with John Wenck*, pp. 26–27.

19. Hans Blumenberg has called Cusanus's thought of a circle whose radius becomes infinite—a thought offered to the reader as a representation of the *coincidentia oppositorum*—a *Sprengmetapher*: a metaphor meant to stretch what first of all and most of the time binds our understanding beyond the breaking point, seeking to explode those bonds, even as it reminds us of their inescapability. Georg Simmel, Blumenberg continues, invites us, in one of the fragments of his diary, to understand Nietzsche's thought of the eternal recurrence as another such *Sprengmetapher*. See *Schiffbruch mit Zuschauer: Paradigma einer Daseinsmetapher* (Frankfurt am Main: Suhrkamp, 1979), p. 84.

20. Thomas Aquinas, *Summa contra gentiles* I, chap. 46, and *Declaratio quorundam articulorum*, op. 2; quoted in Georges Poulet, *The Metamorphoses of the Circle*, trans. Carley Dawson and Elliott Coleman in collaboration with the author (Baltimore: Johns Hopkins Press, 1967), p. 154.

21. Petrus Auriolus, *Commentarii in Primum "Librum Sententiarum Pars prima"* (Rome, 1596), p. 829; quoted in Poulet, *The Metamorphoses of the Circle*, p. 154.

4   Alberti and Perspective Construction

1. See Edward S. Casey, *The Fate of Place: A Philosophical History* (Berkeley: University of California Press, 1997), pp. 50–71.

2. Aristotle, *Physics* 4.8, 215a; trans. R. P. Hardie and R. K. Gaye. *The Complete Works of Aristotle: The Revised Oxford Translation*, ed. Jonathan Barnes, 2 vols. (Princeton: Princeton University Press, 1984), vol. 1.

3. Elizabeth Brient, "The Immanence of the Infinite: A Response to Blumenberg's Reading of Modernity," (Ph.D. diss., Yale University, 1995), p. 96.

4. Leon Battista Alberti, *On Painting*, trans. and intro. John R. Spencer, rev. ed. (New Haven: Yale University Press, 1966), p. 54; abbreviated in this chapter as A, followed immediately by the page number, and cited parenthetically. See Mark Jarzombek, *On Leon Battista Alberti* (Cambridge, Mass.: MIT Press, 1989).

5. See chapter 10. See also Charles Trinkaus, "Protagoras in the Renaissance: An Exploration," in *Philosophy and Humanism: Essays in Honor of Paul Oskar Kristeller*, ed. Edward Mahoney (New York: Columbia University Press, 1976), pp. 190–213.

6. That Cusanus was interested in Alberti's theory of perspective is shown by his owning a copy of Alberti's later *Elementa Picturae*. And one of Alberti's mathematical treatises *(De Lunularum Quadratura)* derives very directly from a similar one by Cusanus. Here the debt goes in the opposite direction.

7. See Joan Gadol, *Leon Battista Alberti: Universal Man of the Early Renaissance* (Chicago: University of Chicago Press, 1969), pp. 196–197, n. 68. See also Ernst Cassirer, *The Individual and the Cosmos in Renaissance Philosophy*, trans. Mario Domandi (New York: Harper and Row, 1963), p. 50, and Leonardo Olschki, *Die Literatur der Technik und der angewandten Wissenschaften vom Mittelalter bis zur Renaissance* (Leipzig: Olschki, 1919), pp. 42, 81, 108.

8. See Hugo Damisch, *The Origin of Perspective*, trans. John Goodman (Cambridge, Mass.: MIT Press, 1995), p. 71; Gadol, *Alberti*, p. 27.

9. Franco Borsi, *Leon Battista Alberti: The Complete Works* (New York: Rizzoli, 1989), p. 205; the characterization is by Damisch, *The Origin of Perspective*, p. 71.

10. Gadol, *Alberti*, p. 193. But see Robert H. Tuson, *The Log of Christopher Columbus* (Camden, Me.: International Maritime Publishing, 1992), pp. 27–29:

With regard to Columbus's nautical chart, there is still prevalent belief that it was furnished to him in about 1481 by the Florentine physician Paolo del Pozzo Toscanelli. Toscanelli is said to have written a letter in 1474 to Fernan Martins, a canon in Lisbon, urging king Alfonso V of Portugal to pioneer the Atlantic route to Asia. Upon learning of this correspondence, Columbus reputedly wrote to Toscanelli, who sent him a copy of the original letter, along with a chart. Fernando, in the *Historie*, provides a second letter from Toscanelli to the Admiral.

I am inclined to agree with Henry Vignaud, however, that this entire correspondence was forged after the deaths of all the parties concerned, in order to squelch a rumor that Columbus originally picked up on the idea of an Atlantic crossing from a dying Portuguese sailor who had already accomplished the feat.... The best evidence that the

Toscanelli correspondence was a fake rests with the fact that the information in the letters is ridiculously out of date. No informed scholar in Florence would have written such a letter in 1474.

11. Gadol, *Alberti*, p. 186 n. 68.

12. "We note this here all the more, because when we consider phenomenology as a transcendent optics, we also think a transcendent perspective and a language of appearance (*Schein*), and accordingly can extend these concepts along with the concept of illusion to their true generality." Johann Heinrich Lambert, *Neues Organon oder Gedanken über die Erforschung und Bezeichnung des Wahren und dessen Unterscheidung von Irrtum und Schein*, 2 vols. (Leipzig: Wendler, 1764), 2:220. See also Johannes Hoffmeister's introduction to Georg Friedrich Wilhelm Hegel, *Phänomenologie des Geistes*, 6th ed. (Hamburg: Meiner, 1952), pp. vii–xii.

13. Carlo Marsuppini (1398–1453), "Epitaph Commemorating Brunelleschi," in *Brunelleschi in Perspective*, ed. Isabelle Hyman (Englewood Cliffs, N.J.: Prentice-Hall, 1973), p. 24.

14. On the tradition that credits Brunelleschi with the discovery of one-point perspective construction, see Damisch, *The Origin of Perspective*, pp. 59–72, and J. V. Field, *The Invention of Infinity: Mathematics and Art in the Renaissance* (Oxford: Oxford University Press, 1997), pp. 20–42.

15. Antonio di Tuccio Manetti, "From *The Life of Brunelleschi* (1480's)," in Hyman, *Brunelleschi in Perspective*, pp. 65–66.

16. William M. Ivins, Jr., *On the Rationalization of Sight: With an Examination of Three Renaissance Texts on Perspective* (New York: Da Capo, 1973), p. 10.

17. Field, *The Invention of Infinity*, pp. 6–7.

18. Ibid., 14.

19. Cf. ibid., p. 7: "On the whole, in the Middle Ages, as in ancient times, philosophers were agreed that seeing was an active process. That is, the eye sent out beams. The suggestion that the eye merely received light from external objects was indeed put forward, most notably by the Islamic mathematician and natural philosopher Ibn al-Haytham (AD 965–c. 1040, usually known in the West as Alhazen), but received rather little attention."

20. See ibid., pp. 29–40.

21. See Erwin Panofsky, *Perspective as Symbolic Form*, trans. Christopher S. Wood (New York: Zone Books, 1997), pp. 30–36. I do, however, find misleading his claim that "Exact perspectival construction is a systematic abstraction of the structure of this psychophysiological space" (p. 30). "Abstraction" does not

capture the way Alberti's construction violates our experience of space. You cannot get from the latter to the former by a process of abstraction. Also, as Hubert Damisch observes, "It is only too true that the author of 'Perspective as Symbolic Form' blurred the distinction between vision and the optical process leading to the formation of an image on the internal, concave surface of the retina; just as it is clear that it was this confusion that led him to accord *costruzione legittima* only a relative validity" (*The Origin of Perspective*, pp. 5–6).

22. Damisch, *The Origin of Perspective*, p. 35. See also Martin Kemp, "Leonardo and the Visual Pyramid," *Journal of the Warburg and Courtauld Institute* 11 (1977), pp. 128–149.

23. Damisch, *The Origin of Perspective*, p. 36.

24. Martin Heidegger, "Die Zeit des Weltbildes," *Holzwege*, in *Gesamtausgabe* (Frankfurt am Main: Klostermann, 1977), 5:75–113.

5   Curious Perspectives

1. Reprinted in William M. Ivins, Jr., *On the Rationalization of Sight: With an Examination of Three Renaissance Texts on Perspective* (New York: Da Capo, 1973).

2. All parenthetical page references in this chapter are to Leon Battista Alberti, *On Painting*, trans. and intro. John R. Spencer, rev. ed. (New Haven: Yale University Press, 1966); abbreviated as A, followed immediately by the page number.

3. For a discussion and summary of the *Asclepius*, see Frances A. Yates, *Giordano Bruno and the Hermetic Tradition* (Chicago: University of Chicago Press, 1979), especially pp. 35–40. See also St. Augustine, *The City of God*, trans. Marcus Dods (1872; reprint, New York: Modern Library, 1950), 8.23, pp. 270–272.

4. *Asclepius*, translated in Yates, *Bruno*, p. 37.

5. Augustine, *The City of God* 8.24, pp. 273, 272.

6. Plato, *Republic* 10.596, trans. Benjamin Jowett (New York: Random House, 1960).

7. Jacques Maritain, *Art and Scholasticism, and the Frontiers of Poetry*, trans. Joseph W. Evans (New York: Scribner, 1962), p. 52.

8. See Karsten Harries, *The Bavarian Rococo Church: Between Faith and Aestheticism* (New Haven: Yale University Press, 1983), especially "The Insufficiency of Perspective," pp. 146–150.

9. Friedrich Ohly, *Schriften zur mittelalterlichen Bedeutungsforschung* (Darmstadt: Wissenschaftliche Buchgesellschaft, 1977), pp. 15, 35–37.

10. Hubert Damisch, *The Origin of Perspective*, trans. John Goodman (Cambridge, Mass.: MIT Press, 1995), pp. 80–81.

11. Richard H. Popkin, *History of Scepticism from Erasmus to Descartes*, rev. ed. (New York: Harper Torchbooks, 1964), pp. 84, 202.

12. Michel de Montaigne, "An Apology for Raymond Sebond," in *The Essays of Michel de Montaigne*, trans., ed., intro., and notes by M. A. Screech (London: Penguin, 1991), p. 514.

13. Ibid., pp. 678–679.

14. Ibid., p. 680.

15. See Mary F. S. Hersey, *Holbein's "Ambassadors": The Picture and the Men* (London: George Bell, 1900), and Jean-Louis Ferrier, *Holbein, "Les Ambassadeurs"* (Paris: Denoel/Gauthier, 1977).

16. Jurgis Baltrušaitis, *Anamorphoses: ou, Magie artificielle des effets merveilleux* (Paris: Perrin, 1969), pp. 61–62. For illustrations see also the catalogue of the exhibition *Anamorphoses: Games of Perception and Illusion in Art*, organized by Michael Schuyt and Joost Elffers (New York: Abrams, 1975). See also Fred Leeman, *Hidden Images: Games of Perception, Anamorphic Art, Illusion*, trans. Ellyn Childs Allison and Margaret L. Kaplan, concept, production, and photographs by Joost Elffers and Mike Schuyt (New York: Abrams, 1976).

17. Cf. Carcavi's letter to Descartes of July 9, 1649; in *Oeuvres de Descartes*, ed. Charles Adam and Paul Tannery (Paris: J. Vrin, 1984), 5:372. This edition is hereafter cited as AT.

18. For illustrations see Leeman, *Hidden Images*, figs. 46–50. Descartes's interest in Maignan is documented by his correspondence with Carcavi. See his letter of August 17, 1649, in AT 5:392.

19. Ovid, *Metamorphoses* 8, trans. Mary M. Innes (Harmondsworth: Penguin, 1971), p. 184.

20. Ibid., p. 186.

21. I cannot agree with Anne Hollander that "The sun comes dazzling toward us across the water, rising as we watch; the shadows cast by the plow seem to move." *Moving Pictures* (Cambridge, Mass.: Harvard University Press, 1991), p. 94.

22. I am indebted to Beat Wyss, *Pieter Bruegel: Landschaft mit Ikarussturz: Ein Vexierbild des humanistischen Pessimismus* (Frankfurt am Main: Fischer, 1990), pp. 9–12.

23. See Jacques Maritain, *The Dream of Descartes together with Some Other Essays*, trans. Mabelle L. Andison (New York: Philosophical Library, 1944), p. 15.

6 The Thread of Ariadne

1. John Amos Komensky (Comenius), *The Labyrinth of the World and the Paradise of the Heart*, ed. and trans. Count Lützow (New York: Dutton, 1901), p. 67.

2. Ibid., p. 275.

3. René Descartes, *Meditation II*, in *The Philosophical Works of Descartes*, trans. Elizabeth Haldane and G. R. T. Ross, 2 vols. (New York: Dover, 1955), 1:149; *Oeuvres de Descartes*, ed. Charles Adam and Paul Tannery, 8 vols. (Paris: J. Vrin, 1964), 7:24. These editions are hereafter abbreviated as HR and AT, respectively.

4. Comenius, *The Labyrinth of the World*, p. 299.

5. See René Hocke, *Die Welt als Labyrinth: Manier und Magie in der europäischen Kunst* (Hamburg: Rowohlt, 1957), p. 103. See also Gerhart Schröder, *Baltasar Graciáns "Criticon"* (Munich: Fink, 1966).

6. Francis Bacon, *Novum Organum*, I, XLI, in *The Works of Francis Bacon*, ed. J. Spedding, R. Ellis, and D. Heath, 14 vols. (London: Longmans, 1854–1874); the Latin text is in 1:70–365, trans. J. Spedding as *The New Organon* in 4:39–248.

7. Bacon, *Novum Organum:* I, LXXXII, p. 190. Cf. Martin Heidegger's revision of Bacon's use of the figure of the forest clearing. In this connection the five sentences that introduce his *Holzwege*, in *Gesamtausgabe*, vol. 5 (Frankfurt am Main: Klostermann, 1977), are of special interest.

8. See Karsten Harries, "Descartes and the Labyrinth of the World," *International Journal of Philosophical Studies* 6, no. 3 (1998): 307–330. This chapter develops the argument of the article.

9. See Albert van Helden, *The Invention of the Telescope*. Transactions of the American Philosophical Society, vol. 67, part 4 (Philadelphia: American Philosophical Society, 1977), for an excellent discussion. Van Helden concludes that the telescope was discovered first in the Netherlands, not long before September 1608. See also Edward Rosen, *The Naming of the Telescope* (New York: Henry Schumann, 1947).

10. See Hans Blumenberg, *Die Genesis der kopernikanischen Welt* (Frankfurt: Suhrkamp 1975), pp. 762–782.

11. Joseph Glanvill, *The Vanity of Dogmatizing* (1661; facsimile reprint, New York: Columbia University Press, 1931), p. 5.

12. See Heinrich C. Kuhn, *Venetischer Aristotelismus im Ende der aristotelischen Welt: Aspekte der Welt und des Denkens des Cesare Cremonini (1550–1631)* (Frankfurt am Main: Peter Lang, 1996). See also Blumenberg, *Die Genesis*, p. 764, and chapter 15, section 1, above.

13. Galileo Galilei, *Discoveries and Opinions of Galileo*, trans. and intro. Stillman Drake (Garden City, N.Y.: Doubleday, 1957), p. 73.

14. Ibid., p. 175. Note, however, that in Galileo we also meet with a Platonic distrust of the eyes. See chapter 14 above.

15. Descartes, *Meditation III*, in HR 1:164; AT 7:43. On this point Descartes would seem to have agreed with Kepler. See Job Kozhamthadam, *The Discovery of Kepler's Laws: The Interaction of Science, Philosophy, and Religion*. (Notre Dame, Ind.: University of Notre Dame Press, 1994), pp. 62–63.

16. Plato, *Republic* 10.602b, trans. Benjamin Jowett (New York: Random House, 1960); this translation is hereafter cited parenthetically in the text.

17. J. Sirven, *Les années d'apprentissage de Descartes (1596–1628)*, diss. Paris (Albi, 1928), p. 324.

18. AT 10:7.

19. Descartes, letter to *** of September 1629?, in AT 1:21. Sirven, *Les années d'apprentissage*, p. 336.

20. Cf. Descartes's letter to Ferrier of June 18, 1629, in AT 1:13–16.

21. See Jurgis Baltrušaitis, *Anamorphoses: ou, Magie artificielle des effets merveilleux* (Paris: Perrin, 1969), pp. 61–62.

22. Descartes, *Discourse on the Method* I, in HR 1:83; AT 6:6.

23. For a discussion of Mersenne's critique of the Hermetic tradition, see Frances A. Yates, *Giordano Bruno and the Hermetic Tradition* (Chicago: University of Chicago Press, 1979), pp. 432–447.

24. AT 10:215–216.

25. René Descartes, *Dioptric* IV, in *Philosophical Writings*, trans. Norman Kemp Smith (New York: Modern Library, 1958), pp. 146–147; AT 6:113.

26. Heinrich Cornelius Agrippa von Nettesheim, *Magische Werke* (Stuttgart: Scheible, 1850), 2:10–13. See Sirven, *Les années d'apprentissage*, p. 111.

27. See Frances Yates, *The Rosicrucian Enlightenment* (London: Routledge and Kegan Paul, 1975), p. 12: "De Caus had constructed many grottoes in the gardens, containing scenes enlivened with music from mechanical fountains and formed of mythological figures, Parnassus with the Muses, or Midas in a cave. Very striking was a statue of Memnon, a Hercules-Memnon with a club. This statue gave forth sounds when the sun's rays struck it as in the classical story." De Caus published engravings of these works and explained the mechanism that made them possible.

28. See Baltrušaitis, *Anamorphoses*, p. 66.

29. Cf. Galileo Galilei, *The Assayer*, in *Discoveries and Opinions*, p. 246: "If Sarsi and

others think that certainty of a conclusion extends much assistance in the discovery of some means for realizing it, let them study history. There they may learn that Archytas made a dove that flew, that Archimedes made a mirror which kindled fires at great distances, and many other remarkable machines. . . . By reasoning about these they may easily discover, to their great honor and profit, how to construct such things."

30. Descartes, Rule XIII, in HR 1:52–53; AT 10:435–436.

31. Descartes, *Discourse V,* in HR 1:115–116; AT 6:56.

32. Descartes, *Treatise on Man,* in AT 11:120, 131.

33. De Caus's work is dedicated to Elizabeth, wife of the Palatine Elector Ferdinand V, whose daughter, also named Elizabeth, was to become Descartes's favorite student. See Baltrušaitis, *Anamorphoses,* p. 36.

34. Comenius, *The Labyrinth of the World,* p. 302.

35. Ibid., p. 279.

36. Lüder Gäbe, *Descartes' Selbstkritik: Untersuchungen zur Philosophie des jungen Descartes* (Hamburg: Meiner, 1972), pp. 53, 77–78.

37. See Descartes, Rule XII, in HR 1:37. In the *Rules* Descartes does not deny that such abstraction may fail to do justice to reality. "For the young Descartes mathematics is not a metaphysical science of the essence of matter, but nothing more than an art *bene metiendi* and this is the ground for its fertility." Lüder Gäbe, introduction to Descartes, *Meditationes de Prima Philosophia* (Hamburg: Meiner, 1959), p. xviii. Cf. Rule XIV, in HR 1:55: "Similarly if in the magnet there be any sort of nature the like of which our mind has never yet known, it is hopeless to expect that reasoning will ever make us grasp it; we should have to be furnished either with some new sense or with a divine intellect. But we shall believe ourselves to have attained whatever in this matter can be achieved by our human faculties, if we discern with all possible distinctness that mixture of entities or natures already known which produces just those effects which we notice in the magnet." If there are indeed occult qualities in things, we shall not know them. We can know things only to the extent that we can measure them.

38. Descartes, Rule XII, in HR 1:38.

39. See Gäbe, *Descartes' Selbstkritik,* p. 90.

40. See Descartes, Rule VIII, in HR 1:26: "But nothing seems to me more futile than the conduct of those who boldly dispute about the secrets of nature, the influence of the heavens on these lower regions, the predicting of future events and similar matters, as many do, without yet having ever asked whether human reason is adequate to the solution of these problems." Kepler appears to have

been caught up in such futility when he sought to show how God created the universe. Not that the mathematical physics Descartes envisions in the *Rules* will be able to explain all that we would like to explain, although Descartes is confident that it will explain all that occurs without any aid from reason. On his view, human action will exceed the scope of such explanations. But if so, and if nature is understood as the product of divine action, should we not suspect that it, too, will exceed the scope of physical explanations? Here we have a key to understanding why the approach taken in the *Rules* left Descartes dissatisfied and why that work remained incomplete.

41. Gäbe, *Descartes' Selbstkritik*, p. 37.

42. See Alexandre Koyré, *Entretiens sur Descartes* (New York: Brentano's, 1944), p. 84.

43. Glanvill, *The Vanity of Dogmatizing*, p. 175.

44. Descartes, Rule XIII, in HR 1:53; AT 10:436.

45. "Ad Lectorem de Hypothesibus Huius Operis," in Nicolaus Copernicus, *Das neue Weltbild, Drei Texte: Commentariolus, Brief gegen Werner, De revolutonibus I*, Lateinisch-deutsch, trans., ed., and intro., Hans Günter Zekl (Hamburg: Meiner, 1990), p. 62; trans. Edward Rosen as *Three Copernican Treatises: The "Commentariolus" of Copernicus, the "Letter against Werner," the "Narratio Prima" of Rheticus*, 2nd ed. (New York: Dover, 1959), p. 25.

46. Kepler, quoted in Alexandre Koyré, *From the Closed World to the Infinite Universe* (New York: Harper Torchbook, 1958), pp. 60, 61.

47. See chapter 3, section 3, above.

48. Glanvill, *The Vanity of Dogmatizing*, pp. 209–212.

49. Jacques Maritain, *The Dream of Descartes together with Some Other Essays*, trans. Mabelle L. Andison (New York: Philosophical Library, 1944), p. 39.

50. Alexandre Koyré, *Essai sur l'idée de Dieu et les preuves de Son existence chez Descartes* (Paris: Leroux, 1922), p. 93, and Étienne Gilson, *Études sur le role de la pensé médievale dans la formation du système cartésien* (Paris: Vrin, 1930), p. 12.

51. Martin Heidegger, *Sein und Zeit*, 7th ed. (Tübingen: Niemeyer, 1953), p. 229.

7   Truth as the Property of God

1. See Hans Blumenberg, "Die humanistische Idealisierung der Weltmitte," in *Die Genesis der kopernikanischen Welt* (Frankfurt am Main: Suhrkamp, 1975), pp. 237–246.

2. Pierre Duhem, *Medieval Cosmology*, ed. and trans. Roger Ariew (Chicago: University of Chicago Press, 1985), pp. 4, 197. Cf. Edward S. Casey, *The Fate of*

Place: A Philosophical History (Berkeley: University of California Press, 1997), pp. 106–129. For the text, see P. Mandonnet, *Siger de Brabant et l'averroisme latin aux XIIIme siècle*, 2me partie, textes inédites (Louvain: Institut superieur de philosophie de l'Université, 1908), pp. 175–191, and Roland Hissette, *Enquète sur les 219 articles condamnés à Paris le 7 mars 1277*, Philosophes médiévaux vol. 22 (Louvain: Publications Universitaires, 1977). Trans. "The Condemnation of 1277," in *Philosophy in the Middle Ages*, ed. Arthur Hyman and James J. Walsh, 2nd ed. (Indianapolis: Hackett, 1973), pp. 582–591. The numbering of the propositions in this translation, quoted hereafter in the text, follows the Mandonnet edition.

3. See Siger of Brabant, "Question of the Eternity of the World," in Hyman and Walsh, *Philosophy in the Middle Ages*, pp. 490–502.

4. See Friedrich Heer, *Europäische Geistesgeschichte* (Stuttgart: Kohlhammer, 1953), p. 162.

5. Ibid.

6. Siger, "The Eternity of the World," p. 494.

7. Ibid., p. 500.

8. Duhem, *Medieval Cosmology*, p. 369.

9. The following discussion is indebted to Blumenberg, *Die Genesis*, pp. 174–182. Blumenberg relies on Anneliese Maier, *Zwei Grundprobleme der scholastischen Naturphilosophie*, 2nd ed. (Rome: Edizioni di Storia e Letteratura, 1951, pp. 166 ff., and Marshall Clagett, *The Science of Mechanics in the Middle Ages* (Madison: University of Wisconsin Press, 1959), pp. 526–531.

10. Franciscus de Marchia is quoted in Blumenberg, *Die Genesis*, p. 177.

11. Blumenberg, *Die Genesis*, p. 181.

12. Ibid.

13. Jean Buridan, *Questions on the Eighth Book of Aristotle's "Physics,"* in Hyman and Walsh, *Philosophy in the Middle Ages*, p. 769.

14. Ibid., p. 770.

15. See Blumenberg, *Die Genesis*, pp. 182–188.

16. Buridan, *Questions*, p. 770.

17. Ibid., p. 771.

18. Duhem, *Medieval Cosmology*, p. 181.

19. Ibid., pp. 181–182.

20. Ibid., p. 369.

21. Nicole Oresme, *Traité du Ciel et du Monde*, chap. 4, fol. 5, col. d; quoted in Duhem, *Medieval Cosmology*, p. 478.

22. Ibid., p. 477.

23. Duhem, *Medieval Cosmology*, p. 477. See chapter 2, section 4, above.

24. Ibid.

25. Aristotle, *Metaphysics* 1.1, 980a22–27, trans. W. D. Ross in *The Complete Works of Aristotle: The Revised Oxford Translation*, ed. Jonathan Barnes, 2 vols. (Princeton: Princeton University Press, 1984), vol. 2; this translation is hereafter cited parenthetically in the text.

26. Plato, *Theaetetus* 173d–174a, trans. F. M. Cornford in *The Collected Dialogues of Plato, Including the Letters*, ed. Edith Hamilton and Huntington Cairns (Princeton: Princeton University Press, 1961); this translation is hereafter cited parenthetically in the text.

27. See Hans Blumenberg, *Die Legitimität der Neuzeit* (Frankfurt: Suhrkamp, 1966), pp. 201–432. Especially important here is Blumenberg's critique of a paragraph in *Being and Time* that links theoretical curiosity to inauthenticity: see Martin Heidegger, *Sein und Zeit*, 7th ed. (Tübingen: Niemeyer, 1953), par. 36.

28. St. Augustine, *Confessions*, trans. Edward B. Pusey (New York: Modern Library, 1949), book 10; pp. 231–232.

29. Ibid., p. 232.

8 The Infinity of Space and the Infinity of Man

1. Joseph Addison, *Spectator*, no. 412 (June 23, 1712); reprinted in Joseph Addison and Richard Steele, *Selected Essays from "The Tatler," "The Spectator," and "The Guardian,"* ed. Daniel McDonald (Indianapolis: Bobbs-Merrill, 1973), pp. 464–465.

2. Immanuel Kant, *Kritik der Urteilskraft*, par. 23, A 75/B 76; trans. J. H. Bernard as *Critique of Judgment* (New York: Hafner, 1951), p. 83.

3. Ibid., par. 29, A 109–110/B 111; trans., p. 105.

4. Francesco Petrarca, *La lettera del Ventoso: Familiarum Rerum Libri IV, 1, Testo a Fronte*, preface by Andrea Zanzotto, trans. by Maura Formica, commentary and notes by Mauro Formica and Michael Jakob (Verbania: Tarara, 1996), p. 43; see also p. 62 n. 40.

5. Ibid., pp. 33, 57 n. 1. The note refers the reader to Giovanni Carducci, "Il Petrarca alpinista," published in *Il Secolo* (Milano) in 1882.

6. Jacob Burckhardt, *The Civilization of the Renaissance in Italy*, trans. S. G. C. Middlemore (New York: Modern Library, 1954), pp. 219–220. Hans Blumenberg considers the day of Petrarch's ascent of Mont Ventoux one of those great

moments that join and separate two epochs. See *Der Prozess der theoretischen Neugierde* (Frankfurt am Main: Suhrkamp, 1973), pp. 142–144.

7. Francesco Petrarca, "The Ascent of Mont Ventoux," trans. Hans Nachod, in *The Renaissance Philosophy of Man*, ed. Ernst Cassirer, Paul Oskar Kristeller, and John Herman Randall, Jr. (1948; reprint, Chicago: University of Chicago Press, 1971), p. 36.

8. St. Augustine, *The Confessions*, trans. Edward B. Pusey (New York: Modern Library, 1949), book 10, p. 205.

9. Petrarca, "The Ascent of Mont Ventoux," pp. 36–37. This translation is hereafter cited parenthetically in the text.

10. See the commentary by Formica and Jakob in Petrarca, *"La lettera del Ventoso,"* pp. 33–56, which also includes useful bibliographical notes.

11. St. Augustine, *The Confessions*, book 10, p. 205.

12. Petrarch is quoting Seneca the Younger, *Epistle* 8.5.

13. St. Augustine, *The Confessions*, book 8, pp. 166, 167.

14. Ibid., p. 167.

15. See the commentary by Formica and Jakob in Petrarca, *"La lettera del Ventoso,"* p. 38.

9   The Infinity of Man and the Infinity of God

1. Meister Eckhart, "Adolescens, tibi dico: surge!" in *Meister Eckharts Predigten*, ed. and trans. Josef Quint, 3 vols. (Stuttgart: Kohlhammer, 1936–1976), 2:305; trans. Raymond B. Blakney in *Meister Eckhart* (New York: Harper, 1957), p. 134 (translation modified).

2. See Stephen Menn, *Descartes and Augustine* (Cambridge: Cambridge University Press, 1998), pp. 251–254.

3. See Karsten Harries, "The Infinite Sphere: Comments on the History of a Metaphor," *Journal of the History of Philosophy* 13, no. 1 (1975), pp. 10–11.

4. Eckhart, "Adolescens, tibi dico: surge!" 2:305; trans. *Meister Eckhart*, p. 134.

5. Cf. Nicholas of Cusa, *Idiota de Sapientia*, trans. Jasper Hopkins as *The Layman on Widsom* in *Nicholas of Cusa on Widsom and Knowledge* (Minneapolis: Banning, 1996), p. 101: "And for every [intellectual] spirit it is delightful to ascend continually unto the Beginning of its life, although [this Beginning] remains inaccessible."

6. Meister Eckhart, "Scitote, quia prope est regnum dei," in *Meister Eckharts Predigten*, 3:305; trans. *Meister Eckhart*, p. 130.

7. Ibid.

8. Blakney, introduction to Eckhart, *Meister Eckhart*, p. xxiv; and see Eckhart, "The Defense," in ibid., pp. 258–305.

9. See Friedrich Heer, introduction to Meister Eckhart, *Predigten und Schriften* (Frankfurt am Main: Fischer Bücherei, 1956), pp. 12–19.

10. Norman Cohn, *The Pursuit of the Millennium*, 2nd ed. (New York: Harper Torchbooks, 1961), p. 166.

11. Heer, introduction, pp. 14–15.

12. See Franz-Josef Schweitzer, *Der Freiheitsbegriff der deutschen Mystik: Seine Beziehung zur Ketzerei der "Brüder und Schwestern vom Freien Geist," mit besonderer Rücksicht auf den pseudoeckartischen Traktat "Schwester Katrei" (Edition)* (Frankfurt am Main: Lang, 1981).

13. Cohn, *The Pursuit of the Millennium*, p. 164.

14. Ibid., p. 150.

15. Schweitzer, *Der Freiheitsbegriff der deutschen Mystik*, p. 111; Cohn, *The Pursuit of the Millennium*, p. 184.

16. Schweitzer, *Der Freiheitsbegriff der deutschen Mystik*, pp. 26, 126–127.

17. Cohn, *The Pursuit of the Millennium*, p. 152. Cf. Schweitzer, *Der Freiheitsbegriff der deutschen Mystik*, p. 87.

18. Cohn, *The Pursuit of the Millennium*, p. 165.

19. Schweitzer, *Der Freiheitsbegriff der deutschen Mystik*, p. 122; Cohn, pp. 165, 169, 171.

20. See Schweitzer, *Der Freiheitsbegriff der deutschen Mystik*, p. 122–129; Heer, introduction, p. 17.

21. Heer, introduction, p. 17.

22. Cohn, *The Pursuit of the Millennium*, p. 181, quoting Wilhelm Preger, *Beiträge zur Geschichte der religiösen Bewegung in den Niederlanden in der zweiten Hälfte des vierzehnten Jahrhunderts, Abhandlungen der königlich bayerischen Akademie der Wissenschaften* (Historische Classe), vol. 21, part 1 (Munich, 1894), pp. 62–63.

23. Ibid., quoting B. Ulanowski, *Examen testium super vita et moribus Beguinarum . . . in Sweydnitz*, in *Scriptores Rerum Polonicarum* (Cracow, 1890), 13:247.

24. Francesco Petrarca, "The Ascent of Mont Ventoux," trans. Hans Nachod, in *The Renaissance Philosophy of Man*, ed. Ernst Cassirer, Paul Oskar Kristeller, and John Herman Randall, Jr. (Chicago: University of Chicago Press, 1948), p. 45.

25. Cohn, *The Pursuit of the Millennium*, p. 184, quoting Jan van Ruusbroec, "Van den XII Beghinen," in *Werken*, naar het standhandschrift van Groenendaal uitgegeven door het Ruusbroec-Genoootschap te Antwerpen, ed. Leonce

Reypens and Marcellus F. Schurmans, 4 vols. (Mechelen: Het Kompas, 1932–1934), 4:42–43.

26. Meister Eckhart, "Beati pauperes spiritu, quia ipsorum est regnum coelorum," in *Meister Eckharts Predigten*, 2:492–494; trans. *Meister Eckhart*, pp. 228–229 (translation modified). Surprisingly Norman Cohn does not note this connection; indeed, he hardly mentions Eckhart in his *Pursuit of the Millennium*, (Eckhart does not appear in the index). Cohn does point out that *Schwester Katrei*, one of only two fragments (of what must have been a substantial literature produced by the adepts of the Free Spirit) to have survived the Inquisition's persecution, "was protected by being ascribed—quite wrongly—to the great Dominican mystic Meister Eckhart" (p. 151).

27. Cf. Schweitzer, *Der Freiheitsbegriff der deutschen Mystik*, p. 24.

28. Meister Eckhart, "Defense," in *Meister Eckhart*, p. 266.

29. Eckhart, "Adolescens, tibi dico: surge!" 2:305–306; trans. *Meister Eckhart*, p. 134 (translation modified).

30. Meister Eckhart, "Dum medium silentium tenerent omnia et nox in suo cursu medium iter haberet . . . ," in *Deutsche Mystiker des 14. Jahrhunderts*, ed. Franz Pfeiffer, vol. 2, *Meister Eckhart, Predigten und Traktate* (Leipzig: G. J. Goschen, 1857), 1; Meister Eckart, *Deutsche Predigten und Traktate*, trans. Josef Quint (Munich: C. Hanser, 1955), p. 57; trans. M. O'C. Walshe in *Meister Eckhart: German Sermons and Treatises*, with intro. and notes by O'Walshe, 3 vols. (London: Watkins, 1979–1987), 1:3. Cf. *Meister Eckhart*, pp. 95, 316 n. 1.

31. Ibid.

32. Eckhart, in "Dum medium silentium tenerent omnia," in *German Sermons and Treatises*, 1:4.

33. Cf. Martin Heidegger, "Der Feldweg (1949)," in *Aus der Erfahrung des Denkens, Gesamtausgabe* (Frankfurt am Main: Klostermann, 1983), 13:87–90, where Heidegger invokes Eckhart as the master who can teach us how to read and how to live ("der alte Lese und Lebemeister Eckehardt," p. 89) and concludes with an interpretation of the call of the field path that leaves us wondering who here is really speaking: the soul, the world, or God?—"Der Zuspruch des Feldweges ist jetzt ganz deutlich. Spricht die Seele? Spricht die Welt? Spricht Gott?" (p. 90).

34. Eckhart, "Dum medium silentium tenerent omnia," in *German Sermons and Treatises*, 1:11 (translation modified).

35. Meister Eckhart, "Ubi est qui natus est rex Judaeorum," Pfeiffer 2; *Deutsche Predigten und Traktate*, p. 58. Trans. in *German Sermons and Treatises*, 2:21; cf. *Meister Eckhart*, p. 107.

36. Meister Eckhart, "In his, quae Patris mei sunt, oportet me esse," Pfeiffer 3. Trans. in *German Sermons and Treatises*, 3:29–30; cf. *Meister Eckhart*, p. 112.

37. Meister Eckhart, "Et cum factus esset Jesus annorum duodecim, etc.," Pfeiffer 4; *Deutsche Predigten und Traktate*, p. 59. Trans. in *German Sermons and Treatises*, 3:40–41; cf. *Meister Eckhart*, 119.

38. Meister Eckhart, "Haec dicit dominus: honora patrem tuum," in *Meister Eckharts Predigten*, 2:469–470, 471–472; trans. *Meister Eckhart*, pp. 147–148, 148 (translation modified).

39. Meister Eckhart, "Moyses orabat dominum, deum suum, in *Meister Eckharts Predigten*, 2:13–14; trans. *Meister Eckhart*, p. 176 (translation modified).

40. Meister Eckhart, "In occisione gladui mortui sunt," in *Meister Eckharts Predigten*, 1:132; trans. *Meister Eckhart*, p. 171 (translation modified).

41. See Friedrich Heer, *Europäische Geistesgeschichte* (Stuttgart: Kohlhammer, 1953), p. 180.

42. Eckhart, "Dum medium silentium tenerent omnia," in *German Sermons and Treatises*, 1:8; cf. *Meister Eckhart*, p. 100.

43. Meister Eckhart, "Qui audit me, non confudetur," in *Meister Eckharts Predigten*, 1:196–197; trans. *Meister Eckhart*, p. 204 (translation modified).

44. Meister Eckhart, "Nolite timere eos, qui corpus occidunt, animam autem occidere non possunt," in *Meister Eckhart*, p. 226. Cf. Blackney's comment, p. 328 n. 1: "Quint shows that this sermon is widely quoted in early manuscripts as being Eckhart's. It reveals the Eckhart of the later years." But if so, this Eckhart could be appropriated effortlessly by the brothers and sisters of the Free Spirit.

45. Eckhart, "Nolite timere eos," p. 226.

46. Cf. Reiner Schürmann, *Meister Eckhart: Mystic and Philosopher* (Bloomington: Indiana University Press, 1978), p. 16: "One of the key terms in the very rich vocabulary of detachment is *gelazenheit*, in modern German *Gelassenheit*. . . . We can translate this word by 'infinite resignation' and by 'serenity.'"

47. Meister Eckhart, "In hoc apparuit caritas Dei in nobis," in *Meister Eckharts Predigten*, 1:91–92; trans. *Meister Eckhart*, p. 127 (translation modified). The sermon brings to mind the rose of Angelus Silesius's *Cherubinischer Wandersmann*, which blooms "without a why": "Die Ros ist ohn warum; sie blühet, weil sie blühet / Sie acht nicht ihrer selbst, fragt nicht ob man sie siehet." Heidegger's discussion of the verse demonstrates his closeness to Meister Eckhart. See Martin Heidegger, *Der Satz vom Grund* (Pfullingen: Neske, 1957), pp. 67–75.

48. Meister Eckhart, "Convescens praecepit eis, ab Ierosolymis ne discrederent,

etc.," in *Meister Eckharts Predigten*, 2:79–80; trans. *Meister Eckhart*, p. 193 (translation modified).

49. Heinrich Seuse, *Das Buch der Wahrheit, Daz buechli der warheit*, ed. Loris Sturlese and Rüdiger Blumrich, intro. Loris Sturlese, trans. Rüdiger Blumrich, Mittelhochdeutsch–Deutsch (Hamburg: Meiner, 1993), pp. 56–57. Cf. Cohn, *The Pursuit of the Millennium*, p. 186.

50. Loris Sturlese, introduction to Seuse, *Das Buch der Wahrheit*, pp. xv–xxi.

10 Homo Faber: The Rediscovery of Protagoras

1. Meister Eckhart, "Haec dicit dominus: honora patrem tuum," in *Meister Eckharts Predigten*, ed. and trans. Josef Quint, 3 vols. (Stuttgart: Kohlhammer, 1936–1976), 2:469–470; trans. Raymond B. Blakney, in *Meister Eckhart* (New York: Harper, 1957), p. 148.

2. Leon Battista Alberti, *On Painting*, trans. and intro. John R. Spencer, rev. ed. (New Haven: Yale University Press, 1966), p. 55. Alberti also refers to Protagoras in book 2 of his *Libri della famiglia*, dating from roughly the same time. See Charles Trinkaus, "Protagoras in the Renaissance: An Exploration," in *Philosophy and Humanism: Essays in Honor of Paul Oskar Kristeller*, ed. Edmund Mahoney (New York: Columbia University Press, 1976), p. 195.

3. Trinkaus, "Protagoras in the Renaissance," p. 194.

4. Paul O. Kristeller, " A Latin Translation of Gemistos Plethon's *De Fato* by Johannes Sophianos Dedicated to Nicholas of Cusa," in *Nicolò Cusano: Agli Inizi del Mondo Moderno*, Atti del Congreso internazionale in occasione del V centenario della morte di Nicolò Cusano, Bressanone, 6–10 Settembre 1964 (Florence: Sansoni, 1970), pp. 84–85. Kristeller bases himself on Girolamo Mancini, *Vita di Leon Battista Alberti* (Florence, 1882), p. 137.

5. Nicholas of Cusa, *De Beryllo*, in *Opera Omnia*, ed. Hans G. Senger and Karl Bormann, vol. 11 (Hamburg: Meiner, 1988), p. 6; trans. Jasper Hopkins, as *On [Intellectual] Eyeglasses*, in *Nicholas of Cusa: Metaphysical Speculations* (Minneapolis: Banning, 1997), pp. 36–37.

6. Nicholas of Cusa, *De Beryllo*, p. 7; trans. *On [Intellectual] Eyeglasses*, p. 37.

7. Ibid., p. 65; trans., p. 68.

8. Trinkaus, "Protagoras in the Renaissance," p. 203. On the phrase *la più grassa Minerva*, see John R. Spencer's introduction to his translation of Alberti, *On Painting*, pp. 18–19.

9. Nicholas of Cusa, *De Beryllo*, p. 69; trans. *On [Intellectual] Eyeglasses*, p. 70.

10. Ibid.

11. Cf. Trinkaus, Protagoras in the Renaissance," p. 193.

12. Aristotle, *Metaphysics* 10.1, 1053a31–1053b4, trans. W. D. Ross in *The Complete Works of Aristotle: The Revised Oxford Translation*, ed. Jonathan Barnes, 2 vols. (Princeton: Princeton University Press, 1984), vol. 2; this translation is hereafter cited parenthetically in the text.

13. See chapter 3, section 3, above.

14. Plato, *Theaetetus* 152a, trans. F. M. Cornford in *The Collected Dialogues of Plato, including the Letters*, ed. Edith Hamilton and Huntington Cairns (Princeton: Princeton University Press, 1961).

15. Nicholas of Cusa, *Idiota de Mente* 1, in *Opera Omnia* 11:170; trans. as *The Layman on Mind* in Jasper Hopkins, *Nicholas of Cusa on Wisdom and Knowledge* (Minneapolis: Banning, 1996), p. 171.

16. See Maurice de Gandillac, *Nikolaus von Cues: Studien zu seiner Philosophie und philosophischen Weltanschauung*, rev. German ed., trans. Karl Fleischmann (Düsseldorf: Schwan, 1953), p. 152. Gandillac refers to a sermon from 1455 where Cusanus appeals to Albertus, *De Anima*, and also refers us to Aquinas, *De veritate* X, art. 1, *In sent.* 1.35.1: *Mens dicitur a metior, metiris*.

17. Plato, *Republic* 7.524e–525a, trans. Benjamin Jowett (New York: Random House, 1960).

18. See Ernst Cassirer, *Das Erkenntnisproblem in der Philosophie und Wissenschaft der neueren Zeit*, 4 vols. (Darmstadt: Wissenschaftliche Buchgesellschaft, 1994), 1:32 ff. See also Ernst Hoffmann, *Platonismus und christliche Philosophie* (Zurich: Artemis, 1961), pp. 367 ff., 429 ff.

19. Ernst Cassirer, *Philosophie der symbolischen Formen* (Berlin: Cassirer, 1923), 1:9.

20. Nicholas of Cusa, *Idiota de Sapientia*; trans. as *The Layman on Wisdom* in Hopkins, *Nicholas of Cusa on Wisdom and Knowledge*, pp. 87–155.

21. Thomas Aquinas, *Summa Theologica* 1.11.2, in *The Basic Writings of St. Thomas Aquinas*, ed. Anton C. Pegis, 2 vols. (New York: Random House, 1945).

22. Plato, *Timaeus* 69b–c. See Elizabeth Brient "The Immanence of the Infinite: A Response to Blumenberg's Reading of Modernity," (Ph.D. diss., Yale University, 1995), pp. 113–114.

23. Nicholas of Cusa, *On Learned Ignorance*, trans. Jasper Hopkins (Minneapolis: Banning, 1981), I.11, trans. p. 61.

24. Nicholas of Cusa, *De Beryllo*, p. 56; trans. *On [Intellectual] Eyeglasses*, p. 63.

25. Nicholas of Cusa, *On Experiments Done with Weight-Scales*, in Hopkins, *Nicholas of Cusa on Wisdom and Knowledge*, pp. 319–371.

26. Ibid., p. 321.

NOTES

27. Ibid., p. 337.

28. Ibid., p. 365.

29. Ibid., p. 365.

30. Alexander Koyré, *From the Closed World to the Infinite Universe* (New York: Harper Torchbook, 1958), p. 19.

31. See Ernst Cassirer, *The Individual and the Cosmos in Renaissance Philosophy*, trans. Mario Domandi (New York: Harper and Row, 1963), pp. 15–24.

32. Nicholas of Cusa, *De Beryllo*, p. 55; trans. *On [Intellectual] Eyeglasses*, pp. 61–62.

33. Jasper Hopkins has taken issue with what he takes to be my claim that "all putative empirical knowledge is fundamentally poetic knowledge," and more generally with those interpreters who, following Cassirer, interpret Cusanus as an anticipation of Kant or German idealism. "Nicholas's thought is historically fascinating because of the ways in which it veers from Thomas's, not because of the fictively imagined ways in which it anticipates Kant's" (*Nicholas of Cusa on Widsom and Knoweldge*, pp. 73, 490 n. 292). But as I pointed out in the passage to which Hopkins refers, to call knowledge poetic is not to deny that what we know retains its measure in the reality we are trying to understand. The task is to recognize in just what way what I have called here the principle of perspective makes such a veering necessary and prescribes its direction, a direction hinted at already by the passage from *Republic* 7.524e–525a quoted above. See Karsten Harries, "Problems of the Infinite: Cusanus and Descartes," *American Catholic Philosophical Quarterly* 63, no. 1 (1989), pp. 89–110.

34. Nicholas of Cusa, *De Beryllo*, pp. 55–56; trans. *"On [Intellectual] Eyeglasses,"* p. 62.

11 The Dignity of Man

1. Frances A. Yates, *Giordano Bruno and the Hermetic Tradition* (Chicago: University of Chicago Press, 1979), p. 13.

2. See Paul Oskar Kristeller, *The Philosophy of Marsilio Ficino*, trans. Virginia Conant (New York: Columbia University Press, 1943), pp. 16–17.

3. Ibid., pp. 12–13.

4. Ibid., p. 15.

5. Ibid., p. 14, quoting Ficino's *Pimander.*

6. Ibid., p. 17.

7. Did Ficino know Cusanus? Citing Raymond Klibansky, *The Continuity of the Platonic Tradition during the Middle Ages: Outlines of a Corpus Platonicum Medii Aevi* (London: Warburg Institute, 1939), pp. 42, 47, Yates claims that Ficino regarded Cusanus as an important link in the great chain of Platonists (*Bruno,*

p. 124). Ernst Cassirer, too, would have us understand him as such a link, but points out that Ficino mentions him only once, in a letter, misspelling his name (*The Individual and the Cosmos in Renaissance Philosophy*, trans. Mario Domandi [New York: Harper and Row, 1963], p. 46 n. 2). See also Kristeller, *Ficino*, p. 27. Willehad P. Eckert seems right to question whether either Ficino or Pico owed much to Cusanus. See "Nikolaus von Kues und Johannes Reuchlin," in *Nicolò Cusano: Agli Inizi del Mondo Moderno*, Atti del Congraso internazionale in occasione del V centenario della morte di Nicolò Cusano, Bressanone, 6–10 settembre 1964 (Florence: Sansoni, 1970), pp. 199–200.

8. Plotinus, *Enneads* 1.6.8, trans. Stephen MacKenna (London: Faber, 1956); this translation is hereafter cited in the text.

9. See Yates, *Bruno*, pp. 64–65.

10. Ibid., pp. 64–66. Cf. Kristeller, *Ficino*, p. 314.

11. Marsilio Ficino, "Five Questions Concerning the Mind," trans. Josephine L. Burroughs, in *The Renaissance Philosophy of Man*, ed. Ernst Cassirer, Paul Oskar Kristeller, and John Herman Randall, Jr. (1948; reprint, Chicago: University of Chicago Press, 1971), pp. 193–194.

12. Plato, *Symposium* 211e–212a, trans. Michael Joyce in *The Collected Dialogues of Plato, Including the Letters*, ed. Edith Hamilton and Huntington Cairns (Princeton: Princeton University Press, 1961).

13. Plato, *Phaedo* 72e–76c, trans. Hugh Tredennick in ibid.

14. Nicholas of Cusa, *De Beryllo*, in *Opera Omnia*, vol. 11, ed. Hans Senger and Karl Bormann (Hamburg: Meiner, 1988), p. 56; trans. Jasper Hopkins as *On [Intellectual] Eyeglasses*, in *Nicholas of Cusa: Metaphysical Speculations* (Minneapolis: Banning, 1998), p. 63.

15. Yates, *Bruno*, p. 60. See also Kristeller, *Ficino*, pp. 310–312.

16. Cf. Cassirer, *The Individual and the Cosmos in Renaissance Philosophy*, pp. 101–102.

17. Ficino, *"Five Questions,"* p. 195. This work is hereafter cited parenthetically in the text.

18. See Brian P. Copenhaver and Charles B. Schmitt, *Renaissance Philosophy* (Oxford: Oxford University Press, 1979), pp. 163–176.

19. Giovanni Pico della Mirandola, "Oration on the Dignity of Man," trans. Elizabeth Livermore Forbes, in Cassirer, Kristeller, and Randall, *The Renaissance Philosophy of Man*, p. 239.

20. Yates, *Bruno*, p. 111, quoting Pico, "Oration."

21. Pico della Mirandola, "Oration," p. 223. This work is hereafter cited parenthetically in the text.

22. Kristeller, *Ficino*, p. 407.

23. Sophocles, *Antigone*, lines 332–375, trans. R. C. Jebb in *The Complete Greek Drama*, ed. Whitney J. Oates and Eugene O'Neill, Jr., 2 vols. (New York: Random House, 1938), 1:432.

24. *Asclepius*, translated in Yates, *Bruno*, p. 35; see also pp. 110–111.

25. Cited in Yates, *Bruno*, p. 36.

26. See the commentary in Cassirer, Kristeller, and Randall, *The Renaissance Philosophy of Man*, p. 216 n. 4.

12 Copernican Anthropocentrism

1. See chapter 6, section 4.

2. "Ad Lectorem de Hypothesibus Huius Operis," in Nicolaus Copernicus, *Das neue Weltbild: Drei Texte: Commentariolus, Brief gegen Werner, De revolutionibus I*, Lateinisch-deutsch, trans., ed., and intro. Hans Günter Zekl (Hamburg: Meiner, 1990), p. 62; trans. Edward Rosen, in *Three Copernican Treatises: The "Commentariolus" of Copernicus, the "Letter against Werner," the "Narratio Prima" of Rheticus*, 2nd ed. (New York: Dover, 1959), p. 25.

3. Aristotle, *Metaphysics* 12.8, 1074a10–17, trans. W. D. Ross in *The Complete Works of Aristotle: The Revised Oxford Translation*, ed. Jonathan Barnes, 2 vols. (Princeton: Princeton University Press, 1984), vol. 2.

4. Ptolemy, *Ptolemy's "Almagest*," trans. and annotated by G. J. Tomer (Princeton: Princeton University Press, 1998), 11.1–2; pp. 419–423.

5. Thomas Aquinas, *Summa Theologica*, 2.32, art. 1 ad 2, *Commentaria in libr. Arist. de caelo et mundo*, 12.17.

6. Giese is cited in Copernicus, *Das neue Weltbild*, p. xxiv.

7. Rosen, *Three Copernican Treatises*, p. 24; see especially n. 68. On Bruno, see this volume, chapter 13.

8. Copernicus, *De Revolutionibus*, "Praefatio" and 1.5, in *Das neue Weltbild*, pp. 72, 100.

9. Plato, *Laws* 8.809d, trans. A. E. Tayor in *The Collected Dialogues of Plato, Including the Letters*, ed. Edith Hamilton and Huntington Cairns (Princeton: Princeton University Press, 1961).

10. Copernicus, *De Revolutionibus*, "Proemium," p. 82.

11. Copernicus, *De Revolutionibus*, "Proemium," p. 72.

12. See Copernicus, *De Hypothesibus Motuum Coelestium a Se Constitutis Commentariolus*, in *Das neue Weltbild*, pp. 2–3.

13. Copernicus, *De Revolutionibus*, "Proemium," p. 72. Cf. Ptolemy, *Ptolemy's "Al-*

magest" 9.2, p. 423: "we know, finally that some variety in the type of hypotheses associated with the circles [of the planets] cannot plausibly be considered strange or contrary to reason . . . ; for, when uniform circular motion is preserved for all without exception, the individual phenomena are demonstrated in accordance with a principle which is more basic and more generally applicable than that of similarity of the hypotheses [for all planets]." With his insistence that the hypotheses advanced by science have to be arrived at by following a method based on principles that are certain, Copernicus is following Ptolemy, even though such principles no longer are taken to demand geocentrism.

14. Plato, *Timaeus* 34a; trans. Benjamin Jowett in *The Collected Dialogues*.

15. Alberto Pérez Gómez and Louis Pelletier, *Architectural Representation and the Perspective Hinge* (Cambridge, Mass.: MIT Press, 1997), pp. 158–159; Fernand Hallyn, *The Poetic Structure of the World: Copernicus and Kepler*, trans. D. M. Leslie (New York: Zone Books, 1993), pp. 203–209.

16. Copernicus, *Commentariolus*, p. 4.

17. Copernicus, *De Revolutionibus*, "Introduction," p. 84; trans. *Three Copernican Treatises*, p. 269.

18. Copernicus, *De Revolutionibus*, "Proemium," p. 70.

19. Ibid., p. 74.

20. "Ad Lectorem de Hypothesibus Huius Operis," p. 62; trans. Copernicus, *Three Copernican Treatises*, p. 25.

21. Francesco Petrarca, "On His Own Ignorance and That of Many Others," trans. Hans Nachod, in *The Renaissance Philosophy of Man*, ed. Ernst Cassirer, Paul Oskar Kristeller, and John Herman Randall, Jr. (1948; reprint, Chicago: University of Chicago Press, 1971), p. 82.

22. Ibid., p. 82, quoting Cicero, *De natura deorum* 2.90.

23. Ibid., pp. 84–85, quoting Cicero, *De natura deorum* 2.97–98.

24. Ibid., p. 85, quoting Romans 1:19–20.

25. Ibid., p. 86.

26. Ibid., p. 87, quoting Cicero, *De natura deorum* 2.167.

27. "Ad Lectorem de Hypothesibus Huius Operis," p. 62; trans. Copernicus, *Three Copernican Treatises*, p. 25.

28. Aquinas, *Summa Theologica* 2.32, art. 1 ad 2, *Commentaria in libr. Arist. de caelo et mundo* 12.17; he follows Simplicius, *In Arist. de caelo* 32. See the commentary of Hans Günter Zekl, pp. 218–219.

29. Ptolemy, *Ptolemy's "Almagest"* 9.1, p. 419.

30. See Copernicus, *De Revolutionibus* 1.10. The following discussion is indebted to

Hans Blumenberg; see *Die Genesis der kopernikanischen Welt* (Frankfurt am Main: Suhrkamp, 1975) pp. 272–299, here especially p. 277.

31. Blumenberg, *Die Genesis*, pp. 286, 291.

32. Ibid., pp. 303–307.

33. Ibid., pp. 305.

34. Galileo Galilei, *Dialogue Concerning the Two Chief World Systems—Ptolemaic and Copernican*, trans. Stillman Drake, 2nd ed. (Berkeley: University of California Press, 1967), pp. 188–189; see also 132. See Blumenberg, *Die Genesis*, pp. 312–313.

35. Blumenberg, *Die Genesis*, p. 310.

36. Ibid., p. 311, citing Domenico Berti, *Il processo originale di Galileo Galilei, pubblicato per la prima volta* (Rome: Cotta, 1876), p. cxxxv.

37. Nicolò Machiavelli, *The Discourses*, in *The Portable Machiavelli*, ed. and trans. Peter Bodanella and Mark Musa (Harmondsworth: Penguin, 1979), p. 170.

38. Galileo, *Dialogue*, pp. 188–189.

39. For a discussion of how Copernicans dealt with this passage, see Blumenberg, *Die Genesis*, pp. 317–324.

40. Ibid., p. 321.

41. Ibid., p. 328, citing Simon Starowalski, *Vita Copernici*, ed. F. Hipler, in *Zeitschrift für die Geschichte und Alterthumskunde Ermlands* 4 (1869), p. 359.

42. Ibid., p. 336, quoting Johann Christoph Gottsched, *Gesammelte Schriften*, ed. Eugen Reichel, 6 vols. (Berlin: Gottsched Verlag, 1903–1906), 6:141–142.

43. Ibid., p. 375, citing Martin Luther, *Tischgespräche*, ed. Johann Aurifaber (1566), in *D. Martin Luthers Werke, Kritische Gesamtausgabe* (Weimar: Böhlau, 1883–), I, Nr. 855.

44. Ibid., p. 393.

45. Ibid., n. 110, quoting Philipp Melanchthon, *Commentarius in Genesin II*, in *Corpus Reformatorum Philippi Melanchthonis Opera Quae Supersunt Omnia*, ed. Carolus Gottlieb Bretschneider, 28 vols. (Halle: Schwetschke, 1834–1860), 13:774.

13   The Crime of Bruno

1. Frances A. Yates, *Giordano Bruno and the Hermetic Tradition* (Chicago: University of Chicago Press, 1979), pp. 444–445, quoting M. Mersenne, *L'Impiété des Déistes* (Paris, 1624), 1:229–230. For a discussion of Mersenne's critique of the Hermetic tradition, see pp. 432–447.

2. Paul-Henri Michel, *The Cosmology of Giordano Bruno*, trans. R. E. W. Maddison (Paris: Hermann; Ithaca, N.Y.: Cornell University Press, 1973), p. 10; Sidney

Thomas Greenburg, *The Infinite in Giordano Bruno, with a Translation of His Dialogue, "Concerning the Cause, Principle, and One"* (New York: Octagon, 1978), p. 4.

3. Yates, *Bruno*, pp. 433, 52.

4. Ibid., p. 215, in a discussion of Bruno's *Spaccio della bestia trionfante*.

5. Giordano Bruno, *The Ash Wednesday Supper*, ed. and trans. Edward A. Gosselin and Lawrence S. Lerner (Hamden: Archon, 1977). Page references, given parenthetically in the text, are to this edition. For a critical edition of the original, see Giordano Bruno, *La cena de le ceneri*, ed. Giovanni Aquilecchia (Turin: G. Einaudi, 1955).

6. Vincenzo Spampanato, *Vita di Giordano Bruno*, con documenti edite e inedite, vol. 1 (Messina: Principato, 1921), pp. 579–597. See also Gosselin and Lerner, introduction to Bruno, *The Ash Wednesday Supper*, pp. 11–53; Hans Blumenberg, *Die Legitimität der Neuzeit* (Frankfurt am Main: Suhrkamp, 1966), pp. 524–584, and *Die Genesis der kopernikanischen Welt* (Frankfurt am Main: Suhrkamp, 1975), pp. 416–454.

7. Gosselin and Lerner, introduction, p. 22; Spampanato, *Vita*, pp. 582–583.

8. See Gosselin and Lerner, introduction, p. 22; Yates, *Bruno*, p. 355. On Campanella, see John M. Headley, *Tommaso Campanella and the Transformation of the World* (Princeton: Princeton University Press, 1997), p. 30.

9. Documenti romani XI; in Spampanato, *Vita*, p. 786.

10. Spampanato, *Vita*, pp. 460–461; Documenti veneti, in ibid., pp. 679–704. See also Michel, *The Cosmology of Giordano Bruno*, pp. 17–19.

11. See Mocenigo's statement of March 23, 1592, Documenti veneti I, pp. 679–681.

12. Spampanato, *Vita*, pp. 669–786. A summary of the trial was discovered and published by Angelo Mercati: *Il sommario del processo di Giordano Bruno*, Studi e testi, vol. 101 (Vatican City: Biblioteca apostolica vaticana, 1942). For a discussion of the contents and significance of this summary, see Michel, *The Cosmology of Giordano Bruno*, pp. 18–20.

13. Michel, *The Cosmology of Giordano Bruno*, p. 20.

14. Documenti veneti XIII (June 3, 1592), in Spampanato, *Vita*, p. 733.Cf. Blumenberg, *Legitimität*, p. 326.

15. Yates, *Bruno*, p. 181, quoting Bruno's *Spaccio della bestia trionfante*.

16. Documenti veneti IV, in Spampanato, *Vita*, p. 685. Cf. Yates, *Bruno*, pp. 340–346.

17. Documenti veneti XIII, in Spampanato, *Vita*, pp. 734–735.

18. Documenti veneti XI, in Spampanato, *Vita*, pp. 706–714.

NOTES

19. As the translators inform us, Grunnio Corocotta refers to "A suckling pig whose Last Will and Testament was a schoolboy's joke of long standing." (Bruno, *The Ash Wednesday Supper*, p. 132 n. 87).

20. See Greenburg, *The Infinite in Giordano Bruno*, p. 169. See also pp. 16–18, 43–44.

21. Andreas Osiander, "To the Reader, Concerning the Hypotheses of This Work," in Nicolaus Copernicus, *Three Copernican Treatises: The "Commentariolus" of Copernicus, the "Letter against Werner," the "Narratio Prima" of Rheticus*, trans. Edward Rosen, 2nd ed. (New York: Dover, 1959), p. 25.

22. See the discussion by Gosselin and Lerner in Bruno, *The Ash Wednesday Supper*, p. 166 n. 19.

23. See Michel, *The Cosmology of Giordano Bruno*, pp. 37–41.

24. See Yates, *Bruno*, pp. 313–315.

25. See Gosselin and Lerner's comment in Bruno, *The Ash Wednesday Supper*, p. 228 n. 23.

26. For a brief account by Bruno himself of his early years, see Documenti veneti VIII, pp. 696–698.

27. Gosselin and Lerner, introduction p. 16.

28. Ibid., p. 18. See also C. F. A. Yates, "Giordano Bruno's Conflict with Oxford," *Journal of the Warburg and Courtauld Institutes* 2 (1938–1939), pp. 227–242, and R. McNulty, "Bruno at Oxford," *Renaissance News* 13 (1960), pp. 300–305.

29. Documenti veneti VII, in Spampanato, *Vita*, p. 692.

30. Yates, *Bruno*, p. 155.

31. Bruno appears to have been one of the first to plead for *philosophica libertas* in his valedictory oration to the professors at Wittenberg (1588). Campanella and Galileo were to reiterate that plea. See Headley, *Campanella*, pp. 172–173 n. 109.

32. Documenti tedeschi III, in Spampanato, *Vita*, p. 664. See also Documenti veneti XI, in ibid., p. 711, where Bruno explains to the inquisitors his understanding of third person of the Trinity, "modo pittagorico," as the life-granting soul of the universe.

33. See Norman Cohn, *The Pursuit of the Millennium*, 2nd ed. (New York: Harper Torchbooks, 1961).

34. Yates, *Bruno*, p. 364.

35. Headley, *Campanella*, p. 3. See also Yates, *Bruno*, pp. 360–397.

36. Arthur Lovejoy, *The Great Chain of Being: A Study of the History of the Idea* (1936; reprint, Cambridge, Mass.: Harvard University Press, 1964), pp. 116–121.

37. See Documenti veneti XI, in Spampanato, *Vita*, pp. 712–713.

38. Franz Rosenzweig, *Briefe* (Berlin: Schocken, 1935), p. 211, quoted by Hans Blumenberg in *Die Genesis*, p. 439 n. 146.

39. Cf. Nicholas of Cusa, *On Learned Ignorance* 2.12, trans. Jasper Hopkins (Minneapolis: Banning, 1981), p. 120.

40. Friedrich Nietzsche, "Über Wahrheit und Lüge im aussermoralischen Sinne," in *Sämtliche Werke: Kritische Studienausgabe*, ed. Giorgio Colli and Mazzino Montenari, 15 vols. (Munich: Deutscher Taschenbuch Verlag; Berlin: de Gruyter, 1980), 1:875; trans. as "On Truth and Lie in an Unmoral Sense," in *Philosophy and Truth: Selections from Nietzsche's Notebooks of the Early 1870's*, trans. and ed. Daniel Breazeale (Atlantic Highlands, N.J.: Humanities Press, 1979), p. 79.

14   Insight and Blindness of Galileo

1. See Hans Blumenberg, *Die Genesis der kopernikanischen Welt* (Frankfurt am Main: Suhrkamp, 1975), pp. 453–502.

2. Galileo Galilei, *The Assayer*, in *Discoveries and Opinions of Galileo*, trans. and intro. Stillman Drake (Garden City, N.Y.: Doubleday, 1957), pp. 237–238.

3. Galileo Galilei, *The Starry Messenger*, in *Discoveries and Opinions*, p. 57.

4. Joseph Glanvill, *The Vanity of Dogmatizing* (1661; facsimile reprint, New York: Columbia University Press, 1931), p. 5. See chapter 6, section 1, above.

5. Ibid., p. 140.

6. Galileo, *The Starry Messenger*, p. 28.

7. Ibid., pp. 28–29.

8. Glanvill, *The Vanity of Dogmatizing*, p. 174.

9. Galileo, *The Starry Messenger*, p. 34.

10. Giovanni Ciampoli, Letter to Galileo, from the end of February 1615 cited in "Introduction: Third Part," in Galileo, *Discoveries and Opinions*, p. 158.

11. Galileo, *The Starry Messenger*, p. 45.

12. Blumenberg, *Die Genesis*, pp. 758–761.

13. Galileo, *The Assayer*, p. 253.

14. Ibid., p. 255.

15. Ernst Cassirer, *The Individual and the Cosmos in Renaissance Philosophy*, trans. Mario Domandi (New York: Harper and Row, 1964), pp. 168–169. See also Cassirer, *Das Erkenntnisproblem in der Philosophie und Wissenschaft der neueren Zeit*, 4 vols. (Darmstadt: Wissenschaftliche Buchgesellschaft, 1994), 1:389–390. What separates Galileo from Plato is similarly stressed by Husserl: "For Platonism the

real had a more or less perfect methexis in the ideal. This afforded ancient geometry possibilities of a primitive application to reality. [But] through Galileo's mathematization of nature, nature is idealized under the guidance of the new mathematics; nature itself becomes—to express it in a modern way—a mathematical manifold." Edmund Husserl, *The Crisis of European Sciences and Transcendental Phenomenology: An Introduction to Phenomenological Philosophy*, trans. David Carr (Evanston, Ill.: Northwestern University Press, 1970), p. 23.

16. Job Kozhamthadam, *The Discovery of Kepler's Laws: The Interaction of Science, Philosophy, and Religion* (Notre Dame, Ind.: University of Notre Dame Press, 1994), p. 170.

17. Ibid., pp. 22, 73–80.

18. Maurice A. Finocchiaro, introduction to *The Galileo Affair: A Documentary History* (Berkeley: University of California Press, 1989), pp. 32–33.

19. Ibid., p. 291. Sentence (22 June 1633)

20. Quoted in "Introduction: Third Part," in Galileo, *Discoveries and Opinions*, pp. 162–163.

21. Ibid., pp. 166–167.

22. Ibid., p. 166.

23. Ibid., p. 168.

24. Ibid.

25. Ibid., p. 163.

26. Galileo Galilei, *Dialogue Concerning the Two Chief World Systems—Ptolemaic and Copernican*, trans. Stillman Drake, 2nd ed. (Berkeley: University of California Press, 1967).

27. See the relevant documents in Finocchiaro, *The Galileo Affair*, pp. 206–216.

28. Galileo Galilei, "Letter to the Grand Duchess Christina," in *Discoveries and Opinions*, p. 193.

29. Galileo Galilei, "Ending of the Dialogue" (1632), trans. in Finocchiaro, *The Galileo Affair*, p. 218. Cf. Blumenberg, *Die Genesis*, p. 496.

30. Blumenberg, *Die Genesis*, p. 454.

31. Ibid., p. 763.

32. Husserl, *Crisis*, pp. 48–53.

15   The Reef of the Infinite

1. On Cremonini, see Heinrich C. Kuhn, *Venetischer Aristotelismus im Ende der aristotelischen Welt: Aspekte der Welt und des Denkens des Cesare Cremonini (1550–1631)* (Frankfurt am Main: Peter Lang, 1996).

2. For a fuller account of the esteem in which Cremonini was held, see ibid., pp. 17–24.

3. Ibid., p. 17.

4. Joseph Newman (josephnewman@earthlink.net), *The Energy Machine of Joseph Newman*, "Section 1, Special Report," mirrored on a number of sites, February 18, 1996, and later; e.g., see <http://www.angelfire.com/biz/Newman/section1.html> (accessed September 3, 2000).

5. Kuhn, *Cremonini*, p. 51.

6. Ibid., pp. 126–131.

7. Ibid., p. 399, citing P. K. Feyerabend, *Wider den Methodenzwang*, (1983).

8. As reported by Magini's student Martin Horky in a letter to Kepler (April 27, 1610). Magini himself writes to Kepler in his letter of May 26 of the need to get rid of these new servants of Jupiter. See Hans Blumenberg, *Die Genesis der kopernikanischen Welt* (Frankfurt am Main: Suhrkamp, 1975), p. 764.

9. Kuhn, *Cremonini*, pp. 399–400, relying on Feyerabend, *Wider den Methodenzwang*.

10. Ibid., pp. 400–401, quoting Sizi's text.

11. On Sizi, see Blumenberg, *Die Genesis*, pp. 766–781.

12. Francis Bacon, *Novum Organum*, I, XLI, in *The Works of Francis Bacon*, ed. J. Spedding, R. Ellis, and D. Heath, 14 vols. (London: Longmans, 1854–1874); the Latin text is in 1:70–365, trans. J. Spedding as *The New Organon* in 4:39–248.

13. For my understanding of the significance of the direction taken by Descartes, I am indebted to Lüder Gäbe, *Descartes' Selbstkritik: Untersuchungen zur Philosophie des jungen Descartes* (Hamburg: Meiner, 1972).

14. René Descartes, *Meditation III*, in *The Philosophical Works of Descartes*, trans. Elizabeth Haldane and G. R. T. Ross, 2 vols. (New York: Dover, 1955), 1:164; *Oeuvres de Descartes*, ed. Charles Adam and Paul Tannery, 8 vols. (Paris: J. Vrin, 1964), 7:43—these editions are hereafter abbreviated as HR and AT, respectively. On this point Descartes would seem to have agreed with Kepler. See Kozhamthadam, *The Discovery of Kepler's Laws*, pp. 62–63.

15. Descartes, Rule VIII, in HR 1:26. See Gäbe, *Descartes' Selbstkritik*, p. 90.

16. Descartes, *Discourse on Method*, in HR 1:119; AT 6:62. Cf. also Bacon's call for a *Scientia Activa* in *Instauratio Magna*, "Distributio Operis," *Works* 1:134.

17. See Gäbe, *Descartes Selbstkritik*, pp. 96–111.

18. Bacon, *Novum Organum* I, XLV.

19. Bacon, *Novum Organum* I, LI.

NOTES

20. Bacon, *Novum Organum* I, XLVIII. See Gäbe, *Descartes' Selbstkritik*, pp. 96–111. Cf. Descartes's letters to Mersenne of January 23, 1630, December 10, 1630, and May 10, 1632; in AT 1:109, 195–196, 251–252.

21. I cannot agree, however, with Stephen Menn's understanding of the similarity of Descartes's and Augustine's metaphysics in his admirable *Descartes and Augustine* (Cambridge: Cambridge University Press, 1998). Koyré, Gilson, and Henri Gouhier seem to me closer to the mark when they suggest that Descartes is "pursuing radically anti-Augustinian ends" (p. 8). I agree with Gilson in "regard[ing] Descartes as essentially a mathematical physicist who, wishing to apply his 'mathematical method' to the natural world, must pass 'idealistically' from thoughts to objects. To execute this passage, Descartes requires a metaphysics and 'surrounded by Augustinians, Descartes needed no more than a short conversation to see opening before him the path of a metaphysics along which his method might proceed'" (pp. 8–9; citing Étienne Gilson, *Études sur le rôle de la pensée médiévale dans la formation du système cartésien* [Paris: Vrin, 1930], pp. 289–294). Descartes's debt to Augustine is inseparably tied to his quite un-Augustinian interest in and promise of a practical philosophy that would render us the masters and possessors of nature.

22. See chapter 5, section 6, above.

23. Karsten Harries, "Problems of the Infinite: Cusanus and Descartes," *American Catholic Philosophical Quarterly* 16, no. 3 (winter 1989), pp. 89–110.

24. René Descartes, letter to Chanut, June 6, 1647; in Descartes, *Philosophical Letters*, trans. and ed. Anthony Kenny (Minneapolis: University of Minnesota Press, 1981), p. 221. Descartes had insisted on this distinction already in his reply to Caterus. See *Reply to Objections* I, in HR 2:17. Descartes goes on there to distinguish between the formal notion of the infinite and the thing that is infinite: the former we understand only in a certain negative fashion, namely from the fact that we preceive no limitation in the thing; but the thing that is infinite is itself positively understood. Descartes wants to claim both: that we have a positive understanding of God, yet cannot comprehend his infinity (HR 2:17–18).

25. René Descartes, *Principles of Philosophy*, trans. Valentine Rodger Miller and Reese P. Miller (Dordrecht, Boston, Lancaster: Reidel, 1983), I.26, p. 13. This edition is hereafter cited parenthetically in the text.

26. Nicholas of Cusa, *De Docta Ignorantia* I.3, trans. Jasper Hopkins as *On Learned Ignorance* (Minneapolis: Banning, 1981), p. 52.

27. Descartes, *Meditations* IV, in HR 1:174.

28. Descartes, *Meditations* IV, in HR 1:175.

29. Descartes, *Passions of the Soul* I.34, in HR 1:347.

30. Descartes, *Objections* V, in HR 2:201.

31. Descartes, *Objections* IV, in HR 2:89.

32. Descartes, *Reply to Objections* IV, in HR 2:110.

33. Descartes, *Passions of the Soul* I.7, 10; in HR 1:334, 335, 336.

34. Descartes, *Passions of the Soul* I.31, in HR 1:345, 346.

35. Cf. chapter 3, section 5, above.

16 Copernican Revolutions

1. Hans-Georg Gadamer, *Truth and Method*, trans. [William Glen-Doepel, ed. Garrett Borden and John Cumming] (New York: Seabury, 1975), p. 235.

2. Hans Blumenberg, *Die Genesis der kopernikanischen Welt* (Frankfurt am Main: Suhrkamp, 1975), p. 611. For a good account of Lambert's life and achievements, see Stanley L. Jaki, introduction to Johann Heinrich Lambert, *Cosmological Letters on the Arrangements of the World Edifice*, trans. with notes by Stanley L. Jaki (New York: Science History Publications, 1976), pp. 1–7.

3. Johann Heinrich Lambert, *Neues Organon oder Gedanken über die Erforschung und Bezeichnung des Wahren und dessen Unterscheidung von Irrtum und Schein*, 2 vols. (Leipzig: Wendler, 1764), 2:220.

4. Jaki, introduction, p. 7. See Johann Heinrich Lambert, *Schriften zur Perspektive*, ed. and intro. Max Steck (Berlin: Lüttke, 1943); Blumenberg, *Die Genesis*, pp. 616–621.

5. For the following account, see Jaki's introduction, pp. 1–2. Jaki relies on the account given by Dieudonné Thiébault in his *Mes souveniers de vingt ans de séjour à Berlin*, published in Paris in 1804, in an English translation the following year. See also Blumenberg, *Die Genesis*, pp. 611–615.

6. Jaki, introduction, p. 1.

7. Ibid., p. 2.

8. Lambert, *Cosmological Letters*, pp. 120–127. Cf. Blumenberg, *Die Genesis*, p. 617.

9. Lambert, *Cosmological Letters*, p. 62; see also pp. 174–175. Cf. Blumenberg, *Die Genesis*, p. 647.

10. Immanuel Kant, *Der einzig mögliche Beweisgrund zu einer Demonstration des Daseyns Gottes*, A 13, footnote. Jaki, introduction, p. 23.

11. Lambert, *Cosmological Letters*, p. 175. Cf. Blumenberg, *Die Genesis*, p. 650.

12. Bertrand Russell, *Human Knowledge: Its Scope and Limits* (New York: Simon and Schuster, 1948), p. 9. Cf. Blumenberg, *Die Genesis*, p. 709.

13. Immanuel Kant, *Kritik der reinen Vernunft*, B xvi.

14. See Karsten Harries, "Meta-Criticism and Meta-Poetry: A Critique of Theoretical Anarchy," *Research in Phenomenology* 9 (1979), pp. 54–73.

15. Roland Barthes, "Science versus Literature," in *Introduction to Structuralism*, ed. Michael Lane (New York: Basic Books, 1971), p. 414.

16. Martin Heidegger, *Being and Time*, trans. John Macquarrie and Edward Robinson (New York: Harper, 1962), p. 272 (translation modified).

17. Johann Gottfried Herder, "Eine Metakritik zur Kritik der reinen Vernunft" (1799), *Aus Verstand und Erfahrung*, in *Sprachphilosophie, Ausgewählte Schriften*, ed. Erich Heintrel (Hamburg: Meiner, 1960), pp. 183–227.

18. Friedrich Nietzsche, "Über Wahrheit und Lüge im aussermoralischen Sinne," in *Sämtliche Werke: Kritische Studienausgabe*, ed. Giorgio Colli and Mazzino Montinari, 15 vols. (Munich: Deutscher Taschenbuch Verlag; Berlin, de Gruyter, 1980), 1:879; hereafter this edition is abbreviated KSA. Trans. as "On Truth and Lie in an Unmoral Sense," in *Philosophy and Truth: Selections from Nietzsche's Notebooks of the Early 1870's*, trans. and ed. Daniel Breazeale (Atlantic Highlands, N.J.: Humanities Press, 1979), p. 82.

19. Ibid., pp. 880–881; trans., p. 84.

20. Richard Rorty, *Philosophy and the Mirror of Nature* (Princeton: Princeton University Press, 1979), pp. 328–333. See also Karsten Harries, "Copernican Reflections and the Tasks of Metaphysics," *International Philosophical Quarterly* 23, no. 3 (September 1983), pp. 235–250.

21. Arthur Schopenhauer, *The World as Will and Representation*, trans. E. F. J. Payne, 2 vols. (New York: Dover, 1966), 1:95.

22. Friedrich Nietzsche, *Die fröhliche Wissenschaft* V.354, KSA 3:593.

23. Geoffrey Hartman, "Literary Criticism and Its Discontents," *Critical Inquiry* 3, no. 2 (Winter 1976), p. 216.

24. See Theodor Litt, *Mensch und Welt: Grundlinien einer Philosophie des Geistes* (Munich: Federmann, 1948), pp. 214–231.

25. Werner Heisenberg, *Das Naturbild der heutigen Physik* (Hamburg: Rowohlt, 1955), pp. 15–16.

17 Epilogue: Astronautics and Astronoetics

1. Hans Blumenberg, *Die Vollzähligkeit der Sterne*, 2nd ed. (Frankfurt am Main: Suhrkamp, 1997). All parenthetical page references in this chapter are to this work.

   A version of this concluding chapter was first given as the keynote address at the symposium *"Curiously Invisible: Work on Blumenberg,"* New York University, April 23, 1998.

2. Hans Sedlmayr, *Der Verlust der Mitte* (Munich: Ullstein, 1959).

3. Vitruvius, *The Ten Books of Architecture*, trans. Morris Hicky Morgan (New York: Dover, 1960), 2.1.1, p. 38.

4. Hans Blumenberg, *Die Genesis der kopernikanischen Welt* (Frankfurt am Main: Suhrkamp, 1975), pp. 793–794.

5. Al Gore, quoted in *New York Times*, March 14, 1998, p. A7.

6. Blumenberg, *Die Genesis*, p. 794.

7. See Hans Blumenberg, *Schiffbruch mit Zuschauer: Paradigma einer Daseinsmetapher* (Frankfurt am Main: Suhrkamp, 1979), pp. 70–74.

8. Ibid., p. 74, citing Paul Lorenzen, "Methodisches Denken," *Ratio* 7 (1965), pp. 1–13.

9. Ibid., p. 74.

10. Hans Blumenberg, *Lebenszeit und Weltzeit* (Frankfurt am Main: Suhrkamp, 1986), p. 306.

11. Ibid.

Index